"For decades, pioneering contem[
FitzGerald has been creatively exp[
Carmelite tradition can help addre[ss] [our] contemporary experience of impasse and darkness, and our deepest desires for personal and social transformation, in the face of so many current crises. Gathered here are seven of her most important essays, together with contributions from a variety of theologians, who draw upon her insights as they grapple with such issues as the COVID-19 pandemic, economic injustice, environmental degradation, violence and dehumanization, systemic racism, and the oppression of women and minorities. Sometimes provocative, always thought provoking and change-oriented, this anthology is a rich resource for all those 'urgently longing' for a timely reintegration of theology, contemplation, and the struggle for social justice."

—Steven Payne, OCD, author of *The Carmelite Tradition: Spirituality in History*

"Laurie Cassidy and M. Shawn Copeland have performed an astonishing service to the Christian community in collecting seven of Constance FitzGerald's essays on profound themes, specifically dark night experiences, in the works of St. John of the Cross that shed light on and offer guidance in confronting several situations of impasse in contemporary society. Although FitzGerald rarely directly alludes to her personal experience in prayer in her appropriation of the teaching of John of the Cross for our times, there are moments when the reader catches glimpses when FitzGerald's own experience all but merges with that of John of the Cross."

—Janet Ruffing, RSM, PhD
Yale Divinity School

"At once eternal and timely, this book is the most rare of treasures for those who want to think deeply about the spiritual journey of our time, one shaped by twin pandemics, 'the coronavirus disease and white racist supremacy.' FitzGerald's singular wisdom invariably invites greater intimacy with God, but particularly so during this time of impasse. She illuminates the path of prophetic hope. In this book, FitzGerald's outstanding interpreters lay bare the enduring fecundity of her contribution. By any measure, a must read."

—Nancy Pineda-Madrid
Loyola Marymount University

"Wonderful and unusual in equal parts, this is truly an extraordinary book. It may be that this collection of essays illumines Karl Rahner's remark that the Christian of the future will be a mystic or will not exist at all. But what is undoubtedly true is that it reveals how prayerful theology today needs to be if it is to help to lead us beyond the many impasses of our times."

—Paul Lakeland
Fairfield University

"In this generous book we encounter a secret treasure: the wide, wise heart and mind of a great lover of the divine and of humanity. Shawn Copeland and Laurie Cassidy have done theologians, 'nones,' and lovers everywhere an enormous service by introducing Constance FitzGerald and her cloud of witnesses to a broader audience. May their light shine long and brightly."

—Dr. Wendy Farley
Graduate School of Theology
Redlands University

"What a rare marvel this book is. While emphatically celebrating the God awareness, spirituality, and theological prowess of Carmelite contemplative theologian Sister Constance FitzGerald, these essays deeply engage FitzGerald's understanding of desire, darkness, hope, passion, impasse, and prayer—all in her yearning for and union with God. These essays are a timely invitation into the spiritual life of FitzGerald as she offers hope and wisdom in these disconcerting times."

—Maurice J. Nutt, CSsR
Convener, Black Catholic Theological Symposium

"This volume is an invaluable contribution to the deepening reflection in the theological academy on the role of the Christian (especially the Carmelite) mystical tradition in the project of engaging the most important issues of personal and social transformation in our time. It makes available seven of the now classic studies of that tradition by Carmelite scholar, Constance FitzGerald, OCD, which are each engaged by scholars with expertise in the areas in question."

—Sandra M. Schneiders, IHM
Jesuit School of Theology of Santa Clara University

Desire, Darkness, and Hope

Theology in a Time of Impasse

Engaging the Thought
of Constance FitzGerald, OCD

Edited by
Laurie Cassidy and M. Shawn Copeland

LITURGICAL PRESS
ACADEMIC

Collegeville, Minnesota
www.litpress.org

Cover design by Monica Bokinskie. *Jesus Calms the Storm*, oil on canvas, 2005–2006, by Daniel Bonnell.

4 5 6 7 8 9

Library of Congress Cataloging-in-Publication Data

Names: Cassidy, Laurie M., editor. | Copeland, M. Shawn (Mary Shawn), editor. | McDermott, Brian L., writer of foreword. | FitzGerald, Constance. Works. Selections. | Ackerman, Colette. Constance FitzGerald, OCD, contemplative.

Title: Desire, darkness, and hope : theology in a time of impasse : engaging the thought of Constance FitzGerald, OCD / edited by Laurie Cassidy and M. Shawn Copeland.

Description: Collegeville, Minnesota : Liturgical Press Academic, [2021] | Includes bibliographical references. | Summary: "An introduction to seven of the works of Sister Constance FitzGerald, OCD, with responsive essays written by ten theologians"—Provided by publisher.

Identifiers: LCCN 2020055662 (print) | LCCN 2020055663 (ebook) | ISBN 9780814688014 (paperback) | ISBN 9780814688267 (epub) | ISBN 9780814688267 (mobi) | ISBN 9780814688267 (pdf)

Subjects: LCSH: FitzGerald, Constance. | Mysticism—Catholic Church.

Classification: LCC BV5082.3 .D47 2021 (print) | LCC BV5082.3 (ebook) | DDC 248.2/2—dc23

LC record available at https://lccn.loc.gov/2020055662

LC ebook record available at https://lccn.loc.gov/2020055663

With Deepest Gratitude

to

Constance FitzGerald, OCD

Carmelite, Contemplative Theologian, Friend of God, and Prophet,

whose passionate desire

illumines a way in the deepest darkness that is God

Contents

Foreword

Constance FitzGerald, OCD, who is the stimulus for these theological articles, is widely recognized as a contemplative theologian. This is manifest in both *how* she writes and *what* she writes.

In recent years, I have come to know first-hand how Sister FitzGerald operates as a writer. Everything she publishes gives evidence of profound wrestling with God, of careful pondering over that *agonia,* and of the great labor of finding the least inaccurate way of interpreting the experience, first for herself and then for others. But the evidence is indirect, it is hinted at, because Sister FitzGerald does not display her own religious experience for all the world to see. What arrives on the page is the fruit of the dialogue in her of her experience with her appropriation of Scripture and Tradition in its broadest sense. This is what ensures that her writings will be of perennial interest to scholars and seekers. But behind the prose is an author who tests the truth of what she writes on the anvil of her own heart. Her actual thinking and writing of each article is a way of the cross for her, a sharing in the paschal mystery. I am not dramatizing here: she suffers her way into print.

For example, if Sister FitzGerald writes about impasse and dark night, you know that the very writing of that classic essay is the fruit of engaging with impasse in her own life as she contemplatively takes in the sin and violence of our world. All the while she remains rooted, by raw faith, in the hidden Christ who gives her the strength to move *through* the impasse to the new hope beyond hopes, which comes to her as gift and in no way achievement. But I must say again that this very personal wrestling is always drawn into dialogue with the sources of revelation and with classical and contemporary philosophical, theological, and literary resources.

For example, her extensive study of Paul Ricoeur and Hans-Georg Gadamer has made her hermeneutically savvy, and this protects her from any naïve understandings of experience and its validity.

Of course, Sister FitzGerald's primary guides are St. Teresa of Avila and St. John of the Cross. The Carmelite world and beyond recognizes in her a true and reliable interpreter of their classic texts, the fruit of years of study and of instructing young nuns in formation, and many years of involvement in the Carmelite Forum, which met for many years in South Bend, Indiana.

A privileged way in which I have been able to experience Sister FitzGerald as a writer involved spending a couple of years working with her on the interconnections between Carmelite spirituality and Ignatian spirituality. The context we have been using is that of human evolution, taking our cue from Pierre Teilhard de Chardin, SJ, who insisted that the future of evolution will come to pass on the level of human consciousness and its corresponding embodiments, personal and social. For this reason, we focused on the evolution of Christ consciousness (Christ union) and its corresponding embodiments and how these two traditions contributed, and continue to contribute, to that evolution.

Sister FitzGerald is deeply versed, of course, in John of the Cross and Teresa of Avila, and I know something about Ignatius of Loyola and *The Spiritual Exercises.* The new learning for both of us was first of all with regard to the significant influence of two young (but helpful) Jesuit spiritual directors on Teresa and of her influence on them during the three years when she lived outside a Carmelite monastery. We learned that she "made" major portions of Ignatius' Exercises, in particular receiving graces proper to the First Week (knowledge of her sinfulness and experience of its forgiveness) and the Second Week (rediscovering the human Jesus), as well as learning from them about the discernment of spirits, which she masterfully uses in *The Interior Castle* when she shows how to determine the authenticity of visions, locutions, and other forms of embodied prayer. Second, we came to a new appreciation of Teresa's experience of those visions, locutions, ecstasies, and levitations, as temporary, anticipatory experiences of sharing in the eschatological gift of resurrected life. Carmelites tend to be silent about such experiences, and Jesuits ordinarily haven't known how to deal with them. We came to see them as transient but grace-given experiences of the evolution of Christ consciousness *in its corresponding embodiments.*

Our collaboration in this area has strengthened our shared conviction that there is a deep complementarity between these two major streams of Christian spirituality. Three of the major contributions that the Ignatian tradition can offer those who find their principal guidance from the Carmelite perspective are (1) a pathway—or, if you will, a method—for growing in union with Christ in his humanity as revelatory of his relationship with the one he called "Abba"; (2) a generous array of methods of prayer for those who find discursive praying helpful; and (3) guidelines for learning how to notice and identify spiritual movements in oneself and then how to identify the various "spirits" from which they proceed, as well as wisdom regarding some of the kinds of evidence God gives a person who is seeking to do God's will.

Those in the Ignatian tradition need to familiarize themselves with Carmelite tradition regarding the dark nights of the senses of the spirit. Many of them will at some point find themselves in a place with God where the Ignatian conceptuality and vocabulary will be inadequate. John of the Cross and Teresa of Avila "map" the path for those whom the Holy Spirit leads into deeper purification and union. And, for sure, spiritual directors in the Ignatian tradition must have a basic awareness of Carmelite wisdom if they are not to confuse and frustrate those they accompany who are being led into the deeper waters where the Spirit is forming them to *attain* God's way of loving God, world, and self.

The contributors to this volume give eloquent witness to the fruitfulness of Constance FitzGerald's *oeuvre* by showing how her theological work has stimulated their own theological reflection. My hope is that their testimony will encourage seekers, spiritual directors, retreat directors as well as young and mature theologians to continue to discover the awesome potentiality of human experience, both personal and corporate, as a theological *locus*.

Brian O. McDermott, SJ, Dr. Theol.
Georgetown University

Acknowledgments

This collection grew out of years of conversations between the editors and contributors—conversations that probed the relationship of theology to spirituality and that relationship to the prevailing culture and society, the fractured way in which we, in the United States, live. In this way, we were led—some jointly, others independently—to deeper exploration of the spiritual traditions of our Catholic faith. Our encounters with Carmelite spirituality and theology through engagement with the thought and heart of Sister Constance FitzGerald, OCD, remain an inestimable and demanding gift. Editors and contributors all are grateful.

We are deeply appreciative of the patience, wisdom, and unfailing support of our publisher, Hans Christoffersen of Liturgical Press. We thank Lauren Murphy and Stephanie Lancour for meticulous editing, and the Boston College Association of Retired Faculty for financial assistance.

Finally, we are grateful that these many bleak months have been brightened by the presence, calm, and love of Barbara Bzura and John Sabo.

Laurie Cassidy
M. Shawn Copeland
December 14, 2020
The Feast of St. John of the Cross

Introduction

Rowing Toward God in an Anguished World

M. Shawn Copeland

> I am mooring my rowboat
> at the dock of the island called God.[1]

> One day [Jesus] got into a boat with his disciples, and he said to them, "Let us go across to the other side of the lake." So they put out, and while they were sailing he fell asleep. A windstorm swept down on the lake, and the boat was filling with water, and they were in danger. They went to him and woke him up, shouting, "Master, Master, we are perishing!" And he woke up and rebuked the wind and the raging waves; they ceased, and there was a calm.
> —Luke 8:22-24

The selection of Daniel Bonnell's painting, *Jesus Calms the Storm*, for the cover of *Desire, Darkness, and Hope* takes inspiration, not only from the familiar story found in Luke's gospel, but also from this poignant fact: we peoples of planet Earth *all* are in the same boat. We *all* are battered by the same coronavirus pandemic, *all* struggling for survival and safety, *all* anguished and yearning for life.

1. Anne Sexton, "The Rowing Endeth," in *The Awful Rowing toward God* (Boston: Houghton Mifflin, 1975), 85.

As this volume comes to publication, we in the United States still find ourselves writhing under twin pandemics: the coronavirus disease *and* white racist supremacy. These lethal outbreaks confuse and confound, mock medical science and technological possibility, uncover and indulge virulent racism. Hundreds of thousands of our fellow citizens have died and are dying of the disease, while millions have been diagnosed with it.[2] Healing possibilities may not be far off. In record time, selfless medical scientists and researchers around the globe have generated vaccines for COVID-19, and the human community has reasonable expectation of preventive measures and treatments, if not a cure.

The same cannot yet be said of white racist supremacy.[3] According to a CBS News report, in the first eight months of 2020, 164 black youth, women, and men have died either at the hands of police or their designated agents or under suspicious circumstances while in police custody or during police tactical responses.[4] More than six hundred Central American children have been separated from their parents in the attempt to cross the US border, and quite likely most of these children will never see their parents again.[5] We cannot forget that in August 2019, a man murdered twenty-three Hispanic and Latinx women and men in a Walmart store in El Paso, Texas.[6] We cannot forget that in October 2018, a man murdered eleven and injured ten Jewish women and men during worship at the Tree of Life Synagogue in Pittsburgh, Pennsylvania.[7] We cannot forget that in June 2015,

2. Around our global village, the coronavirus disease has sickened more than 60,000,000 and more than 1,500,000 have died; https://www.nytimes.com/interactive/2020/world/coronavirus-maps.html.

3. A lexical note: The editors have decided not to impose consistency on the capitalization of the words "black" and "white" but to allow each writer to exercise her or his determination.

4. See https://www.cbsnews.com/pictures/black-people-killed-by-police-in-the-u-s-in-2020/.

5. Josh Marcus, "US Still Hasn't Reunited 666 Children with Parents after 'Zero Tolerance' at Border," *Independent*, November 10, 2020, https://www.independent.co.uk/news/world/americas/separated-child-migrants-us-mexico-border-trump-b1720053.html.

6. Patrick Wood Crusius is accused of this mass shooting.

7. Robert Gregory Bowers is accused of this mass shooting and was injured.

a man murdered nine African American women and men during Bible study at Mother Emanuel AME Church in Charleston, South Carolina.[8] *We cannot forget*. We cannot forget the names of Oscar Grant, Trayvon Martin, Andy Lopez, Michael Brown, Sandra Bland, Breonna Taylor, George Floyd.[9]

These and other acts of resentful, biased violence tear at those brittle scabs that ever so thinly cover the festering wounds beneath the epidermal layer of our society. Our nation's fragile racial ecology has been aggravated: resentments coddled to anger, anger sharpened to willful falsehood, willful falsehood shaped into policies, policies boiled to a violence that de-creates and disposes, detains and incarcerates, kills and chokes.

In the thick of our global anguish, the Lukan story and Bonnell's painting witness to our human need for help and guidance in plague and racial hurt, in anguish and storm. Yet, story and painting also witness to our deep human desire for more: for holding out for and holding on to hope, for life, for loving union and communion—with God and others. In the thick of our

8. Dylan Roof is charged with this shooting.

9. Oscar Grant III, a twenty-two-year-old African American man, was killed in Oakland, California, by BART Police Officer Johannes Mehserle on January 1, 2009. Trayvon Martin, an unarmed seventeen-year-old African American teenager, was shot in Sanford, Florida, by neighborhood watchman George Zimmerman on February 26, 2012. Andy Lopez, a thirteen-year-old Mexican American teenager, was killed in Santa Rosa, California, by Deputy Sheriff Erick Gelhaus as he walked through a vacant lot carrying an airsoft gun designed to resemble an assault rifle on October 22, 2013. Michael Brown, an unarmed eighteen-year-old African American teenager, was shot in Ferguson, Missouri, by police officer Darren Wilson on August 9, 2014. Sandra Bland, an unarmed twenty-eight-year-old African American woman, having been stopped by police for failing to signal while switching lanes, was arrested for allegedly assaulting a police officer and was found hanged in a jail cell in Waller County, Texas, on July 13, 2015. Ahmaud Arbery, an unarmed twenty-five-year-old African American man, was pursued and murdered while jogging by Travis McMichael, Gregory McMichael, and William Bryan in Glynn County, Georgia, on February 23, 2020. Breonna Taylor, a twenty-six-year-old African American woman, was killed by police who forced entry into her apartment as she slept on March 13, 2020. George Floyd, an unarmed forty-six-year-old African American man, was killed during an arrest as police officer Derek Chauvin knelt on his neck for roughly eight minutes and forty-six seconds on May 25, 2020.

global anguish, we turn to the wisdom, symbols, practices, rituals, texts, and language of our religious traditions "for orienting our desire,"[10] for nurturing our hope. Indeed, our religious traditions, as Wendy Farley affirms, "enable us to speak together about this desire and to find ways to speak together about this desire and to find ways to live more deeply into this desire."[11]

Having steeped herself in the texts of St. John of the Cross, Carmelite theologian Constance FitzGerald perceives the gravity and possibility of our situation, naming that situation as one of "impasse," as "the dark night of the world."[12] Few theologians or spiritual writers capture so well the connection between spirituality and the ordinary or the here-and-now, between spirituality and our global material context with its cruel and spreading "zones of abandonment."[13] Even fewer writers have done so with as much intellectual acuity, psychological sensitivity, and spiritual insight as has Sister FitzGerald. Surely and sadly, we recognize our world, our nation, ourselves in her account of impasse, that situation from which there is

> no rational escape from, what imprisons [us]. . . . [E]very normal manner of acting is brought to a standstill, and ironically, impasse is experienced not only in the problem itself but also in any solution rationally attempted. Every logical solution remains unsatisfying, at the very least. . . . Any movement out, any next step, is canceled and the most dangerous temptation is to give up, to quit, to surrender to cynicism and despair, in the face of the disappointment, disenchantment, hopelessness, and loss of meaning.[14]

10. Wendy Farley, *The Wounding and Healing of Desire: Weaving Heaven and Earth* (Louisville: Westminster John Knox, 2005), 14.

11. Farley, *The Wounding and Healing of Desire*, 14.

12. Constance FitzGerald, "Impasse and Dark Night," in *Living with Apocalypse: Spiritual Resources for Social Compassion*, ed. Tilden H. Edwards (San Francisco: Harper & Row Publishers, 1984), 94.

13. Joao Guilherme Biehl, "Vital: Life in a Zone of Social Abandonment," *Social Text* 68, vol. 19, no. 3 (Fall 2001): 131–49; see also Ivan Petrella, *Beyond Liberation Theology: A Polemic* (London: SCM Press, 2008), loc. 705–43, Kindle ed.

14. FitzGerald, "Impasse and Dark Night," 94.

Impasse: the strange and discomfiting societal situation that we ourselves have made through our refusals *to live mindfully, attentively, reasonably, responsibly, and lovingly* in relation to the Divine, to other human persons, and to the entire created order.

For nearly four decades, Constance FitzGerald's theological thought and spiritual insight have been a well-known secret among Carmelite religious, members of other religious orders of women and men, spiritual directors or advisers, academic students and practitioners of Christian spirituality and mysticism, and theologians. Widely recognized as an expert on the writings of St. Teresa of Avila and St. John of the Cross, FitzGerald has taught and lectured on spirituality and has advocated for and assisted communities of cloistered nuns in adaptation and renewal. In 2009, Sister FitzGerald was the first cloistered nun to address the Catholic Theological Society of America (CTSA).[15] In 2017, the Leadership Conference of Women Religious (LCWR)[16] honored her for her profound impact on women religious in the United States. And the highly regarded Cambridge University theologian David Ford wrote that FitzGerald's interpretation of Thérèse of Lisieux "reads like an illustration of Ricoeur's 'self as another.'"[17]

Desire, Darkness, and Hope: Theology in a Time of Impasse aims to introduce FitzGerald's work to a wider and more diverse audience, particularly laywomen and laymen, young people and "the Nones,"[18] theologians—any and all who hunger to sharpen the

15. The Catholic Theological Society of America (CTSA) is the primary professional association of Catholic theologians in the United States and Canada; its membership numbers about 1,300.

16. The Leadership Conference of Women Religious (LCWR) is an organization of 1,350 members representing nearly 80 percent of 44,000 women religious in the United States.

17. David Ford, *Self and Salvation: Being Transformed* (New York: Cambridge University Press, 1999), 225n49.

18. Frank Newport, "Millennials' Religiosity amidst the Rise of the Nones," *Polling Matters*, October 29, 2019, https://news.gallup.com/opinion/polling-matters/267920/millennials-religiosity-amidst-rise-nones.aspx. The term "nones" refers to the increase of Americans who, when interviewed by researchers about their religious affiliation, say "none."

"searching character"[19] of their lives, who yearn to deepen personal or scholarly theological reflection on spirituality, who endeavor to make sense of perplexing and dispiriting times. To that end, this volume gathers and makes available several of Sister FitzGerald's most vital essays. At the same time, it includes essays by social activists, contemplatives, spiritual directors, and theologians who take inspiration from and *engage* her thought. Perhaps the inclusion of these essays suggests that this book is a *festschrift* or celebratory volume prepared in Sister FitzGerald's honor; after all, the book is dedicated to her. It is not. As the reader quickly will ascertain, these interpretative essays function neither as simplistic agreement nor as naïve tribute. Rather, the authors *engage* critically with FitzGerald's thought to draw out ways of responding and relating to their own desire *to act, to live, to be* for God and for neighbor in the midst of the dark night of our world. Moreover, their critical *engagement* aims to facilitate the reader's own encounter, *engagement*, dialogue, even wrestling with FitzGerald's thought, but, more important, the reader's response to the pull of that grounding desire of all desires—union with God.

Constance FitzGerald's Theology: Desire, Passion, Prayer

Constance FitzGerald's life has been galvanized by a single-minded pursuit of the luminous end of contemplative prayer, the passionately sought fulfillment of that grounding desire of all desires—union with God. Sister FitzGerald radiates what the great Spanish Carmelite mystic John of Cross teaches: the human person has an infinite capacity for God. At the same time, her life in Carmel for God reflects a motto of the Order of Preachers—*contemplare contemplata aliis tradere*, to contemplate and to hand on the fruit of contemplation. Hence, two characteristics come readily to mind when thinking of her theological thought and writing—passionate and perceptive.[20] This choice is not ran-

19. Roger Haight, *Spirituality Seeking Theology* (Maryknoll, NY: Orbis Books, 2014), 4.

20. FitzGerald clarifies this in "Passion in the Carmelite Tradition: Edith Stein," *Spiritus: A Journal of Christian Spirituality* 2, no. 2 (Fall 2002): 217–35:

dom; indeed, FitzGerald identifies three questions as shaping her theological work:

> First, where do we really find passion or excess in the Carmelite tradition? Second, how does the passion of the Carmelite tradition meet the hunger of our own time for spirituality and even mystical experience, the thirst for the divine and for community? Third, how does the Carmelite tradition move out from the familiar, from an enclosure of language and esotericism into new social and cultural situations?[21]

FitzGerald commits herself to the rigorous activity of understanding, appropriating, explicating, and interpretating the writings of the Carmelite tradition, with particular attention to John of the Cross. In this endeavor, the leading edge of her work has been to illuminate the meaning and power of *passion* in the spiritual life—passion as love and desire for union with God and, through that passion, passionate compassion for an anguished and suffering world, for suffering others.

For example, in "Passion and the Carmelite Tradition: Edith Stein," FitzGerald tracks the transformation of a young scholar's "raw passion for greatness that can only be assuaged by the absorption of self into an overwhelming plan beyond her own personal life" through to its evolution into "complete, unconditional commitment to God and the Cross in radical solidarity with her own Jewish People."[22] The deep passion that runs through the course of Stein's life allows FitzGerald to conclude that

> in her life as an intellectual, in her death in the Holocaust as a voluntary scapegoat, Edith broke through the traditional form of the Carmelite nun, a stone rejected and yet destined to become, in the twenty-first century, a cornerstone in Carmel. This is why we dare

"The Carmelite tradition transmits a legacy of profound passion. . . . The way the Carmelite prayer tradition helps and educates is by showing us how passion for God matures, that is, how desire grows in ardor, how communion and being God's partner in love comes about in our lives" (217).

21. FitzGerald, "Passion in the Carmelite Tradition: Edith Stein," 232–33n1.

22. Ibid., 219.

> not minimize the extent of the influence of her passionate intellectual life upon her equally passionate contemplative prayer life nor the radicality of her total involvement in the social situation.[23]

Might we say much the same of Sister FitzGerald? We ought not to minimize the interactional influence of FitzGerald's own passionate intellectual life upon her passionate contemplative prayer life and sharp grasp of the complex cultural and social situation within which she finds herself. To read FitzGerald's work is to encounter a probing, subtle, and capacious mind at home in history, theology, philosophy, psychology, modern science, feminist thought, and the literature of diverse cultures—to name areas in which she has become far more than conversant, even expert. FitzGerald's work bears the mark of close, conversational, open-ended reading—reading that spirals into further questions and leads to new responses; these in turn rebound in fresh questions and provoke new answers. Such reading "motivates abiding" with the text.[24] Abiding, waiting patiently, with the text enables FitzGerald to reach not only subtle understanding that is alert to the historical situatedness of author and text but fitting re-interpretation in and for new and different contexts. FitzGerald builds up insights so that categories generative in one context might be transposed adequately and vividly into another context. A good example of this is found in the way in which FitzGerald grapples with Stein's appropriation of classical theologies of salvation and their resulting categories of sacrifice, satisfaction, substitution, and expiation. If contemporary Christians recoil from these notions, expiation in particular, during the 1930s and 1940s these ideas flooded the commonsense religious consciousness of the church at large and certainly were "operative, viable theological constructions [that were] profoundly influential and inspiring in the spiritual life of Carmel."[25] Thus, FitzGerald

23. Ibid., 232. I have been reading FitzGerald through Stein.

24. Hans-Georg Gadamer, "Zwischen Phänomenologie und Dialektik," *Hermeneutik* II, 9, cited in Frederick G. Lawrence, *The Fragility of Consciousness: Faith, Reason, and the Human Good* (Toronto: University of Toronto Press, 2017), 38.

25. FitzGerald, "Passion in the Carmelite Tradition: Edith Stein," 226.

renders Stein's understanding of expiation and her death in Auschwitz as "an opening of [Stein's] heart to God's freely offered love" for liberation from resentment and an absorption of the evil all around.[26] In light of Stein's passion, FitzGerald critiques our modern/postmodern loss of "passion as evidenced by a certain spiritual fatigue, softness and malaise." She continues:

> Modernity, with its often one-sided emphasis on the development and realization of the autonomous self without adequate concern for the common good or multipersonal community, has left us bereft of passion, and herein, I suggest, lies a radical call to self-transcendence. Our passionless, "so-what" society needs a new language of selflessness or of the Cross that describes and supports the loss of possessive selfhood. Such a forfeiture is indispensable in the contemporary quest for the transforming love, universal communion and cosmic consciousness that seem today beyond the achievement of human ability.[27]

Then, in an explanatory note, FitzGerald acknowledges the grave harm that self-transcendence, so improperly deployed, has done to women:

> I am aware that some have difficulty with a call to "self-transcendence." They see it as a denial of the human, of the need for a strong, well-developed sense of self. This is especially threatening and even unfair for women, many of whom have come so belatedly into full selfhood. Nevertheless, the summons to a cosmic consciousness is so urgent and the spiritual experience of some women so compelling that I think we must speak of self-transcendence until we have another word that expresses the real radicality of the challenge today.[28]

FitzGerald's theological method may be characterized as *critical contemplative trialectics*.[29] This method refers to varied cognitive

26. Ibid., 227.
27. Ibid., 218.
28. Ibid., 233n8.
29. There is considerable debate about method among scholars who research, write, and teach the academic study of spirituality. Biblical scholar and expert on Christian spirituality Sandra M. Schneiders claims that there is no single method

acts or operations, including attentiveness to and questioning of history and society, of sociality, of spaciality; interrupting and unsettling, marshalling and weighing, reviewing and reflecting, embracing silence, attentive judging and deciding and interpreting. At the same time, the nature of cloistered Carmelite communal life requires and creates space for the interior growth of each individual nun (hermit) even as that life weaves strong and thick, yet translucent, webs of relationships. For FitzGerald, her community *stands* as the indispensable finite ground of her theological thought and praxis:

> [T]he heart of my dream and my community's dream has been the reinterpretation of the Carmelite tradition for the times in which we live. In other words, we want to offer a contemporary interpretation that is accessible, comprehensible and relevant for people so the ancient mystical tradition might serve as both a guide and stimulus for a deeper spiritual life. This dream is the basis for everything that we have done, and it has guided all our practical decisions about contemplative life.[30]

---

for the study of spirituality; rather, such study necessarily requires an interdisciplinary approach. See her "Spirituality in the Academy," *Theological Studies* 50 (December 1989): 676–97. Mary Frohlich has pushed this question of method forward in her essay "Spiritual Discipline, Discipline of Spirituality: Revisiting Questions of Definition and Method," *Spiritus* 1, no. 1 (2001): 65–78. In a later essay, Schneiders cites three approaches to the academic study of spirituality—the historical, the theological, and the anthropological. See "Approaches to the Study of Christian Spirituality," in *The Blackwell Companion to Christian Spirituality*, ed. Arthur Holder (Oxford: Blackwell Publishing Ltd., 2005), 15–33, at 19–28.

My interpretation of Sister FitzGerald's theological thought and method takes cues from the theological work of Wendy Farley, Howard Thurman, and Bernard Lonergan. I am particularly grateful to Joy Bostic for the notion of *trialectics* that dovetails so well with my working out of critical contemplative dialectic. See Joy Bostic, *African American Female Mysticism: Nineteenth-Century Religious Activism* (New York: Palgrave Macmillan, 2013), 3, 45; see Copeland, "What Is Poetics? A Response to Mayra Rivera," https://syndicate.network/symposia/theology/poetics-of-the-flesh/.

30. FitzGerald, "Pursuing Our Dreams in Times of Darkness," in *Transformational Leadership: Conversations with the Leadership Conference of Women Religious*, ed. Annmarie Sanders (Maryknoll, NY: Orbis Books, 2015), 12. The choice of the word *stands* is significant. On more than one occasion (e.g., the nuns' funerals

On Bernard Lonergan's account, this method and the theology that emerges from its exercise are rooted in the theologian's authenticity expressed as self-transcendence through the threefold conversions—intellectual, religious, and moral. "This threefold conversion is, not a set of propositions that a theologian utters," Lonergan declares, "but a fundamental and momentous change in the human reality that a theologian is."[31] Moreover, religious conversion remains the specifically theological principle.[32] Theology emerges from love, is rooted in falling in love with God; thus, FitzGerald's theology begins in loving conversation with God, which overflows in love of neighbor. FitzGerald's theology begins on her knees.[33]

Sister FitzGerald's theological thought arises from and is the result of differentiated consciousness. In ordinary or common-sense usage, consciousness refers to awareness, but, Lonergan observes, "more properly, 'consciousness' is an awareness of oneself or of some aspect of oneself."[34] While undifferentiated consciousness pertains to the manner or operations of common sense, differentiated consciousness denotes complex comprehension and control of a realm or realms of religion, art, theory,

---

or jubilee celebrations), FitzGerald has quoted Susan Griffin's "The Way We Stand," in *Woman and Nature: The Roaring Inside Her* (New York: Harper & Row Publishers, 1978, 1980), 220–21. The passage describes trees in a forest, growing together, leaning together in the same direction, dead limbs leaning on living ones that grow around them.

31. Bernard Lonergan, *Method in Theology* (New York: Herder & Herder, 1972), 270.

32. In this introduction of Sister FitzGerald's theological thought and method, her spiritual life and practice are assumed implicitly. Hence, falling in God as religious conversion forms the specifically theological principle.

33. In "Approaches to the Study of Christian Spirituality," Schneiders begins with a general definition of spirituality as "the actualization of the basic human capacity for transcendence." Then, for the purposes of that particular essay, Schneiders specifies spirituality as "the experience of conscious involvement in the project of life-integration through self-transcendence toward the horizon of ultimate value one perceives" (15, 17).

34. Bernard Lonergan, "Prolegomena to the Study of the Emerging Religious Consciousness of Our Time," in *A Third Collection: Papers by Bernard J. F. Lonergan, S.J.*, ed. Frederick E. Crowe (New York/Mahwah, NJ: Paulist Press, 1985), 55.

scholarship, interiority.[35] Scholarly and religiously differentiated consciousness are of significance in interpreting and appreciating Sister FitzGerald's thought. Hence, Lonergan again:

> Religiously differentiated consciousness is approached by the ascetic and reached by the mystic. In the latter there are two quite different modes of apprehension, of being related, of consciously existing, namely, the commonsense mode operating in the world mediated by meaning and the mystical mode withdrawing from the world mediated by meaning into a silent and all-absorbing self-surrender in response to God's gift of [divine] love.[36]

Sister FitzGerald's skill in understanding and interpreting history and texts (including spiritual, theological, scientific, philosophic texts) discloses scholarly differentiation of consciousness. In other words, while critically recognizing and disciplining the common sense of her own place and time, FitzGerald ably combines this recognition and discipline "with a commonsense style of understanding that grasps meanings and intentions in the words and deeds" of writers such as John of the Cross or Teresa of Avila or Thérèse of Lisieux or Edith Stein.[37] Religiously differentiated consciousness as grace-given fruition of union with God is the aspiration of Carmelite (mystical) life. Such life, such union can never be attained, only gifted by Gift. But to write of that gifted life—to grasp its grace-given possibility and radical incarnational character; to interpret its inner exigences with delicate openness, stark honesty, and fierce reverence; to invite and encourage others to respond to the desire and embrace of Divine Love—to do this is to carve from the rock of contemplation a rekindled hope, a path toward a new consciousness.

35. Lonergan, *Method in Theology*, 273. He notes: "Fully differentiated consciousness is the fruit of an extremely prolonged development" (*Method in Theology*, 257).

36. Lonergan, *Method in Theology*, 273. Lonergan notes here the manifold character of mystical attainment—there are mystics of Christianity, Judaism, Islam, Hinduism, Indigenous religions, etc.

37. Lonergan, *Method in Theology*, 274; see also, pp. 257–62, 302–5.

Since the 1990s, Sister FitzGerald's reading, study, writing, and speaking have given increasing attention to the relation between theology and modern science. More than twenty years ago, she addressed the need for a "quantum leap" in human consciousness in order to address the lag of the "mental machinery" of our species in evolving quickly enough to address the monumental global problems we face.[38] Echoing the early appeals of Vaclav Havel and Thomas Berry, Robert Ornstein and Paul Ehrlich, Sister FitzGerald turns with passion and acute perception to the evolutionary possibility of contemplation, to the transformation of individual human consciousness for global change.[39] We can no longer, Sister FitzGerald insists,

> afford to bypass contemplation, interiority, or desire for God, as though they were esoteric experiences for the lazy or unbalanced elite, but not for us who value above all else reason, sanity, and the ability to control our destinies. Certainly without contemplative prayer and the transformation it really can effect, the deepest dimension of the human person and of humanity itself lies forever dormant and beyond our reach. But even more, without it the true evolutionary possibilities completely dependent on the inbuilt purpose and aspirations of the human soul are beyond us. . . . [T]his is the era of contemplation and the stakes are very high.
>
> We need to understand and to speak, therefore, of the unleashed power, influence and freedom of contemplative love and wisdom, of their ability to pass beyond the limits by which both person and humanity are confined, the boundaries within which human consciousness, desire, culture, evolution and religion are now enclosed.[40]

Such is the vision of being human and human be-*ing*, of Christian spirituality, of mysticism to which the theology of Constance

38. FitzGerald, "The Desire for God and the Transformative Power of Contemplation," in *Light Burdens, Heavy Blessings: Challenges of Church and Culture in the Post Vatican II Era, Essays in Honor of Margaret R. Brennan, IHM*, ed. Mary Heather MacKinnon, et al. (Quincy, IL: Franciscan Press Quincy University, 2000), 213–14.

39. Ibid., 215.

40. Ibid., 215–16.

FitzGerald invites us. This vision breaks through signs of decline, breakdown, and death and turns us toward healing, creating, and new life. This vision summons us to recognize, acknowledge, and accept God's great and gracious desire for us—the Divine Desire who lights the dark night of our world and guides our rowing to open arms of Holy Mystery.

The Impact of the Contemplative on Contemporary Theology

For several decades, theologians have bemoaned theology's break or estrangement from spirituality, from mysticism. Healing this rupture begins where theology exists—the minds and hearts and prayer and lives of theologians. In a homily given at the convention liturgy of the annual meeting of the Catholic Theological Society of America, Dominican William Hill declared that if theologians are to speak and write of God meaningfully, we must "show who God will be for [humankind] and what humankind must be for God." This requires, Hill said,

> undertaking an inner spiritual voyage with no set itinerary. And if we are to tell God's people of it . . . we must travel it ourselves. And it is a pilgrimage which takes place in the deep places of our spirit, in that country of the heart whose native language is prayer. Not prayer simply as a means and a method, but as a mode of being, as living in and with Christ.[41]

The contributors to *Desire, Darkness, and Hope* are theologians—critical thinkers, skilled readers of religious texts, perceptive interpreters of our national and global material contexts. Their academic theological specializations include systematic, philosophical, pastoral, black, liberation, political, feminist, and womanist theology; theological and social ethics; critical race theory;

41. William Hill, "The Theologian: On Pilgrimage with Christ; Appendix B: Homily, Convention Liturgy," *Proceedings of the Catholic Theological Society of America* 40 (1985): 230–32, at 230. Retrieved from https://ejournals.bc.edu/index.php/ctsa/article/view/3320.

cultural, gender, and peace studies. Their reading, research, and writing reflect their commitment not only to intellectual rigor but to theology as mediation of God's active and abiding presence in the dark night of our world, to the inner journey, to prayer as a mode of being, as living in and with Christ.

These theologians risk encounter with the contemplative.[42] At the heart of differentiated consciousness lies interiority that "promotes us from consciousness of self to knowledge of self."[43] Such knowledge is the fruit of self-appropriation through which not only do we affirm and verify cognitional activities[44] but such self-knowledge renders our living authentic. And it is Constance FitzGerald's authenticity, her fidelity to the pull of the divine call to self-transcendence that, in turn, calls and attracts—nudges and turns them to attend to their own interiority, to embark on the inner spiritual journey.

These theologians risk grappling with contemplation. They recognize and

> point to an incarnational depth in the world in which Christian faith and teaching might renew itself. If that depth also requires . . . a disciplined unknowing, it is not as an escape from knowledge. Rather it lends contemplative attention to the opacity of our own self-constitution in an intimate multiplicity of relations.

42. Of course, we should not overlook the double meaning of "contemplative" in the context of this volume. Like every human person, Constance FitzGerald remains a mystery even to those who love and cherish her dearly. And, just like each of us, she remains a mystery, not because she is an enigma, but because she cannot be contained or confined by simplistic categorization or convenient labeling. Sister FitzGerald is a cloistered nun, yet cloister has taken her to distant and near places in the world. She is a contemplative, yet contemplative life has made her an activist for contemplatives and contemplative life, for theology. She lives in solitude, yet her solitude thrives on community, collaboration, and friendship. She is sophisticated and humble, gregarious and disciplined, direct and street-smart, serious and fun loving. And above all, Constance FitzGerald is thoroughly in love with Jesus-Sophia.

43. Lonergan, *Method in Theology*, 259.

44. Ibid., 14–15.

> Otherwise we may miss the point at which the planetary multitude lays its specific claim, its truth, and its justice, upon our gifts.[45]

These theologians contest postmodernity's infatuation with abstraction—its distancing relation to history, the world, the flesh, the body as well as its ambivalent relation to religion. These writers seek solidarity with wounded flesh and bodies—children, youth, women, and men. Through word, the theologian or writer makes present flesh and blood, bread and wine, life and water to open, excite, comfort, honor, inspire, and accompany the reader's famished heart and soul. These essays evoke and seek to prepare us for another kind of transfiguration through which the ordinary life radiates the holy, performs another kind of transubstantiation (confects another kind of *eucharist—of thanksgiving*). *The dark night of the world is (re)charged not only with the grandeur and glory but also with the mystery of God.*

Desire, Darkness, and Hope invites reading as spiritual and contemplative practice. Such practice calls for slow, deliberate, patient, and open-ended reading and reflection; for testing one's own experience in coming face-to-face with that of another; for waiting, even in the tension of activism. The volume opens with Sister FitzGerald's essay on the great voices of the Carmelite tradition, "A Discipleship of Equals: Voices from the Tradition—Teresa of Avila and John of the Cross." The current prioress of the Baltimore Carmel, Colette Ackerman, OCD, situates Sister FitzGerald within cloistered contemplative religious life and considers the renewal of that life as prompted by the Second Vatican Council (1958–1963). Sister Ackerman emphasizes the importance of community (hermits living together) and clarifies the meaning of the five-hundred-year-old Carmelite tradition for twenty-first-century women.

"Impasse and Dark Night"[46] remains the most well known and most often cited of Sister FitzGerald's publications. Strikingly prescient, this classic essay continues to nourish the hearts and

45. Catherine Keller and Laurel C. Schneider, eds., "Introduction," in *Polydoxy: Theology of Multiplicity and Relation* (London: Routledge, 2011), 4.

46. FitzGerald, "Impasse and Dark Night," 93–116.

minds and souls of hundreds who hunger for God and yearn to embrace the world in passion and compassion and yet who are painfully self-aware of crusted barriers of personal and cultural and societal limitation, of forfeiture and powerlessness and failure and loss—of impasse. These themes are reiterated in "Desolation as Dark Night: The Transformative Influence of Wisdom in John of the Cross."[47] Laurie Cassidy, Roberto Goizueta, and Margaret Pfeil consider societal impasses presented by white racist supremacy, the abandonment of the poor, and the spiraling collapse of the natural environment.

Cassidy faces squarely the impasse that white supremacy presents not only to the "ever more perfect union" of the United States but to the development and flourishing of the interior lives of white women and men. Cassidy explores the possibilities of a contemplative approach through which white women and men might open themselves to God in the midst of societal dark night—not only for themselves, but for relations of mutuality and communion for future generations. Goizueta considers the relation between impasse and liberation theology's notion of the preferential option for the poor. In his reading of Gustavo Gutiérrez's liberation theology, Goizueta retrieves the Peruvian theologian's indebtedness to the thought of Christian mystics and, thus, enacts a conversation between Gutiérrez and FitzGerald that allows Goizueta to conclude that "in the experience of impasse, the mystic and the revolutionary are revealed as one." Pfeil analyzes narrative accounts of the effects of the global climate crisis in order to deepen our understanding of the collective experience of impasse. Pfeil argues that FitzGerald's work leads us to turn with humility and openness to the transformative power of contemplation, which well might be the way that we inhabitants of Earth grasp the interrelationship of the whole of God's creation.

47. FitzGerald, "Desolation as Dark Night, the Transformative Influence of Wisdom in John of the Cross," *Ignatian Prayer: The Way Supplement* 82 (Spring 1995): 96–108. Here FitzGerald accords critical attention to consciousness and personal transformation through encounter with the feminist apprehension of Wisdom, of Jesus-Sophia.

Concern for integrating the role of dark night and impasse experience in personal and societal crises features in the contributions of Maria Teresa Morgan and Susie Paulik Babka. Morgan uses recollection of her childhood experience of being lovingly carried on the shoulders of her father, the "watchman," as he walked each evening through the streets of their town. Morgan brings together John of the Cross, Rainer Marie Rilke, and FitzGerald in order to propose an understanding of dark night that opens possibilities for personal and communal interpretations during the present fearful COVID-19 pandemic. Babka sets up a dialogue between catastrophe and impasse. Her essay works upward from personal grief at the tragic death of her father to a reflection on societal grief. She focuses on catastrophic suffering—COVID-19, HIV/AIDS, and the Ebola outbreak (2014–2016)—and its barbarism made manifest in shattered families, broken lives, economic hardship, anxiety, loneliness, death. With FitzGerald, Babka recognizes the "suffering Other as the locus of the desire for God."

Like Cassidy, Alex Mikulich and Bryan Massingale probe Sister FitzGerald's emphasis on the transforming power of contemplation in grappling with white racist supremacy in the United States. Beneath evident displays of personal and institutional racism and of the persistent dominative colonial matrix of power, Massingale and Mikulich, respectively, uncover white supremacy as a culture, a worldview, and uncover "the darker side of Western Modernity."[48] Mikulich reads FitzGerald's critique of modernity and radical concern for contemplative transformation as an expression of decolonial praxis. He proposes that we must unlearn modernity's fateful *habitus*;[49] to do so requires that we retrieve

48. Walter Mignolo, *The Darker Side of Western Modernity: Global Futures, Decolonial Options* (Durham, NC: Duke University Press, 2011), 16.

49. The term *habitus* as deployed by French sociologist Pierre Bourdieu refers to "a product of history, produces individual and collective practice in accordance with the schemes generated by history. . . . As an acquired system of generative schemes, the habitus makes possible the free production of all thoughts, perceptions and actions inherent in the particular conditions of its production—and only those" (*The Logic of Practice*, trans. Richard Nice [Stanford: Stanford University Press, 1980/1990], 54, 55).

and relearn our differentiated and interconnected pasts in order to realize new and communal futures for the flourishing of all creation. Analyzing the "soul-sickness" that infects people from white racist supremacy, Massingale insists on a spiritual (r)evolution.

"Suffering and confusion," Wendy Farley states simply, "are intrinsic to the process of transformation."[50] Andrew Prevot's essay engages Sister FitzGerald's interpretation of philosopher and Carmelite Edith Stein; M. Catherine Hilkert considers the contribution her thought might make to preachers as they proclaim the wisdom of the cross in an anguished world. Both FitzGerald and Prevot describe the sexism and anti-Semitism to which Stein was subjected in Nazi-occupied Germany; both take into account Stein's conversion to Catholicism and her entrance to Carmel; both emphasize the significance of Stein's Jewish familial and philosophical formation for her contemplative life and theology, for her example of discipleship in a world of violence. Hilkert's essay urges preachers to attend carefully to contemporary signs and experiences of impasse and dark night. Indeed, Hilkert quotes Pope Francis in *Evangelii Gaudium*, "a preacher has to contemplate the word, but [the preacher] also has to contemplate [the] people, . . . paying attention 'to actual people, to using their language, their signs and symbols, to answering the questions they ask.' "[51] Such attention, Hilkert argues, begs for cultivation of empathy, solidarity, and communion with those children, youth, women, and men who endure personal and societally imposed suffering.

These essays *stand* as critical reflection on religious faith that yearns to *become flesh* in knowledge and love in the radical transformation of oppressive systems; that *abandons* ideological or dogmatic certitudes and makes an intentional option for openness to the unknown, the unforeseen, and the impossible; that *embraces* the interrelatedness and multiplicity of existence and existents; that engages "critical *apophasis* or critical nonknowingness as an energy of epistemological and theological integrity."[52]

50. Farley, *Wounding and Healing of Desire*, 135.

51. Pope Francis, Apostolic Exhortation *Evangelii Gaudium/The Joy of the Gospel* 154 (Washington, DC: United States Conference of Catholic Bishops, 2013), 78.

52. Keller and Schneider, "Introduction," 3.

Docking on the Island Who Is God

The Lukan story of Jesus calming not only the storm but the fear and anxiety of his disciples and Daniel Bonnell's rendering of this account turn us toward the One who equips us for growth, for life, for life beyond impasse, for flourishing beyond the dark night of our world. The theologians writing here disclose the impact of contemplative prayer and practice not only on themselves as Christian thinkers but on theology. Taking inspiration from the theological thought and work of Constance FitzGerald, in confrontation with impasse, with the dark night of our world, these theologians advocate passionately for justice, truth, solidarity, and equity through radical attentiveness to development of the interior life, through spiritual transformation.

The rower pulls and is pulled. The rower seeks Transcendent Holy Mystery—Truth, Beauty, Goodness, and Justice. Still, the rower cannot see the form; the light in its excess dazzles. There is "no option but faith," Constance FitzGerald counsels.

> It is precisely as broken, poor, and powerless that one opens oneself to the dark mystery of God in loving, peaceful waiting. When the pain of human finitude is appropriated with consciousness and consent and handed over in one's own person to the influence of Jesus' spirit in the contemplative process, the new and deeper experience gradually takes over, the new vision slowly breaks through, and the new understanding and mutuality are progressively experienced.[53]

We row on to the Island who is God.

53. FitzGerald, "Impasse and Dark Night," 104, 103.

1

A Discipleship of Equals

Voices from Tradition—Teresa of Avila and John of the Cross

Constance FitzGerald, OCD

Introduction

In the epilogue of *In Memory of Her,* Elisabeth Schüssler Fiorenza suggests that in the past women's relationship to God has been defined by their sexual relationship to men and through the patriarchal structures of family and church. Now a Christian feminist spirituality wants to probe and to define women's relationship to God in their concrete experience of being called today beyond patriarchal structures into "a discipleship of equals."[1] What the great mystics like Teresa of Avila and John of the Cross teach us is that it is in the very development of their relationship with God that both women *and men* will first of all discover and then finally embrace their equality in life and discipleship. In the dark fire and the bright living flame of God's Spirit, equality is inescapably appropriated, even when this is not consciously recognized because of the pressures of culture and education. This means that the *experience* of equality and solidarity in a common humanity

1. See Elisabeth Schüssler Fiorenza, *In Memory of Her* (New York: Crossroads, 1983), 349.

is conditioned by the depth of one's interiority or religious consciousness or relationship with God.

In the sixteenth-century reform of the ancient Carmelite Order, the Spanish mystics Teresa of Avila and John of the Cross stand together through time and mirror in their lives and writings this experience of equality. Teresa, older by twenty-seven years, is the charismatic leader who envisioned, initiated and directed the reform of Carmel, first for the women and later for the men. John looked to her as the mother of the Teresian Carmel, not only for her gifts of vision and leadership—she taught him practically how to live in the new reform—but also because she embodied in her life and writings the deepest experiences of God the human person can know. In his own incomparable mystical works, he refers to her writings to enlarge on or complete his own.[2]

John, on the other hand, is the father. He went with Teresa to open the first house for men in the reform. His poems, the primary expression of his experience of God, are thought by many in our day to be the greatest poetry in the Spanish language. They have been the fire in the Teresian Carmel for four hundred years. John was the father of Teresa's soul, her confessor and confidant in prayer from at least 1572–1575, during which time she experienced the most profound depths of communion with God in the "spiritual marriage." In a letter to Mother Ann of Jesus, Teresa sings John's praises and urges Ann and her sisters in Beas to "talk to him with the utmost frankness, for I assure you," she says, "that you can talk to him as you would to me, and you . . . will find great satisfaction, for he is very spiritual and of great experi-

2. See John of the Cross, *The Collected Works of St. John of the Cross* (*CW*), trans. Kieran Kavanaugh and Otilio Rodriguez (Washington, D.C.: Institute of Carmelite Studies, 1973), *The Spiritual Canticle,* 13.7; *The Living Flame,* 2.9-12. The following abbreviated titles for John's works are used in the footnotes that follow: *Ascent, Dark Night, Canticle, Flame*. In references to *The Ascent* and *The Dark Night*, the first number indicates the book, the second number refers to the chapter, the third number refers to the paragraph. For example, *Ascent* 2.17.3 refers to book 2, chapter 17, paragraph 3. Similarly, for *The Spiritual Canticle* and *The Living Flame* the first number refers to the stanza, and the second number to the paragraph. Thus, *Canticle* 4.2 is a reference to stanza 4, paragraph 2 of *The Spiritual Canticle*. Italics in quotations are mine.

ence and learning. Those who were brought up on his teaching miss him greatly."[3]

An often-told story illustrates the character and extent of the collaboration, communion, and equality of this great woman and man. On the feast of the Blessed Trinity, John was talking to Teresa about the profound mystery of the feast "when suddenly both of them were seized by the ardor of the Spirit and raised aloft" in ecstasy.[4] In this context of a common experience of God's Spirit, it is significant that while Teresa's writings were published before John's and she was also canonized before he was, he, a man, was declared a Doctor of the Church nearly fifty years before the structures of the patriarchal Church could bestow that same highest approval of her writings upon Teresa, a woman.

Now, in our time, we ask if the writings and the lives of these two saints and doctors can contribute to a Christian feminist vision of a "discipleship of equals"? Can they function for both the liberation and development of women and for the ultimate equality of women and men? What do these two giants of contemplation, these two friends and companions, tell us about the process of becoming equal?

To examine this question, I want to do two things. First of all, I will try to trace the evolution of Teresa's image of Christ

3. John, *CW*, Introduction, 23; See Teresa of Avila, *The Collected Works of St. Teresa of Avila*, (CW), trans. Kieran Kavanaugh and Otilio Rodriguez, 3 vols. (Washington, D.C.: Institute of Carmelite Studies, 1976–1985), vol. 1: *Spiritual Testimonies*, 31; vol. 2: *The Interior Castle* 6.9.17 with note 14. (This article's extensive notes are provided as an aid for in-depth study of Teresa's and John's texts. I have, however, in some cases grouped a number of references for a single section into one note.) The following abbreviated titles are used in the footnotes that follow: *Life*, *Way (Way of Perfection)*, *Castle*, *Testimonies*. In references to the *Life* and *Way of Perfection*, the first number refers to the chapter and the second number to the paragraph. Therefore, *Life* 3.5 refers to *The Book of Her Life*, chapter 3, paragraph 5. Regarding *The Interior Castle*, the first number refers to the dwelling place, the second to the chapter and the third to the paragraph. Thus, Castle 6.2.4 refers to the sixth dwelling place, chapter 2, paragraph 4. In references to the *Spiritual Testimonies*, the first number refers to the number of the *Testimony*, the second to the paragraph. Italics in quotations are mine.

4. John, *CW*, Introduction, 30.

by analyzing the complex symbolism of her visions of Jesus. Secondly, I will look at Teresa's development in the light of specific teaching of John of the Cross. In this way, we will see Teresa's lifelong movement from confusion of heart, inferiority and fear of abandonment to connectedness, mutuality and equality. If Christology has, indeed, been used to subordinate and exclude women, as Elizabeth Johnson suggests, I want to study Teresa's visions to see if her experience of Jesus Christ validates that subordination and exclusion.[5] It is my hope that the deepest meanings of her life, revealed in the imagery through which her psyche expressed its experience of God, will intersect with our questions and struggles and even re-describe our reality. The functioning of the image of Christ in Teresa's life really transformed her self-image, and an investigation of the development of her God-image may transform our self-understanding as well.

Symbolism of Desire and the Image of Christ in John of the Cross

We can begin to study the process of becoming equal by concentrating on the symbolism of desire and friendship, or relationship, which is central in any interpretation of Teresa's and John's works. Teresa and John are always talking about desire—the desire of the human person, first of all, but also the desire of God. God, says John, has only one desire for a person and that is to exalt her and make her equal.

> If anything pleases him, it is the exaltation of the soul. Since there is no way by which he can exalt her more than by making her equal to himself, he is pleased only with her love. For the property of love is to make the lover equal to the object loved. Since the soul in this state possesses perfect love, she is called the bride of the Son of God, *which signifies equality with him.* In this equality of friendship the possessions of both are held in common, as the Bridegroom himself said to his disciples: I have now called you

5. See Elizabeth Johnson, "Jesus, the Wisdom of God: A Biblical Basis for Non-Androcentric Christology," *Ephemerides Theologicae Lovanienses* (Dec. 1985): 263.

> my friends, because all that I have heard from my Father I have made known to you. . . . As a result they are truly gods by participation, equals and companions of God.[6]

The person, on her part, can never be satisfied, will never have what she desires, says John, until she has attained this equality of love, until God has "put her somehow in himself and made her his equal."[7] The desire of God and the desire of the human heart coincide, therefore, although we often feel they are at odds with each other. It took Teresa many years to understand and to accept this reality and the equality it implied.

The itinerary of meaning we find in Teresa's experiences will be understood better if we look briefly at John of the Cross' teaching on the image of Christ. John counsels his readers to immerse themselves in the Jesus of the Gospels so that Christ will gradually become the focus of meaning in their lives. He wants them, in this way, to build up more and more conscious references to Jesus Christ in order to redirect their deepest desire toward him. In this prayer process, an image of Jesus, unique for each person, slowly forms within and is the basis for any relationship with Jesus Christ. Furthermore, it is the basis for the experience of equality. All our life experience becomes a part of and is in dialogue with this image in some way or other. In the poem, *The Spiritual Canticle*, John sings:

> O spring like crystal!
> If only, on your silvered over face,
> you would suddenly form
> the eyes I have desired,
> Which I bear sketched deep within my heart.

Commenting on this stanza, John says: the person "experiences within herself a certain sketch of love . . . and she desires the completion of the sketch of this image, the image of her Bridegroom, the Word, the Son of God, who . . . is the splendor of

6. *Canticle* 28.1; 39.6; see also 30.6.
7. *Canticle* 32.6; 38.3-4.

his glory and the image of His substance." When John, therefore, decries the destructive counsel of inexperienced spiritual directors, it is because they cause their directees to "lose the sublime image God was painting within [them]."[8] In Teresa's visions of Christ we see a very explicit illustration of John's doctrine.

Teresa's Development—A Dialogue: Self-Image and Image of Christ

Basic to any study of Teresa's visions is an understanding of the way of prayer she learned, during the solitude of a prolonged illness, from Francisco Osuna's *Third Spiritual Alphabet* which was given to her by her uncle when she was a young, sick nun. "I tried as hard as I could," she writes, "to keep Jesus Christ, our God and our Lord, present within me, and that was my way of prayer. If I reflected upon some phase of the Passion, I represented him to myself interiorly." Even though this was difficult for her and she often resorted to good reading to collect her thoughts and quiet herself into God's presence, still she insists that beginners "must strive to consider the life of Christ" and use their own creativity and ingenuity to do this.

> The soul can place itself in the presence of Christ and grow accustomed to being inflamed with love for his sacred humanity. It can keep him ever present and speak with him, asking for its needs and complaining of its labors, being glad with him in its enjoyments and not forgetting him because of them, trying to speak to him not through written prayers but with words that conform to its desires and needs. . . . I consider the soul advanced who strives to remain in this precious company and to profit very much from it, and who truly comes to love this Lord to whom we owe so much.[9]

According to Teresa's self-report, however, her life was a story of vacillating desire. At one time the focus of her desire was a

8. *Canticle* 12; 11.12; *Flame* 3.45; see also *Ascent* 1.13.3; 14.2; *Canticle* 37.
9. *Life* 4.7; 11.9; 12.2-3; see also 13.11; 12.22; *Way* 26 and 27 and 28.3-4.

human love; at another time the focus of her longing was Jesus Christ. She is quick to tell us when someone is her friend. She always mentions when someone loves her. Her life energy came from friendship. Yet for many years she was certain that God and others—"the world"—were in competition for her affection.[10] She found out very slowly, and not without mistakes, just *how* Jesus Christ was the fulfillment of her deepest desire.

Teresa felt that the almost reckless desire for God and eternity that characterized her youth was in adolescence dimmed and overshadowed by the desire for pleasure, vanity, romance, approval and honor. In the company of her young friends and cousins, her desire for God grew cold.[11] Later, during her prolonged illness, after the fervor of her first years in religious life, Teresa's heart wavered again and rested in an intimate friendship with her confessor who was involved in a "sinful" relationship with a local woman.

We should note just how much Teresa appropriated without reflection the prevalent patriarchal attitudes toward woman as the temptress, the one who leads man into sin:

> . . . Men [should] be on their guard with women who desire to carry on in this way. Men should believe that since these women have lost their shame before God (*for women are obliged to more modesty than men*) they can be trusted in nothing, for they will stop at nothing in order to hold on to this friendship and passion the devil has placed in them.

While the woman, herself, *may* have been the seducer, neither equality of responsibility, nor the reality of men who seduce and then desert, were part of Teresa's awareness when she wrote her

10. According to Colin P. Thompson, *The Poet and The Mystic* (Oxford: Oxford University Press, 1977), 10: "One of the most insistent calls echoing through the whole [western] tradition is the renunciation of the self and everything created for God. Its roots lie in pre-Christian antiquity and it occurs in other faiths." See note on R.C. Zaehner's *Mysticism Sacred and Profane* (Oxford: Oxford University Press, 1961) in Thompson.

11. *Life* 2.1-8.

Life. Furthermore, Teresa paints herself as one who also "seduces" the priest!

This confessor loved Teresa for her goodness and she "loved him deeply." She used his affection for her to win him away from the woman, and though her intention was good and the priest was converted and "died a very good death," Teresa always felt guilty about the relationship. It was somehow competitive and diverted her desire from God, she thought. It placed her in danger of almost dying in mortal sin. "Damned be such loyalty [friendship] that goes against the law of God," she writes.[12] It should be noted that when Teresa saw herself as one whose salvation was in jeopardy she blamed it on the poor guidance of confessors who did not understand the significance and seriousness of misdirected desire.

Because of her divided heart, Teresa marveled she could endure suffering so patiently and associated it with the deep prayer experiences she was having. "All my conversations were with him [Jesus Christ] . . . the Lord [who] raised me from the dead," she writes.[13] In the frightening experience of nearly dying, Teresa felt her desire swing again toward Jesus Christ. But *this* time of focused attention on God was not to last either.[14]

Here Teresa brings two important symbols—*abandonment* and the *hand* of Jesus—into relationship with the image of Christ as one who not only relates in interpersonal *dialogue* but even *raises up* and makes whole. Because Teresa seemed to fear abandonment all through her life, she was very sensitive to the vacillation and treachery of her own heart. *She* abandoned the conversations of intimate prayer for human conversation and superficial pastimes, and though Christ held out his hand to her, she did not want it. She felt unfit to face Christ because of her human friendships and was therefore "ashamed to return to the search for God by

12. Ibid., see 5.4-5 for her description of the relationship with the priest.

13. Ibid., 5.8 and 11.

14. As Teresa here describes her fervent life and her carefulness of conscience, one is reminded of the description she wrote years later of the good, reasonable, careful person in the third dwelling place. See *Life* 6 and *Castle* 3.

means of a friendship as special as is that found in the intimate exchange of prayer . . ." She writes:

> It seemed impossible, my Lord, to abandon you so completely. And since I did forsake you so many times I cannot but fear. For when you withdrew a little from me, I fell to the ground. Although I abandoned you, you did not abandon me so completely as not to turn to raise me up by always holding out your hand to me.[15]

In response, as it were, to her self-understanding and world view came Teresa's first *vision* of Jesus Christ.[16] While she was actually with a friend, she "saw" a very severe looking Christ before her making her understand his disapproval of such friendships. It is hardly coincidence that this vision reflected and validated Teresa's own fragile self-image. Nor is it inconsequential that at this same time she described and found meaning in the appearance of a large ugly toad (a well-known symbol of evil) in the middle of the day moving more quickly than usual toward her and her friend.[17] There seems to be a profound relationship both here and in her other visions between Teresa's image of herself and her image of God. Each calls forth and responds to the other in some mysterious way giving a much deeper meaning than we might suspect to the *dialogic* character of Teresian prayer, which Teresa, herself, describes

15. *Life* 7.1; 6.9.

16. In *The Seeing Eye: Hermeneutical Phenomenology in the Study of Religion* (University Park and London: The Pennsylvania State University, 1982), 78–79, Walter L. Brenneman et al. write: "Seeing in a metaphor for a broad spectrum of cognitive experiences, including visions that come from beyond the boundaries to which senses and reason extend and revelations that have radically changed people's 'views' of the world and of the meaning of life. . . . Sight involves a realization of what was previously undisclosed . . . and it implies a prior blindness to that which was always there to be seen if only one had had the 'eyes' to see it."

17. *Life* 7.6-9; see also J.E. Cirlot, *A Dictionary of Symbols* (New York: Philosophical Library, 1971) for the entry on "toad" to understand the fascinating and even lethal effect of a toad's gaze; see also *Life* 22.13 where Teresa compares the person at this stage of development to a toad who tries to fly on its own.

> . . . as nothing else than an intimate sharing between friends; it means taking time frequently to be alone with Him who we know loves us.[18]

Teresa, however, continued her "worldly" conversations. She *needed* friendship and she did not want to face the warnings she received. Her desire was focused elsewhere! It was only in the terrible wrenching caused by the sickness and death of her beloved and holy father, "who was everything to [her]," that she slowly and with good guidance began to pray regularly again. And even though she never again abandoned prayer, neither did she forego her frivolous pastimes for "almost twenty years." Thus, she was torn in two and found happiness in neither God nor her worldly enjoyments. *Teresa's* God wanted everything! Her experience of Christ's severe judgement of her seemed only to validate this perception and widen the gulf between friendship with God and friendship with the world.[19]

What is the full import of these initial images of Christ? First of all, *hand* functions as an important symbol from the beginning of Teresa's prayer life all the way through to its fulfillment in the spiritual marriage. Putting out one's hand is the first simple gesture of friendship, a movement of concern and reassurance. The hand can be a promise of tenderness and delicate care, even intimate union. But there is a long way between the *touch* of a hand and that kind of communion. Moreover, the hand can be withdrawn along the way. A hand can be stretched out to touch in acceptance and encouragement or pulled back in rejection and condemnation, as the image of the severe, judging Christ indicates. From the other side, a stretched-out hand can be refused because of the guilty confusion within one's own heart, or out of the fear of being abandoned in the end.

When Christ holds out a hand not only to touch but also to *raise up* Teresa, the hand also signifies strength, power, authority and even superiority. There is a certain inequality implied in the support, just as there is inequality implied in the severe judge-

18. *Life* 8.5.
19. Ibid., 8.2; 7.6; 8.3.

ment of Christ. This inequality is carried further in the symbol of being raised up *from death* which, while it does speak of potentiality and new life, seems to emphasize the disintegration, powerlessness, and brokenness of the one who is lifted up. In this powerlessness, we circle back to the symbol of abandonment which recurs throughout Teresa's life and is parallel to the symbol of death and resurrection. To feel abandoned or to fear abandonment is, according to J. E. Cirlot, "to feel forsaken by the 'god within us'; [it is] to lose sight of the eternal light in the human spirit." It points to Teresa's sense of estrangement from her own deepest self, her own Center, and God as she imagines God to be. Abandonment as a recurring symbol indicates the need for deeper interiority.[20] Furthermore, it underlines Teresa's experience of a deadly evil within herself. "I wanted to live," she writes, "for I well understood that I was not living but was struggling with a shadow of death, but I had no one to give me life, and I was unable to catch hold of it. He who had the *power* to give it to me was right in not helping me, for so often had he brought me back to himself; and so often had I abandoned him."[21]

It was an image of the "wounded Christ," a statue, that finally stirred up resonances in Teresa's weary, broken, tired soul and called her, through the words of Augustine's *Confessions*, to conversion. Only a human God, broken by human life, could have spoken into the life of this woman wounded by years of conflicting priorities and vacillating desires. She identified with Jesus Christ and tried to picture him within her in the Gospel scenes where he was more alone. It seemed to her that being alone and afflicted and in need, he had to accept her as she tried to companion him in the darkness of her own faith life.[22] We see here the first faint seed of equality that will bear fruit in the difficult experience of the dark night.

20. See Cirlot, *Dictionary*, 1, "abandonment." Although we cannot pursue this here, we become aware at this point of significant relationships between some of the major symbols in Teresa's writings: garden, castle, way, and even water which is given little by little, in relationship to abandonment and death/resurrection.

21. *Life* 8.12.

22. *Life* 9.1-7.

For now, Teresa began to experience the *feeling* of God's presence, tenderness, and love, entering and pervading her life as she dwelt with increasing attention and care on the humanity of Jesus, particularly the poor, suffering Jesus. The pendulum of her desire swung once again and she reached for satisfaction toward a God who was tender, who comforted, who gladdened, who satisfied, who gifted her. Now *she* placed herself in the *"hands of God,"* and while she desired to speak of nothing but Jesus Christ who was showing her such love, she was overcome with her ignorance and lack of education as a woman, her weakness and unworthiness as a person, and her general inability to measure up to the favors of *her* God. These very favors made her inferior, not only to a strong and powerful God, but even to men. In the context of trying to give an account of her gifts to her male advisors and confessors, she says: " . . . Just being a woman is enough to have my wings fall off—how much more being both a woman and wretched as well."[23]

Her self-doubt, complicated, or perhaps *caused*, by the marginal position of women in her society, battled with the inner affirmation she received. Even the experience of a God comforting as a mother and tender as a lover could not reassure her in the face of the negative, masculine evaluations of her life and prayer. Still, she persevered in prayer and really began to love "the most sacred humanity." She thought she was ready to forfeit everything for Christ until her confessor was transferred to another place! Then her "soul was left as though in a desert, very disconsolate and fearful." In the face of this abandonment, the old fear reasserted itself and with it one of Teresa's deepest life questions: Is abandonment the finality? Is there anyone for me who is ultimately trustworthy? The need for reassurance and friendship was overpowering. She was too fragile to give up her friendships, and, therefore, her new confessor advised her to commend the whole matter to God.[24]

In response, the dialogue extended itself to *inner words*, effective words heard and understood, that changed her heart and

23. Ibid., 10.8; see also all of chap. 10; 22.12; 23. This is the prayer of quiet.
24. Ibid., 24.4-5.

could never be forgotten. Teresa, in her first rapture, heard deep within her being words *verifying her own suspicions* that her human friendships conflicted with her relationship with Jesus Christ: "No longer do I want you to converse with men but with angels."[25] Concerned chiefly with her conflict over the incompatibility of her relationships, Teresa did not understand, at first, the extent of the liberation offered her: No longer was she to be victim to human words of wisdom, controlled by human words of love and assurance, but she was to own her own life and be guided by her own inner voice. The challenge of the word was to find the locus of motivation, of wisdom, within her own heart, but Teresa made this transfer only with difficulty. However, in the light of this inner assurance, Teresa's motivation did shift again and she made a decisive choice of the heart for Christ—Wisdom who speaks, changes, refreshes, quiets, makes strong. Out of this experience, Teresa articulated certain basic beliefs about human friendship, and later she developed these extensively in the *Way of Perfection*. Although she never seemed *consciously* to grasp the full import of the word, she expresses her freedom. " . . . I have never again been able to tie myself to any friendship or to find consolation or bear particular love for any other persons than those I understand love Him and strive to serve Him."[26]

While the inner autonomy, freedom, and strength that Teresa experienced in herself grew, she discovered her appropriation of them was only partial when she was faced with the negative evaluations of her numerous locutions by learned and wise *men*. When they decided that her experience was clearly from the devil(!), Teresa was terrified and "her fear made her forget her self-worth." As a *woman* in sixteenth-century Spain, she needed their reassurance and approval. In challenging the truth of Teresa's inner word and attempting to lead her away from her own interior wisdom, the words of these "wise" *men* drove this *woman* into deeper inferiority. It was they who quite unconsciously spoke the word of the devil, whose "aim . . . is [always] regression or stagnation in

25. Ibid., 24.5; see also 25.1 and *Ascent* 2.31.
26. *Life* 24.6; see *Way* 4, 6, 7.

what is . . . inferior . . ." according to Cirlot.[27] In the dichotomized world of patriarchal Spain, Teresa's inner experience was either from God or from the devil (or her own deluded self). The devil here stands as such a strong archetypal symbol of societal domination, control and power-over. It surfaces in every age and exerts its demonic influence whenever a person, a group, or a nation appropriates power and structure to keep a race, a sex, a people, in an inferior, powerless, oppressed position.

Teresa's agitated feeling of being deluded, alone, and without any human support was answered by another word in the dialogue. This word effected peace, strength, courage, and security: "Do not fear, daughter, for I am, and I will not abandon you; do not fear." Teresa's whole person was touched by reassurance as the pathway back to her own Center opened up. She began to experience a sporadic, though often fearless, mastery over not only human condemnation but even her own inner contradictions:

> O, my Lord, how you are my true friend . . . Oh, who will cry out for you, to tell everyone how faithful you are to Your friends! All things fail; you, Lord of all, never fail. O my God, who has the understanding, the learning and the *new words* with which to extol your works as my soul understands them? All fails me . . . , *but if you will not abandon me, I will not fail you.* Let all learned men rise up against me, let all created things persecute me, let the devils torment me [but] do not you fail me, Lord.[28]

One can feel her remembering the intimidation she suffered when she writes a few years later to her nuns in the *Way of Perfection* that "since the world's judges are sons of Adam and all of them men, there is no virtue in women they do not suspect."[29]

But, the Lord did not fail Teresa. When in 1559, the Inquisitor General published an Index of forbidden books which prohibited the reading in the vernacular of many books on prayer she enjoyed, Teresa was very upset. The Lord said to her: "Don't be sad

27. Cirlot, 80; see *Life* 25.14-15.
28. *Life* 25.17-19.
29. *Way* 3.7.

for I shall give you a living book." In retrospect, she understood this as a promise of the visions to come in which Jesus, eternal Wisdom, became the "true book" in which she saw all the truth she needed impressed upon her forever.[30]

This whole period was a turning point for Teresa. In the experience of numerous words of Wisdom, Teresa, the woman, was being given to herself and empowered to claim her own inner wisdom. She was being lifted out of her inferiority and fear. She saw she was "another person" and "would have disputed with the entire world that these words came from God." Later she was to pray to possess "all human eloquence and wisdom together" in order to know how to explain clearly the path to the knowledge of God.[31]

The fact remains that Teresa was so affirmed as a woman by this "Master of wisdom . . . Wisdom itself, without beginning, without end, without any limit to [her] works" that her view of herself changed and she began to see women from the perspective of God. Her later writings stand as a clear and forceful defense of women's wisdom; so forceful, in fact, that the censors of her writings sometimes intervened, and Teresa was forced to revise her work.

Some years later, in an era still suspicious of interior prayer and wary of false mysticism, especially in women, Teresa wrote to her nuns with bold conviction in *The Way of Perfection*:

> You will hear some persons frequently making objections: "there are dangers"; "so and so went astray by such means"; "this one was deceived"; "another who prayed a great deal fell away"; "it's harmful to virtue"; "it's not for women, for they will be susceptible to illusion"; "it's better to stick to their sewing"; "they don't need these delicacies"; "the Our Father and Hail Mary are enough." This last statement, Sisters, I agree with. And indeed they are sufficient.[32]

Teresa, the woman, was no longer to be intimidated by the oppressive words and decisions of fearful men into dichotomizing

30. *Life* 26.5.
31. *Way* 22.6.
32. Ibid., 22.6; 21.2-3.

deep, interior prayer and vocal prayers—the Our Father and the Hail Mary. Now she trusted her own inner wisdom and did not hesitate to point accusingly at the senselessness of what was being urged upon women.

> Well, what is this, Christians, that you say mental (interior) prayer isn't necessary? Do you understand yourselves? Indeed, I don't think you do, and so you desire that we all be misled. You don't know what mental prayer is, or how vocal prayer should be recited, or what contemplation is, for if you did you wouldn't on the one hand condemn what on the other hand you praise.[33]

Realizing that the only real danger lay in the neglect of the interiority in which the God of wisdom would call them to own their own lives, Teresa urged her sisters not to pay any attention to the fears men raised or to the picture of the dangers they painted. She exclaimed with determination, with inner authority, and even a hint of sarcasm: "Hold fast, daughters, for they cannot take from you the Our Father and the Hail Mary." Kavanaugh explains:

> Here the censor, quick to catch the point, intervened and, going a step further than his usual method of simply crossing out the passage, wrote in the margin: "It seems she is reprimanding the Inquisitors for prohibiting books on prayer."[34]

Teresa's visions apparently began in earnest after the locution mentioned above. Although she was counselled to pray to be led along a different path, her own inner experience prevented her from sincerely wanting this "deliverance." Nevertheless, she was torn apart by the controversy and her own efforts to be obedient.

> There were enough things to drive me insane . . . [and] I didn't know what to do other than raise my eyes to the Lord. For the opposition of good men to a little woman, wretched, weak, and fearful like myself, seems to be nothing when described in so few

33. Ibid., 22.2.
34. Ibid., Introduction, 25; see also chap. 25.

> words . . . if the Lord hadn't favored me so much, I don't know what would have happened to me.[35]

But, the lifelong dialogue did continue and the Lord urged Teresa deeper into the inner Mystery in ways that defied her expectations. She felt Jesus Christ *beside her* even though she did not see him with her eyes or even, she thought, with her imagination. Yet she *saw* it was he who was *speaking* to her—a human person who shared life with her (accompanied her and witnessed her life) in a deep mutuality of understanding, friendship, and love. They were like two people who love each other very much and who even without signs, with only a glance, understand each other perfectly. She writes:

> The Lord puts what he wants the soul to know very deeply within it, and there he makes it known without image or explicit words. . . . And this manner in which God gives the soul understanding of his desires, and great truths and mysteries is worthy of close attention.[36]

What are the specifics of what Teresa here calls "vision"? Along with the "impressions of the Divinity" that Teresa felt earlier, in the prayer of quiet, it was now Jesus in his *humanity* who was present, who "spoke," who was, above all, known with an intuition "clearer than sunlight." This knowledge was engraved upon her mind, her understanding, with a clarity and permanence that could not be erased or doubted, that could not have even been *consciously* desired. It was, she explains, as if someone who had never even tried to learn to read suddenly possessed all knowledge. This woman who was so convinced of her own inadequacy and ignorance could say, "The soul sees in an instant that it is wise."

It is intriguing that in the intersubjective union that was slowly taking over Teresa's consciousness, it was the *human* Jesus, son of Mary, whom she knew and enjoyed. But her experience was

35. *Life* 28.18.

36. Ibid., 27.6; see also nos. 2-3 for Teresa's description of an intellectual vision.

subtle and profound. In her determination to forego dependence on human approval and honor, in identification with this man who suffered such contempt and rejection for her sake, she realized that the clearsighted wisdom she discovered in herself was closely related to this Jesus who was not only man but also divine Wisdom. She says, "How rich will [she] find that [she] is, [she] who has left all riches for Christ. . . . How wise will [she] be, [she] who rejoiced to be considered mad because that is what they called *Wisdom Himself*!"[37]

When one looks at Teresa's experience of inner wisdom and self-affirmation, the growing ability, we see in her writings, to trust that experience and inner truth, and the strong conviction of feminine worth she later passes on to her sisters, we are reminded of the investigations of feminist theologians today regarding *Sophia*. If the New Testament does identify Jesus with Sophia, and if we can speak, therefore, as Elizabeth Johnson suggests, of the union of female Divine Wisdom (Sophia) and male humanity in Jesus, we can understand better the dynamics of Teresa's appropriation of her own feminine truth.[38] Divine Wisdom, who is Jesus, was, as it were, a mirror in which Teresa saw the reflection of herself as a wise *woman*. Teresa, in a sense, became what she saw, for in Jesus, eternal Wisdom, the feminine was lifted up and cherished. In a society where *weak, ignorant* women lived on the margins of knowledge, in subordination to the men who controlled them, Teresa's sexual identity was affirmed by God. Therefore, even though church men continued to warn her of the danger of deception, she was reassured from within and con-

37. *Life* 27.14. Using the "categories of interiority" of Bernard Lonergan and his concept of intersubjective union, James Robertson Price III of Georgia State University has done a helpful study called *Lonergan and the Foundations of a Contemporary Mystical Theology*. One would think the study was done using Teresa, herself, as a subject for the research. See Lonergan's *Method in Theology* (New York: Herder & Herder, 1972), 3–25.

38. See Elizabeth Johnson, "Incomprehensibility of God and the Image of God Male and Female," *Theological Studies* (1984): 462–63; see also Susan Cady et al., *Sophia* (San Francisco: Harper & Row, 1986). While Teresa's development, supported by John of the Cross' experience and teaching, may throw light from the mystical tradition on Wisdom studies, feminist research will, I suspect, open up new horizons in the interpretation of John and Teresa.

scious of being brought to new "frontiers."[39] Had the culture and theology of the sixteenth century fitted Teresa to articulate this, she might have echoed the words from *for colored girls who have considered suicide/when the rainbow is enuf*:

> I found God in myself
> And I loved Her
> I loved Her fiercely.[40]

While Teresa experiences and writes of Jesus as Wisdom, John is the one who clearly validates the identity and place of Wisdom in mystical union, particularly in the *Living Flame* and the latter part of *The Spiritual Canticle*. For him, Jesus Christ is uncreated Wisdom, and union with God is seen as transformation in Divine Wisdom. He says, "[The] soul . . . will then be transformed into . . . Wisdom, the Son of God." And, at the end of the second book of the Dark Night, John explains that when the person is ready "Divine Wisdom unites herself with the soul in a new bond of the possession of love."[41]

It is critical to note, however, that even though Teresa experienced growing inner certitude, the symbols which appear in her descriptions of her visions continue to point also toward connectedness, relationship and tenderness, suggesting that autonomy and intimacy are not mutually exclusive but rather integrally connected. She writes:

> . . . The Lord desired to show me only *his hands* which were so very beautiful. . . . After a few days I saw also that *divine face* which it seems left me completely absorbed. Since afterward he granted me the favor of *seeing him entirely*, I couldn't understand why the Lord showed himself to me . . . little by little until later I understood that his Majesty was leading me in accordance with my natural weakness.[42]

39. *Life* 27.11; 28.1.

40. Ntozake Shange, *for colored girls who have considered suicide/when the rainbow is enuf* (New York: Macmillan, 1977), 63.

41. *Ascent* 2.15.4; *Dark Night* 2.24.3; see also *Canticle* 37.2.

42. *Life* 28.1; Teresa tells us that she was always afraid of each *new* experience of Jesus Christ.

Let us look at *hands*, masculine hands, held out to support and strengthen, perhaps even to convey power and authority. But these are beautiful hands. They are somehow *for* Teresa. They promise deeper self-donation and though they initially frighten because of their other-worldly splendor, they invite trust. Teresa frequently mentions her surrender to, or withdrawal from, "the hands of God." Jesus' hands have a power over Teresa all the way through to the spiritual marriage.

The image of "so beautiful a face" complements the hand image, but it is a different metaphor. It is one thing to hold a hand, to be held in another's hands, even to be caressed by hands. It is another experience to look into a beautiful light-filled face. I cannot recall without tears the words my mother wrote to me on my fiftieth birthday: "I still remember," she said, "the first time I looked into your beautiful little face," and I reflect on the meaning of a mother's face in a baby's life and development. Whether a child sees herself as beloved or blamed, worthwhile or inferior, is dependent on what she has seen in the face of her mother. Face has a primary association with mother.

In her work on Julian of Norwich, Elizabeth Koenig draws on an essay by D. W. Winnicott who argues that "the mother's face is the precursor of the mirror in its contribution to the sense of personal identity."[43] This essay intrigues me because in one of the last visions Teresa describes in the *Life*, Jesus is a mirror filling her soul. Koenig tells us that when an infant looks at her mother, what the baby sees is not the mother but the baby herself. The mother is looking at the baby but what she looks like [to the baby] is related to what she, herself, sees. If she is so pre-occupied with herself that she only reflects her own mood or, worse still, the rigidity of her own defenses, the baby may spend a lifetime trying to find someone who can give her to herself. If the mother's face is not a mirror in which the baby may learn about herself, she

43. Elizabeth Koenig writes about this in her doctoral dissertation *The Book of Showings of Julian of Norwich: A Test Case for Paul Ricoeur's Theories of Metaphor and Imagination*. Koenig draws on D. W. Winnicott's "Mirror-role of Mother and Family in Child Development," *Playing and Reality* (New York: Basic Books, Inc., Publishers, 1971).

will move through life attempting to be seen in a way that will make her feel she exists and is worthwhile.

When we reflect on Teresa's early descriptions of her own self-image, we sense she needed to receive something of herself from the face of another. This can throw new light on the significance for Teresa of the face of Jesus Christ which she says "gives the most intense delight to the sight" in its splendor and soft whiteness and beauty. It suggests that the Face functions as a maternal, feminine symbol even when the face belongs to a friend, a lover, or a god. To look into a face that is *for us*, in whose beauty and total regard we see our own unsuspected beauty and potential, is expressive of a whole new level of self-understanding.

Here we see, as John of the Cross suggests, that God moves through human ways of knowing, according to the mode of the soul, according to the way the human person is made. God does not violate our deepest needs but fulfills slowly in our life situations our most profound desires for reassurance, unconditional love, tenderness, and special regard.[44] We see also that God, like a mother, is on the side not of lifelong subordination and inferiority but of development characterized by mutuality.

This was Teresa's learning as the experience of Jesus risen imprinted itself on her heart as a vibrant living image. Then she discovered that although she had sinned and was weak, she really was an image of God. When she compares the light of this vision to the sun and assures us the brightness of the sun appears very tarnished beside the glorified Jesus, she could be describing the movement of her own self-understanding. "It's like the difference between a sparkling, clear water that flows over crystal and on which the sun is reflecting and a very cloudy, muddy water flowing along the ground." Teresa saw very clearly, as did those who knew her, that these experiences had radically changed her. Even her health improved![45]

44. See *Ascent* 2.17. This is a key passage in understanding the developmental aspect of John's teaching. Moreover, it reveals his epistemology.

45. *Life* 8.5, 11, 13; see also *Castle* 6.1.4.

What must be stressed here again is the all-pervasive presence of the dialogue, or the dynamic of reciprocity, between Jesus and Teresa. Each responded to the other in a day by day companionship that stretched over the years and changed both Teresa and God. Jesus Christ accommodated his presence to Teresa's moods and the circumstances of her life. She tells us that although it was the risen Jesus who accompanied her, when she was suffering and when she was wounded by misunderstanding and persecution, he appeared on the cross or in the garden, wounded or crowned with thorns. In fact, he took her part and guided her through the misunderstandings, suspicions, and poor counsel of her confessors who continued to believe she was deceived by the devil and should resist her visions.

When men continued to press her to repudiate her own inner experience, a challenge was thrown to Teresa (and perhaps to Jesus!). Would she repudiate the love experience, would she choose self-hatred over self-acceptance, would she accept the self being shown and given to her by Jesus—a self connected, related, possessed—rather than the isolated self being forced upon her? We sense the struggle and more than a hint of humor when she tells us that Jesus seemed annoyed when she was forbidden to practice prayer. "He told me to tell them that now what they were doing was tyranny and He gave me signs for knowing that the vision was not from the devil." Furthermore, when she tried to obey the command to reject and resist her experiences, "there was a much greater increase in them." Jesus taught her what she should say and gave her so many adequate reasons that she felt "completely secure."[46]

We get the full import of Teresa's internal conflict in Jesus' next move. He took in his own hands the cross Teresa was holding to drive him away. When he returned it to her, it was made of precious stones. After that, she always saw the cross this way, but no one saw it except her! This is powerful symbolism to express not only the continual challenge to Teresa to accept her own inner truth, her whole humanity, but also the integration of

46. For this whole section see *Life* 29.2-7.

many seemingly contradictory elements in her life: outer obedience with inner freedom and certitude; conflict and opposition with genuine maturation; personal autonomy and strength with fidelity and surrender in relationship; inner light with inner darkness. All this was the fruit of the experience of being in love with God. And she was in love with God precisely because she, herself, was loved without restriction.

Teresa's life and desire, therefore, stood open to God's next move in the dialogue! She had reached another intersection. She tells us:

> I saw close to me . . . an angel in bodily form . . . very beautiful, and his face was so aflame that he seemed to be one of those very sublime angels that appear to be all afire. I saw in his hands a large golden dart and at the end of the iron tip there appeared to be a little fire. It seemed to me this angel plunged the dart several times into my heart and that it reached deep within me. When he drew it out, I thought he was carrying off the deepest part of me; and he left me all on fire with great love of God.[47]

In the beautiful fiery angel, we see the antithesis of the devil who was, according to many, the cause of Teresa's visions of Christ. As a symbol of the world of God, the angel is, first of all, another confirmation of Teresa's very self and a promise of eventual victory over the power of evil. The experience of an angel complements the visions of devils and hell, which we see in Teresa's *Life* at this time, and brings to consciousness Teresa's on-going struggle to understand her own humanity even more deeply and to integrate into a wholesome self-image both the light and the darkness in her own heart. But there is much more in this rich symbolism.[48]

47. Ibid., chap. 29, nos. 13, 10; see *Castle* 6.2.4.

48. Teresa writes at length about seeing the devil. This is one of the ways she describes the dark night. See, for example, chap. 31.2.9. Darkness weaves its way in and out of Teresa's experience over a lifetime, as we see in her writings. Because I have written elsewhere about earlier phases of the dark night, I have chosen to concentrate later in this paper on Teresa's most profound experience of abandonment, just prior to the spiritual marriage. See note 66.

Standing as it did just before the beginning of her reform of the Carmelite Order, at a time of intense persecution and suffering, this vision signaled a *painful* breakthrough to a whole new level of life, motivation and energy for Teresa. The awesome configuration of symbols—the fire, the arrow, the pierced heart, the wound—tell of a shattering intrusion, and of a demand for total self-donation and availability. The heart with all its great, conflicting desires was torn open, pierced to its very depths, possessed by a compelling power capable of either destroying what it touched, or changing it into itself. Teresa, in a sense, became the fire; she did not surrender to destruction. Instead, her insatiable desire and passion absorbed the fire and were transformed into boundless spiritual energy. But we must not miss the implication that this creativity was bought at a price: disintegration—change—for the sake of God.

Heart is one of the basic, primordial images of the self. To see it thrust itself into Teresa's consciousness with such intensity and power clearly manifests that a process of unusual spiritual maturation and fulfillment is going on in the depths of her soul. The psyche is moving toward its full expansion in a decisive moment of illumination. This means that while the *heart* pierced and wounded with the *flaming arrow* indicates, in Teresa, an explicit awareness of an intersubjective union of love with God, the emotional identification with that God that we see here is only possible because of the unity and wholeness of the self that have slowly developed in the life-long relationship with Jesus Christ.[49] Because her self-image had been purified, to some extent, of its sinful tendencies toward inferiority and excessive self-depreciation, Teresa could surrender to being loved and claimed by God. Stripped of concern for human respect, she could receive the creative energy of love that would issue in an alternative vision, new life and service in the sixteenth century Church.

John of the Cross clearly understood the relationship of this experience to Teresa's role as foundress and/or reformer. He writes explicitly about her in *The Living Flame*:

49. In an article on Therese of Lisieux I have written at more length about the symbol of heart. See Constance FitzGerald, "Contemplative Life and Charismatic Presence," *Spiritual Life* (Spring 1983): 18–30.

> The soul feels its ardor strengthen and increase and its love become so refined in this ardor that seemingly there are seas of loving fire within it, reaching to the heights and depths of the earthly and heavenly spheres embuing all with love. It seems to it that the entire universe is a sea of love in which it is engulfed, for, conscious of the living point or center of love within itself, it is unable to catch sight of the boundaries of this love. . . . The soul is converted into the immense fire of love. . . . Few persons have reached these heights. Some have, however; especially those whose virtue and spirit was to be diffused among their children. For God accords to founders, with respect to the first fruits of the spirit, wealth and value commensurate with the greater or lesser following they will have in their doctrine and spirituality.[50]

A deep reading of Teresa's text allows us to see that the God of Teresa did not want a fearful, subservient woman. The expectations of the friendship were far too demanding for that. Only a strong woman capable of capitalizing on her own inner experience to create imaginative life alternatives could bear to hear the Lord's next "compelling" words in the dialogue which commanded her to strive to found a new monastery—no matter how others would judge the venture. We have to read chapters 32–34 of Teresa's *Life*, where she describes the reactions of her own community, her confessors, superiors, and even the people of Avila, to understand the dramatic and sometimes comical dialogue between Jesus and Teresa. Beneath it, we touch Teresa's profound life struggle between self-doubt and fear, on the one hand, and a whole new vision of reality, on the other. Teresa was being urged to take the image of Christ that had slowly been etched into her inner being and to create in her own social milieu, far beyond the boundaries of her own soul, a likeness of that love-image.[51] Because she was being pushed toward an autonomy stronger than her society allowed or would approve, she cried out:

> My Lord, how is it that you command things that seem impossible? For if I were at least free, even though I am a woman! But

50. *Flame* 2.10-12.

51. In the *Life* 37.4 Teresa writes: "The vision of Christ left upon me an impression of his most extraordinary beauty, and the impression remains to this day."

> bound on so many sides, without money or the means to raise it or to obtain the brief or anything, what can I do, Lord?[52]

During this time Teresa's obsession with self-doubt, with fear of deception, with a consciousness of her own sinfulness, was balanced by repeated moments of inner affirmation and assurance. While so many around her condemned her, belittled her, and attempted to stop the new foundation, she vacillated between extreme anxiety and an amazing ability not to take the reprimands to heart. That she was growing steadily in self-esteem and trust in her own inner wisdom is evidenced by a plethora of images in her numerous visions and locutions. For instance, she experienced herself clothed in a robe of shining brightness by our Lady and St. Joseph who promised to watch over her and who placed around her neck, as a sign, a beautiful golden necklace. Our Lady took Teresa *by the hands* and encouraged her to make the foundation of St. Joseph's. Moreover, she says, "I was given to understand that I was now cleansed from my sins." Later she saw Christ who seemed to be receiving her with great love and who placed a crown on her head and thanked her for what she did for his Mother.

Teresa's God was forcing her to believe in herself in spite of a patriarchal culture which put little store in the wisdom, judgement, or abilities of women. The Lord told her to proceed and not to listen to the various opinions because few would counsel her prudently! Furthermore, she wasn't to be distressed about making the foundation under the protection of the Bishop of Avila and, therefore, not giving obedience to the Order, for "the Lord had told me," she said, "it wasn't suitable to give it to my superiors! He gave me the reasons why it would in no way be fitting that I do so. But he told me I should petition Rome in a certain way . . . and that he would take care that we get our request. And so it came about."[53]

Teresa's ability to envision and then pursue creative life alternatives was not based on an isolated, autonomous, go-it-alone ego. Rather it was rooted in a deep connectedness and identifica-

52. Ibid., 33.11.

53. Ibid., 33.14, 16; 36.24; 34.2.

tion with *Another* to whom she was related in unconditional love. Hence, she could say with a hint of exasperation when everything seemed to be failing: "Lord, this house is not mine; it was founded for you; now that there is no one to take care of its affairs, you . . . must do so." And earlier when she was worried that the house and grounds she had were much too small for a monastery, she heard an irritated Lord say to her: "Oh covetousness of the human race, that you think you will be lacking even ground! How many times did I sleep in the open because I had no place else."[54]

The easy familiarity and affirmation of this constant companionship signaled a growing feeling of equality with others, even with the nobility. Teresa tells us that she conversed with them with the freedom she would have felt had she been their equal in social position. Even more significant, though, is the subtle experience of equality with Jesus Christ. She admits:

> I began to talk to the Lord in a foolish way, which I often do without knowing what I am saying. It is love that is then speaking, and . . . the soul is so transported that *I don't know the difference there is between it and God.*[55]

In the context of this identification and equality, we finally see the resolution of Teresa's life-long conflict over human friendship. When after many years she met again the Dominican Garcia de Toledo, they were drawn irresistibly to share their life experiences with each other. Since Teresa liked him so much, she longed for him to give himself totally to God and God's service and so she prayed: "Lord, you must not deny me this favor. See how this individual is fit to be *our* friend." Then she adds, "O the goodness and great humanity of God!" But then Teresa was overcome with great affliction and guilt lest she had seriously offended God. She was not yet consciously at peace with her human loves. The Lord, however, gave her a message for the priest through which he turned completely to God. Later when Teresa was rejoicing over the graces given to the man and thanking God for *fulfilling*

54. Ibid., 36.17; 33.12.
55. Ibid., 34.8.3; see also *Castle* 6.8.4.

her desires, and making "a little old woman wiser . . . [than] a very learned man," she was overcome by rapture and she tells us:

> I saw Christ with awesome majesty and glory showing great happiness over what was taking place. Thus he told me and wanted me to see clearly that he is always present in conversations like these and how much he is pleased when persons so delight in speaking of him.[56]

Here we see a reversal in Teresa's God. Before she was to talk with angels, not human persons. Now her God not only rejoiced in her human conversations and loves but understood her love and concern and compassion for others as an extension of the love that was flooding her life. Now her God rushed to answer her prayers for others and to verify her relationships, even with those who had died.[57] Teresa's awareness had changed and she no longer saw her human friendships as conflictual. It was as if they were given back to her. In her deep emotional identification with the humanity of God, she herself experienced a new solidarity with everything human in herself and others.[58]

In one of her "most sublime visions" she *saw* with deep inner knowledge the humanity of Jesus, and *humanity in Jesus,* being taken into the bosom of the Divinity in whose presence she experienced herself to be. What did it mean for humanity to be taken into God? Certainly, she could never be the same. In fact, this vision was symbolic of a radically altered world view. She tells us she understood with contemplative intuition what Truth is and what it is for a human person "to walk in truth before Truth itself." She *knew* finally that just as every truth imaginable depended upon this Truth, so all her human loves were a part of this love, and every grandeur she could know was a reflection of this Grandeur.[59]

56. Ibid., 34.17; see also 34.8-12.

57. Ibid., see vision in 39.1 and chaps. 38 and 39 to see how and why Teresa's prayers for others were answered.

58. See *Testimonies* 2.4.

59. See *Life* 38.17-18; 40.1-4; *Castle* 6.10.7.

In the symbolism of one of the last experiences she describes in the book of her *Life*, we glimpse the extent to which she passed over into the perspective of God regarding both her own self-understanding and her whole vision of reality. She writes:

> [My soul] seemed to me to be like a brightly polished mirror, without any part on the back or sides or top or bottom that wasn't totally clear. In its center Christ our Lord was shown to me. . . . It seemed to me I saw him clearly in every part of my soul, as though in a mirror. And this mirror also . . . was completely engraved upon the Lord himself by means of a loving communication I wouldn't know how to describe.[60]

There is no vision in the whole of Teresa's writings that thrills me like this imagery. Teresa looked into herself, a mirror, and she saw Christ. There was nothing but this completed imprint of Christ, etched within her, totally filling the mirror. She looked at Christ and yet she saw herself—engraved upon the Lord. Christ, the self-knowledge of humanity, gave her to herself. We marvel at such mutual indwelling, such mutual imprinting, that speaks not only of radical self-donation but just as strongly of self-possession. Teresa's heart had found its dwelling place. Yet, she herself was a dwelling place. She was at home in her own house, her Self! "Each is transfigured in the other," says John. The truth of the self and the truth of the other were revealed, and the desire of the human heart was fulfilled without restriction. Teresa truly experienced herself and her acts united to the self and acts of Christ. John of the Cross writes in The *Spiritual Canticle* that Christ "will really transform her into the beauty of both his created and uncreated Wisdom, and also into the beauty of the Word with his humanity."[61] Could there be any deeper answer for Teresa to the question of ultimate reliability or the fear of abandonment? The

60. *Life* 40.5 with note 6; see also *Castle* 6.10.2; *Way* 28.9-12; *Testimonies* 20.13-14.

61. *Canticle* 38.1; see Cirlot, *Dictionary*, "mirror," 211–12; *Castle* 7.2.8; *Flame* 1.9-13. To understand the kind of affirmation Teresa received, see *Life* 39.22; 40.12.

mirror is a striking symbol of mystical consciousness all through spiritual literature. It shows us Teresa, the woman mystic, effectively connected in reciprocal mutuality with God and with the entire universe.

For not only is her soul a mirror, not only is Christ a mirror, but for Teresa, Divinity is, as it were, a mirror or a very clear diamond, "much greater than all the world," in which she clearly sees everything in the universe joined together, everything part of the whole. All things are held in God—good and evil and all loves. And God is, after all, the embrace of human love, of friendship. The experience of Teresa deals a death blow not only to going it alone, but even going it alone with God.[62]

Dark Night

One might think that now Teresa's development was complete, but she tells of a time of deep pain and insatiable desire when she was overcome by a sense of total estrangement and extreme desolation. Her human powers were paralyzed from the pain.

> The soul begins to grow so weary that it ascends far above itself and all creatures. God places it in a desert so distant from all things, that however much it labors, it doesn't find a creature on earth that might accompany it . . . it desires only to die in that solitude.[63]

The desert symbolizes Teresa's experience of human powerlessness before the incomprehensible mystery of salvation. It was Teresa's final temptation to disavow her self-worth and to succumb in despair to inferiority, subordination and "wretchedness." She stood on the brink without a final answer to the question of ultimate reliability and value. She was challenged to see in the mirror without any defenses, filters, or support, not only

62. *Life* 40.9-10.

63. Ibid., 20.9; see 20.8-16; 30.8-14. Teresa tells us this time of estrangement occurred after everything else she writes of in her *Life*. However, she completed that work long before she died and before she reached the Spiritual Marriage.

the stark reality of her own darkness, which was hard enough, but even the evil of humanity, and still believe in unconditional love.[64] This is the blackest time of night, John of the Cross tells us, when the last delicate shading of the image of Jesus, crucified and abandoned, is being sketched within the human heart in total darkness and absolute silence. He says, "The soul cannot see herself in the beauty of God unless she is transformed in the Wisdom of God" (divine Wisdom) . . . and made to resemble her . . . "who is the Word, the Son of God." But the gate entering into the fullness of these riches of Wisdom is the cross of Jesus. It seems that a final phase of the transfiguration of Teresa and Jesus in each other could only occur in the dispossession of the Cross and the desperate scream of the heart, "My God, why have you abandoned me?" The image was, as it were, being finished when Teresa no longer had any consciousness of it, when she no longer saw it, or when all the images she had known had lost their cogency.[65] When we realize the power and the fullness of the image or vision of Christ in Teresa's experience over a lifetime, we can grasp the significance and extent of this deprivation.

In the dark night we are, in fact, always purified and transformed through what we cherish and through what gives us security and support. In other words, for Teresa, the relationship itself became the cause of pain. Its intense reciprocity actually highlighted human limitation, and even the limitations of God. This was Teresa's most profound experience of abandonment, and it preceded what both she and John call the spiritual marriage. For Teresa and John, God seemed to walk away, seemed to break the connectedness: "Where have you hidden, Beloved, and left me to my moaning. You fled like the stag after wounding me; I went out calling you and you were gone."[66]

64. See *Flame* 1.20, and *Life* 40.10.

65. *Canticle* 36.7, 8, 13; see *Life* 20.11.

66. *Canticle* poem 1; see *Testimonies* 22.2. In my article "Impasse and Dark Night," in *Living with Apocalypse* (San Francisco: Harper & Row, 1984), 94–116, I deal with dark night in the sense mentioned here. There I draw on Michael J. Buckley, "Atheism and Contemplation," *Theological Studies* 40 (1979).

John throws a very clear light on this experience of Teresa. I want to move, therefore, to him for an understanding of this dark night which, he says, shows us the whole person deprived in her entire life situation. John, a man and a theologian, writes from the side of the powerless, the inferior, the poor and the abandoned. He tells of the darkness enwrapping their minds, their empty terror and hopelessness in the face of the overpowering burden of their memories, the anguished longing for a lost hope, a lost dream, a lost love. John's God of the dark night has such power over him, such power to disturb and control. He says:

> God divests the faculties, affections and senses, both spiritual and sensory, interior and exterior. He leaves the intellect in darkness, the will in aridity, the memory in emptiness, and the affections in supreme affliction, bitterness and anguish, by depriving the soul of the feeling and satisfaction it previously obtained from spiritual blessings.[67]

If we attempt to interpret John's teaching, we discover that here there is no reassurance or affirmation that one can discern. All supports drop from one's consciousness and only the experience of emptiness, vulnerability and abandonment remain. In earlier times, the desert had woven its way in and out of life bringing dryness, boredom and the absence of pleasure, but now the dark desert night eclipses the very support systems that have given life meaning and value and through which reassurance has been forthcoming. When John says the intellect is empty and in darkness, he seems to suggest that everything the person has understood and has accumulated by way of knowledge, everything that has given it *faith* and *God*—its concepts, theology, systems of thought, symbolic structures, relationships, institutions, etc.—become meaningless. Nothing makes any sense, so that the mind, while full on one level of everything the person *knows*, is in total darkness on another level, the level of meaning. The knowledge, the understanding, that has provided support for a lifetime becomes a vast, painful, dark emptiness. In other words, nothing

67. *Night* 2.3.3; see also 2.4.1; 2.16.1.

Teresa understood from her past experience gave her satisfaction or security. She explains:

> The fact is that it seems everything the soul understands then adds to its pain, and that the Lord doesn't want it to profit in its entire being from anything else.[68]

When John describes the emptiness of the memory, our minds stumble because we know human memory is *full* of experience. But in the afflicted, anguished memory, memories once so life-giving, significant, and affirming now rise like piled ash in a bottomless void. The imagination can no longer connect life's memories to produce meaning and hope. One can speak of emptiness in the memory, not because one remembers nothing, but because all that the memory holds, which once provided motivation and security, which engendered trust, hope, and promise for the future, now mocks the abandoned heart. Memories do not mean now what one thought or imagined they did. The memory is indeed empty, holding only the scattered remains of cherished experiences—experiences one thought revealed God and were the ground in which trust in the "Other" germinated and grew. Someone has written that the day will come when one must go on *in spite of* memories.[69]

Yes, one must will to go on even when the will is touched by sorrows, deadness, affliction, and painful longing. We have to understand that abandonment and the seeming betrayal of trust and love are the heart of this dark experience. What one wants and needs and clings to more than anything in life, that which one cherishes above all else, is withdrawn, taken away, denied. Moreover, the loved one, the very focus of one's love and desire, becomes the cause of one's agony and distress. There is nothing so destructive of affirmation and, therefore, of motivation and meaning, as the seeming rejection and abandonment by one who has loved you, who has touched your naked vulnerability, and on whom you have counted with complete assurance.

68. *Testimonies* 59.14.

69. See *Ascent* 2.2.3; 9.5; *Life* 30.8.

The destruction of mutuality, with its deep frustration of desire, is a humiliation, a dispossession, and a death which leaves the person (the *will*) unable to grasp anything affectively. A transcendence is forced upon a person in which she is not at home, against which she rebels. Depression invades the whole structure of personality with the certainty that one's life is over and that there is nothing to live for because one's good is gone forever. Life becomes absurd when one feels that there is no one anywhere who is *for me*. With no home within or without, the thought of a deeper union than one formerly knew is beyond comprehension. One looks, therefore, with the eyes of absolute doubt toward a hell of eternal nothingness. An eternal life where affectivity and desire are fulfilled is a mockery. Bitterness, anger, and hate well up like an uncontrollable flood, from the very heart of one's frustrated desire and betrayed love, to threaten destruction and collapse. Rejection and abandonment surface so much human "shadow" and all the unintegrated contents of the human soul.[70]

Let us look at the dynamic in Teresa. The intensity of mutuality between her and Jesus Christ put in strong relief human limitation and even the "limitations" of God. In the mirror, everything was seen; there was too much self-knowledge and the feeling of extreme unworthiness resulted. Her love was not great enough, she thought, and she was too "wretched" to be loved. Therefore, she was being abandoned once and for all. The temptation to inferiority was overpowering and, in her depression, she was angry not only with herself but with those others who could not measure up to her expectations of human life. She describes her experience:

> Nor does its will appear to be alive, but it seems to be in so great a solitude and so forsaken by all that this abandonment cannot be described in writing. For the whole world and its affairs give it pain, and no created thing provides it with company, nor does it want any company but only the Creator . . . it . . . dies with the longing to die.

70. To understand this interpretation see *Dark Night* 2.4-12; *Flame* 1.20-22; *Life* 32.1-4.

> The devil gives a spirit of anger so displeasing that it seems as if I want to eat everyone up, without being able to help it.[71]

The only way to get a new perspective on this impasse, John tells us, is to accept the alternative vision of faith, hope, and love and so pass over into the perspective of God.

> We must lead the faculties of the soul to these three virtues and inform each faculty with one of them (faith in the intellect, hope in the memory, and love in the will) by stripping and darkening it of everything which is not conformable to these virtues.[72]

We know the theological virtues are gifts of God, but we act and speak as if we can muster them up in crisis. So, we hear it said, "She had such strong faith. Her faith got her through." This is, of course, true to some extent. However, in *this* darkness and hopelessness, when we no longer feel any faith or any hope, when we hang over the abyss of atheism, absolute doubt and total loss of trust, we truly learn *they are gifts* "made possible and effective by the divine self-bestowal itself," as Karl Rahner explains in his "Theology of Hope."[73] They become the only way, the only response, to an *unsought*, inescapable darkness and emptiness. They are gifts that bring us blindness and agony, gifts we all but reject in our despair. They must overcome an anger, fear, and rebellion that want to refuse grace rather than be left with *nothing*. These gifts are known *only in retrospect* by their power to catch and bind the falling, desperate person to God. Perhaps, we learn the critical importance of the theological virtues only at this stage of development! What is harder to understand is *why* we only believe and hope in God truly, theologically, when nothing else any longer sustains us. John must have struggled deeply to find the answer to human suffering to write as he does.

71. *Testimonies* 54.14; *Life* 30.13.

72. *Ascent* 2.6.6; see all of chap. 6 for John's doctrine on the theological virtues; also see *Dark Night* 2.21.11; 13.11.

73. Karl Rahner, *Theological Investigations X* (New York: Seabury, 1977), 245–47.

Thus, he explains, faith causes darkness in our very power to understand. Now it is at cross purposes with our ability to make *logical* sense out of life, death and eternity, out of loss, rejection, and abandonment. Faith moves us into Mystery which is incomprehensible, unimaginable and uncontrollable. Only in some kind of searing loss, it seems, do we begin to know experientially that God is indeed *the darkness* beyond all our concepts, images, experiences, feelings, and perceptions, and that, as John writes, no knowledge or feeling bears any resemblance to God.[74]

The horizon of the mind is boundless. The one we call God dwells in this nameless and pathless expanse of our consciousness. When Jesus Christ seems to recede from our consciousness, when nothing human satisfies because of losses without and bitterness within, and we, therefore, come to the very limits of human understanding, is this a signal that God waits over the brink? When we look back and nothing is left, when ahead we see only meaninglessness, when the images and representations of life are empty, is God then the unimaginable darkness over the brink?[75]

> This [night] guided me
> more surely than the noon
> to where he waited for me
> —Him I knew so well—
> in a place where no one else appeared.[76]

The hopelessness and emptiness of the dark night are precisely the conditions that make hope in the strictly theological sense possible. Hope can come into play only when we are radically at the end, absolutely unable to find any further resources within ourselves to connect the memories, feelings, images and experi-

74. See *Ascent* 2.3 for John's teaching on faith; see also 2.4.1-3; 2.8-9; *Dark Night* 2.16.8, par. 2; *Life* 30.12.

75. Juan Luis Segundo calls this the passage from anthropological faith to authentic faith in *Faith and Ideologies* (Maryknoll, N.Y.: Orbis Books, 1984), 166. Karl Rahner has helped me to bring John of the Cross' teaching into dialogue with contemporary experience. See "The Experience of the Spirit," *Theological Investigations XVIII* (New York: Crossroads, 1983), 196–97.

76. *Dark Night* poem, 4.

ences of life into a meaningful pattern or a promising future. Yet, it is hard to surrender to hope, hard to believe there is a possession worth possessing beyond everything we have known. Hope, as John of the Cross and Karl Rahner see it, is free and trustful commitment to the impossible, to that which cannot be built out of what one possesses. In hope we allow ourselves finally to be grasped and drawn out of ourselves by the absolutely uncontrollable, who is God. Hope, therefore, perfects the memory [and imagination], John says, and prepares it for union with God.[77]

Estrangement and abandonment administer the final test of love—genuine love of the self that continues to believe in its own worth, and a love of the other that will not surrender in the end to hate or violence. This love overcomes the will to die, to give up, to commit suicide literally or figuratively, and, instead, truly lives with the pain of its woundedness and longing. We can identify this experience in a woman, or a man, who is abandoned after many years of marriage, or after total, self-giving love, and who does not surrender finally to cynicism and hate. We see it when a spouse or child is taken away, tortured, and murdered, and a person continues to labor for the well-being and freedom of those left behind.

Any feeling of superiority or exclusivity is destroyed in this experience. In this sense, dark night is, indeed, a leveler. Love, care, compassion for *us*, a common humanity, flower here. When we stand in this kind of nakedness, with all our masks ripped away, we see our common bonding and we know that we are "equal."[78] Then faith affirms *for us* a wisdom and light beyond our own reason. It affirms life and meaning beyond any carefully reasoned plans for meaningless destruction. Then, hope is exercised *for all* against domination, abandonment and final annihilation. Then,

77. *Dark Night* 2.21.11; *Ascent* 3.15.1; 3.7.2; 3.11.1-2; see Karl Rahner, "On the Theology of Hope," *Theological Investigations X*, 242–59; "Theology of Death," *Theological Investigations XIII* (New York: Crossroads, 1983), 176–84.

78. Marie Celeste Fadden, OCD, of Reno Carmel has captured the reality of this solidarity in a painting of incredible power and feeling that she executed for Edith Stein's beatification. It shows Edith at the gate of Auschwitz identified and one with the Jewish men, women and children being herded to their death.

love affirms *for us* the bondedness, communion, and equality of all women and all men beyond rejection, violence, and inequality.

Transformation after Darkness

Teresa's sense of herself survived the onslaught of the fire of self-knowledge. Fidelity in this dark faith, hope, and love completed her transformation and she was transfigured by the love, wisdom, and power of God.[79] The fear that had repeatedly made her a victim of male domination gave way to the experience of inner Power. Her feelings of inferiority and ignorance were put to rest in the certainty of the wisdom she possessed. Her questions about ultimate exclusion, rejection, and abandonment were finally answered in the experience of a mutuality of love and gifts that could not be doubted. John explains Teresa's experience of wholeness in *The Spiritual Canticle*:

> This is the transformation in the three persons in power, wisdom and love and thus the soul is like God through this transformation. God created her in his image and likeness that she might attain such resemblance.[80]

Teresa speaks of this "imprinting" of the Blessed Trinity in the center of her being as an experience of indescribable understanding and communion. In her use of the word "imprinting," we realize that the image of Christ that had been in process over a lifetime was completed. She truly was a likeness of God. John says: "The Spouse will really transform her into the beauty of both created and uncreated Wisdom, and also into the beauty of the union of the Word with his humanity."[81]

The totality and depth of Teresa's relationship to God was symbolized in a beautiful vision of the risen Jesus when she was

79. For John of the Cross, purification and transformation are two sides of a single coin. The same fire that burns the log black causes the blackened wood to burst into brilliant flame. This realization pervades *The Living Flame*. See, for example, stanza 1.1-25, especially no. 1.

80. *Canticle* 39.4.

81. Ibid., 38.1; 42; *Castle* 7.1.6, 7.

fifty-seven years old. He gave her his right *hand,* as one gives his hand in marriage to his bride, and told her that now it was time that she consider as her own what belonged to him and that he would take care of what was hers. The hand which Teresa experienced in so many ways throughout her life was finally the symbol of the fulfillment of her desire, for Jesus said to her:

> Behold this nail; it is a sign you will be my bride from today on. Until now you have not merited this; from now on not only will you look after my honor as being the honor of your Creator, King and God, but you will look after it as my true bride. My honor is yours and yours mine.[82]

In the nail we understand that all the painful past was brought into this union. The nail sealed forever Teresa's identification with the dying, abandoned Jesus. Because they had shared a common pain, all their possessions were now held in common. John tells us the soul is called the bride of the Son of God to signify her equality with him. God, he says, "makes her love him with the very strength with which he loves her. Transforming her into his love . . . he gives her his own strength by which she can love him . . . he always desired this equality . . . for a lover cannot be satisfied if [she] fails to feel that [she] loves as much as [she] is loved."[83] For God and for Teresa, the heart of equality is love. Only love creates equality. Love gives equality. Love receives equality.

It is interesting to see honor appear as a symbol of the spiritual marriage. It is another symbol of equality. In sixteenth-century Spain, honor was prized more than life itself. It was *the* value that determined personal worth and social acceptance. In her writings and her reform, Teresa was, like the people of her time, "obsessed with honor which stands out everywhere and in the most unexpected passages."[84] Here we see Teresa's concern for honor (the material of ordinary human life and culture) transformed into a

82. *Testimonies* 31.

83. *Canticle* 38.3-4; see also *Flame* 3.78-79 for equality.

84. Teofanes Egido, OCD, "The Historical Setting of St. Teresa's Life," trans. Michael Dodd and Steven Payne, *Carmelite Studies* 1 (Washington, D.C.: ICS Publications, 1980), 152.

symbol of equality and love and made the heart of the mutuality. The nail of Jesus' cross, the honor of Teresa's Spain: real life symbols to show the total sharing of life in God's world.

Now, John tells us, the person "always walks in festivity" and so John of the Cross sings for Teresa at this point:

> Let us rejoice, Beloved,
> Let us go forth to behold ourselves in your beauty,
> To the mountain and to the hill,
> To where the pure water flows,
> And further, deep into the thicket.[85]

This means, he says, "Transform me into the beauty of Divine Wisdom and make me resemble [her] which is the Word, the Son of God." And then "she asks that he inform her with the beauty of this other lesser wisdom, contained in his creatures. . . . The soul cannot see herself in the beauty of God unless she is transformed in the Wisdom of God, in which she sees herself in possession of earthly and heavenly things. . . . God permits it in this state to discern its beauty and he entrusts to it the gifts and virtues he has bestowed."[86]

Beyond anything she could have dreamed of, Teresa, *the woman*, was affirmed in a definitive way. In the face of eternal Wisdom, she saw the giftedness of her own self, precisely as woman, and the power and possibilities of the insight she now possessed. With God's view of things—her mind united to the mind of God, her will to the will of God, her memory attuned "so as to have in its mind the eternal years"—she saw a new way of life rooted in the reality of what she experienced: love, connectedness, relationship, communion and equality.[87]

She envisioned, in fact, a new social order where all were to be equal.[88] In her small communities of contemplative women, Teresa set in motion a reversal of the social and religious order

85. *Canticle* 36.
86. Ibid., 36.6-8; *Flame* 1.31.
87. *Flame* 1.32; 2.34; 1.22; 4.5-7; *Canticle* 37.3; 39.11.
88. *Way* 27.6.

by a spiritual one that would eradicate the highest principles of the established order and undermine the current images of social status. Her fearless struggle to destroy concern for honor and wealth and, therefore, uphold the value of person over money and ancestry; her unswerving struggle for the recognition of women's rights to deep interior prayer and, therefore, to significant service in the Church at a time of great ecclesial danger and turmoil: these constituted the framework on which she built her renewal of the Carmelite Order in the sixteenth-century church, as well as her teaching on prayer, wholeness, and union with God.[89]

While John was also a major figure in the Reform of Carmel and contributed deeply to its spiritual formation, his creativity lives majestically and, above all else, in his poetry which has survived for four hundred years. It witnesses, as nothing else can, to the grandeurs of an equality of love with God. John was so affirmed by God in his life that nothing could destroy his self-confidence. Though he was persecuted, blamed, and pushed aside after Teresa's death, he could die singing of the treasures of God and the beauty of the human person living in communion and equality with God. It is significant that one of the reasons he was removed from a leadership position and deprived of influence in the Carmelite Order was his defense of the rights of the Carmelite nuns, the daughters of that great woman Teresa who was, he knew, his companion and equal, not only in the depth and intensity of her experience of God, but also in her ability to write about the ways of God.

Conclusion

John of the Cross obviously writes from his own experience. However, he also describes Teresa's experience, and he describes the experience of many women past and present. His teaching on the dark night raises the painful, paradoxical question: Is it necessary for women today to *accept* the place in which they find themselves and stand without the comfortable connections and

89. See Egido, "The Historical Setting of St. Teresa's Life," 130.

belongingness and loves they have known; to stay in the place where previous understandings and memories are not consolations but only burdens, and where *faith and hope* in the face of the unacceptable, the totally unfathomable, are the only doorway to insight, healing, vision, creative new life, the intimate touch of communion, and equality? Must we be able to stand without the God we once *saw* and even, to some degree, the understanding and support of men and institutions, as Teresa did? In *The Living Flame,* John answers through the author of the Book of Wisdom: "If the spirit of the One who has power descends upon you, do not abandon your place (the place and the site of your probation), for the cure will make great sins cease."[90]

Our dark night comes to us because of our particular time and place in history. The consciousness of our age shapes it, just as the particular awareness of Teresa's time shaped hers. When we can respond with enduring faith, hope and love to the dark presence of an incomprehensible God, who calls us to something new, we will perhaps, like Teresa, be led finally to the fulfillment of our deep human desires in a relationship of love and equality. Then we might know how to create and express a vision of connectedness and equality in our own groups and communities, and, thereby, move our world and our Church beyond the unequal power relations that are tearing them apart. The only question is this: Can we, women and men, do it without becoming mystics? In Teresa, we see that becoming a mystic, a contemplative, is possible for fragile human people like us. In her transformation we understand just how true it is that the degree of our religious consciousness, the depth of our communion with God, does indeed condition the depth of our experience of equality and solidarity.

In tracing the image of Christ through Teresa's writings, and following the movement of her self-understanding from inferiority, confusion of heart, and fear of abandonment to connectedness, mutuality, and equality of love, we grasp the centrality of Jesus Christ in the Christian mystical experience. Moreover, an analysis of her complex experience/visions reveals a Christology

90. *Flame* 1.19.

that certainly does not validate either the subordination or the exclusion of women. On the contrary, the "world" of these texts reveals quite a different vision of reality, a vision that confronts and challenges our personal and societal lives. Here I can only say that as I have appropriated these texts in this study, the inequalities we maintain, one toward another, in so many of our relationships and structures, appear absurd to me—the work of the evil one who prefers inferiority, exclusion, and submission to equality of love.

Teresa makes an interesting comment about women at the end of the book of her *Life*. I want to close with this:

> There are many more women than men to whom the Lord grants these favors. This I heard from the saintly Friar Peter of Alcantara—and I, too, have observed it—who said that women make much more progress along this road than men do. He gave excellent reasons for this, all in favor of women; but there's no need to mention them here.[91]

Perhaps, John agreed because he wrote both the commentary of *The Spiritual Canticle* and *The Living Flame* for women.

91. *Life* 40.8.

2

Constance FitzGerald, OCD, Contemplative

Colette Ackerman, OCD

The Second Vatican Council (1962–1965) opened the Roman Catholic Church to the contemporary world and called for *aggiornamento* or *renewal* in nearly every aspect of Catholic life. Religious congregations of women and men responded to this invitation by researching, studying, and reappropriating the early inspiration of their foundations. For Carmelites this meant a "*return to the sources*." Carmelite renewal called for reading again the great mystics St. Teresa of Jesus and St. John of the Cross and other Carmelite saints. Then, with a new perspective, Carmelite nuns could study *the signs of the time* and interpret how to respond with gospel understanding and the call of contemplative ministry.

By the early 1980s, Constance FitzGerald, OCD, was widely recognized as a vowed religious woman who had contributed theologically, substantively, and creatively to this renewal and the ongoing development of contemplative life in the United States. She had helped to organize and to guide both Carmelite Communities Associated (CCA) and the Association of Contemplative Sisters (ACS). The ACS had blossomed after a meeting of contemplative sisters from many traditions held at Woodstock, Maryland, in August 1969. Sister Connie had the original idea for this gathering and had approached Father George Wilson, SJ, about using the Woodstock facility for this meeting. These groups, both ACS and CCA, provided significant networks for helping contemplative communities to collaborate around the ongoing education and formation of their members—initiatives that continue to bear fruit.

In 1984, Sister Connie's essay "Impasse and Dark Night" was published in Tilden Edwards's volume, *Living with Apocalypse: Spiritual Resources for Social Compassion*. This piece, of all her writings, has become so well and widely known, so frequently quoted and interpreted that it might itself be a classic text.

> My Beloved is the mountains,
> And lonely wooded valleys . . .
> Silent music, sounding solitude
> (John of the Cross, *Spiritual Canticle* 13, 14)

Constance FitzGerald's story is a story of *desire*, the soul's desire for God, attention to God and God's response in mercy and love. As a young girl attending school at St. Joseph's, Connie was introduced by the parish priest to a young woman travelling to California in order to join the Carmelite nuns in Santa Clara. This incident, meeting the woman who would become Sister Josepha, defined Connie's vocation and future life. *She would be a Carmelite.* So began her longing for the Wisdom of God and the desire to know Jesus Christ and his grace, the grace that could transform her soul, her life. Nurtured by the geographic landscape of her place, the place of her birth, mountains became the symbol of God's revelation, God's call, the manifestation of God's Spirit. Connie would, eventually, connect this early, earthy experience of God with the works of her beloved St. John of the Cross. She would spend her life interpreting the meanings of John's mystical writings, making them accessible for all those who sought to learn the ways of contemplative prayer, all those others who longed for the Wisdom of God.

Sister Constance FitzGerald was born in Ogden, Utah, and spent her early childhood living among an extended family of deep Northern Italian heritage. They were part of a small Catholic community living in the midst of Utah's Mormon culture and influence. Educated by the Holy Cross Sisters in Ogden and later by the Sisters of St. Joseph at Chestnut Hill, Philadelphia, Connie graduated from Mount Saint Joseph Academy in 1951. She entered Baltimore Carmel in that year at the age of seventeen. Her friend from high school, Patricia Scanlan, was a novice in the community, having entered the year before. They would both move with the sisters to a new monastery near Towson, Maryland, in 1961—a momentous undertaking as the community had lived on Biddle Street in Baltimore for almost ninety years. Also momentous at the time was the Second Vatican Council, which began urging religious communities to reflection, to adaptation, and sometimes to change.

> There He gave me His breast;
> There he taught me a sweet and living knowledge;
> And I gave myself to Him,
> Keeping nothing back
> (*Spiritual Canticle* 18)

What the young Carmelite, like Connie, walks into and what the old Carmelite has walked through is a story of grace, sometimes costly grace. How wisdom is found cannot be planned; what is most precious cannot be purchased. It can only be received. The life of a Carmelite nun is, as our Rule states, "to live in allegiance to Jesus Christ . . . meditating day and night on the Word of the Lord and keeping vigil in prayer, unless occupied with other lawful activities" (prologue and chap. 7). This is the life Connie embraced. She has described our life in community quite simply in her recent profession exhortation for the solemn vow ceremony of our Sister Cecilia: "We are given something quite specific, extremely focused in contemplative life: the daily privileged sharing of Christ's presence in bread and wine, the ever-recurring liturgical cycle marking Jesus' life, ministry, death, resurrection, sending of the Spirit—year after year, the word of scripture read and meditated upon day after day, the psalms sung hour by hour, the precious but exacting solitude and intimacy of personal prayer so essential to the Carmelite, the leisure and discipline of spiritual reading and contemplative study, the faithfulness and demands of shared meals and personal relationships, the community work and our ministry to and with our people" (FitzGerald, May 12, 2019).

Flowing from this life of prayer and work come integrity and service, creativity and the imagination of faith. The contemplative life of a Carmelite calls forth a greater love that hopes that the world will believe (John 17:21). Connie has, for almost seventy years, traversed this Carmelite terrain and been immersed in her own experience of prayer, her passion for God. And this love, this passion, carried over to ministries in and for the community. Her major work in the community, emerging from her contemplative prayer and study, has been the dedication of her life to the intellectual education and formation of the sisters. Connie has invited theologians for retreats and lectures and fostered theological reading and study for the community. Beside this lifetime ministry, she has served as prioress, worked in initial formation and devoted much time and energy to archive our organization and our history. She has had oversight of community finances and, with our financial committee and a small cadre of sisters, helped raise money for the two major renovations of our monastery. She shares in the daily life of relationships, ideas, plans, and work.

St. Teresa of Jesus taught to her sisters a community life that was to be rooted in equality, deep commitment to one another, relationships that are open and sincere, where joys and sorrows are shared. Teresa's famous quote comes from her *Way of Perfection* (4.7): "All must be friends, all must love one another, all must be cherished, and all must help one another." If anything, the small communities of Teresian nuns, hermits living in community, reflect the grammar of a theology of accompaniment. Carmelite nuns sometimes speak of the connection between community living and the seasons of an individual's life. We live together for most of our lives in a relatively stable environment; we experience one another from season to season, from year to year, really from generation to generation. In all this blending, Teresa hopes for deeper fidelity and friendship among the sisters, the constant increase of faith, hope, and love, and the generativity for the community to go forward and incorporate newer members. Connie's life among us and with us in discernment of future planning has, over the years, helped us hear the call of God for us as contemplative women living in our contemporary world.

Our community has made many decisions related to our living and being, which contextualize the community we have become. Chief among these is the decision to have daily Eucharist together and daily meals together. In a sense, these decisions concern obvious, seemingly simple things, but they have sustained us during all the years of adaptation and change and are reflective of our gospel focus and our Teresian spirit. "I have called you friends" (John 15:14-15). Friends witness to love and mutuality, to real, genuine happiness; they pray together and eat and drink together. They can be together in peace, along with the difficulties, compromises, and vagaries of life. Eucharist, the Body and Blood of Jesus Christ, sustains this gift of communion and oneness and enables us to bring forth the Wisdom of God on this planet.

Our community took another decision as we celebrated our bicentennial in 1990 and renovated the chapel and guest wing of the monastery. This decision was settled after many years of the wider community of laypeople, families, and young people who, in their yearning for God, asked us to share with them our mode of contemplative prayer by making our facilities accessible for retreats, teaching prayer, and providing spiritual direction. We agreed to renovate one room with basic facilities for a single retreatant, redesigned our conference and community meeting room so that it might be available for retreat groups or meetings, and began to think about teaching prayer and how we sisters might be prepared for spiritual direction. This process led us to decide that perhaps we could support ourselves by sharing contemplative prayer, our life's real focus and meaning. We believed that the people and friends who came to the chapel for Sunday Eucharist and others who came on occasion for meetings or prayer or retreat, would enable us to include them in our charism of prayer and leave us free of financial concerns.

Amazingly this has worked! Our contemplative ministry has flourished and brought tremendous solidarity between our community and our "congregation" and among the people themselves who join us. Our prayer at Eucharist can highlight the search for justice in our world or the life of a Carmelite saint. It can focus on a contemporary issue like gun violence or saving our Earth. The effort toward inclusion of the contemporary life of God's people has deepened our empathy with those who suffer and struggle to bring about "the new heavens and the new earth" (Rev 21:1).

Given her intense study of the works of Teresa and John, Connie felt that trying to teach prayer to young adults not only could help shape their lives but might also lead to vocations to religious life for the community. Many people, and especially the young in our more secularized world, long to know God's Spirit in their lives, want some measure of transcendence to open new paths to freedom and a self-giving love. We believe the mystical texts of our Carmelite saints lead to knowledge of how to pray and how to meditate on the Scriptures; we believe in the change this prayer can bring to a life. This transmission of the teachings of Carmelite spirituality has taken many forms for us over the years through liturgy, writing, and sharing with groups who come to the monastery. But, perhaps, the most inspiring and productive has been teaching young people the practice of prayer. We have done this in various ways and at different times and it has proved to be a very powerful experience. This ministry is now continuing with our next generation of sisters. It is always a new venture!

In the mid-1960s Connie began to work with Father Thomas Kilduff, OCD, a Carmelite scholar, who had just finished a term on the General Council of the Carmelite Friars in Rome. Fr. Thomas was committed to assisting the nuns in the United States with renewal of our lifestyle, formation, and education. With this impetus, Connie planned serious theological education for our community. We invited speakers and had tapes on the documents and theology of Vatican II, on Scripture studies, on systematic theology, and on Christology. All this to inform and deepen our own prayer and to help in guiding others who desired a life of contemplation. Not separate from any of this was the study of the classic texts of Teresa and John and our Carmelite saints. Our formation program for new members was imbued with reflection on the ancient and classic texts of our order, which Connie was well-equipped to teach.

At the same time there were works of collaboration stirring among the Carmelite nuns in the United States. A journal, titled

Encounter, begun as a response to Vatican II by the sisters, was published over the course of eleven years. It is a treasure house for its historical notes in many areas as the sisters and their communities developed through the 1960s and 1970s. Connie helped coordinate a meeting of almost two dozen Carmelite monasteries, whose representatives met at Marriottsville, Maryland, in February 1970. The result was an interim committee whose task was to plan a meeting that would lead to formation of a national association of Carmelite nuns. As part of this committee Connie encouraged that those who would attend the first meeting reflect on papers written by the nuns themselves on various aspects of the Carmelite charism. This was one of the first steps toward the self determination of the nuns in the United States. We reflected on the various aspects of our life as they were presented by the sisters who lived that life. Carmelite Communities Associated was also established as a grassroots association or organization, not limited to the prioress and/or a delegate, but open to any member of the community who wanted to participate in the national meetings. Over the years, this has fostered bonds of friendship and has led to many kinds of collaboration among the sisters and communities.

> When you looked at me
> Your eyes imprinted your grace in me
> (*Spiritual Canticle* 23)

This vocation of Connie's, to study, to understand, and to interpret the works of classic Carmelite texts and put her knowledge in writing, is the grace of her life. It might be called a vocation within a vocation. Her voice is a voice for contemplative women who for centuries have carried the flame of love and passion for God in our world. In our time these voices need to be heard. The truth of self-giving love might even be an antidote to the dark voices of individualism, despair, and violence that haunt our societies. The deep communion that authentic prayer effects with God and with others could help our world move into a new consciousness of wisdom and hope where all creation will flourish.

Connie's work of writing is her art; it is a field of dreams as you will see in her work and in the contributions to this volume. In her interpretations of John of the Cross, Teresa of Jesus, Therese of Lisieux, or Edith Stein, people are helped to negotiate their lives with God or self or the world of relationships that surround them. This is another perspective on the theology of accompaniment.

The Leadership Conference of Religious Women (LCWR) gave their 2017 Outstanding Leadership Award to Connie in recognition of her writing and her role as an adviser to them from a contemplative perspective and the Carmelite tradition. This award was also given to honor her continuing support, help, and inspiration to many sisters working in active ministry. Religious communities, at the time of their general chapters and other periods of reflection, have drawn on Connie's two essays, "Impasse and Dark Night" (1984) and "From Impasse to Prophetic Hope: Crisis of Memory" (CTSA, 2009), for wisdom and direction.

During the celebration of the fourth centenary of Teresa of Avila's death in 1982, held by the Discalced Carmelite Friars in Washington, DC, Connie presented an audiovisual program on Teresa's four waters of prayer drawn from *The Book of Her Life*. This program, *The Woman, the Water and the Way*, has had a remarkable and enduring life. It is beautiful and instructive at the same time.

While this conference was in progress, Connie met with the provincial of the Friars of the Ancient Observance, Father John Malley, OCarm, and Father Ernest Larkin, OCarm. They began exploring the possibilities for an organized teaching body to share Carmelite spirituality with the wider public. Father Malley and Father Larkin were enthusiastic. With financial support from the Carmelites of the Ancient Observance, what resulted was the Carmelite Forum, which hosted two-week programs at St. Mary's College in South Bend, Indiana, for twenty-five years. Connie was part of the core group of usually about eight Carmelites (men and women) who presented lectures and workshops each summer. This program was appreciated for the content it imparted and for the opportunity it provided Carmelites, the Secular Order groups, and so many others to be together in a special setting for study of Carmelite prayer and spirituality.

In 1989 and 1990, our community celebrated its bicentennial—two hundred years of continuous life in the Archdiocese of Baltimore. The Carmelite nuns in Baltimore are the first community of sisters founded in the thirteen original States. Three of the foundresses were Maryland women: Mother Bernardina Matthews and her nieces, Sisters Mary Eleanora and Mary Aloysia Matthews. They returned home after some years in the Carmel of Hoogstraet, Belgium. The fourth foundress, Sister Clare Joseph Dickinson, was from the English-speaking Antwerp Carmel. These Carmels were founded by English recusant families in the low countries following the persecution of Catholics that began in England at the time of Henry VIII and the Reformation. The sisters returned to Maryland by way of a three-month ocean voyage accompanied by their Jesuit chaplain, Father Charles Neale. The Jesuits were a constant spiritual support to the nuns in both the low countries and in Maryland, a relationship that continues to this day. Sister Clare Joseph kept an amazing, handwritten journal of the ocean voyage. Connie published this journal, *The Carmelite Adventure*, with extensive historical notes, as part of our bicentennial celebration.

By 1990, the community had moved three times and lived in four successive monasteries; the sisters directed a school for young women for twenty years (1831–1851) when they first moved to Baltimore from Port Tobacco, Maryland, in order to support themselves. The community had ties with many of the first bishops of the country and were close to families who were friends and benefactors in Maryland. This long communal history gives us a certain pride, strength, and stability.

At the conclusion of the year-long celebration of the bicentennial in August 1990, we had a six-day symposium held at Loyola University (Baltimore) titled "Carmel 200: Contemplation and the Rediscovery of the American Soul—History and Spirituality." Connie, as chairperson of the Bicentennial Committee, and the community coordinated this event and brought together speakers on the Carmelite tradition and contemplative prayer who offered perspectives on history and spirituality in relation to American society. Through the presentations and discussion, the hope was to further contemporary attempts to reclaim the Western mystical tradition and bring it into dialogue with the challenges we face as North Americans and citizens of the world.

> Let us rejoice, Beloved,
> And let us go forth to behold ourselves in your beauty,
> To the mountain and to the hill,
> To where the pure water flows,
> And further, deep into the thicket.
> (*Spiritual Canticle* 36)

Connie has continued this work of theology engaging the strengths of Carmelite contemplative prayer with the hopes and worries we face in our world and on our planet. In June 2009, she gave a keynote address to the Catholic Theological Society of America: "From Impasse to Prophetic Hope: Crisis of Memory." This lengthy and sometimes complex paper describes the deep transformation of soul explained in the work of John of the Cross as he discusses the purification of memory in our developing life of prayer. It is, in a sense, a companion piece to Connie's 1984 essay on "Impasse." Through her reflection and writing as a "contemplative theologian," Connie has helped to inform and ground the lives of theologians, persons in religious life, and laypeople with a supportive voice that calls for the deepening of contemplative prayer and the possibility of personal and communal transformation. This work has also drawn Connie to study the ways we humans develop new consciousness and how science and our evolution are connected to any change of consciousness. In recognition of this scholarship Notre Dame University, Maryland, conferred on Connie an honorary doctorate in 1984, as did Chestnut Hill College in 2011.

The most recent focus for Connie has been work with the "newer members" group of our Carmelite association, CCA. During summer sessions in 2017 and 2019, she presented extensively on Carmelite spirituality and the history of the Discalced Nuns. This history was to be the focus of lectures Connie would present in Ghent, Belgium at a scheduled symposium in May 2020. The meeting was planned to celebrate the four hundredth anniversary of the first foundation of English-speaking Carmelite Nuns at Antwerp, established on May 1, 1619. Because of the COVID-19 pandemic, the meeting was cancelled and these lectures are being video recorded. They will be available for all Carmelites and those interested in Carmelite history and spirituality.

To all of this and what has gone before in our Carmelite life, Constance FitzGerald, OCD, has made an enduring and remarkable contribution. Connie's soul, shaped by the early desires of her heart, has borne the fruit of spiritual generativity. She has helped to stretch our consciousness in understanding the immense depths of ardor and love that can transform the soul that gives itself wholly to God and others in contemplative prayer. This transformation is not just an individual endeavor or longing, however, but also a thirst for the mutuality and communion that our world, in its darkness and division, desires to claim. It is the urging of prophetic hope and Connie's desire as a prophet of hope.

3

Impasse and Dark Night

Constance FitzGerald, OCD

A number of issues in contemporary Christian spirituality under-pin and influence the theological interpretation developed in this chapter. Today our spirituality is rooted in experience and in story: the experience and story of women (poor women, black women, white women, exploited women, Asian women, Native American women, etc.); the experience of the poor and oppressed of the world; the experience of the aging; the experience of the fear of nuclear holocaust and the far-reaching evils of nuclear buildup for the sake of national security, power, and domination; the experience of the woundedness of the earth and the environment.

This experience is nourished with meaning by history. It values, therefore, the interpretation of and dialogue with classical sources, with the story of the tradition. Within this framework, Christian spirituality remains attentive to the centrality of the self—to stages of faith development, to passages, to crises of growth—in one's search for God and human wholeness. It reaches, moreover, with particular urgency in our own time for the integration of contemplation and social commitment.

Against this background, I hope to interpret John of the Cross' concept and symbolism of "dark night" (including his classical signs concerning the passage from meditation to contemplation) to show what new understanding it brings to the contemporary experience of what I would call impasse, which insinuates itself inescapably and uninvited into one's inner life and growth and into one's relationships.[1] What is even more significant today is that many of our societal experiences open into profound impasse, for which we are not educated, particularly as Americans.

This brings me to two assumptions. First, our experience of God and our spirituality must emerge from our concrete, historical situation and must return to that situation to feed it and enliven it. Second, I find a great number of dark night or impasse experiences, personal and societal, that cry out for meaning. There is not only the so-called dark night of the soul but the dark night of the world. What if, by chance, our time in evolution is a dark-night time—a time of crisis and transition that must be understood if it is to be part of learning a new vision and harmony for the human species and the planet?

To discover meaning, there is value in bringing contemporary impasse into dialogue with the classical text of John.[2] In unfolding the mystery of dark night and unpacking its symbolism in response to the experience of impasse, I would hope to help others understand, name, and claim this experience of God and thereby direct their own creative and affective energy.

Impasse

By impasse, I mean that there is no way out of, no way around, no rational escape from, what imprisons one, no possibilities in the situation. In a true impasse, every normal manner of acting is brought to a standstill, and, ironically, impasse is experienced not only in the problem itself but also in any solution rationally

1. See David Tracy, *The Analogical Imagination: Christian Theology and the Culture of Pluralism* (New York: Crossroads, 1981), chap. 3, "The Classic."

2. Not only Tracy has influenced my methodology, but also Thomas H. Groome, *Christian Religious Education* (San Francisco: Harper & Row, 1980), 185–222, and John Shea, *Stories of Faith* (Chicago: Thomas More Press, 1980), 76–90. These three studies are helpful in dealing with the dialogue between tradition and contemporary story or issues.

attempted. Every logical solution remains unsatisfying, at the very least. The whole life situation suffers a depletion, has the word *limits* written upon it. Dorothee Soelle describes it as "unavoidable suffering," an apt symbol of which is physical imprisonment, with its experience of being squeezed into a confined space. Any movement out, any next step, is canceled, and the most dangerous temptation is to give up, to quit, to surrender to cynicism and despair, in the face of the disappointment, disenchantment, hopelessness, and loss of meaning that encompass one.

It is not difficult to imagine how such attitudes affect self-image and sense of worth and turn back on the person or group to engender a sense of failure, to reinforce a realization—not always exact—that their own mistakes have contributed to the ambiguity.

Moreover, intrinsic to the experience of impasse is the impression and feeling of rejection and lack of assurance from those on whom one counts. At the deepest levels of impasse, one sees the support systems on which one has depended pulled out from under one and asks if anything, if anyone, is trustworthy. Powerlessness overtakes the person or group caught in impasse and opens into the awareness that no understandable defense is possible. This is how impasse looks to those who are imprisoned within it. It is the experience of disintegration, of deprivation of worth, and it has many faces, personal and societal.

There is, however, another dimension of impasse that philosophers and psychologists, sociologists and theologians, poets and mystics, have reflected upon from their particular perspectives. Belden Lane, director of historical theology at Saint Louis University, indicates it in his article, "Spirituality and Political Commitment":

> . . . in a genuine impasse one's accustomed way of acting and living is brought to a standstill. The left side of the brain, with its usual application of linear, analytical, conventional thinking is ground to a halt. The impasse forces us to start all over again, driving us to contemplation. On the other hand, the impasse provides a challenge and a concrete focus for contemplation. . . . It forces the right side of the brain into gear, seeking intuitive,

> symbolic, unconventional answers, so that action can be renewed eventually with greater purpose.[3]

The negative situation constitutes a reverse pressure on imagination so that imagination is the only way to move more deeply into the experience. It is this "imaginative shock," or striking awareness that our categories do not fit our experience, that throws the intuitive, unconscious self into gear in quest of what the possibilities really are.

Paradoxically, a situation of no potential is loaded with potential, and impasse becomes the place for the reconstitution of the intuitive self. This means the situation of being helpless can be efficacious, not merely self-denying and demanding of passivity. While nothing seems to be moving forward, one is, in fact, on a homeward exile—*if* one can yield in the right way, responding with *full consciousness* of one's suffering in the impasse yet daring to believe that new possibilities, beyond immediate vision, can be given.

It must be stressed, writes Dorothee Soelle, that insofar as the experience of impasse, or suffering, is repressed, "there is a corresponding disappearance of passion for life and of the strength and intensity of its joys" and insights.[4] The person caught in impasse must find a way to identify, face, live with, and express this suffering. If one cannot speak about one's affliction in anguish, anger, pain, lament, at least to the God within, one will be destroyed by it or swallowed up by apathy. Every attempt to humanize impasse must begin with this phenomenon of experienced, acknowledged powerlessness, which can then activate creative forces that enable one to overcome the feeling that one is without power.[5]

3. Belden C. Lane, "Spirituality and Political Commitment: Notes on a Liberation Theology of Nonviolence," *America*, March 14, 1981; see also Urban T. Holmes III, *Ministry and Imagination* (New York: Seabury, 1981), 89–93, for a good treatment of right- and left-brain thinking. Holmes works out of the contributions of Jerome S. Bruner, *On Knowing: Essays for the Left Hand* (New York: Atheneum, 1971), and Robert E. Ornstein, *The Psychology of Consciousness* (New York: Viking, 1972), 57–64.

4. Dorothee Soelle, *Suffering* (Philadelphia: Fortress, 1975), 36.

5. See ibid., 76, 11.

A genuine impasse situation is such that the more action one applies to escape it, the worse it gets. The principles of "first order change"—reason, logic, analysis, planning—do not work, as studies by three Stanford psychiatrists try to show. Thorough-going impasse forces one, therefore, to end one's habitual methods of acting by a radical breaking out of the conceptual blocks that normally limit one's thinking.

Genuine change occurs through a "second order" response, "one which rethinks the solution previously tried and suggests something altogether unexpected. The quality of paradox is at the heart of 'second order change.' "[6] It implies that the unexpected, the alternative, the new vision, is not given on demand but is beyond conscious, rational control. It is the fruit of unconscious processes in which the situation of impasse itself becomes the focus of contemplative reflection.[7]

The psychologists and the theologians, the poets and the mystics, assure us that impasse can be the condition for creative growth and transformation *if* the experience of impasse is fully appropriated within one's heart and flesh with consciousness and consent; *if* the limitations of one's humanity and human condition are squarely faced and the sorrow of finitude allowed to invade the human spirit with real, existential powerlessness; *if* the ego does not demand understanding in the name of control

6. Lane, "Spirituality and Political Commitment," 198. Lane's discussion of the theory of Paul Witzalawick, John Weakland, and Richard Fisch in *Change: Principles of Problem Formation and Problem Resolution* (New York: Norton, 1974).

7. There are other models to explain and verify this experience: e.g., the creative process as it is described by Ralph J. Hallman, "Aesthetic Pleasure and Creative Process," *Humanitas* 4 (1968): 161–68, or *Journal of Humanistic Psychology* 6 (1966): 141–47; the process of individuation developed by Carl Jung and described by John Welch, OCarm, *Spiritual Pilgrims: Carl Jung and Teresa of Avila* (New York: Paulist Press, 1982), esp. 136–37, 141–43, 151–62; the model of structure and anti-structure developed by Victor W. Turner, *The Forest of Symbols: Aspects of Ndembu Ritual* (Ithaca: Cornell University Press, 1967), 93–101, *The Ritual Process: Structure and Anti-Structure* (Chicago: Aldine, 1969), *Dramas, Fields and Metaphors: Symbolic Action in Human Society* (Ithaca: Cornell University Press, 1974). See Holmes, *Ministry and Imagination*, 119–36, for material on Turner's structure and anti-structure.

and predictability but is willing to admit the mystery of its own being and surrender itself to this mystery; *if* the path into the unknown, into the uncontrolled and unpredictable margins of life, is freely taken when the path of deadly clarity fades.

Dark Night in John of the Cross

When I am able to situate a person's experience of impasse within the interpretive framework of dark night, that person is reassured and energized to live, even though she feels she is dying. The impasse is opened to meaning precisely because it can be redescribed.

In order to understand dark night, it is important to realize that John of the Cross begins and ends with love and desire in his poems and prose writings.[8] He is intent on showing what kind affective education is carried on by the Holy Spirit over a lifetime. He delineates, therefore, the movement from a desire, love, that is possessive, entangled, complex, selfish, and unfree to a desire that is fulfilled with union with Jesus Christ and others. In the process of affective redemption, desire is not suppressed or destroyed but gradually transferred, purified, transformed, set on fire. We go *through* the struggles and ambiguities of human desire to integration and personal wholeness.

This means there is a dark side to human desire, and the experience of dark night is the way that desire is purified and freed.[9] What is important to realize is that it is *in* the very experience of darkness and joylessness, in the suffering and withdrawal of accustomed pleasure, that this transformation is taking place. Transfiguration does not happen at the end of the road; it is in the making now. If we could see the underside of this death, we

8. See John of the Cross, *The Collected Works of St. John of the Cross*, trans. Kieran Kavanaugh and Otilio Rodriguez (Washington, DC: Institute of Carmelite Studies, 1973), *The Ascent of Mount Carmel*, Book I, chap. 13, no. 3; chap. 14, no. 2; poem, "The Dark Night," p. 296; poem, "The Spiritual Canticle," pp. 410–15; *The Dark Night*, Book II, chap. 9, no. 1; *The Living Flame*, stanza 3, nos. 1, 3, 7.

9. See John of the Cross, *CW, The Dark Night*, Book I, chaps. 1–8, for a view of the dark side of human desire. John calls this dark side the faults of beginners.

would realize it is already resurrection. Since we are not educated for darkness, however, we see this experience, because of the shape it takes, as a sign of *death*. Dark night is instead a sign of *life*, of growth, of development in our relationship with God, in our best human relationships, and in our societal life. It is a sign to move on in hope to a new vision, a new experience.

Night in John of the Cross, which symbolically moves from twilight to midnight to dawn, is the progressive purification and transformation of the human person *through* what we cherish or desire and through what gives us security and support.[10] We are affected by darkness, therefore, where we are mostly deeply involved and committed, and in what we love and care for most. Love makes us vulnerable, and it is love itself and its development that precipitate darkness in oneself and in the "other."

Only when love has grown to a certain point of depth and commitment can its limitations be experienced. Our senses are carried to deeper perception, as it were, by exhaustion. A fullness in one way of being and relating makes one touch its limits. This is not a question of disgust, as it often appears and feels like, but of a movement through sensual pleasure and joy to deeper, stronger faithfulness and to the experience of a love and a commitment, a hope and a vision, unimagined and unexpected on this side of darkness.

We all need some satisfaction of our desire in order to begin and go on in prayer, relationship, or ministry, but it is the withdrawal of pleasure and the confrontation with limitation (our own and others') that signals the transition or growth crisis of the dark night. The test is whether we can, in the last analysis, maintain the direction or momentum of our life without either glancing off permanently into another direction to escape, or succumbing to the darkness of total despair.[11]

10. See Michael J. Buckley, "Atheism and Contemplation," *Theological Studies* 40 (1979): 696; see also John of the Cross, *CW, The Spiritual Canticle*, stanzas 3-7, to grasp how one moves through that which one cherishes, the self, the world, relationships, to deeper love for God.

11. See John of the Cross, *CW, The Dark Night*, Book I, chap. 7, no. 5; chap. 8, no. 3.

Love (romance!) makes us hunger for the unambivalent situation. Yet it is in the very light of love that we encounter the opaqueness of our own humanness and experience the destructiveness within ourselves and the "other." Ambiguity arises, on the one hand, from human inadequacy; it arises, on the other hand, from the Spirit of God calling us beyond ourselves, beyond where we are, into transcendence. We are being challenged to make the passage from loving, serving, "being with," because of the pleasure and joy it gives us, to loving and serving regardless of the cost. We are being challenged to a reacceptance of the "other."[12]

Every God relationship, every significant human love, every marriage, every ministry, every relationship between a person and a community, and perhaps every human group and every nation will come to this point of impasse, with its intrinsic demands for and promise of a new vision, a new experience of God, a quieter, deeper, freer, more committed love. And it will come precisely when imagination seems paralyzed, when intimacy seems eroded, and when desire feels dead.

This brings us to John of the Cross' signs for discerning the genuineness of the dark night purification. Traditionally, they have been recognized as theological signs of the passage in prayer from discursive meditation to contemplation and are, therefore, descriptive of one's spiritual development, one's intrapersonal life. A careful reading of John of the Cross, integrated with concrete human experience, would seem to indicate, however, that the interpretation of these signs must be extended to one's in*ter*personal life as well, and perhaps even to one's societal life. I submit that a societal interpretation of these signs, and dark night in general, throws considerable light on the contemporary experience of societal impasse.

Although John seems to delineate a smooth transition, his developmental model includes breakdown and failure. This is why the signs speak to us of death, even though they are in reality signs of development and growth. There are two sets of signs, one in the second book of *The Ascent of Mount Carmel* (chap.

12. See ibid., Book 1, chap. 9, no. 4.

13.2-4), the other in the first book of the *The Dark Night* (chap. 9.2-8). Although the perspective is different in each (the *Ascent* signs are given from the side of the person's faith response, the *Dark Night* signs from God's side), the signs are the same and can be correlated.

The first set of signs underlines one's powerlessness to pray with one's reason or rational mind "since God does not communicate himself through the senses as he did before, by means of the discursive analysis and synthesis of ideas, but begins to communicate himself through pure spirit by an act of simple contemplation in which there is no discursive succession of thought." The senses cannot attain to this contemplation, and dryness results.[13]

Basic to the experience of disintegration or dark night is apparent breakdown of communication and a powerlessness to do anything about it. One's usual way of functioning, or relating, provides no satisfaction and does not work. What formerly was essential for growth and fidelity (e.g., an active choice and decision for Christ in reasoned meditation) now hinders growth.[14] Nothing happens in meditation. One cannot relate to the loved one as before. The system on which one depends breaks down. Certainty and pleasure give way to ambiguity, misunderstanding, and dryness or boredom.

It is difficult to realize, except by hindsight, that a new kind of love and deeper level of communication, transcending the former love, is developing and is already operative (contemplation). Accustomed to receiving love and insight in one way, one perceives this communication and situation as darkness. What is, in fact, a call to a new vision and to deeper, more genuine intimacy with God, with the "other," and with the world, is experienced as less commitment and less love, precisely because the call comes when intimacy seems to be falling apart and limitation looms large. There seems no possibility of movement backward or forward but only imprisonment, lack of vision, and failure of imagination.

13. For the first set of signs, see ibid., Book I, chap. 9, no. 8; *Ascent of Mount Carmel*, Book II, chap. 13, no. 2.

14. John, *CW*, *The Dark Night*, Book I, chap. 9, no. 7.

"Everything seems to be functioning in reverse," writes John, in this forced passage from rational, analytical, linear thinking to intuitive, metaphorical, symbolic consciousness.[15]

In his probing article, "Atheism and Contemplation," Michael J. Buckley shows that John of the Cross, like Feuerbach, is very "sensitive to the humanization consciousness works on its God." John is acutely aware, with Freud, that the religious movement toward God can emerge either from the desire for satisfaction or from the drive for reassurance.[16] In other words, John is conscious of the tendency of religion to become projection and is always subtly asking the question, What is the focus of your desire, of your religious awareness and its commitment? "He takes the theological dictum, 'Whatever is received is received according to the mode of the one receiving it,' and he applies it to a person's conceptions and images of God."[17]

> Because in the initial stages of the spiritual life, and even in the more advanced ones, the sensory part of the soul is imperfect, it frequently receives God's spirit with this very imperfection.[18]

We make our God, or gods, in our own image. "Our understanding and our loves are limited by what we are. What we grasp and what we long for is very much shaped and determined by our own nature and personality-set," writes Buckley. If this is not changed by the Spirit of Jesus gradually permeating individual experiences and influencing patterns of development and growth, "there is no possibility of [the] contemplation of anything but our own projections."[19] John of the Cross is at pains to show how our images of God are progressively and of necessity changed and shattered by life experience. The very experience of dark night does, in fact, critique our present images of God. As Buckley writes,

15. Ibid., Book I, chap. 8, no. 3.
16. Buckley, "Atheism and Contemplation," 694.
17. Ibid., 693, see also 690.
18. John, *CW, The Dark Night*, Book I, chap. 16, no. 2.
19. Buckley, "Atheism and Contemplation," 694.

> The continual contemplative purification of the human person is a progressive hermeneutic of the nature of God. The self-disclosure of God . . . is finally only possible within the experience of the contradiction of finite concepts and human expectations. The darkness and its pain are here, but they are finely dialectical movements in which the human is purified from projection by a "no" which is most radically a "yes." The disclosures of God contradict the programs and expectations of human beings in order to fulfill human desire and human freedom at a much deeper level than subjectivity would have measured out its projections.[20]

When, in the first sign, we reflect on the breakdown of communication and relationship, therefore, we are assuming also a change and a shattering of one's images. This causes confusion and a sense of loss and meaninglessness.

This is not a defense of Christian masochism, as Dorothee Soelle calls it, nor a sadistic understanding of God, but rather a recognition of the ongoing process of self-acceptance and re-acceptance of the "other" that is necessary for real, enduring love and progressive, mutual insight and creativity. This process presupposes that, in every significant relationship, we come to the experience of limitation, our own and others'. We come to the point where we must withdraw and reclaim our projections of God, of friend, of ministry, of community, and let the "others" be who and what they are: mystery.

The emphasis in the second set of signs is on emptiness in life experience and deadness of desire. Not only is prayer dry, but life is dry, relationship is dry, ministry is dry.

> Souls do not get satisfaction or consolation from the things of God [and] they do not get any out of creatures either. Since God puts a soul in this dark night in order to dry up and purge its sensory appetite, he does not allow it to find sweetness or delight in anything.[21]

20. Ibid., 696–97.

21. See John, *CW, The Dark Night*, Book I, chap. 9, no. 2; for correlating signs, see also *Ascent of Mount Carmel*, Book II, chap. 13, no. 3.

John assures us the time must come in our development when neither God, nor the "other," nor one's life project satisfy, but only disappoint, disillusion, and shatter one's naive hope.

Because desire seems dead, because there is no inclination to do anything about the situation, because one really ceases to care, the temptation to quit, to walk away, becomes overpowering. Hopelessness and worthlessness invade one's perception and one's psyche. It is in the throes of this crisis that people abandon God and prayer, a marriage, a friend, a ministry, a community, a church, and forfeit forever the new vision, the genuine hope, the maturity of love and loyalty, dedication and mutuality, that is on the other side of darkness and hopelessness. Darkness is the place where egoism dies and true unselfish love for the "other" is set free. Moreover, it is the birthplace of a vision and a hope that cannot be imagined this side of darkness.

John can write about self-knowledge as a primary effect of the dark night for two reasons. First, the light and development of contemplative love show up one's limitations. Second, the withdrawal of accustomed pleasure in life, and the consequent frustration of desire, trigger one's seemingly destructive tendencies and move them into action on a level that is beyond conscious control.[22]

What must be remembered at all costs is that desire is not destroyed. Rather, right in this situation of unassuaged emptiness and apparent deadness of desire, in the very area of life in which one is most involved and therefore most vulnerable, desire is being purified, transformed, and carried into deeper, more integrated passion. Dark night mediates the transfiguration of affectivity, and obstacles conceal within themselves untold, hidden energy.

Here we sense what powerful symbolism dark night is. It is an image of productivity and speaks of life buried in its opposite: life concealed, life invisible, life unseen in death.

Thus the third set of signs has two different moments, moving from painful anxiety about culpability to a new and deeper

22. See John, *CW, The Dark Night*, Book I, chap. 14, where he speaks of the spirit of fornication, blasphemy, and confusion (*spiritus vertiginis*), or what I would call frustrated desire. See also Welch, *Spiritual Pilgrims*, 141–46.

level of appreciation of God and/or the "other" in a quiet, loving attentiveness. John describes the suffering side of this experience when he writes,

> The memory ordinarily turns to God solicitously and with painful care, and the soul thinks it is not serving God but turning back, because it is aware of this distaste for the things of God.[23]

Here it is a question of being obsessed with the problem. How much easier it would be to bear the darkness were one not conscious of one's failures and mistakes. The most confusing and damnable part of the dark night is the suspicion and fear that much of the darkness is of one's own making. Since dark night is a limit experience, and since it does expose human fragility, brokenness, neurotic dependence, and lack of integration, it is understandable that it undermines a person's self-esteem and activates anxious self-analysis.

The only way to break out of this desperate circle of insoluble self-questioning is to surrender in faith and trust to the unfathomable Mystery that beckons onward and inward beyond calculation, order, self-justification, and fear. John continues, therefore:

> The third and surest sign is that a person likes to remain alone in loving awarenss of God, without particular considerations, in interior peace quiet and repose. . . .
>
> If those in whom this occurs know how to remain quiet, without care and solicitude about any interior or exterior work, they will soon in that unconcern and idleness delicately experience the interior nourishment.[24]

It is precisely as broken, poor, and powerless that one opens oneself to the dark mystery of God in loving, peaceful waiting. When the pain of human finitude is appropriated with consciousness and consent and handed over in one's own person to the

23. John, *CW, The Dark Night*, Book I, chap. 9, no. 3.

24. John, *CW, Ascent of Mount Carmel*, Book II, chap. 13, no. 4; *The Dark Night*, Book I, chap. 6, no. 2.

influence of Jesus' spirit in the contemplative process, the new and deeper experience gradually takes over, the new vision slowly breaks through, and the new understanding and mutuality are progressively experienced.

At the deepest levels of night, in a way one could not have imagined it could happen, one sees the withdrawal of all one has been certain of and depended upon for reassurance and affirmation. Now it is a question, not of satisfaction, but of support systems that give life meaning: concepts, systems of meaning, symbolic structures, relationships, institutions. All supports seem to fail one, and only the experience of emptiness, confusion, isolation, weakness, loneliness, and abandonment remains. In the frantic search for reassurance, one wonders if anyone—friend or spouse or God—is really "for me," is trustworthy. But no answer is given to the question.[25]

The realization that there is *no* option but faith triggers a deep, silent, overpowering panic that, like a mighty underground river, threatens chaos and collapse. This "scream of suffering contains all the despair of which a person is capable, and in this sense every scream is a scream for God," writes Soelle.[26] In this experience of the cross of Jesus, what the "soul feels most," John explains, "is that God has rejected it and with abhorrence cast it into darkness."[27] And Soelle continues:

> All extreme suffering evokes the experience of being forsaken by God. In the depth of suffering people see themselves as abandoned and forsaken by everyone. That which gave life its meaning has become empty and void: it turned out to be an error, an illusion that is shattered, a guilt that cannot be rectified, a void. The paths that lead to this experience of nothingness are diverse, but the experience of annihilation that occurs is the same.[28]

Yet it is the experience of this abandonment and rejection that is transforming the human person in love. This is a possession,

25. See Welch, *Spiritual Pilgrims*, 145.
26. Soelle, *Suffering*, 85.
27. John, *CW, Ascent of Mount Carmel*, Book II, chap. 6, no. 2.
28. Soelle, *Suffering*, 85.

a redemption, an actualizing and affirmation of the person that is not understood at the time. Its symbolic expression is dispossession and death.[29]

John seems to say that one leaves the world of rejection and worthlessness by giving away one's powerlessness and poverty to the inspiration of the Spirit and one moves into a world of self-esteem, affirmation, compassion, and solidarity. Only an experience like this, coming out of the soul's night, brings about the kind of solidarity and compassion that changes the "I" into a "we," enabling one to say, "we poor," "we oppressed," "we exploited." The poor are objects until we are poor, too. This kind of identification with God's people, with the "other," is the fruit of dark night.[30]

Some years ago it became evident to me that in our most significant human relationships we go through precisely the kind of suffering John describes concerning the soul's journey to God. In our ministries, moreover, we inevitably come to personal impasse. John's signs of passage and development, refashioned for the present time, should be a valuable tool for discernment. They relate to the breakdown of marriages, to departures from priesthood and religious life, and to the contemporary phenomenon of burnout, among other things.

Societal Impasse

I want to bring together dark night and societal impasse because, as I said, our experience of God and our spirituality must emerge from our concrete historical situation and because our time and place in history bring us face to face with profound societal impasse. Here God makes demands for conversion, healing, justice, love, compassion, solidarity, and communion. Here the face of God appears, a God who dies in human beings and rises in human freedom and dignity.

We close off the breaking in of God into our lives if we cannot admit into consciousness the situations of profound impasse we

29. See Buckley, "Atheism and Contemplation," 696.

30. See Constance FitzGerald, "Contemplative Life as Charismatic Presence," *Contemplative Review* 11 (1978): 45, or *Spiritual Life* 29 (1983): 28.

face personally and societally. If we deal with personal impasse only in the way our society teaches us—by illusion, minimization, repression, denial, apathy—we will deal with societal impasse in the same way. The "no way out" trials of our personal lives are but a part of the far more frightening situations of national and international impasse that have been formed by the social, economic, and political forces in our time.

We are citizens of a dominant nation, and I think that as a nation we have come to an experience of deep impasse and profound limitation. On the other side of all our technology, we have come to poverty and to dark night. We can find no escape from the world we have built, where the poor and oppressed cry out, where the earth and the environment cry out, and where the specter of nuclear waste already haunts future generations. We can find no way out of the horror of nuclear stockpiles but more sophisticated and deadly weapons systems.

As Americans we are not educated for impasse, for the experience of human limitation and darkness that will not yield to hard work, studies, statistics, rational analysis, and well-planned programs. We stand helpless, confused, and guilty before the insurmountable problems of our world. We dare not let the full import of the impasse even come to complete consciousness. It is just too painful and too destructive of national self-esteem. We cannot bear to let ourselves be totally challenged by the poor, the elderly, the unemployed, refugees, the oppressed; by the unjust, unequal situation of women in a patriarchal, sexist culture; by those tortured and imprisoned and murdered in the name of national security; by the possibility of the destruction of humanity.

We see only signs of death. Because we do not know how to read these kinds of signs in our own inner lives and interpersonal relationships, we do not understand them in our societal or national life, either. Is it possible these insoluble crises are signs of passage or transition in our national development and in the evolution of humanity? Is it possible we are going through a fundamental evolutionary change and transcendence, and crisis is the birthplace and learning process for a new consciousness and harmony?

Let us examine the signs. Our impasses do not yield to hard, generous work, to the logical solutions of the past, to the knowledge and skills acquired in our educational institutions. The most farsighted economists said some years ago that the economic solutions of past decades do not fit the present economic crisis in the world. It is argued that the whole economic, social, and political system would collapse were we to feed the poor with surplus crops and stop the wars, the exploitation, the oppression, in which we are involved. Not only God and the loved one fail us, our institutions fail us.

We are obsessed with the problem and with the need for new insight and breakthrough; we are disillusioned with a political system that contributes to international oppression, violence, and darkness. Is it any wonder we witness the effects of impasse among us—anger, confusion, violence—since real impasse or dark night highlights destructive tendencies? Frustrated desire fights back.

Recently, a Jesuit on our local Peace and Justice Commission described the stance of a prominent Roman Catholic theologian, a layman, at a meeting of theologians, bishops, and others on the nuclear question. It was the focused awareness, the incredible logic and rationality, of this man who favored nuclear superiority and denied that a nuclear freeze was a good idea that made such a negative impression on pro-freeze participants. Reason, left to itself, moved to a basically destructive position, unrecognized and unacknowledged in the speaker.

Dark night shows up the "shadow," the dark side of desire. If we refuse to read the signs of dark night in our society and avoid appropriating the impasse, we see cold reason, devoid of imagination, heading with deadly logic toward violence, hardness in the face of misery, a sense of inevitability, war, and death. And we witness the projection of our national shadow on others, "the inevitable shadow of over-rational planning," as Irene de Castillejo calls it.[31]

31. See Irene Claremont de Castillejo, *Knowing Woman: A Feminine Perspective* (New York: Harper & Row, 1974), 32, 39; see also 17–18 for a very interesting analysis of the different levels on which people discuss nuclear weapons.

Today, instead of realizing that the impasse provides a challenge and concrete focus for prayer and drives us to contemplation, we give in to a passive sense of inevitability, and imagination dies. We do not really believe that if we surrender these situations of world impasse to contemplative prayer that new solutions, new visions of peace and equality, will emerge in our world. We dare not believe that a creative revisioning of our world is possible. Everything is just too complex, too beyond our reach. Yet it is only in the process of bringing the impasse to prayer, to the perspective of the God who loves us, that our society will be freed, healed, changed, brought to paradoxical new visions, and freed for nonviolent, selfless, liberating action, freed, therefore, for community on this planet earth. Death is involved here, a dying in order to see how to be and to act on behalf of God in the world.[32]

This development suggests two questions: Do we really expect anything at all of the contemplative process of prayer in our world today? And how does the failure of imagination and creativity in our national life relate to the breakdown of the contemplative process of prayer and transformation in people's lives? With these questions concerning the intersection of impasse and contemplation, I move into my concluding reflection, on women's religious experience today.

Feminine Impasse

I submit that the feminine experience of dark night, if we read it, interpret it, understand it, and live it through, is in itself a critique of religious consciousness and, therefore, ultimately of Christianity, with its roots in a sexist, patriarchal culture. It is not my intention simply to apply a Christian theme, dark night, to a contemporary issue, women. Rather, I am probing a resource within the theological-mystical tradition in order to understand the contemporary feminist experience of God and to see if John

32. See Holmes, *Ministry and Imagination*, 154. The entire chapter 6, "Dying to Image," 137–64, is excellent supplementary reading to my development.

of the Cross' dark night can function in the struggle of women for liberation and equality.[33]

Behind every new spirituality and any creative re-visioning of the world, at the root of any real theology, is an experience of God. Yet every religious experience comes from a meeting with a new and challenging face of God in one's own time and social situation. I suspect that although it is imperative, for example, for feminist theologians to develop new interpretive paradigms that function to liberate people, only women's *experience* of God can alter or renew our God images and perhaps our doctrine of God. I want, therefore, to examine the feminist experience of God in impasse, because this is where many women in the Church, and in the world, find themselves. "We have only begun to experience the depth of women's alienation from Christian belief systems and from the existing Churches," writes Elisabeth Schüssler Fiorenza.[34]

Today feminists struggle with the Judeo-Christian image of a male God and a male Church. Just as Marxism sees religion as the opiate of the people and Christianity's doctrine of God as a support of oppression and misery, so the feminists see a patriarchal system that visualizes God, and consequently Church, in almost exclusively patriarchal terms as basically destructive. The masculine image of God is experienced as unsatisfying and confusing because it serves to reinforce male domination, a patriarchal value system, and an entire male world view.

This is an impasse for women, since their past religious experience has come to them through these images and this inherited

33. See Anne Carr, BVM, "Is a Christian Feminist Theology Possible?" *Theological Studies* 43 (1982): 282, 292; Elisabeth Schüssler Fiorenza, "Toward a Feminist Biblical Hermeneutics: Biblical Interpretation and Liberation Theology," in *The Challenge of Liberation Theology*, ed. Mahan, 109: "Theological interpretation must also critically reflect on the political pre-suppositions and implications of theological 'classics' and dogmatic or ethical systems. In other words, not only the content and traditioning process within the Bible, but the whole of Christian tradition should be scrutinized and judged as to whether or not it functions to oppress or liberate people."

34. Elisabeth Schüssler Fiorenza, "Sexism and Conversion," *Network* (May–June 1981): 21.

symbol system, which does not function for women now as it did before. There is no going back to what was, what gave comfort and clarity and brought feminists to their present stage of religious development and commitment, but there is no satisfactory going forward either. There seems to be no way out of this God-less situation because no genuine evolution of God images has really occurred. We touch this in Alice Walker's latest novel, *The Color Purple,* a story of a black woman, Celie, who moves from being oppressed and brutalized to self-actualization and religious transformation. What is significant is that Celie's transcendence requires or coincides with a radical redefinition of God. "The author's choice of the genre of the epistolary novel, in this case composed entirely of letters for which there is no direct response," places the whole story in a prayer context.[35] In the first fifty-five letters Celie writes the story of her life to God, because she is ashamed to talk to him about it. Abused by the man she thought to be her father and deprived by him of the children she consequently bore, dehumanized by her husband and deprived by him of any knowledge of or communication with her sister, she is loved by one woman, Shug Avery. Aware finally, under the influence of Shug's love and affirmation, of the extent of her exploitation, Celie rebels not only against men but against God and can no longer write to *him.* She writes instead to her sister:

> What God do for me? I ast. . . .
>
> [H]e give me a lynched daddy, a crazy mama, a lowdown dog of a step pa and a sister I probably won't ever see again. Anyhow, I say, the God I been praying and writing to is a man. And act just like all the [other] mens I know. Trifling, forgitful and lowdown. . . .
>
> All my life I never care what people thought bout nothing I did, I say. But deep in my heart I care about God. What he going to think. And come to find out, he don't think. Just sit up there glorying in being deef, I reckon. But it ain't easy, trying to do

35. Sue E. Houchins, "I Found God in Myself and I Loved Her / I Loved Her Fiercely: A Study of Suffering in the Archetypal Journey of Alice Walker's Female Heroes," a chapter of a dissertation in progress, 15.

> without God. Even if you know he ain't there, trying to do without him is a strain.

When Shug asks what her God looks like, Celie senses the incongruity of her image but replies:

> He big and old and tall and graybearded and white. He wear white robes and go barefooted.
>
> Blue eyes? she ast.
>
> Sort of bluish gray. Cool. Big though. White lashes. I say. . . .
>
> Ain't no way to read the bible and not think God white, she say. Then she sigh. When I found out I thought God was white, and a man, I lost interest. You mad cause he don't seem to listen to your prayers. Humph! Do the mayor listen to anything the colored say? . . .
>
> Here's the thing, say Shug. The thing I believe. God is inside you and inside everybody else. You come into the world with God. But only them that search for *it* inside find it. And sometimes it just manifest itself even if you not looking, or don't know what you looking for. Trouble do it for most folks, I think. . . .
>
> . . . [U]s talk and talk about God, but I'm still adrift. Trying to chase that old [white] man out of my head. I been so busy thinking bout him I never truly notice nothing God make. Not a blade of corn (how it do that?) not the color purple (where it come from?). Not the little wildflowers. Nothing. [. . .]
>
> Man corrupt everything, say Shug. He on your box of grits, in your head, and all over [the] radio. He try to make you think he everywhere. Soon as you think he everywhere, you think he God. But he ain't. Whenever you trying to pray, and man plop himself on the other end of it, tell him to git lost, say Shug. Conjure up flowers, wind, water, a big rock.
>
> But this [is] hard work, let me tell you. He been there so long, he don't want to budge. He threaten lightening, floods and earthquakes. Us fight. I hardly pray at all. Every time I conjure up a rock, I throw it.
>
> Amen[36]

36. Alice Walker, *The Color Purple* (New York: Harcourt Brace Jovanovich, 1982), 164–68. [Italics added by FitzGerald.—Eds.]

Thus feminists, unable to communicate with the God of patriarchy, are imprisoned in a night of broken symbols. They ask how the idea of God undergoes transformation.

Is it by changing our religious language? By feminizing God, uncovering feminine images and attributes of God in the Scriptures? Is it by the desexualization of God and a move toward deism? Or is it by contemplation? (A step in the criticism of Marxism is implied here. Can experience really be altered simply by changing language?) What our programs to eliminate sexist language in our theological, devotional, and liturgical life have shown us is that our solutions are unsatisfactory and confusing. We find impasse not only in the problems but even in the solutions.

So-called postpatriarchal theologians and philosophers have suspected this for some time and, in consequence, have moved beyond Judeo-Christian religion. These radical feminist thinkers claim feminine consciousness and Christian faith are contradictions in terms. Aware, like John of the Cross, of the tendency of religion to become projection, they have rejected the Christian God that patriarchy projects. But is this the only option? Here the advance of postpatriarchy intersects with the development of contemplation. If one admits that religious belief and desire can be analyzed into episodes of projection, does the force of this discovery indicate a movement toward the total rejection of the God of patriarchy, or can it equally indicate that faith and desire must move into contemplation, one movement of which is apophatic? Is the alternative either to deny the reality of the God of Christianity or to insist that the evolution of faith and desire must pass through the darkness and the cross, in which the meaning of the night is found? It is imperative to emphasize, as Buckley observes,

> that apophatic theology is not primarily one which does or does not make statements about God. It is primarily an experiential *process*, a process of entering into the infinite mystery that is God, so that gradually one is transformed by grace and this grace moves through the intense experience of darkness [impasse] into the *vision* of the incomprehensible God [the God who transcends present images and symbols]. Apophatic theology involves both interpretation and criticism, conceptualization and theological argument. But all of these are descriptive of *a process in which one*

> *is engaged*, a process in which *one must be engaged* in order to grasp its interpretation in any depth.[37]

If the impasse in which feminists find themselves *is* dark night, then a new experience of God, transformative of alienating symbols, is already breaking through even though it is not comprehensible yet, and impasse is a call to development, transcendence, new life, and understanding. Ultimately, therefore, impasse is a challenge to feminists to be mystics who, when human concepts disillusion, symbols break, and meanings fail, will let their "faith . . . relocate everything known within a new horizon in which it is radically reinterpreted and transvaluated."[38] Feminists need to realize that the gap that exists between human, patriarchal concepts of God and what is internalized by them in impasse is exactly what promises religious development and is the seed of a new experience of God, a new spirituality, and a new order—what Elizabeth Janeway calls the "Great Myth, as yet unborn," to which Madonna Kolbenschlag refers in her article, "Feminists, the Frog Princess, and the New Frontier of Spirituality."[39]

I believe there is no alternative for feminists except contemplation, if they are to avoid the trivialization of their own religious experience in dark night. The experience of God in impasse is the crucible in which our God images and language will be transformed and a feminine value system and social fabric generated. All the signs (of dark night) indicate this is the next step in any positive, creative re-visioning of the future, in any genuinely feminine generativity. Theology is dependent on this experience, which cannot be created by theological reflection alone. Dark night is, as was stated before, "a progressive hermeneutic of the nature of God." If this passage is not recognized and traversed, a certain kind of atheism and permanent cynicism are inevitable.

The contemplative love experience, which is beyond conscious control and is not given on demand, is concerned not for the image of God, as political theologians are, but with God, who

37. Buckley, "Atheism and Contemplation," 690; italics mine.

38. Ibid., 695.

39. Quoted by Madonna Kolbenschlag, "Feminists, the Frog Princess, and the New Frontier of Spirituality," *New Catholic World* (July–August 1982).

does in the end transcend our images and expectations. What is critical to see is that one has to *allow* the experience to take place through a love that is gradually welling up from the ground of one's being and that serves as a basis for contemplation. Only this experience can give to theology the insight it needs "to search out a new doctrine of God which is related to the intellectual, practical, and ethical concerns of the present situation of women and which suggests transformation or emancipative possibilities for the future."[40]

Contemplation, and ultimately liberation, demand the handing over of one's powerlessness and "outsider-ness" to the inspiration and power of God's Spirit. How imperative it is that women take possession of their pain and confusion; actively appropriate their experience of domination, exploitation, and oppression; consent to their time in history; and hold this impasse in their bodies and their hearts before the inner God they reach for in the dark of shattered symbols. Although the God of the dark night seems silent, this God is not a mute God who silences human desire, pain, and feeling, and women need to realize that the experience of anger, rage, depression, and abandonment is a constitutive part of the transformation and purification of the dark night. This very rage and anger purify the "abused consciousness" of women in the sexism they have internalized.[41]

If there is, as we suggest, an incipient experience of God, this presence of God will necessarily throw light on woman's "shadow" and reveal her to herself with all the destructive power she has and all the repressed possibilities or "lost alternatives" that cry within her for a voice. It is in the experience of this kind of night, when women put all the power of their desire, not in ideology, but here before the inner God, that the real bonding of women takes place, and purified of violence, they are readied for communion with their God, for sisterhood, equality, liberation and mutuality.

40. Carr, "Is a Christian Feminist Theology Possible?" 293.

41. Here I am addressing the call of Schüssler Fiorenza for "a spirituality that understands anger, persecution, defamation, violence and suffering in political-theological terms." See "Sexism and Conversion," 20–21.

Impasse internalizes the option for the poor and effects an identification with and compassion for all "women whose cry for liberation is so basic and unmistakable that it shouts out for all of us in our common quest for equality."[42] In one's own womanhood, one holds every woman before God, women of the present and women of the past. This is an experience, not a theory! Though one lives in Baltimore or Atlanta or California or Washington, one's life is lived within the bleeding borders of El Salvador and Guatemala, Lebanon and South Africa, Afghanistan and Cambodia. Though one lives at the end of the twentieth century, the voiceless sorrow of women long dead is felt as one's own. One senses this in Alice Walker's essay "In Search of Our Mothers' Gardens":

> When [the poet] Jean Toomer walked through the South in the early twenties, he discovered a curious thing: black women whose spirituality was so intense, so deep, so *unconscious*, that they themselves were unaware of the riches they held. They stumbled blindly through their lives: creatures so abused and mutilated in body, so dimmed and confused by pain, that they considered themselves unworthy even of hope. In the selfless abstractions their bodies became to the men who used them, they became more than "sexual objects," more even than mere women: they became "Saints." Instead of being perceived as whole persons, their bodies became shrines: what was thought to be their minds became temples suitable for worship. These crazy Saints stared out at the world, wildly, like lunatics—or quietly, like suicides; and the "God" that was in their gaze was as mute as a great stone. . . .
>
> . . . [T]hese grandmothers and mothers of ours were not Saints, but Artists; driven to a numb and bleeding madness by the springs of creativity in them for which there was no release. They were Creators, who lived lives of spiritual waste, because they were so rich in spirituality—which is the basis [of] Art—that the strain of enduring their unused and unwanted talent drove them insane. Throwing away this spirituality was [their] pathetic

42. Maureen Fiedler, "The Equal Rights Amendment and the Bonding of Women," *LCWR Newsletter* 8 (1980): 5.

> attempt to lighten the soul to a weight [their] work-worn, sexually abused bodies could bear.[43]

Such a time is past: the time of throwing away one's spirituality in order to survive.

It is regrettable that the possible liabilities of dark night theology cannot be dealt with in full here. Although some *interpretations* of dark night could reinforce passivity and women's internalized inferiority, subordination, lack of self-esteem and self-actualization, John of the Cross sings of the affirmation of the person by God within and of the redemption or transformation of affectivity that dark night effects. Dark contemplation is not a validation of things as they are or a ploy to keep women contented "outcasts of the [patriarchal] land"[44] but a constant questioning and restlessness that waits for and believes in the coming of a transformed vision of God; an affirmation of the self as woman that comes from deep inside and the consequent maturing to wholeness as a complete person; and a new and integrating spirituality capable of creating a new politics and generating new social structures.

Contemplation is what Dorothee Soelle calls revolutionary patience and is the epitome of passionate desire, activity, self-direction, autonomy, and bondedness.[45] It is a time bomb and will explode in new abilities and energy in women that cannot be conquered. Ultimately, it is the mystic, the contemplative woman, who will be reassured, affirmed, and loved, who will see and love, and for whose sake the world will be given sight, language, reassurance, and love. And she will understand Celie's final epistle, a letter to God: "Dear God. Dear stars, dear trees, dear sky, dear peoples. Dear Everything. Dear God."

43. Alice Walker, "In Search of Our Mothers' Gardens," in *Working It Out*, ed. Sara Rudick and Pamela Daniels (New York: Pantheon, 1977), 93.

44. Houchins, "I Found God in Myself," quoted from Anne Pratt, *Archetypal Patterns in Women's Fiction* (Bloomington: Indiana University Press, 1981), 5.

45. Dorothee Soelle, *Revolutionary Patience* (Maryknoll, NY: Orbis, 1977); see also Marianne Katoppo, *Compassionate and Free: An Asian Woman's Theology* (Maryknoll, NY: Orbis, 1980), 21.

4

Contemplative Prayer and the Impasse of White Supremacy

Laurie Cassidy

> "If I ever find out you are white, then I'm through with you. And if I find out you are black, I'll try my best to kill you when I get to heaven."[1]

These gut-wrenching words are Anne Moody's prayer to God after the bombing of Birmingham's Sixteenth Street Baptist Church in 1963. This prayer is a profound statement of the theological and spiritual problem that white supremacy poses for Christians in America—and particularly for white people who call themselves Christians.[2] Carmelite contemplative theologian Constance FitzGerald explains that our image of God "is what effects the character and quality of our human living."[3]

1. Anne Moody, *Coming of Age in Mississippi* (New York: Dial Press, 1968), 318.

2. The rising tide of white nationalism in the United States and Europe is the context of this essay. See Vegas Tenold, *Everything You Love Will Burn: Inside the Rebirth of White Nationalism in America* (New York: Nation Books, 2018). Also Adam Nossiter, "'Let Them Call You Racists': Bannon's Pep Talk to National Front," *New York Times* (March 10, 2018) at https://www.nytimes.com/2018/03/10/world/europe/steve-bannon-france-national-front.html.

3. Constance FitzGerald, "Transformation in Wisdom: The Subversive Character and Educative Power of Sophia in Contemplation," in *Carmel and Contemplation:*

On Sunday morning September 15, 1963, a bomb planted by white supremacists exploded in the Sixteenth Street Baptist Church in Birmingham, killing four young girls and injuring many other people in this African American congregation.[4] Moody's rage exposes what is hidden for white people, which is the image of god that legitimizes the death-dealing mechanics of white supremacy in America. Moody also models a way of praying that is a radical presence to herself, to human suffering, and to God. As white people what enables us to hear this rage and learn from the deep desire for God in Moody's prayer?

To begin this essay with God and white supremacy is dangerous because just the term "white supremacy" alone triggers strong reactions for many people.[5] Taken together, God and white supremacy create a cognitive dissonance stopping us in our tracks. Often, we white people resist using the term "white supremacy" because it conjures a specter of the hooded members of Ku Klux Klan, skinheads, and neo-Nazi hate groups. When we balk at this term, we stop the process of genuine and honest engagement as to why and how white supremacy forms us as Americans and impacts our faith as Christians. For example, we distance ourselves from exploring this reality by sincerely declaring, "I'm not racist. I abhor any action to kill black people!"

Transforming Human Consciousness, ed. Kevin Culligan and Regis Jordan (Washington, DC: Institute of Carmelite Studies, 2000), 284.

4. Denise McNair, Cynthia Wesley, Addie Mae Collins, and Carol Robertson were in the basement of the church preparing for the youth choir when killed in this bombing. See Carolyn Maull McKinstry, *While the World Watched: A Birmingham Bombing Survivor Comes of Age During the Civil Rights Movement* (Carol Stream, IL: Tyndale House Publishers, 2011); T.K. Thorne, *Last Chance for Justice: How Relentless Investigators Uncovered New Evidence Convicting the Birmingham Church Bombers* (Chicago: Lawrence Hill Books, 2013) and Spike Lee's documentary film *4 Little Girls* (1997).

5. I use the term "white supremacy" throughout this essay because this is the system that legitimizes the economic, political, social, and cultural system of the United States and is built into all the institutions of America. This term also enables inquiry into how race, class, gender, and other forms of oppression intersect. See the very helpful summary by Elizabeth Martínez at SOA Watch, https://www.nosue.org/app/download/7244496066/what-is-white-supremacy.pdf.

> I hope to make clear that white supremacy is something more pervasive and subtle than the actions of explicit white nationalists. White supremacy describes the culture we live in, a culture that positions white people and all that is associated with them (whiteness) as ideal.[6]

The pervasiveness and subtlety of white supremacy is often invisible to those of us who are white because we are socialized *not to see* race as something *we have*. White supremacy is the very architectural framework of our nation; we live in "the house built on race."[7] How, then, can we be ignorant of our being white? The violence briefly described at the beginning of this essay may be all too familiar for readers. Like a landscape painting, however, racism can be interpreted as "out there" adversely impacting people of color. We are socialized to believe that if we do not intentionally do bad things to people of color we are not involved in this "social problem" in the American landscape. Being white is a frame of reference—for us—that is unquestioned, invisible, and unnamed.[8]

We are socialized or formed by white supremacy, through our being ignorant of how we are involved and shaped by the system in which we live. Ironically this is how the system is maintained by white people and reproduced in our everyday life.[9] By beginning this essay with talk of God, prayer, and white supremacy I want to bring home the urgency of our reality, throw a spotlight on the inner reach of racism as it imprints itself upon the human

6. Robin Diangelo, *White Fragility: Why It's So Hard for White People to Talk about Racism* (Boston: Beacon Press, 2018), 33.

7. M. Shawn Copeland, "Racism and the Vocation of the Christian Theologian," *Spiritus* 2 (2002): 25. This metaphor of America as a house built on race is found in the work of Joe Feagin. He explains that this metaphor is critical to understanding that white supremacy is not an "add on" to the structure of our country but the very foundation. This framing of the house is not only a systemic reality but also our worldview. Joe Feagin, *The White Racial Frame: Centuries of Racial Framing and Counter-Framing* (New York: Routledge, 2013), x.

8. Bryan Massingale, *Racial Justice and the Catholic Church* (Maryknoll, NY: Orbis Books, 2010), 22.

9. Feagin, *The White Racial Frame*, 11.

spirit. "Only an invasion of divine love will shatter the small images of God that enable us to live undisturbed by the racism that benefits some and terrorizes so many."[10] We must face that our being white impacts how we pray, how we imagine God, and where we see signs of hope.

Our collective inability to use the term "white supremacy" is, as FitzGerald describes, an element of our societal impasse in America. As white people we can feed the intransigence in our bristling at even the mention of the term. For example, recall the controversy in the United States over the phrase "Black Lives Matter."[11] Some people react by declaring, "All Lives Matter."[12] The standoff over this language makes it impossible to inquire into why Black, Brown, and Red men and women were (and are) being killed going to the corner store, visiting a relative, playing in the backyard, going for a run, or at home asleep.[13] Even how we

10. Bryan Massingale, "The Assumptions of White Privilege and What We Can Do about It," *National Catholic Reporter* (June 1, 2020) at https://www.ncronline.org/news/opinion/assumptions-white-privilege-and-what-we-can-do-about-it.

11. Please see https://blacklivesmatter.com/. For a theological interpretation of this phrase and the movement, see Nichole M. Flores, "Martin Luther King Jr. and the Dignity of Black Lives Matter Network," *America* (March 23, 2018) at https://www.americamagazine.org/arts-culture/2018/03/23/martin-luther-king-jr-and-dignity-black-lives-matter-network.

12. For an excellent commentary of this phrase, see German Lopez, "Why You Should Stop Saying 'All Lives Matter,' Explained in Nine Different Ways," *Vox* (July 11, 2016) at https://www.vox.com/2016/7/11/12136140/black-all-lives-matter.

13. This is an ongoing reality that can be seen in the murder of Ahmaud Arbery, who was shot while out jogging his neighborhood. Khushbu Shah, " 'They Lynched Him': Ahmaud Arbery's Father on the Killing of His Son," *Guardian* (May 10, 2020) at https://www.theguardian.com/us-news/2020/may/09/ahmaud-arbery-father-marcus-georgia-running. Also the fatal shooting of Breonna Taylor while sleeping in her own home. Josh Wood, "Breonna Taylor Shooting: Hunt for Answers in Case of Black Woman Killed by Police," *Guardian* (May 14, 2020) at https://www.theguardian.com/us-news/2020/may/14/breonna-taylor-louisville-police-shooting-kentucky. Please see Sara Hylton, "A Well of Grief: The Relatives of Murdered Native Women Speak Out," *Guardian* (January 13, 2020) at https://www.theguardian.com/us-news/2020/jan/13/a-well-of-grief-the-relatives-of-murdered-native-women-speak-out.

structure our language about race makes Asian Americans invisible and erases their history in this country.[14] This heated dispute regarding language is a symptom of the gridlock regarding racism and the reality of white supremacy that shapes our shared life together in America. This impasse is not just a political problem or social issue but a dynamic that "jeopardizes that which makes us most human—our capacity for relationships."[15]

My essay explores a contemplative approach for white people to our impasse in this "house built on race." John of the Cross describes the dark night using words such as "self-knowledge," "attachment," and "purification of desire."[16] The understanding of

14. Please see Ki Joo Choi, *Disciplined by Race: Theological Ethics and the Problem of Asian American Identity* (Eugene, OR: Cascade Books, 2019). See also Edward Chang and Carol Park, *Korean Americans: A Concise History* (Riverside, CA: The Young Oak Kim Center for Korean Studies at the University of California, 2019); Jonathan Lee, ed., *Japanese Americans: The History and Culture of a People* (Santa Barbara, CA: ABC-CLIO, 2018); Beth Lew-Williams, *The Chinese Must Go: Violence, Exclusion, and the Making of the Alien in America* (Cambridge, MA: Harvard University Press, 2018); Sucheng Chan, ed., *The Vietnamese American 1.5 Generation: Stories of War, Revolution, Flight and New Beginnings* (Philadelphia: Temple University Press, 2006); Anthony Christian Ocampo, *The Latino of Asia: How Filipino Americans Break the Rules of Race* (Stanford, CA: Stanford University Press, 2016). This very limited list of texts is simply to point to what is lost in our understanding of America and when Asian Americans are made invisible in racial discourse. And as Ki Joo Choi argues we are also at a loss in our understanding of the operations of racism. For example, how does knowing these histories help us to understand and contest the racist political narratives about the origins of COVID-19 virus?

15. Copeland, "Racism and the Vocation," 15.

16. There are a number of authors critiquing what they regard as a misuse of the category of the dark night in John of the Cross. For example, Elizabeth Anderson writes, "Very often in contemporary Western Christianity, the phrase 'dark night of the soul' is tossed around uncritically to cover any and all experiences of dryness, depression, emptiness, or despair, stretching the term far beyond what John of the Cross ever intended it to encompass" ("The Experience of Abandonment by God in Syriac Christian Ascetical Theology," *Spiritus* 20 [2020]: 80). Anderson's comment deserves sustained critical engagement. Who are the contemporary Christians using this term in an uncritical way? How does this "misuse" indicate a desire of contemporary Christians to find in

these words can be reduced to only indicating interior "spiritual" movements in prayer.[17] FitzGerald's work challenges this reduction and marginalization by demonstrating that "the interpretation of these signs must be extended to one's interpersonal life as well, and perhaps even to one's societal life."[18] Her interpretation of John of the Cross reveals the connection of our own inner life and our life as a nation.[19] I want to push forward FitzGerald's contention that "societal interpretation of these signs, and dark night in general, throws considerable light on the experience of

---

the tradition ways of engaging negativity, limit, and powerlessness? Anderson's critique cuts to the core of contemporary appropriation of the works of John of the Cross—as classic with a surplus of meaning beyond what he intended.

17. For more on the history of this reduction, see Grace M. Jantzen, *Power, Gender, and Christian Mysticism* (New York: Cambridge University Press, 1995).

18. Constance FitzGerald, "Impasse and Dark Night," in *Living with Apocalypse: Spiritual Resources for Social Compassion*, ed. Tilden Edwards (New York: Harper & Row, 1984), 99.

19. There is a way of interpreting and teaching the wisdom of Carmel that is ahistorical, which can be seen in the sustained study of the intense, interior, and extraordinary experiences in the writings of Teresa of Avila and John of the Cross. Teófanes Egido, OCD, argues that this ahistorical approach actually undermines understanding Carmelite wisdom. In writing on Teresa of Avila, Egido explains, "To detach her from the historical conditions of sixteenth century Spain, from the particular circumstances of the Church in which she lived, can ultimately obscure her supernatural experience and her ecclesial work of reform; on the other hand, attention to her human qualities is an increasingly indispensable condition for understanding her total work." See Teófanes Egido, "The Historical Setting of St. Teresa's Life," in *Carmelite Studies*, vol. 1: *Spiritual Direction*, ed. John Sullivan (Washington, DC: Institute for Carmelite Studies, 1980), 122. This point is critical for FitzGerald's contemporary interpretation of Teresa and John. For FitzGerald, "The mystics not only give us paradigms from the past that enable us to interpret our present experience, but they also provide the materials to create new paradigms that unlock a way into the future" (Constance FitzGerald, "The Desire for God and the Transformative Power of Contemplation," in *Light Burdens, Heavy Blessings: Challenges of Church and Culture in the Post Vatican II Era*, ed. Mary Heather MacKinnon, Moni McIntyre, and Mary Ellen Sheehan [Quincy, IL: Franciscan Press, 2000], 217). FitzGerald's contemporary appropriation of Carmelite classics is compared to the hermeneutics of Paul Ricoeur. See David F. Ford, *Self and Salvation: Being Transformed* (New York: Cambridge University Press, 1999), 225n49.

societal impasse."[20] By placing the experience of the impasse of racism and white supremacy in dialogue with the classic text of John of the Cross, FitzGerald helps us understand, name, and claim our experience of God "and thereby direct [our] own creative and affective energy" for God's work of personal and social transformation.[21] In other words, using FitzGerald's work as a lens we can understand, desire, and embody what personal and social transformation looks like concretely in America.

In this essay I draw on FitzGerald's profound approach to societal impasse in a spiral of three interrelated turns. First, I explore how contemplative prayer may enable those of us who are white to be present to impasse. Fully acknowledging the religious and theological implications of white supremacy for our faith may bring about a form of self-knowledge that John of the Cross describes as "not gentle but afflictive."[22] Paradoxically, this self-knowledge can create the possibility for genuine change and transformation because we are disposed for God's loving action and passionate desires in the midst of impasse. For FitzGerald, "John's framework allows us to believe, to hope and to continue to desire."[23] Second, I explore images of God that function to justify white supremacy. FitzGerald explains, "Our gods have to die before we can be for the God who is beyond all our human images and projections and who waits for us over the brink of the known in the darkness."[24] To concretize this insight I reflect on the mosaic *Christ in Majesty* in the upper church of the National Shrine of the Immaculate Conception in Washington, DC. This mosaic acts as lens to study how god legitimizes white supremacy in America.[25] This artistic representation confronts us with the depth to which Christianity, and particularly Catholicism, in America is

20. FitzGerald, "Impasse and Dark Night," 94.

21. Ibid.

22. John of the Cross, *The Living Flame of Love* 1.19.

23. FitzGerald, "The Desire for God and the Transformative Power of Contemplation," 213.

24. Ibid., 219.

25. To view this mosaic and see its location within the basilica, please see https://www.nationalshrine.org/art-architecture/.

cast in white. This image not only reveals what we believe about God but also acts as a mirror revealing how we define ourselves. Finally, for FitzGerald impasse can be a site of tremendous potential and hope. By utilizing the framework of the dark night in relationship to the impasses of white supremacy, we "unveil the horizons to which contemplation, or the love-embrace of God's spirit, throws us open and makes us available as a people" to hearing the prayer of Anne Moody and people of color in America.[26]

I. "Today We Come with the World inside Us"[27]

Twenty years ago, FitzGerald prophetically described the connection of our own personal prayer and the cries of the world. She noted then that in times past people approached God by turning from the world, but today the world is inside of us.

> We come as a last resort, in a sense, because as Americans we have lost faith and hope in human power and human reason. We are driven to interiority, to contemplation, to the desire for the experience of God's love by the poor and oppressed, by, in fact, the image of God in the world and on the face of the earth.[28]

In this passage FitzGerald points out that our prayer is provoked by our desire for transformation of the causes of the pain, horror, and anguish. What if those causes come from inside of us? What if our very interiority as white people offers us *one* way of participating in the transformation of white supremacy?

26. FitzGerald, "The Desire for God and the Transformative Power of Contemplation," 217.

27. Ibid., 209.

28. Ibid. I believe that some forms of contemporary contemplative practice are used to transcend our historical moment. See Christena Cleveland, "So Much of the Privileged Life Is about Transcendence," *On Being* (July 7, 2017) at https://onbeing.org/blog/christena-cleveland-so-much-of-the-privileged-life-is-about-transcendence/. I am very grateful to Martin Byrne, CFC, for introducing me to Cleveland's insightful work.

When FitzGerald writes that "[t]oday we come with the world inside us,"[29] she is describing a contemplative stance, an interiority that is a site of transformation. This interiority is not cordoned off from the world but suggests that the one who prays is integrally related to and participating in the world. Exploring the world inside of us becomes a contemplative way of disposing ourselves to God's love as transformation of human consciousness.

While contemplative forms of prayer are becoming more popular the fatal violence of white supremacy in America continues, unabated and often unnoticed.[30] What is the function of prayer in the face of the death-dealing violence of white supremacy? In American society to offer prayers in the aftermath of violence "has become a model of performative sympathy and inaction."[31] In the face of this ongoing carnage do we throw up our hands in powerlessness and despair and think, "I can't do anything about this, but at least I can pray!" Within popular culture "thoughts and prayers" are met with a rightful amount of cynicism and eye rolling.[32] Is our turn to prayer a spiritual bypass and evasion of our reality? Do I sincerely prayer for "them"? Do I pray for an end to racial violence? Probing into these questions and our feelings of powerlessness is essential to examining our

29. FitzGerald, "The Desire for God and the Transformative Power of Contemplation," 209.

30. For example, eight million Americans have turned to daily practices of meditation. This statistic is considered a "conservative" number and is cited in a 2012 survey by the National Health Interview Survey found at https://nccih.nih.gov/research/statistics/NHIS/2012.

31. Tara Isabella Burton, "9 Faith Leaders on 'Thoughts and Prayers'—and Action—after Tragedy," *Vox* (February 15, 2018) at https://www.vox.com/identities/2017/10/3/16408658/9-faith-leaders-action-after-tragedy-florida-shooting-majory-stoneman-douglas.

32. See the video game called *Thoughts and Prayers: The Game* (https://www.thoughtsandprayersthegame.com/) and the fifth episode of season 4 of *BoJack Horseman* titled "Thoughts and Prayers," https://bojackhorseman.fandom.com/wiki/Thoughts_and_Prayers. What is troubling is "thoughts and prayers" are sent out after the mass shooting of white people but not in response to the ongoing killing of people of color. This absence of even "performative sympathy" deserves its own commentary.

deeply held assumptions about prayer for which we must urgently make an accounting. FitzGerald names our conundrum:

> We do not really believe that if we surrender these situations of world impasse to contemplative prayer that new solutions, new visions of peace and equality, will emerge in our world. We dare not believe that a creative re-visioning is possible. Everything is just too complex, too beyond our reach.[33]

We must ask ourselves, "Do we really expect anything at all of the contemplative process of prayer in our world today?"[34] And specifically, can we expect anything of prayer with the tight knot of fear, anger, guilt, defensiveness, and confusion when we even speak of our being white and white supremacy?

If you are white your experience of reading this essay may offer clues into this experience of the impasse of white supremacy. For example, you may urgently long for me to outline a hitherto unknown plan for white people to overcome the problem of racism, "get on with it and tell me what to do!" or "Give me a checklist!" And I am tempted by the illusion that if I clearly and rationally spell out the "spiritual" problem of being white—and offer you something persuasive enough (ironically, even though I am white!)—you will be "converted." The deep desire for "mastery" and control (and even giving the appearance that it is possible) through a step-by-step plan we can work hard to achieve are elements of the very dynamics of our impasse. As white people we have been deeply conditioned to value these ways of operating, so much so that suggesting a different way of operating can be judged to be "doing nothing." Our impasse as white people is that we are being confronted with the dead-end of our habitual methods of acting and are faced with the very bankruptcy of the frameworks of understanding ourselves and seeing the world. We must face our urgent need to find an antiracist checklist. FitzGerald counsels us to notice this experience and to understand its significance.

33. FitzGerald, "Impasse and the Dark Night," 107.
34. Ibid.

> As Americans we are not educated for impasse, for the experience of human limitation and darkness that will not yield to hard work, studies, statistics, rational analysis, and well-planned programs. We stand helpless, confused, and guilty before the insurmountable problems of our world. We dare not let the full import of this impasse even come to complete consciousness.[35]

The experience I describe can be the "concrete focus for prayer and drive us to contemplation."[36] FitzGerald explains that basic to the experience of the dark night is the breakdown and disintegration of the usual ways of operating and functioning. Let's face it, if we are socialized not to see whiteness, and we benefit from being white, how could we possibility imagine we would be able or willing to "solve" white supremacy? "*The only reason for racism's persistence is that white people continue to benefit from it.*"[37]

It is right here at this place of confounding limitation, urgent confusion, frustrated powerlessness, and desperate attachment that *God's passionate love and desire* are drawing us. FitzGerald assures us that this place of impasse can be a source of transformation,

> *if* the experience of impasse is fully appropriated within one's heart and flesh with consciousness and consent; *if* the limitations of one's humanity and human condition are squarely faced and the sorrow of finitude allowed to invade the human spirit with real, existential powerlessness; *if* the ego does not demand understanding in the name of control and predictability but is willing to admit the mystery of its own being and surrender itself to mystery.[38]

One element of our appropriating the experience of the impasse of white supremacy is to turn *toward* the feelings of guilt and defensiveness rather than trying to ignore them, overcome them, fix

35. Ibid., 105.
36. Ibid., 107.
37. Massingale, "The Assumptions of White Privilege," emphasis in original.
38. FitzGerald, "Impasse and the Dark Night," 96.

them, deny them, or justify ourselves.[39] To be present to all the discomfort is one step in opening ourselves to how our experience can enable us to learn about what it means to be white—something we are socialized not to see. As Bryan Massingale passionately explains, "There is no way to tell the truth about race in the country without white people being uncomfortable." Moreover, the violence against people of color for the past four hundred years in America makes it is critical to know and "*understand the difference between being uncomfortable and being threatened.*"[40] Understanding this difference through educating ourselves to our shared history in America may awaken us also to the suffering of our own ancestors.[41] Studying the underside of history we may begin to lament with people of color and cry out, "Where have you hidden, Beloved, and left me moaning?"[42]

Our consent to God's love in our vulnerability—even choosing to be vulnerable—makes change possible: our moving "into that deep place of knowledge" where "terror and loathing of any difference" is rooted.[43] As FitzGerald explains, "Dark night mediates the transfiguration of affectivity."[44] The transfiguration of affectivity is a critical process for authentic social change, change

39. For more on all the ways we have been socialized to defend ourselves against this, please see DiAngelo, *White Fragility*.

40. Massingale, "The Assumptions of White Privilege," emphasis in original.

41. Please see David Roediger, *Working toward Whiteness: How America's Immigrants Became White* (New York: Basic Books, 2018); Noel Ignatiev, *How the Irish Became White* (New York: Routledge, 1995); Jennifer Guglielmo and Salvatore Salerno, *Are Italians White?* (New York: Routledge, 2003); Theodore Allen, *The Invention of the White Race* (New York: Verso, 1994).

42. This the first line of the *Spiritual Canticle*. See *The Collected Works of John of the Cross*, trans. Kieran Kavanaugh and Otilio Rodriguez (Washington, DC: Institute of Carmelite Studies, 1991), 471.

43. This invitation comes from the work of Audre Lorde, whose words we can take to our prayer. "Racism and homophobia are real conditions of all our lives in this place and time. I urge each one of us here to reach down into that deep place of knowledge inside herself and touch the terror and loathing of any difference that lives there. See whose face it wears. Then the personal as the political can begin to illuminate all our choices." As quoted in Iris Marion Young, *Justice and the Politics of Difference* (Princeton: Princeton University Press, 1990), 122.

44. FitzGerald, "Impasse and the Dark Night," 102.

that goes beyond governmental legislation or individual rational assent. Since the era of Civil Rights in the United States we have a discursive commitment to equality. There is a consensus that if as individuals we verbally agree to equality, we are not racist. But this "discursive commitment" belies the fears, aversions, and revulsions that "have gone underground, dwelling in the everyday habits and cultural meanings of which people are for the most part unaware."[45] In other words, we may have a conscious acceptance of people who do not look like "us" but may have unconscious aversion, nervousness, and discomfort.[46] Though sanctioned against legally, the repressed and unspoken aversion is operative in all kinds of decision making and judgments. As Iris Marion Young explains, "Aversion or devaluation of certain groups is displaced onto a judgment of character or competence supposedly unconnected with group attributes."[47]

Contemporary culture is replete with this dynamic of unconscious aversion transmuted into the judgment of competency or character:[48] for example, the critiques of Michelle Obama's appearance during her time as First Lady, even declaring she should cover her arms.[49] One Virginia voter illustrates the power of affectivity in reinscribing white supremacy in comments regarding the Obamas: "I just—I don't like him. . . . Can't stand to look at him. I don't like his wife. She's far from the first lady. It's about time we get a first lady in there that acts like a first lady, and looks like a first

45. Young, *Justice and the Politics of Difference*, 124.

46. Ibid., 130.

47. Ibid., 135.

48. For a theological exploration of this dynamic as it relates to the association of Black bodies and criminality, see Alex Mikulich, Laurie Cassidy, and Margaret Pfeil, *The Scandal of White Complicity in U.S. Hyper-Incarceration: A Non-Violent Spirituality of White Resistance* (New York: Palgrave, 2013).

49. This critique of a Black woman's body is not new; we see such derision in the attempt to humiliate Sojourner Truth. See Brittney Cooper, "A'n't I a Lady? Race Women, Michelle Obama, and the Ever-Expanding Democratic Imagination," *MELUS* 35, no. 4 (2010): 39–57; Shirley Tate, "Michelle Obama's Arms: Race, Respectability and Class Privilege," *Comparative American Studies: An International Journal* 10, nos. 2–3 (2012): 226–38.

lady."[50] The voter denies that this has anything to do with race: "No it's not, I don't care what color she is. It's just she doesn't act and look like a first lady."[51] These comments reveal the deep affective roots of white supremacy. The voter not only demonstrates the aversion to the Obamas' bodies (while simultaneously claiming it has nothing to do with race) but also shows how this affectivity is the foundation of what is deemed to be ideal and therefore normative ("She's far from the first lady"). This voter's comments are illustrative of what Bryan Massingale describes as the soul of whiteness, a worldview that "sees itself as the measure of what is real, standard, normative, and/or normal."[52]

Self-knowledge is a precious fruit of the dark night. "John of the Cross' writings suggest that the clarity of our self-knowledge is in itself the embrace of God we have silenced."[53] In other words, our growth in self-knowledge is a deepening in our capacity to be loved by God. Can we allow ourselves to be affected by the desire of people of color, for us to know ourselves? And can we consider this as reflective of God's desire? Our self-knowledge involves our growing capacity to see this white worldview and understand how it impacts our relationships with God, other people, and ourselves. Ijeoma Oluo declares,

> *White people: I don't want you to understand me better; I want you to understand yourselves. Your survival has never depended upon on your knowledge of white culture. In fact, it's required your ignorance.*[54]

Oluo's challenge is for us to grow in self-knowledge, a knowledge we benefit from not having. This ignorance is not simply a gap in information. If it were, we could simply read books and educate

50. Ari Shapiro, "A Second, Chance Interview with Subject of Controversial First Lady Remarks," *National Public Radio* (September 27, 2012) at https://www.npr.org/sections/itsallpolitics/2012/09/27/161903264/a-second-chance-interview-with-subject-of-controversial-first-lady-remarks.

51. Ibid.

52. Massingale, *Racial Justice and the Catholic Church*, 22.

53. FitzGerald, "The Desire for God and the Transformative Power of Contemplation," 212.

54. Cited in DiAngelo, *White Fragility*, 51; emphasis in original.

ourselves. In contrast, self-knowledge as a fruit of contemplation is not solely intellectual but is a grace that involves, frees, and empowers the whole person. As white people our ignorance is a way of being that is a deeply embodied, collective, intergenerational socialization that is actively (re)produced in everyday life in order to maintain white supremacy.

The grace of self-knowledge is responsive to the depth necessary for unlearning this ignorance. For example, if we are white the vast majority of us "cannot answer the question 'How has race shaped your life?' "[55] This question confronts us with the challenge to explore the specifics of our socialization.[56] How do we unlearn such benighted ignorance? In the *Ascent of Mount Carmel* John of the Cross writes, "To come to the knowledge you have not you must go by a way you know not."[57] Our consent to the discomfort of the impasse of white supremacy can be a way of being led to a "knowledge we have not by a way we know not." FitzGerald explains that a primary effect of the dark night is self-knowledge. She writes:

> [W]ithdrawal of accustomed pleasure in life, and the consequent frustration of desire, trigger one's seemingly destructive tendencies and move them beyond them into action on a level that is beyond conscious control.[58]

For example, Kamilah Majied invites curiosity into the connection of discomfort and attachment. In relationship to the demonstrations

55. Robin DiAngelo, *What Does It Mean to Be White? Developing White Racial Literacy* (New York: Peter Lang, 2016), 193.

56. Linda Martín Alcoff explains, "[W]e clearly need to address the class, ethnicity, and gender heterogeneity among whites." See Alcoff's essay, "Epistemologies of Ignorance: Three Types," in *Race and Epistemologies of Ignorance*, ed. Shannon Sullivan and Nancy Tuana (Albany: SUNY Press, 2007), 50. I cite this source to call attention to specific ways that we are socialized. All of us who are white have varying degrees of privilege and penalty depending on elements of our identity such as education, age, gender, class, physical ability, ethnicity, and sexual orientation.

57. *The Collected Works of John of the Cross*, 150.

58. FitzGerald, "Impasse and the Dark Night," 102.

protesting the murder of George Floyd, Majied asks us to consider, "Is the discomfort that arises connected to attachment to privilege, to not wanting to give up any more time or energy to thinking about anti-Black racism?"[59]

For John of the Cross our growth in self-knowledge is integrally related to growth in knowledge of God. Quoting Augustine, John writes, *"Let me know myself. . . and I will know you."*[60] To take seriously FitzGerald's interpretation of John of the Cross suggests that surrendering to God in the impasse of white supremacy makes possible our being grasped by God who is "alluring us from a future that comes to meet us."[61]

II. "Our Gods Have to Die"[62]

Anne Moody's prayer that began this chapter rejects God as either Black or white. Her rejection expresses profound desire and urgent longing for God. Moody's deep contemplative intuition is in itself openness to the God of Jesus who transcends this binary of Black or white. FitzGerald describes such prayer as already the beginning of communion with God because it is the beginning of the end of our attachment to our images of God and openness to the mystery of God.[63]

We are witnessing the process of our national gods dying in American society, as public monuments are being torn down and there are even calls to remove statues of Jesus "that depict him 'with European features . . . because they support white suprem-

59. Kamilah Majied, "May Disrupting Anti-Black Racism Never Cease," in *Lion's Roar* (June 12, 2020) at https://www.lionsroar.com/may-disrupting-anti-black-racism-never-cease/?mc_cid=aa26006302&mc_eid=03a000d771.

60. John of the Cross, *The Dark Night* 1.12.5 in *The Collected Works of John of the Cross*, 387; emphasis in original.

61. Constance FitzGerald, "From Impasse to Prophetic Hope: Crisis of Memory," in *Carmelite Wisdom and Prophetic Hope: Treasures Both Old and New*, ed. Mary Frohlich (Washington, DC: Institute of Carmelite Studies, 2018), 69.

62. FitzGerald, "The Desire for God and the Transformative Power of Contemplation," 218.

63. Ibid.

acy.' "[64] Is this "tearing down" simply vandalism and a symptom of our political chaos and social upheaval? Should the statues be removed or not? Will white supremacy's grip on America be dismantled with such removal? What statues will authentically represent the message of Jesus? As FitzGerald observes, "We find impasse not only in the problems but even the solutions."[65] However we judge the destruction of statues, FitzGerald's interpretation of the dark night may attune us to a deeper process at work in our current events. She sees in such impasse a call to "development, transcendence, new life, and understanding."[66]

As national monuments and religious statues both have been destroyed, one American bishop asked how we learn from history if these statues are removed. "If we allow the commemorative and visual history of our nation to be destroyed by random groups in the current moment of anger how will we ever learn from history?"[67] The bishop's comments raise the question of how remembering American history may also enable us to examine how it is that the majority of our religious statues equate "the fullness of Catholicism with [white] European culture."[68] He argues that we cannot equate white representations of Christ, the Virgin Mary, and the saints as "inherently signs of white supremacy." But how have we come to even question this equation?[69]

64. "Wisconsin Bishop Denounces Activist's Call to Destroy Statues of Jesus," *Crux* (July 1, 2020) at https://cruxnow.com/church-in-the-usa/2020/07/wisconsin-bishop-denounces-activists-call-to-destroy-statues-of-jesus/.

65. FitzGerald, "Impasse and the Dark Night," 110.

66. Ibid., 111.

67. Jonah McKeown, " 'I Cannot Remain Silent': Madison Catholic Bishop Condemns Destruction of Religious Statues," *Catholic News Agency* (June 24, 2020) at https://www.catholicnewsagency.com/news/i-cannot-remain-silent-madison-catholic-bishop-condemns-destruction-of-religious-statues-77800.

68. Ibid.

69. The challenge to explore the problem of Christ as white is not new. As Catholics we must hear this theological and spiritual challenge that can be traced back to the writings of W.E.B. Du Bois. See W.E.B. Du Bois, *The Souls of Black Folk*, ed. Henry Louis Gates Jr. and Terri Hume Oliver (New York: Norton, 1999). Du Bois writing on Christ as Black is viewed as critical to the development of Black

One example of this white religious imagery is found in the mosaic of Christ in Majesty in the upper church of the National Shrine of the Immaculate Conception in Washington, DC.[70] Historian of the National Shrine Thomas Tweed claims that "No visitor to the Great Upper Church could miss the enormous Byzantine-inspired mosaic Christ in Majesty, from which Jesus looks down on pilgrims, reminding them of the final judgment."[71] The mosaic is 3,610 square feet with Christ's image spanning thirty-four feet across and "is one of the largest mosaics of Jesus Christ in the world."[72] Christ is represented as seated, with his arms outstretched. A red robe covers most of his body, with his left arm and chest exposed, which is youthful and muscular. His skin is a pinkish white and his blond hair is shoulder length in waves. The face of Christ has arched eyebrows, blue eyes, and an aquiline nose with a short blond beard and mustache. Two halos surround Christ's head with flames of fire radiating out in three directions, suggestive of a cross. The artist, Jan Henryk de Rosen (1891–1982), described that this mosaic of Christ was intended to be the culmination of the art in five domes in the upper church of the Shrine. De Rosen explains,

> As in St. Mark's in Venice, the chief characteristics of the interior of the Shrine are a succession of decorated domes. Each dome is a unit in itself, leading to the last dome of the apse of the church, the Christ in Majesty.[73]

What do we make of this image of Christ? How do we interpret the white skin, blond hair, and blue eyes of Jesus in this resurrected Christ? In the crypt of the Shrine diverse communities of Catholics in America are represented, for example, through

---

and Womanist theology in America. Edward Blum, *W. E. B. Du Bois: American Prophet* (Philadelphia: University of Pennsylvania Press, 2007).

70. To view this mosaic and see its location within the basilica, please see https://www.nationalshrine.org/art-architecture/.

71. Thomas A. Tweed, *America's Church: The National Shrine and Catholic Presence in the Nation's Capital* (New York: Oxford University Press, 2011), 9–10.

72. https://www.nationalshrine.org/blog/a-guide-to-basilica-art-mosaics-of-the-great-upper-church/.

73. https://www.trinitydome.org/news/5-domes-national-shrine-story-tell/.

Our Lady of Antipolo, Our Lady of La Vang, Our Lady of Lebanon, and Our Mother of Africa. What is the significance of this image of Christ as white as the culmination of art in center of the Shrine while all the non-European images are in the crypt? The juxtaposition of these images reinforces that even when we create "multicultural" images they are always in response to the dominance of God as white.[74]

In the *Compendium of the Catechism of the Catholic Church* Pope Benedict XVI acknowledges the power of images to communicate faith. He writes that in a culture dominated by the visual, images have a unique way of expressing faith.

> It is an indication of how today more than ever, in a culture of images, a sacred image can express much more than what can be said in words, and be an extremely effective and dynamic way of communicating the Gospel message.[75]

This image of Christ as young, strong, able bodied, white, and male and its placement in the Shrine expresses much more than can be communicated with words. First, Christ is imaged here as "in majesty"; in other words, Christ is raised from the dead and ascended to God. What does the image proclaim about being risen? Will the particularity of Jesus' historical existence be erased? In the risen life does Jesus Christ becomes white? Some argue this image and its place within the Shrine point to an even more hideous and heretical belief. The association of whiteness and divinity is deeply rooted in the conquest of the Americas, which made possible and justified the enslavement of Africans and genocide of Native Americans.[76]

74. For more on this, see Anthony Pinn, "Putting Jesus in His Place," in *Humanism: Essays on Race, Religion and Popular Culture* (New York: Bloomsbury, 2015), 76–92.

75. Benedict XVI, *Compendium of the Catechism of the Catholic Church* (Rome: Libreria Editrice Vaticana, 2005), no. 5 at http://www.vatican.va/archive/compendium_ccc/documents/archive_2005_compendium-ccc_en.html#INTRODUCTION.

76. Willie James Jennings, *The Christian Imagination: Theology and the Origins of Race* (New Haven: Yale University Press, 2010). See also James W. Perkinson, *White Theology: Outing Supremacy in Modernity* (New York: Palgrave Macmillan, 2004).

The significance of the Shrine's location in Washington, DC, demonstrates the connection of political power and religious imagery at work in the mosaic of Christ. The Shrine is a place of worship and is also American Catholicism's claim to civic space, a church "sunk in tradition yet distinctively American."[77]

> In the United States, with its legally sanctioned diversity, faiths have negotiated political power, constructed denominational identity, and secured public visibility by positioning national churches in the nation's capital.[78]

The physical location of the Shrine was critical to American Catholicism's staking a claim to the landscape of political power in Washington, which can be seen in how the Shrine is described as it relates to government buildings in the city. The dome of the Shrine, which holds the mosaic of Christ, has been compared in size and shape to that of the capitol building. At the time of the Shrine's completion one commentator declared that one dome honors the "continent-conquering forefathers" and the other shows the "Catholic ecclesiastical forefathers have erected our spiritual capital there."[79]

Tracing how and why American Catholicism embraced the white Christ and the supremacy it legitimates is not only a historical necessity and a theological imperative but must also be a contemplative commitment.

> The basic theological task in America is not that of establishing the existence of God, but that of discerning the true God from false idols. Today it is no longer meaningful to call one's self a believer; the meaningful thing is to explain in which God one believes. The basic problem is not the existence of God but the presence of God.[80]

77. https://www.nationalshrine.org/art-architecture/.

78. Tweed, *America's Church*, 191.

79. Ibid., 185.

80. Pablo Richard, "Theology in the Theology of Liberation," in *Mysterium Liberationis: Fundamental Concepts of Liberation Theology*, ed. Ignacio Ellacuría and Jon Sobrino (Maryknoll, NY: Orbis Books, 1993), 155. See also Jon Sobrino, "Evil and Hope: A Reflection for Victims," *CTSA Proceedings* 50 (1995): 80.

The destruction of monuments and statues calls us to consider how these images function; in other words, what is their impact on those of us who are white and on those of us who are people of color in America?

FitzGerald declares, "Our gods have to die before we can wait for the God who is beyond all our human images and projections and who waits for us over the brink of the known in the darkness."[81] She explains that acknowledging our gods must die is an experiential process in which we are allowing ourselves to be grasped by Incomprehensible Mystery.[82] This process is not just a passive waiting; the contemplative stance in the dark night involves a constant questioning "and restlessness that waits for and believes in the coming of a transformed vision of God." This contemplative stance is not only transforming of persons but makes possible "new politics and generating new social structures."[83] FitzGerald's description of the contemplative journey of dark night is a deeply engaged process of passionate desire and critical exploration, which makes possible new patterns of relationships not only with God but also with each other. But what kind of questioning and restlessness will make it possible for those of us who are white and Catholic to participate in the coming of a transformed vision of God, as FitzGerald suggests?

American Catholic white feminist theologians have clearly documented the connection of how we image God and how we relate to one another. Elizabeth A. Johnson writes,

> How a group names its God has critical consequences, for the symbol of the divine organizes every other aspect of a religious system. The way a faith community speaks about God indicates what it considers the greatest good, the profoundest truth, the most appealing beauty. In turn, the image of God shapes a community's corporate identity and behavior as well as the individual

81. FitzGerald, "The Desire for God and the Transformative Power of Contemplation," 218.

82. FitzGerald, "Impasse and the Dark Night," 101. Here FitzGerald draws on the work of Michael Buckley, "Atheism and Contemplation," *Theological Studies* 40 (1979): 690.

83. FitzGerald, "Impasse and the Dark Night," 114.

> behavior of its members. . . . The symbol of God functions. It is never neutral in its effects, but expresses and molds a community's bedrock convictions and actions.[84]

Taking Johnson's insight into our present context demands we examine the theological implications of the white Christ for white Catholics in America.[85] For example, Mary Aquin O'Neil explains that exclusively male imagery of the divine not only compromises women's capacity to find their image and likeness of God but also handicaps men from viewing women as *imago Dei*. O'Neil asks, "Is it too strong to say that one who cannot find the other in God cannot love the other as she or he is? I think not."[86] Extending O'Neil's insight, is it too strong to say that if we cannot imagine God not being white, then we cannot truly love people of color as they are? I think not. Do our images form us into people who, "[w]hen we deal with each other, we should do so with the sense of awe that arises in the presence of something holy and sacred[?] For that is what human beings are: we are created in the image of God (Gn 1:27)."[87]

Moreover, this white Christ blinds us to the suffering body of Christ in America. For example, M. Shawn Copeland challenges us to understand the suffering of African people captured to endure the horror of chattel slavery as "time on the cross."[88] Copeland

84. Elizabeth A. Johnson, "Naming God She: Theological Implications," *The Boardman Lecture in Christian Ethics* (October 19, 2000), 1; at http://repository.upenn.edu/boardman/5.

85. There is not adequate space in this essay to account for the profound treasury of Black and Womanist theology that explores racism, the doctrine of God, and theological anthropology. This work has been developing for more than forty years. For a groundbreaking example, please see William R. Jones, *Is God a White Racist?* (New York: Doubleday, 1973).

86. Mary Aquin O'Neil, "The Mystery of Being Human Together," in *Freeing Theology: The Essentials of Theology in Feminist Perspective*, ed. Catherine Mowry LaCugna (New York: HarperCollins, 1993), 159.

87. United States Catholic Bishops, *Economic Justice for All: Pastoral Letter on Catholic Social Teaching and the U.S. Economy* (Washington, DC: USCCB, 1997), no. 28; at http://www.usccb.org/upload/economic_justice_for_all.pdf.

88. M. Shawn Copeland, *Knowing Christ Crucified: The Witness of African American Religious Experience* (Maryknoll, NY: Orbis Books, 2018), 8–9. See also James

documents the "dark and hidden wisdom" of those who clung to Christ crucified to stay human in enslavement. These women and men came to know Jesus as "'God's Black Slave who had come to put an end to human bondage.' Jesus's resurrection meant that slavery would not have the last word."[89] The scandal of the white Christ is in its denial of the "dark and hidden wisdom" within our own history in America. Our collective ignorance of such precious wisdom radically disables our ability to discover, understand, and follow Christ incarnate in our reality today.

The theological problematic of this image in the Shrine is profoundly disturbing on many levels—not simply because the skin is white, but because of how Christ's whiteness functions to form our beliefs about God and what it tells us about being human. "It is time to seriously consider . . . the ways that race and racism has been formative of white Catholicism, and indeed, white U.S. religion writ large."[90] It is easy to think if we pray to images of God that are not white this white Christ in the National Shrine is not our problem, or that we have not participated in the history to which I allude in this chapter. Even if we should paint over the images, this will not necessarily interrupt the radical connection of whiteness and Christ that has been so deeply imprinted on American imagination and legitimizes white supremacy.[91] My purpose here is not to thoroughly explicate what we must reflect on but to explore what the contemplative restlessness and questioning might entail if we take seriously FitzGerald's wisdom for

---

Cone, *The Cross and the Lynching Tree* (Maryknoll, NY: Orbis Books, 2011).

89. Copeland, *Knowing Christ Crucified*, 35.

90. Matthew J. Cressler, "'Real Good Sincere Catholics': White Catholicism and Massive Resistance to Desegregation in Chicago, 1965–1968," *Religion and American Culture: A Journal of Interpretation* (2020): 22.

91. In 1972 Albert Cleage wrote, "You can take anything and paint it Black, but that does not make it black if it is still serving white interests and if it still comes out of the white experience. . . . A thing is not Black because it is painted Black" (Albert Cleage, *Black Christian Nationalism: New Directions for the Black Church* [New York: William Morrow & Company, 1972], 14). Please also see M. Shawn Copeland, "The (Black) Jesus of Detroit: Reflection on Black Power and the (White) American Christ," in *Christology and Whiteness: What Would Jesus Do?*, ed. George Yancy (New York: Routledge, 2012), 180–95.

the dark night in America. John of the Cross's teachings hold out a promise and hope that as our gods die a deeper union with God is being made possible. FitzGerald explains, "In fact, the dark emptiness is already the beginning of this communion."[92]

"There Are Already Signs of New Life and New Vision"[93]

As white people, what is it like to imagine that opening ourselves to God in our dark night may indeed be the opening for ourselves and for future generations of "tender communion, mutuality and an entirely different perspective which we ourselves cannot produce by sheer determination and reason"?[94]

FitzGerald invites us to interpret dark night through the lens of hope. She writes,

> This is actually a hopeful time, when theological faith, hope and love, *the gifts of God,* are being accessed. We are forced, as it were, to accept the alternative vision of faith, hope and love, and so pass over into the perspective of God. The question is this: can we receive the darkness of this *empty time and barren space,* personally and collectively, as the love and care of God in our lives desiring to purify our desire as persons and our national dream as a people?[95]

Across the generations John of the Cross calls to us, to trust Love during this transforming process of dark night. He offers a vision of hope in the darkness that is rooted in God's longing for intimacy with us.[96] John's life is an example of this hope. While im-

92. FitzGerald, "The Desire for God and the Transformative Power of Contemplation," 218.

93. Ibid.

94. Ibid.

95. FitzGerald, "The Desire for God and the Transformative Power of Contemplation," 213; emphasis in original.

96. Kevin Culligan, OCD, writes of John's transformation in prison. He explains that John's writing does not offer a plan for this transformation but rather describes attitudes and dispositions that are our consent to God in the experience. Culligan reflects at length John's teaching of "lifting first movements to God." Please see Kevin Culligan, "From Imprisonment to Transformation: John of the Cross in Toledo," in *Carmel and Contemplation: Transforming Human*

prisoned John sang in praise of God's love, a passionate, intimate love, between lover and beloved.[97] "O night that has united the Lover with his beloved, transforming the beloved into her lover."[98]

FitzGerald reiterates John's vision, as she writes that the dark night "begins and ends with love and desire."[99] She describes the new life arising in dark night: "Darkness is the place where egoism dies and true unselfish love for the 'other' is set free." The dark night is a powerful symbol of hope because the darkness "speaks of life buried in its opposite: life concealed, life invisible, life unseen in death."[100]

Where do we see "life buried in its opposite"? As we experience the wrenching events in our country can we dare hope in signs of life? In 1990 FitzGerald wrote, "In the midst of the signs of death, there are already signs of new life and new vision not accessible ten or fifteen years ago."[101] In 2020, following FitzGerald's direction, one such sign of new hope and new vision not accessible a decade ago can be seen in the actions of the Standing Rock Sioux Tribe as "water protectors" resisting the Dakota Access oil pipeline. Former Chief Dave Archambault describes the emergence of their plan at a 2016 tribal meeting:

> At the meeting, a medicine man asked the spirits how we could stop the pipeline. The spirits said: with prayer and with peace, the pipeline can be stopped; but with any form of violence, the pipeline would go under the river.[102]

Consciousness, ed. Kevin Culligan and Regis Jordan (Washington, DC: Institute of Carmelite Studies, 2000), 209–39.

97. For details regarding John's imprisonment, see Federico Ruiz et al., *God Speaks in the Night: The Life, Times and Teaching of Saint John of the Cross*, trans. Kieran Kavanaugh (Washington, DC: ICS Publications, 1991), 157–88.

98. John of the Cross, *The Dark Night*, stanza 5 in *The Collected Works of John of the Cross*, 359.

99. FitzGerald, "Impasse and the Dark Night," 97.

100. Ibid., 102.

101. FitzGerald, "The Desire for God and the Transformative Power of Contemplation," 213.

102. Alison Cagle, "Still Standing: Youth Activism and Legal Advocacy Work Hand in Hand in the Fight for Justice" (July 6, 2020) at https://earthjustice.org/features/standing-rock-still-standing.

Following this spiritual vision young people from the Standing Rock Nation set up a camp called "Sacred Stone" where the pipeline was proposed to cross the Missouri River. Their actions inspired thousands of people from around the world to join them. "A generation of young, mostly Native activists found new ways to organize, fueling parallel movements around the world."[103] This is only one example; by contemplating this sign of hope and new vision we allow our hearts to expand into broader and deeper discoveries. FitzGerald explains that the emergence of new life is the other side of our emptiness and powerlessness "that paradoxically is bringing us closer to God but also purifying our desire and imagination and moving them toward transcendence of what has been."[104]

FitzGerald explains that the time of dark night is an "omen of radical revolution." She contends that for all oppressed people dark night is a sign of liberation. It is in this dark night that an awakening consciousness emerges, which is painful yet is "energy for the struggle toward new life." Can't we see this dynamic resonating in the work of Black Lives Matter, in the organization Dignity and Power Now, and in the activism of Idle No More?[105] FitzGerald describes this time as radical. God is transforming us at the roots of who we understand ourselves to be and righting all our patterns of relating. This cry for new life "promises . . . the possibility of true liberation and transformation, a whole new view of what it means to be the *human* species on the planet earth."[106]

103. Ibid.

104. FitzGerald, "The Desire for God and the Transformative Power of Contemplation," 218.

105. Dignity and Power Now is a grassroots organization working for the dignity of incarcerated people and their families. For more information, see http://dignityandpowernow.org/. Idle No More is a nonviolent global movement of Indigenous peoples for protection of the earth and for sovereignty; see https://idlenomore.ca/.

106. FitzGerald, "The Desire for God and the Transformative Power of Contemplation," 213.

This contemplative approach to the transformation of white supremacy is no ploy to spiritualize this struggle but rather to consent to our moment in history! This contemplative approach is not a spiritual insouciance but rather the acceptance of our powerlessness that frees a passionate desire for God. It is this desire for God that opens us to a radically different vision of what it means to be human. "The challenge is to understand what is happening in order not to turn away from the faint light of contemplative wisdom that is showing us to ourselves."[107]

107. Ibid.

5

The Sentinel

Maria Teresa Morgan

One of my earliest memories is being carried on my father's shoulders while going for a walk at night on a cool tropical evening. From that somewhat precarious vantage point I had a unique view of the world, and I felt loved and safe. In the quiet of the empty streets we ran into a gentleman known to my parents. My dad told me he was the watchman, tasked with keeping the streets of our town out of harm's way. I figured that must have been an interesting job, being alone through the night, watching over everyone. But it must have also been wearisome, judging from the sleepiness that was quickly overtaking me while thinking that the watchman had to stay awake all night. The images arising from this memory: emptiness and silence, perspective, night, the breeze, being safe and loved, and the watchman, reflect those found in the poetry and descriptions of the night in John and the Cross and weave together the narrative I intend to present.

This chapter offers a reflection on the dark night as a way to meaning, hope, and transformation in the face of the COVID-19 pandemic. The wisdom of the night is explored from three intersecting interpretations. Drawing from John of the Cross, Rainer Maria Rilke, and Constance FitzGerald, OCD, I trace a constructive integration of the role of darkness in personal and societal crises. I first present John of the Cross who through his poetic genius and systematic explanations provides the source for all subsequent understandings and varied applications of the night. I then consider the role of the night in three poems of Rainer Maria Rilke, pointing to correlations between his poetry and that of John of the Cross as well as to the covenantal engagement with "the other" that Rilke underscores in his poetry. Throughout these two sections, key connections will be made with Constance FitzGerald's work on impasse.[1] The third consideration offers a brief recounting of the role of the night in salvation history. The final section resources FitzGerald's thought, locating the COVID-19 pandemic within the framework of societal impasse presented by FitzGerald. My conclusion completes the circle by returning to my experience as a child and discovering God as the Sentinel who carries us in love and safety through the night watches.

I. The Night in the Poetry and Doctrine of John of the Cross

Long accustomed to Carmelite spirituality, this tradition has been an interpretive framework for my experiences and has informed my worldview. Teresa of Avila I knew and loved from infancy because of the religious order that taught me as a child.[2] She was my confidant, was my first experience of "the communion of saints," and has been a companion that often surprises me with reminders of her presence. Her assertiveness and perspicacity while living within the patriarchal societal and ecclesial systems of sixteenth-century Spain made her a heroic trailblazer in my eyes and educated me in the realm of possibilities within my own contextual limitations.

But John of the Cross came to me in my young adulthood by way of literature. Since that initial encounter with his poetry I have carried the burden of a beauty that broke me with the words "on a dark night, aflame with love's earnest yearnings." Those

1. Constance FitzGerald, "Impasse and Dark Night" in *Living with Apocalypse: Spiritual Resources for Social Compassion*, ed. Tilden Edwards (New York: Harper and Row, 1984), 93–116.

2. A Spanish religious congregation, *Compañia de Santa Teresa de Jesús*, whose charism is education and missiology.

lines of *The Dark Night* opened to a different realm than the one presented in the too rational intent of the theology and philosophy classes required at the university. And "I went forth," like so many others, on the unexpected journeys where the night has taken me. Perhaps because of that literature-theology connection, poetry oftentimes becomes my prayer. Scattered lines from here and there break through my all too busy world to anchor me in faith, hope, and love.[3]

It is not my intention in this section to offer a systematic theological construct of the dark night in John of the Cross. Rather, I propose an understanding of the night through weaving poetical texts that open possibilities for personal and communal interpretations such as the present crisis of the COVID-19 pandemic. In doing so, I follow the advice of John of the Cross, who in his "Prologue" to *The Spiritual Canticle* states that "it is more suitable to shed some general light" on his poetry and offer the "broadest" explanations "so that each one may derive profit from them according to the mode and capacity of his spirit, rather than narrow them down to a meaning unadaptable to every palate."[4] In the same manner, he asserts there is "no need to be bound to this explanation" leaving open possibilities to relocate varied situations within the framework of his poetry. FitzGerald proposes this contextualization in contemporary settings arguing the night holds the promise of personal and social conversion.[5] Placing the dark night in relation to the COVID-19 pandemic opens possibilities that the transformative power of the night embraces not only our personal narratives but also the catastrophic quandary confronting the world at present.

3. Boccaccio, commenting on the *Divine Comedy*, said, "Poetry is theology." From a citation by Jacques Maritain found in R. A. Herrera, *Silent Music: The Life, Work and Thought of St. John of the Cross* (Grand Rapids: Eerdmans, 2004), 67.

4. John of the Cross, *The Spiritual Canticle*, prologue, in *The Collected Works of St. John of the Cross*, trans. Kieran Kavanaugh and Otilio Rodriguez (Washington DC: ICS, 1979). All subsequent citations from John of the Cross are taken from this text and edition. In the manner of citing the classics, from now on I will refer to citations from the saint by identifying the book, chapter, and paragraph.

5. FitzGerald, "Impasse and Dark Night," 105–7.

The poetic imaginations of John of the Cross and Rilke create a most appropriate language when seeking meaning in the midst of crisis. For poetry is symbolic and open ended, having the power to redescribe human experience in manifold ways. As FitzGerald asserts, in a true impasse we can no longer find answers through rational analysis.[6] Thus it is my hope that the poetic texts presented here will serve to find meaning and hope in the midst of the present affliction and signal a search for renewed ways of being and acting in the world.

Before I proceed, it is important to provide a brief description of what is meant by "dark night." Beginning with Origen of Alexandria (185–254 CE), the Christian tradition has identified the spiritual life as a journey that corresponds to three progressive stages:[7] purification, illumination, and union. St. John of the Cross draws from his study of patristics,[8] from the apophatic theology of Pseudo-Dionysius (late fifth to early sixth century), and, likely, from the Rhineland mystics such as Meister Eckhart, Johannes Tauler, Henry Suso, and Ruysbroeck.[9]

John of the Cross adapts and expands this long and rich tradition, indicating not only that darkness plays a purifying role in the initial stages but that between the illuminative and unitive way there is a night of the spirit. Furthermore, for John of the Cross the night is a leaven of transformation present not only in the initial stages of the purgative way but also in the proceeding ones

6. Ibid., 105.

7. Ernest Larkin identifies two stages of the spiritual life in the works of Origen. See "The Three Spiritual Ways" in *The Published Articles of Ernest E. Larkin, O.Carm* at http://www.carmelnet.org/larkin/larkin.html. On the other hand, Gregory Higgins points to three stages in Origen's writings. See Gregory C. Higgins, *A Revitalization of Images: Theology and Human Creativity* (Eugene, OR: Cascade Books, 2019), 53.

8. Manuel Diego Sanchez, "La herencia patrística de San Juan de la Cruz," in *Experiencia y Pensamiento en San Juan de la Cruz* (Madrid: Editorial de Espiritualidad, 1990), 83–111.

9. Since John of the Cross intended to transfer to the Carthusians before Teresa of Avila convinced him otherwise with the words, "Are you going to abandon the Order of your Mother?" he may have had access to the fourteenth-century work *The Cloud of Unknowing*, possibly written by a Carthusian.

as well. For instance, in his poem *The Dark Night* the night enfolds the sojourner from the beginning of desire ("aflame with love's earnest longing") to the fulfillment of the encounter ("reclining my face on the Beloved"). Nothing in the poem is visual, for darkness disables the sense of sight.[10] Throughout the poem the night is witness and protagonist, the night creates the condition for the journey, the night is guide and safety, the night makes possible the encounter between the lovers. In the last stanzas, celebrating the delight of union, the Beloved is described through the sense of touch, the breeze is known through touch and hearing,[11] and the lilies are perceived by their perfume.[12]

Central to John of the Cross is that prayer and transformation are rooted in the three theological virtues. Faith corresponds to the intellect, and faith is darkness to the intellect. The progressive nearness to the light of God blinds, disallowing our images and presuppositions about God. Faith is a functional darkness giving us a true perspective.[13] "Therefore, for the soul, the excessive light of faith is darkness."[14] This default of darkness leads to a radical option for faith, as FitzGerald affirms.[15] Unique to John of the Cross is his extensive treatment of the theological virtue of hope.[16] Because of his innovative treatment of Thomistic anthropology, John of the Cross has been called the "doctor of hope."[17] In John of the Cross, hope purifies the memory and becomes the dwelling of desire for God. What before provided joy and satisfaction,

10. Federico Ruiz Salvador, *Introducción a San Juan de la Cruz: el hombre, los escritos, el sistema* (Madrid: B.A.C., 1968), 190.

11. Perhaps an allusion to the theophany in the form of a gentle breeze experienced by Elijah (1 Kgs 19:11-13) whom the Carmelites consider their founder.

12. Lilies are fragrant at night, as anyone who has kept an Easter lily at home knows!

13. Maximiliano Herraiz, "La oración, experiencia teologal," in *Experiencia y Pensamiento en San Juan de la Cruz,* 209–12.

14. II *Ascent* 3.1.

15. FitzGerald, "Impasse and Dark Night," 105.

16. Found throughout III *Ascent* and II *Dark Night*.

17. Father Crisógono de Jesús, OCD, considered one of the most renowned scholars of John of the Cross. Cited in Federico Ruiz Salvador, *Introducción a San Juan de la Cruz,* 467.

affording security in possession and providing the false comfort of complacency, now leaves us with a sense of emptiness and longing for something outside our grasp. For hope, as Gabriel Marcel paradoxically describes it, "is a memory of the future"[18] and becomes the not yet of our longing. Memory, being a present absence of the past, can sequester us from God's unbounded future. FitzGerald elucidates this teaching of John of the Cross by speaking of the progressive education of desire through the dark night, elaborating on the need to unravel the tangled skeins of our selfishness through the purifying pedagogy of the Spirit.[19] In John of the Cross, hope is living and constant, at first purifying the memory and in the union with God infusing love's desire. In his commentary of "the deep caverns of the senses" John of the Cross describes the infinite yearning of a love already possessed.[20] Finally, love purifies the will, harnessing the impulse of its energies. As FitzGerald states, the dark night is the mediator of a transformed affectivity.[21] John of the Cross describes a love that encompasses the manifold dimensions of the human person, even what we would consider unworthy: "That, not despising or excluding anything human from this love, He says: You shall love your God with all your heart, and with all your mind, and with all your soul, and with all your strength."[22]

Three additional points are important to make in relation to the above paragraphs. The first is that the three theological virtues are bound together. Thus we love God in the darkness of faith, "without understanding Him,"[23] and in the fruition of love, hope, as FitzGerald affirms, "opens up the possibility of being possessed by the infinite."[24] The second point is the role of the Holy Spirit, "the artisan of God" (CCC 741). The Spirit who "at first assails

18. Gabriel Marcel, *Homo Viator: Introduction to a Metaphysic of Hope*, trans. Emma Craufurd (Gloucester, MA: Peter Smith, 1978), 53.

19. FitzGerald, "Impasse and Dark Night," 97.

20. *The Living Flame of Love* 3.21.

21. FitzGerald, "Impasse and Dark Night," 102.

22. III *Ascent* 16.1, 2; II *Dark Night* 11.4.

23. II *Night* 12.7; *The Spiritual Canticle*, prologue.

24. FitzGerald, "From Impasse to Prophetic Hope: Crisis of Memory," *CTSA Proceedings* 64 (2009), 21.

[the soul] with the light and heat of His divine flame . . . causing darkness" is the One who with "gentle touch" enfolds the soul in "gladness, glory and love" in transforming union.[25] The third point is that the canopy of darkness offers a nurturing protection. The affirmation that the night provides a safe passage to union with God is key to John's description. Garbed in the white garment of faith, the green garment of hope, and the red garment of love, we journey "in darkness and secure / through the secret ladder disguised" toward the encounter with God.[26]

The reader may think that "the dark night" belongs to an arcane world of theologians and mystics. The above paragraphs have attempted to ground the image of the "dark night" as one born of a lived experience within a spiritual tradition that hearkens to the beginnings of the Christian era and unfolds toward the future. This spirituality confirms that the "lex orandi, lex credendi, lex vivendi" flow one from the other and inform each other.[27] The "Prologue" to *The Ascent* evidences that John of the Cross's intent in explaining the dark night was pastoral rather than apologetic. It is important to state that spiritual classics do not remain static, but rather their message continues to be adapted and applied to diverse circumstances. As FitzGerald asserts, the "dark night" is any crisis that signals an end, a transition, and a begetting of new life, noting that the underside of what is experienced as death bears the seed of resurrection.[28] The dark night can manifest itself in marriage, in relationships, in the loss of a loved one, in a profession, in illness, in failure, and in cataclysmic events such as the COVID-19 pandemic.[29] FitzGerald sees in John of the Cross a spirituality for our times, for in addressing the human experiences of devastating personal and societal transitions the dark night offers validation to the forfeiting of our structures of meaning and

25. *Living Flame* 1.25, 26.

26. II *Night* 21.

27. "As we pray, so we believe, so we live." An ancient Christian axiom adapted from St. Prosper of Aquitaine.

28. FitzGerald, "Impasse and Dark Night," 97.

29. Ibid., 98. See also Augusto Guerra, "Para la integración existencial de la Noche oscura," in *Experiencia y Pensamiento en San Juan de la Cruz*, 225–50.

opens a path to transformation.[30] Let us also remember, in case we are taken aback by depressing interpretations of darkness, that John of the Cross describes the night from the retrospective of a happy ending, where "the soul walks in festivity" with "a song of jubilation to God."[31]

Lest we also interpret the night as a purely individualistic phenomenon elevating the soul to God, this going forth into the night toward the encounter with God is also a going forth toward the other. John's life bears witness to his self-gift to people from diverse walks of life and to the exacting task of the reform of Carmel. In that soaring song of plenitude, "Prayer of the Soul Enkindled with Love,"[32] John of the Cross lays claim not only to "the heavens" ("Mine are the heavens") but also to "the earth" ("and mine is the earth"), not only to "the saints" ("the just are mine"), who are always pleasant to have by our side, but also to "the sinners" ("and mine the sinners"), who caused him and often cause us innumerable troubles. He is able to stake his claim to an embodied love because of the all-encompassing love that lives in him through Christ ("because Christ is mine and all for me").[33] As FitzGerald affirms, among the fruits of the dark night is a passage from the "I" to the "we."[34]

After presenting a brief description of the night I now refer back to the poetry of John of the Cross.

John of the Cross is the mystic and theologian of the night. He was foremost a poet, well versed through his Jesuit education in the Renaissance literary currents brought to Spain toward the end of the fifteenth century. He was gifted with an extraordinary sensitivity to beauty, gleaning beauty for us and becoming a foundational source for theological aesthetics. Hans Urs von Balthasar describes him as "a Dante deprived of all images . . .

30. Constance FitzGerald, "Transformation in Wisdom: The Subversive Character and Educative Power of Sophia in Contemplation," in *Carmelite Studies: Carmel and Contemplation*, ed. Kevin Culligan and Regis Jordan (Washington, DC: ICS, 2000), 281.

31. *Living Flame* 2.36.

32. "Prayer of the soul enkindled with love," *Sayings of Light and Love*, 669.

33. Ibid.

34. FitzGerald, "Impasse and Dark Night," 30.

instead of ditches, cornices and spheres, there is nothing except God."[35] John's baffling commentary on the line from stanza 36 of the *Spiritual Canticle*, "let us see one another in your beauty," repeats the word "beauty" twenty-four times in an incoherent paragraph that remains one of the most obscure in mystical literature, allowing perhaps the only glimpse into his own experience of God.[36] Aware that words transcend their meaning he was also conscious of their margins,[37] indicating he preferred poetry for its capacity to convey various perspectives as well as to bend and break the limits of language. And this he accomplished with exquisite craft. It is said that he would read his poetry to his spiritual disciples, who were mostly women, and they would say, "Father, this is beautiful! . . . But, what does it mean?"[38] And thus he proceeded with scholastic precision[39] to delineate his spiritual doctrine through a commentary on three of his major poems: *The Dark Night, The Spiritual Canticle,* and *The Living Flame of Love.* Line by line he meticulously completed his explanation of these last two poems. He commented on *The Dark Night* twice: in *The Ascent of Mount Carmel* and in *The Dark Night*, but both works end mid-sentence at the first line of the third stanza of the poem. In his life, his poetry, and his theology, John of the Cross shows us the countenance of night, not only to exalt its beauty, but also, as he specifically declares, to be of help in our journey.[40] At first he is shattered by the night, until this darkness transforms itself in the poet's great hymn of love to the night as one that offered guidance and has been loved more than the light of dawn because it made possible the union and transformation of Lover and beloved.[41]

35. Hans Urs von Balthasar, *The Glory of the Lord: A Theological Aesthetics*, trans. A. Louth, J. Saward, M. Simon, and R. Williams, ed. John Richer, 3 vols. (San Francisco: Ignatius Press, 1986), 3:112, cited by Herrera, *Silent Music*, 48.

36. Famously hermetical, he carefully controlled the "I" of his experiences. The puzzling question remains as to why he, being a master of syntax, did not revise this passage.

37. See Prologue to the *Spiritual Canticle* and to the *Living Flame of Love*.

38. Unsourced anecdotes I have heard through the years.

39. *Spiritual Canticle*, Prologue.

40. *Ascent*, Prologue.

41. *Dark Night*, stanza 5.

Having offered a brief description of the night in John of the Cross, I now proceed to consider parallel themes found in another poet of the night, Rainer Maria Rilke.

II. The Night in Three Poems of Rainer Maria Rilke

The verses from Rilke included in this section connect the major themes of this chapter: the dark night of John of the Cross, the nights of God, and the night of the COVID-19 pandemic. The three poems are taken from *The Book of Hours.*

Two notes in Rilke capture my attention. One is how he frequently addresses the subject of his poem with a "You" that falters between a shout, a challenge, and a supplication, charting a path of prayer with his words. The other is the striking correlation between his poetry and that of the Carmelite mystic. Approaching Rilke through the lens of John of the Cross enables interpretive strategies that illuminate the experience of the dark night. Rilke's allusions to the Gospel and to the night provide rich insights into the religious experience of darkness. We find in Rilke's verses the nearness of God throughout an all-encompassing night. Images and metaphors echo the words and teaching of John of the Cross such as darkness, beauty, faith, and prayer.

The first poem from Rilke presented here is "You, neighbor God."[42] The setting of the night provides interwoven associations that break through the verses: God's silent presence; God's vulnerability, waiting in darkness and loneliness; the poet's identification with the Samaritan woman from whom Jesus asked a drink (John 4:4-42); the man bereft of bread whose loud knocks at midnight awaken his friend (Luke 11:5-13). The poem raises the question posed to Jesus leading to the parable of the Good Samaritan, as to who is our neighbor (Luke 10:25-37), plaiting this passage with the great judgment scene in Matthew 25, for that unknown neighbor needing a drink is God. We are left wondering how we can "hearken" to a Presence so silent we "seldom"

42. Rainer Maria Rilke, "You, neighbor God," in *The Book of Hours; Love Poems to God*, trans. Babette Deutsch (New York: New Directions, 2016), Kindle, 98–107.

hear breathing, a quality of contemplative prayer pervading the writings of John of the Cross.[43] FitzGerald elucidates this paradox in her description of the "prayer of no experience" wherein God's presence is felt "not so much as consolation but as a profound peace in the silent unknowing and in the dark empty space of encounter with God."[44] Questions also arise as to the identity of the one "groping in the dark." Is it God, or the poet, or both? These lines direct us to love and service of the "neighbor god" who has "no one . . . there" to give her or him the solace of companionship or to assuage his or her physical needs. These words confront "the complicity of silence"[45] in the face of an increased nationalism that sees in "the neighbor god" a threat to our lifestyle and resources. In our immediate reality, the poem calls us to a listening presence of compassionate service to those affected by the night of COVID-19.

Pointing to images and names that separate the poet from God, Rilke concludes with an iconoclastic longing to batter down the walls of "names and images" that thwart God's mystery, a theme woven throughout the process of the night in John of the Cross.

In the second poem chosen for this section, "You, darkness, of whom I am born,"[46] Rilke considers himself as one begotten of the night and this birthing darkness as more encompassing and inclusive of human experience than the halo of a flame, suggesting the darkness is but the shadow of that "great presence stirring beside" him. Rilke's creedal affirmation "I believe in the night" offers an assurance that in spite of personal and societal crisis, the night has a prophetic role, calling us to that way of solidarity and compassion FitzGerald identifies as a fruit of impasse.

43. See, for example, II *Dark Night* 14.2-3.

44. FitzGerald, "From Impasse to Prophetic Hope," 35.

45. Pope Francis in Inés San Martín, "Pope Francis Hopes after Pandemic, Humanity Has 'Antibodies of Justice, Charity,'" *CRUX: Taking the Catholic Pulse* (April 17, 2020).

46. Rilke, "You, darkness, of whom I am born," in *The Book of Hours; Love Poems to God,* trans. Anita Barrows and Joanna Macy (New York: Riverhead Books, 2005), I.11, 63.

In the third poem considered here, "I love the dark hours of my being,"[47] Rilke connects darkness with an intimate knowledge of "another life that's wide and timeless." We find echoes here of John of the Cross's recounting of the night's grace.[48] These "dark hours" leading to a vast and infinite life allude not only to our vocation to communion in the life of God (CCC 259, 260) but also to the hope that the darkness of our global pandemic will lead to a shared vision of living in new ways.

The lyric metaphors in the poetry of John of the Cross and Rainer Maria Rilke hand over to us their gift of an enkindled night. We have all experienced the many guises of the night in the spirals of life, death, and new beginnings. As we get to know John of the Cross, we realize his life and spirituality cannot be separated, for the night is the critical identifier of John's journey. Misfortune lingered by his side: as an infant he experienced the death of his father; abject poverty followed, which likely caused his brother's death from malnutrition and drove John's mother to place him in an orphanage so he would not suffer the same fate; he was rejected and experienced ethnic marginalization from his father's well-to-do family, probably due to the *morisca*[49] origins of his mother; he also knew abandonment, betrayal, physical and mental abuse, failure, illness, and, under Nicolas Doria and his allies, the final persecution and forced exile by and from the very Discalced Carmelite Order that John was key in establishing and to which he gave the energies and hopes of his adult life. His legacy of love and forgiveness springs from the pain of that last rejection. In his letter to María de la Encarnación, who was grieved by the manner in which he was being treated, John wrote: "[W] here there is no love, put love, and you will find love."[50] Those who by chance or by choice (or a bit of both), like John of the Cross, trek through the sometimes sorry landscape of human

47. Rilke, "I love the dark hours of my being," ibid., I.5, 51.

48. I *Dark Night* 13.10.

49. Identifying term for Muslims (referred to as *moors* in Spain) or their descendants who had been forced to convert to Christianity in Spain at the end of the fifteenth century.

50. Letter of July 6, 1591, 703.

misery may want to access his writings so as to find meaning in "the appalling strangeness of the mercy of God"[51] and to discover the creative impulse that is begotten in the luminous darkness of which he speaks. That same light may well bring hope to a world immersed in tragedy by the COVID-19 pandemic.

It would not seem too difficult, then, to name our nights, for they are part of our common humanity. Neither is it difficult to identify as "dark night" the present pandemic upheaving the world and society. But the most surprising thing for me has been to encounter the nights of God. In the next section I will present various biblical texts that allude to the role of the night in God's economy of salvation.

III. The Role of Darkness in Events of Salvation History

Mystical interpretations and poetical allusions to biblical texts abound in John of the Cross's writings, delighting and educating the reader in the allegorical sense of the Scriptures (CCC 115, 117).[52] John's insistence that the Scriptures be the foundation for his spiritual doctrine allows for exploring parallel visions between the role of the night in salvation history and the role of the night in the transformative process of sanctification.

In an article by Rogelio Zelada, in *La Voz Católica*, the Spanish publication of the Archdiocese of Miami, the author offers an insight into the fundamental role of darkness in the saving action of God.[53] Zelada states that, for the "believing poetry" of the ancient biblical world, primordial darkness preceded the very instant of God's creation and that same darkness is replicated in the great moments of salvation history. Among the biblical nights Zelada

51. Graham Greene, *Brighton Rock* (Penguin, 1991), 246, in "Insights on Mercy: Fyodor Dostoyevsky, Graham Greene, Julian of Norwich, and Eberhard Arnold," November 11, 2015, *Plough Quarterly*, no. 7 (Winter 2016).

52. There are 1,060 citations from the Scriptures in John of the Cross's major works. Francisco de Brändle, *Biblia en San Juan de la Cruz* (Madrid: Editorial de Espiritualidad, 1990).

53. Rogelio Zelada, "La Luz de la noche," *La Voz Católica* (Marzo 2016). Paraphrase is my translation.

points to the night of Genesis (Gen 1:1); the night of exodus (Exod 12); the night of Bethlehem (Luke 2:8); the night of the star guiding the Magi (Matt 2:9); the night memorialized in the Eucharist, "on the night when he was betrayed" (1 Cor 11:23-29); the night of Gethsemane (Matt 26:36-56; Mark 14:32-52; Luke 22:39-53; John 18:1-12); the darkness of Golgotha (Matt 27:45). And the definitive night of our history, the night of the resurrection (John 20:1).

The night in John of the Cross evokes a darkness rooted in God. The very darkness that weaves through the economy of salvation is reflected in the contemplative journey of purification, transformation, and new life. For instance, might not the night preceding the person's transformation and new life be an icon of the primordial darkness before the moment of creation, a darkness that, according to Zelada, is replicated in the great deeds of the biblical narrative? In the same manner, the enveloping darkness of the exodus is repeated in the poem of the *Dark Night*, wherein the soul goes forth toward liberation "in darkness and secure." Commenting on stanza 37 of the *Spiritual Canticle*, John bids us to enter into the knowledge of the mysteries of Christ.[54] One of the most spiritual sections of the *Catechism* repeats John's invitation, stating that "the mysteries of Christ's life are our mysteries" (CCC 512–21) to live and to rejoice, to suffer and to hope, and, in John's description, to delight in the wine of pomegranates.[55] Throughout the Christian journey, we are called to participate in the joyful darkness of Christ's birth, in the darkness of betrayal, and we enter into the night of a new covenant when partaking of the Eucharist. And in the graced splendor of God's Spirit, the debts incurred by every stone that oppressed us are rolled back in the darkness.[56]

The numerous references to the night in the economy of salvation allows also for an interpretation that God also goes forth unseen, "on a dark night, fired with love's earnest longing" to

54. *Spiritual Canticle*, stanza 37, 550.

55. "The pomegranates stand for the mysteries of Christ." Ibid., 552.

56. "And pays every debt." *The Living Flame of Love*, stanza 2.18; 23–33.

encounter humanity. Let us remember that the much maligned eros in Christian tradition is key to the journey, that eros as well as agape abides in God, as Benedict XVI boldly explains in his first encyclical, alerting us to the movement of eros's ascent and agape's descent that forms the basis for the allegorical interpretation of the Song of Songs, a favorite of the mystics (*Deus Caritas Est* 3–8).[57] Based on this scriptural book, John of the Cross describes eros as the spark that sets God and ourselves along the journey of mutual search.[58]

Having offered an analysis of various perspectives of the night, I will now proceed to the final section of this chapter.

IV. The Dark Night of the COVID-19 Pandemic

As I write this chapter, the world is immersed in a classic dark night caused by COVID-19. The world's lament is heard each day in the news. A shrill of contradictions confuses us, and we waver between hope and defeat. Around us is a panic that grips with fear of contagion and terrifying descriptions of the untamable and unpredictable effects of the virus. We have been set adrift by the absence of touch; by the uncomforted grief of not being with loved ones during their final moments; by the loneliness of the elderly and the dying; by the loss of jobs and extending grasp of poverty; by the spread of contagion in refugee camps, in prisons, in "the essential personnel" of meatpacking plants that have become breeding grounds of sickness and death; by the shock of finding that one-third of deaths in the United States have occurred in nursing homes. At the time of writing this (November 29, 2020), an alarming second spike of COVID-19 in the United States has led to 266,813 deaths and counting and 13,363,182 people infected. Hospitals are overwhelmed and healthcare personnel exhausted.

57. In underlining the difference and unity of *eros* and *agape* Benedict makes a distinction between the reduction of *eros* to a sexual commodity and the *eros* that leads to self-gift in human relationships and in our relationship with God. He thus exalts the "human and divine promise" of *eros* and underlines "the true grandeur" of its power.

58. *The Living Flame of Love* 3.28.

Countries are decimated of our old and infirm, and an increasing threat to children and the young hovers on the edges of the pandemic. A virus whose RNA is composed of only fifteen genes[59] has ruptured our lives and the world as we knew it a few months ago. Societal and governmental hubris has been breached, for no walls are impenetrable enough to prevent a miniscule virus from entering our borders and no political posturing can veer away the frightening evidence of our fragility before the destructive power of a microorganism.

In seeking solutions our horizons are muddled. There is evidence of a neo-Malthusianism,[60] seen, for instance, in a sign demanding an end to the lockdown during the first phase of the pandemic: "Sacrifice the Weak." There was also the exhortation from the lieutenant governor of Texas that he would be willing to risk dying for the sake of the economy, stating that many grandparents would follow his example, making a grandiose exit in a last heroic deed. The dystopian results of a populist nationalism endemic in many countries gives rise to new fears, such as those voiced by a former WHO board member as to whether there will be a "vaccine nationalism" that prevents its distribution[61] or is only provided to those who can prove their productivity. Reflecting on a possible aftermath of the pandemic, Pope Francis has said, "The globalization of indifference will continue to threaten our journey."[62]

We look to science to save us with a vaccine and a pharmaceutical development that will neutralize the virus. The economic, mental, and emotional chaos of our post–November 2019 society has, however, exacted a heavy toll and continues its tally for the foreseeable future.

But from the stump arises a fragile hope (Job 14:7). Constance FitzGerald affirms that impasse presents us with a paradox, a cri-

59. Heather Lanier, "Surrendering to Uncertainty," *The Atlantic* (May 16, 2020).

60. Pope Francis in Austen Ivereigh, "Pope Francis Says Pandemic Can Be a 'Place of Conversion,'" *The Tablet* (April 8, 2020).

61. Jane Halton in Paul Karp, "Former WHO Board Member Warns World against Coronavirus 'Vaccine Nationalism,'" *The Guardian* (May 18, 2020).

62. Pope Francis in San Martin, "Pope Francis Hopes after Pandemic."

sis that bears a seed of newness. The author proposes the need to bring global dark nights into dialogue with the dark night of John of the Cross, arguing that "our experience of God and our spirituality must emerge from our concrete historical situation."[63] Her description of the dark night details our present condition in face of the pandemic: "no way out, no way around, no rational escape from . . . no possibilities in the situation . . . every normal manner of acting is brought to a standstill."[64] The author affirms that crises are harbingers of hope and transition, if we but discover their call to "conversion, healing and justice."[65] In considering the personification of Wisdom in the Scriptures, FitzGerald underlines Sophia's dynamic of purification and transformation in peoples and society.[66] In critical moments such as ours, Sophia waits at the gate of our crumbling dwelling and, with gentle and insistent urgency, summons humanity to follow new paths of compassion and righteousness.[67]

FitzGerald raises the question of whether we believe that prayer can bring about change.[68] She affirms that historical situations of deconstruction confront us with a need for a contemplative spirituality and pedagogy leading to "a societal understanding of the contemplative process of transformation."[69]

Relative to prayer and conversion, the powerlessness experienced in the pandemic has led to a new interest in prayer and meditation, and these practices often include an impulse toward solidarity and service. In her article "The Science of Prayer," Elizabeth Bernstein refers to an analysis from the University of Copenhagen that found Google searches for "prayer" increased exponentially in ninety-five countries, and according to a Pew research poll, more than half of Americans have resorted to prayer

63. FitzGerald, "Impasse and the Dark Night," 105.

64. Ibid., 94.

65. Ibid., 105.

66. FitzGerald explains her preference for the word "Sophia" as more representative of the Hebrew *chokmah*, in "Transformation in Wisdom," 283.

67. Ibid., 288, 292, 314, 320.

68. FitzGerald, "Impasse and the Dark Night," 107.

69. FitzGerald, "Transformation in Wisdom," 346, 281.

during the pandemic. Bernstein points out that prayer offers a sense of connection with others as well as providing a way to surrender our control.[70]

Pope Francis voices the challenge to a new vision of solidarity and love for others in two recent interviews. Francis asks for "a memory that yearns and begets hope,"[71] exhorting us to the practice of contemplative prayer and to an ecological conversion.[72] Francis calls Christians to a "creativity that opens new horizons," one that journeys toward God and toward people by adopting "a more austere and humane life that enables an equitable distribution of resources . . . and stop[s] the devastation of the environment."[73]

It is outside of the scope of this paper to delineate the vision of Pope Francis as he reflects on the pandemic. But it is important to mention that his hope for change is also ecclesial. Reflecting on an incident in which a bishop wanted to offer absolution from a hallway to isolated COVID-19 sick and dying patients but was told by canon lawyers that absolution could not be given from a distance, Francis said he hopes for a less institutional church,[74] one rooted in the freedom of the Spirit in the midst of crisis. Francis envisions a creative tension between the disorder brought about by the Spirit and harmony, meaning that the Holy Spirit deinstitutionalizes what is no longer useful. "That is the Church that needs to come out of the crisis," he says.

Conclusion

Perhaps it was that chance encounter with the watchman, now kept as a distant memory of a quiet night when, carried upon

70. Elizabeth Bernstein, "The Science of Prayer," *The Wall Street Journal* (May 17, 2020).

71. Pope Francis in Ivereigh, "Pope Francis Says Pandemic Can Be a 'Place of Conversion.'"

72. Pope Francis in San Martin, "Pope Francis Hopes after Pandemic."

73. Ibid.

74. He told the bishop to "do his priestly duty" and later found out the bishop was giving absolution "all over the place." Ibid.

my father's shoulders, I was safe and loved, that traced my path through the long vigils that followed and drew me toward the aesthetic and mystical theology of John of the Cross. While we can never be sure how our experiences shape our choices, what I have come to know with some degree of certainty is that, like our ancestors in the faith, many of us are descendants of the night, numerous as the stars of God's promise (Gen 26:4), and that every in-breaking of personal or societal darkness leads us on a quest for meaning. At some crossroad in the journey, we might be surprised to discover that God has been the Sentinel all along (Isa 21:11-12; Ps 121:4), watching over our coming and going (Ps 121:8), companioning us in the darkness, and, as beloveds of God, carrying us in safety and love through the shadows (Deut 33:12; Ps 23).

Today, bracketed by personal and communal nights, we grow disheartened and weary. Seeing many besieged by the COVID-19 crisis led me to present in this essay three intertwining facets of the night, summarized in this brief paragraph. Through beauty and scholastic precision, John of the Cross offers a vision of faith, hope, and love indwelling one in the other, showing that the desolation experienced in the darkened fields[75] of faith is but the tillage of the Spirit preparing the harvest of union with God. Three representative poems of Rainer Maria Rilke were chosen for this meditation, as the night weaves like a brooding presence throughout much of his poetry. Rilke's odes to the darkness and the cryptic lyrics he scatters through his verses provide us with a rich lode from which to decode our own experiences of the dark night inviting us to enter into the mystery of the night's generativity. And as we wrestle with the unyielding crisis of COVID-19, Constance FitzGerald assures us that societal nights open to the future of God, if we, as a community, but learn to read its lessons.

In the "Song of the Soul That Rejoices in Knowing God Through Faith," John of the Cross tells the story of a knowledge that flows

75. I am indebted to Susie Paulik Babka for this powerful image. Susie Paulik Babka, *Through the Dark Field: The Incarnation through an Aesthetics of Vulnerability* (Collegeville, MN: Liturgical Press, 2017). See also John of the Cross: "that field is your soul," *Spiritual Canticle* 1.9.

from the very Being of God and is experienced "although it is night" and "because it is night."[76] We too take comfort in the thought that the night will bring us to the Spring whence all creatures and creation flow.

And thus, we find ourselves here, in the company of the "neighbor God" waiting for a signal, waiting like Rilke to be able to say one day: "I believe in the night." And in the night's promises.

76. "For I know well the spring that flows and runs, / although it is night" ("Song of the Soul That Rejoices in Knowing God Through Faith," 723). John of the Cross repeats "although it is night" at the end of stanzas 1 through 9 of said poem, and concludes the poem in stanza 11 with the same subordinating conjunction. In stanza 10, however, he changes "although" to "because": "Here it calls to creatures: and they / are filled with this water, although / in darkness, / Because it is night."

6

The Desire for God and the Transformative Power of Contemplation

Constance FitzGerald, OCD

Introduction

All around us today we see a passion to touch the roots of contemplation or mysticism in our history as a people, to hear a muted desire that has existed often only as a subterranean force and to bring it above ground into the public forum in order to understand its power for transformation in our postmodern world.[1] Even if it is unrecognized and therefore uninterpreted, the desire for God is apparent everywhere in so many different forms. If we are able to reclaim this muted desire that runs through our history and make available centuries of contemplative tradition, Carmelite in this

1. The ideas in this essay were first presented in the keynote address at *Carmel 200: Contemplation and the Rediscovery of the American Soul,* held at Loyola College, Baltimore, August 12–18, 1990, to celebrate the bicentennial of Baltimore Carmel and Carmel in the U.S. This symposium was seen as an enterprise of imagination. It sought to retrieve the personal, relational, and social past of the desire for God, particularly in the 800 year old Carmelite tradition, in order to bring the too often marginalized mystical tradition into conversation with our present reality as North Americans and write a new "text" indicative of the future horizons of contemplation.

case, the dominant paradigms of this tradition may offer some guidance to our nation, North America, the Western world, called as it is by history and socalled "development" to a contemplative time, challenged to mature beyond being first, beyond being the Center of the world. I often feel that only if we are prepared for transformation by contemplation[2] and thereby given a new kind of consciousness and imagination will humanity and the earth, with its various ecosystems, survive.

What the Carmelite contemplative tradition reveals is women and men searching for God, desiring God together. Contemplation cannot be understood except within the context of desire, that is, divine desire coming to meet human desire and igniting in human hearts an unquenchable desire. Those we today call mystics have always upheld the primacy of desire. Their writings are suffused with desire. They know we are propelled by our insatiable desire and keep trying to tell us religion is a message of desire and a hope of its fulfillment. Teresa of Avila and John of the Cross in their classic works tell the story of human desire and delineate how it grows, is educated, purified and finally transformed within the life journey itself. Together, woman and man, they bear witness to the agony and ecstasy of burning desire. This is why after four centuries their writings still educate us to contemplation.

If the contemplative voice is ever really heard again in theology and in the official Church, as it was before the importance given to religious experience gradually separated the patristic theology as found in the monasteries from the theology of the schools, then the primacy of rationality will, according to Brazilian theologian, Maria Clara Bingemer, have to yield a place to "the impulse [passion] of desire that dwells at the deepest level of existence . . ." Bingemer accents the place desire must have:

> Theology, which seeks to be reflection and talk about God . . . cannot but be moved and permeated throughout its whole extent

2. Contemplation has various meanings. In the Carmelite tradition it is understood as a love experience which is also a deep knowing. Hence, John of the Cross speaks of a secret, loving knowledge or the loving inflow of God or dark contemplation or dark night. When John says the dark night is an inflow of God, this inflow is very precisely in terms of secret Wisdom, who is Jesus Christ.

> by the flame of desire. At a particular point in its theological articulation, reason, science and systematic rigor have their role . . . , but they can never suffocate the greater desire, never tame the divine pathos, which, from all eternity, has broken silence and become a loving and calling word, kindling in its turn in the hearts of humankind an irresistible and insatiable desire. . . . Born of desire, theology exists as theology only if it is upheld and supported by desire, in the direction of the desire that is its goal and its horizon.

Bingemer maintains, furthermore, that the future of women doing theology is inseparably linked with desire:

> A woman finds it unthinkable to divide her own being into watertight compartments and treat theological work as a purely rational activity. Moved by desire, a totalizing force, she does theology with her body, her heart and hands, as much as with her head, and the ripe fruit she begins to make available is the result of slow and patient pondering of experiences lived deeply and intensely [in dialogue with the tradition]. . . . When we talk about desire we are talking about human beings at their deepest level, in their deepest and ultimate truth, in their vital force, and therefore in their most authentic and legitimate aspirations. We are talking about what makes our bodies quiver and tremble with pleasure, about our noble and threatened vulnerability, our greatness, which depends on our fragility.[3]

Bingemer concludes by suggesting that the challenge to women doing theology today is to restore the primacy of desire within theological discourse[4] and her challenge suggests a threefold

3. Maria Clara Bingemer, "Women in the Future of the Theology of Liberation," in *The Future of Liberation Theology, Essays in Honor of Gustavo Gutierrez*, ed. Marc H. Ellis and Otto Maduro (Maryknoll, NY: Orbis Books, 1989), 478–79.

4. Margaret Brennan is an example of a woman theologian who has understood this challenge in her life and scholarship. In 1969, she entered the world of contemplative nuns by attending the Seminar for Contemplative Sisters held at Woodstock, Maryland, the former theologate of the Jesuits of the Maryland Province. At that time, as leader of her congregation, she was beginning the House of Prayer movement and came with deep appreciation for the life of prayer and the mystical tradition. She supported the fledgling efforts of the Association

intersection of contemporary feminist theology, the effort to reclaim and reinterpret the mystics, and the experience of the desire for God that pervades this country often unbidden and unseen.

Where Have You Hidden, My Beloved?

In 1984 an article appeared interpreting John of the Cross' teaching on desire and dark night in relation to contemporary experience.[5] This present essay reflects further on the societal aspect of the Dark Night because I sense that our consciousness has changed and as persons and as a nation we are in a different place than we were in the early eighties.

For one thing, *signs of death* seem even more pronounced than they were then, while *signs of new life,* new vision and a new voice, unavailable then, are apparent now. Let us look at the situation in which we live. It is ironic that at the close of a millennium of unprecedented change and "development" which has brought us

---

of Contemplative Sisters founded at Woodstock and continued as President of the Leadership Conference of Women Religious to assist Contemplative Communities in both finding their voice in the Church and renewing their way of life. This was not a comfortable position to assume since, at that time, the Congregation for Religious was discouraging apostolic religious from assisting contemplatives even though the latter had no corporate channel of communication with the Holy See. Outstanding among and typical of her many interventions on their behalf was the address given to the Canon Law Society of America on October 7, 1975. It was fitting that she should close the *Carmel 200* symposium with a presentation entitled "Contemplation Finding Its Prophetic Voice in the Cultural Context of North America." When the history of these years is fully told, Margaret Brennan's contribution to the renewal of Contemplative Life in the U.S. and the retrieval of the Christian mystical tradition will not be small.

5. See Constance FitzGerald, "Impasse and Dark Night," in *Living with Apocalypse,* ed. Tilden Edwards (San Francisco: Harper and Row, 1984). This is presently available with a companion essay, which develops the Dark Night further, "The Transformative Influence of Wisdom in John of the Cross," in *Women's Spirituality,* ed. Joann Wolski Conn (New York: Paulist Press, 1996). A more extensive study, "Transformation in Wisdom: The Subversive Character and Educative Power of Sophia in Contemplation," will appear in *Education for Contemplation,* a collection of articles written by the members of the Carmelite Forum, to be published by the Institute of Carmelite Studies, Washington, DC, in 1997.

into the far depths of the heavens as well as into the inner spaces of the atom, we have such a vivid consciousness of mortality and death, above all, the death of God.

While I hesitate to use words reminiscent of such a short-lived theology, still they express a vivid reality. In a very deep way as a people we are alone. One of the results of the Enlightenment and of the incredible achievements of science and technology is that we are alone in the world. Our own power, accomplishments and sophistication have made us feel we are on our own. For us, success is not necessarily the blessing of God, nor are years of drought or disaster the anger or displeasure of a god. Unlike ancient or simpler civilizations or even earlier generations, we are not sure for what we can turn to God. Good weather? The success of a meeting? Healing in illness? The miracle of a cancer cure? The protection and liberation of the oppressed? Safety for our children? Direction in life? An end to violence and drugs? Peace in the world?

God died in the concentration camps and the totalitarian dictatorships of this century, God was silenced in the Enlightenment and, according to Edward Schillebeeckx, with the disappearance of God, at least in the Western portion of the world, the individual person as a human subject also disappeared. God is dead, and as a consequence so is the human race.[6] The evidence that we have lost our humanity is all around us in organized terror, torture, ethnic cleansing or genocide, political murder, starvation on a mass scale, homelessness, increasing neglect/marginalization of the poor and exclusion of the immigrant.

We see signs of death in racial hatred, in escalating violence and abuse of women and children, in suicide machines and abortion, in drug addiction and drug sales, in the often lonely suffering of AIDS victims and in the escalation of cancer deaths. We see signs of death in an alienation between women and men which shows itself in sexism, divorce, abandonment and rape on the

6. See "Introduction to the International Congress for Theology," in *On the Threshold of the Third Millennium*, Concilium (Philadelphia: Trinity Press International, 1990), 14.

societal level, and in the Roman Church in the absence of more and more women from the Eucharist, on the one hand, and in the inflexible and uncomprehending position of many Church leaders, on the other. The alienation women feel today and their struggle for equality and mutuality is just a part, a deep part, of the much broader alienation of the human species from the rest of the earth community.

When God is dead, not only the human subject is dead, but the cosmos itself is dead as either a subject or an object of respect. When man [*sic*] set himself up as an alternative to God, the human subject began to die and with it reverence for creation. Vaclav Havel, in addressing the situation of the world prior to the failure of communism in Eastern Europe, believes it was due not to East–West tensions but to the spiritual condition of modern civilization. His devotion as a playwright to the theatre of the absurd springs, in fact, from his concern for meaning, inasmuch as the theatre of the absurd throws us into the question of meaning by manifesting its absence. He explains:

> As soon as man [*sic*] began considering himself the source of the highest meaning in the world and the measure of everything, the world began to lose its human dimension, and man began to lose control of it.[7]

We see the destructive effects of modernity's "flight from the world" all around us. Numerous species become extinct every day; the rain forests are being destroyed along with the ozone layer that shields us from the rays of the sun. The air, the water, the land are polluted. We recognize today the real possibility of the death of *the earth*. We have failed for a long time to understand our own place in the earth community and the absolutely essential connections between ourselves as the human species and all other species of life. In consequence, for the first time in the history of the cosmos, we face the possibility of the death of humanity as a species and the death of our home, the earth.

7. See Vaclav Havel, *Disturbing the Peace, Conversations with Karel Huizdala* (New York: Knopf, 1991).

"Where have you hidden, Beloved, and left me to my moaning?" cries John of the Cross in the first lines of his beautiful, classic poem, *The Spiritual Canticle*. While this is the mystic's cry sounding through the ages, *it is our cry, the muted cry of our nation.* This is the cry of desire known by every person who has ever earnestly sought God. The desire for God is everywhere crying out! The miracle is that the contemplative cry of the people, of the whole earth community, is no longer silent and invisible but rather prophetic and revolutionary. It rings through the universe and we must "not lose the thread of desire that from the depths of a disfigured world, groans with unspeakable groans to proclaim the birth of the new creation."[8]

Today the whole world cries out with the desire of the mystics, "Where have you hidden and left me to my moaning?" We hear, on the one hand, the abandoned, the poor, the homeless, the dying, the elderly, the oppressed, the tortured, the martyred, the refugees, the rejected, the starving, the marginalized, the abused, and, on the other hand, we hear our nation, our people, the pleasure-sated and consumer-burdened, the addicts, those wracked by doubt, those disillusioned by government, those committed to justice and equality. All cry out. Even the scarred earth itself cries out and rages against its devastation. Creation groans with its desire and its dream.

All this has become a great cry of desire for life, freedom, and resurrection, a cry to the God of life who brings liberation out of every type of death, a cry for a new vision, a contemplative vision. This cry reaches beyond the collective of the dying communist systems and equally beyond the possessive individualism of capitalism. It is a cry for the recognition of the connectedness of everything in the cosmos, and consequently, a desire for contemplation, for transformation, even though this is unnoticed for what it is by most people. The contemplatives realize it from one side; the theologians, led initially, perhaps, by some of the liberation theologians, realize it from another side, and both stand at a common meeting point trying to understand and articulate the time.

8. Bingemer, 479.

This universal cry, undermining the familiar dichotomy between contemplation and action, experience and theology, is what makes contemplation different today. The cry is within us. My own personal cry is overcome by, engulfed in, the cry of the earth and it is within me. The desire for God becomes sheer passion when joined to the cry of the world. Religious people formerly approached God by turning aside from the world to some degree, but today we come with the world inside us; we are motivated in a very direct way by the earth, the people, the poor, the women and children. The relationship, or better the identification, is profound and it is experienced by many people.

We come, therefore, for the purification of the world, the transformation of human consciousness and human desire, and the completion of the image of Christ. We come as a last resort, in a sense, because we Americans have lost faith and hope in human power and human reason. We are driven to interiority, to contemplation, to the desire for the experience of God's love, by the poor and oppressed, by, in fact, the image of God scarred in the world and on the face of the earth. We cannot continue to manage the world humanity has created with the skills, the minds, the wills, the memories or the imaginative paradigms we have. And it is the poor, the suffering earth, the pleasure-sated that drive us in prayer toward contemplation, toward an understanding of our darkness and to the need for the presence of contemplative vision, wisdom and love in the world, that is, to God's vision. Responsibility for the world, not just for individual wellbeing, moves us to contemplation.

This is the new "text" and this is the contemplative experience today and it rings with the ageless cry of the mystic to the Beloved:

> Where have you hidden? . . .
> Reveal your presence! . . .
> Extinguish these miseries . . .
> Who has the power to heal me? (SC 1, 6, 10, 11)[9]

9. Most references to John of the Cross are inserted in the text. A=*Ascent of Mount Carmel*, DN=*Dark Night*, SC=*Spiritual Canticle*, LF=*Living Flame of Love*.

No gentle nor consoling cry is this as we sometimes imagine when we read John of the Cross' words of yearning and envision him swept away by a love far beyond our reach. Neither does this kind of yearning come at the beginning of the journey, but to those experienced and seasoned by life, often to those who have been generous and creative in using the resources available to them. For John, the mystic's cry of desire is not a disembodied experience but always has a real life context in which there is a profound relationship between interiority and everyday existence.

Refashioning Our Vision and Refashioning the World

This explains why the mystics' painful cry for God in dark contemplation suggests a way of understanding our experience as North Americans. It offers some guidance for our future and some way of redirecting the movement of human desire toward God and refashioning our vision. Today we experience darkness in two distinct though related ways, like two sides of the same coin, that is, in our indissoluble connection or solidarity with the poor and marginalized and in our own personal and societal failures.

Firstly, the poor and the marginalized are our darkness, the darkness of humanity which is backlighted for us today. In "the poor" our violence is unveiled, to use Gil Bailie's dramatic words.[10] We know God's presence precisely because we see so clearly and so painfully the battered people and the scarred earth, an image of the Crucified One who is through time and space the darkness of humanity. In fact, in the poor people and the poor earth we recognize the way the image of Christ has been defaced by human desire.

Secondly, all around us the failures and limitations of our technological world and our philosophy are illuminated. We have rejoiced in the countless wonders of our technological age, in the magnificent exploration of the universe, the incredible life-saving

---

Quotations are from Kieran Kavanaugh and Otilio Rodriguez, *The Collected Works of St. John of the Cross* (Washington, DC: ICS Publications, 1991).

10. After I delivered this talk, Gil Bailie's material was published in *Violence Unveiled* (Spring Valley, NY: Crossroads Publishing Company, 1996).

medical discoveries and the whole evolution of computers and cyberspace, but we seriously question our national ethos of unlimited development. We are proud of the American desire to be free and selfreliant, to reach every frontier, to protect individual rights and provide opportunity for individual advancement, but more and more of us are confused today by our excessive, possessive individualism. Women particularly realize the destructive limitations of the autonomous self and the loss to society when the value of connection and relationship is muted and marginalized for the sake of pleasure, power, advancement, and success. We are burdened by our national pride that must be first at any cost. We recognize the exploitative, oppressive, selfish nature of many of our national social policies and our international relationships. We see the results of our need for comfort and pleasure in a consumer mentality that believes we have a disproportionate right to the world's wealth and resources regardless of the deprivation and mortal affliction it brings to poor, "undeveloped?" peoples, and notwithstanding the destruction of our mortally endangered earth and its eco-systems. Thus, as David Tracy asserts:

> The embrace of modern science, technology and industrialism . . . has helped to render present time for many an empty time—bereft of memory, free of hope, powerless to resist. The consumerism of our age is a relentless attack on the soul of every individual and every tradition.[11]

We experience desire gone awry and the failure of our national vision. As Robert Orstein and Paul Erhlich, authors of *New World, New Mind*, explain, we cannot continue to manage the world humanity has created with the skills, the minds, the imaginative paradigms, the historical memories, or lack thereof, bequeathed to us by modernity.[12]

11. "On Naming the Present," in *On the Threshold of The Third Millennium* (Philadelphia: Trinity Press International, 1990), 69.

12. Robert Ornstein and Paul Ehrlich, *New World, New Mind, Moving Toward Conscious Evolution* (New York: Simon and Schuster Inc., 1989).

We feel some affinity, therefore, for the contemplative experience described by John of the Cross:

> At this stage persons suffer from sharp trials [and darkness] in the intellect, severe dryness and distress in the will, and from the burdensome knowledge of their own miseries in the memory, for their spiritual eye gives them a very clear picture of themselves. (LF 1.20)

Our faith in the god of reason, progress and finally technology has left us without transcendence, without meaning and without hope. The gods of modernity are dying and with them our hope. In fact, one suspects some relationship between the experience of the mortality of humanity as a species and our society's pursuit of immediate pleasure, stimulation (drugs, sex, food) and unparalleled comfort with no thought for the effects on future generations. What kind of unconscious hopelessness drives those who do not even care about, much less provide for, the next generation or future generations?

John of the Cross' writings suggest that the clarity of our self-knowledge is in itself the embrace of the God we have silenced. Furthermore, opening ourselves to the deadendedness and limitation of our national creativity unleashes a thirst for God that we will only feel when we come face to face with the deficiency of our present knowledge and the failure of all we have trusted as a people. When our history and tradition, that is, all we remember and count on for our selfunderstanding, are not sufficient to guarantee our future as a people and as a species, we need to recognize this emptiness as a yearning for God which is only possible when hope in our own abilities fails us. Is it conceivable for us to understand the breakdown of love, mutuality and fidelity, the disappointment of human desire on so many levels, as a hunger for God that we will only sense this profoundly when human desire is thwarted and betrayed? Imbedded within the experience of loss of meaning and imagination abides the possibility of wisdom and new vision; buried within the painful feeling of being abandoned and on our own lies the seed of a mutuality and fulfillment already in process.

In one way, it trivializes the writings of the mystics to suggest our national darkness has any relationship to John of the Cross' contemplative night, but in another way, looking at our national psyche within John's framework allows us to believe, to hope and to continue to desire. The challenge is to understand what is happening in order not to turn away from the faint light of contemplative wisdom and love that is showing us to ourselves.

> Now with the light and heat of the divine fire, [the soul] sees and feels those weaknesses and miseries which previously resided within it hidden and unfelt, just as the dampness of the log of wood was unknown until the fire applied to it made it sweat and smoke and sputter. And this is what the flame does to the imperfect soul. (LF 1.22)

> It is not gentle but afflictive. . . . Neither is the flame refreshing and peaceful but it is consuming and contentious, making a person faint and suffer with selfknowledge. (LF 1.19)

This is actually a hopeful time when theological faith, hope and love, the gifts of God, are being accessed. We are forced, as it were, to accept the alternative vision of faith, hope and love and so pass over into the perspective of God. The question is this: can we receive the darkness of this *empty time and barren space,* personally and collectively, as the love and care of God in our lives desiring to purify our desire as persons and our national dream as a people? Can we hear God calling us to a more contemplative time when we will be able to see and appreciate a new vision, hear within ourselves a new voice, experience a new faith and love capable of creating new paradigms for living as a part of all life on earth and in the universe? We are challenged by the deadendedness around us to mature to a different level of existence. The call for openness to God is radical!

The Need for a Quantum Leap

Ornstein and Erhlich believe that our species cannot evolve quickly enough biologically or even culturally to do this naturally. The human mind is failing to comprehend the world it has created.

> Human inventiveness has created problems because human judgment and humanity's ability to deal with the consequences of its creations lags behind its ability to create. There is now a mismatch between the human mind and the world people inhabit. The mismatch interferes with the relationships of human beings with each other and with their environment [and with all other species on the earth]. . . . The serious and dangerous mismatch is this: civilization is threatened by changes taking place over decades, but changes occurring over decades are too slow for us to perceive readily. . . . At the same time, the changes are much too rapid to allow the biological or cultural evolutionary processes to adapt people to them. We are out of joint with the times, our times.[13]

Biologically we are still programmed for instant response and instant remedies. These are some of the default positions lodged in the human mind which Ornstein and Ehrlich say cannot be transformed or refashioned completely and certainly cannot be genuinely changed in our lifetime. Although we are evolving, our mental machinery will not change biologically in time to help us solve our problems. We cannot wait for the necessary tens of thousands of years until natural selection does its thing in order to solve problems such as runaway population growth, the collapse of ecological systems and the approach of thermonuclear Armageddon. We must therefore find ways of replacing our old minds with new ones by means other than the evolutionary process. Ornstein and Ehrlich suggest a new kind of education, namely, the creation of a process of conscious evolution. They insist we need to be literate in completely new disciplines.

I would like to suggest contemplative interiority as one of these "disciplines" and education for contemplation as essential to the new kind of education required and I suggest it with profound seriousness to educators on every level. We do, indeed, need new minds, as well as new intuitions, new wills, and passionate new desires since many of our highest achievements, Ornstein and Ehrlich explain, represent only a refinement of the old mind, not a new kind of perception.

13. Ornstein and Ehrlich, 10–11. I am completely dependent on their thought in the following paragraph.

Reflection on the sphere of the mind, according to Thomas Berry, the self-styled geologian, is imperative because the other powers of the earth seem now to have given over to the "mind-sphere" the major share of steering the course of earth development. The earth that directed itself instinctively in its former phases seems now to be entering a phase of conscious decision through its human expression. This is the ultimate daring venture for the earth, Berry claims, this confiding its destiny to human decision, the bestowal upon the human community of the power of life and death over its basic systems.[14]

When Vaclav Havel some years ago addressed a joint meeting of the U.S. Congress, he, too, called for "a global revolution in the sphere of human consciousness." He proposed that the salvation of the human world lies nowhere else than in the human heart, in human meekness and human responsibility. This belief in the importance of the transformation of individual consciousness for global change, reinforced by Havel's very life, is supported also in *Megatrends 2000*.

> It is the individual who changes himself or herself first before attempting to change society. Individuals today can leverage change far more effectively than most institutions. . . . [M]ovements (peace, environment, etc.) were built one consciousness at a time by an individual persuaded of the possibility of a new reality.[15]

Is the time of national darkness and national truth (dark contemplation or dark night), evidenced by the breakdown of structures and the awareness of national limitation by many, truly a portent of the kind of global revolution or transformation called for by Vaclav Havel, a call coming out of his own long dark night under communism?

14. See Thomas Berry, *Dream of the Earth* (San Francisco: Sierra Club Books, 1988), 19. Berry enumerates five major components of the earth's functioning: the geosphere, the hydrosphere, the atmosphere, the biosphere and the mindsphere.

15. John Naisbitt and Patricia Aburdene, *Megatrends 2000* (New York: William Morrow and Company, 1990).

John of the Cross, in his commentary on the *Spiritual Canticle* poem, written while he, himself, was in prison, speaks of the time of union with God after the searing purifications of the Dark Night when the person takes on the mind of God, the desire of God, the will of God and the memory of God, in other words, a radically different perspective. Most of us think of such fundamental change as next to impossible in this life. I would like, however, to suggest it as a viable option for the human community, one imbedded in and promised by our Christian tradition, one we cannot continue to undermine, make light of, excuse ourselves from or marginalize. We cannot afford to bypass contemplation, interiority and desire for God as an esoteric experience for the lazy or unbalanced elite but not for us who value above all else reason, sanity and the ability to control our own destiny. Certainly without contemplative prayer and the transformation it really can effect, the deepest dimension of the human person and of humanity itself lies forever dormant and beyond our reach. But even more, without it, the true evolutionary possibilities completely dependent on the inbuilt purpose and aspiration of the human soul are beyond us. I deeply believe this is the era of contemplation—Thomas Berry calls it the "mindsphere"—and the stakes are very high.

We need to understand and to speak, therefore, of the unleashed power, influence and freedom of contemplative love and wisdom, of their ability to pass beyond the limits by which both person and humanity are confined, the boundaries within which human consciousness, desire, culture, evolution and religion are now enclosed. Contemplation can bring within the realm of possibility the purified imagination able to create not only a global economy and *world* community that make a human life more possible for the poor, oppressed and marginalized of the world, but even the paradigm shifts and transformations required to invent a new kind of *earth* community where we re-inhabit the earth in a truly human manner.

John of the Cross seems to imply that if we are to continue to grow and if the desire which constitutes our being is to reach fulfillment, the time will come when God's light will invade our lives and show us everything we have avoided seeing. Then will be manifest the confinement of our carefully constructed meanings, the limitations of our life projects, the fragility of the support systems or infrastructure on which we depend, the boundaries through which we shall never break, the dreams that will never reach fulfillment, the darkness in our own heart. Initially, this is a very dark time but it is also a contemplative experience when God's loving light embraces us with a power that is staggering both in its seeming destructiveness and in its potential for new vision, deeper love, radical transformation. The irony of the situation is that we experience this light as darkness, the nearness of God as unreachable and frightening transcendence, as no experience, in fact. The light is so excessive that we are blinded, we see and believe "nothing."

But this time of dark contemplation is, as has been indicated, an omen of radical revolution. For *the poor and oppressed* it indicates the process of liberation taking place as they become conscious of the desire so long repressed within themselves, let it emerge, release it as a cry of pain, and yet feel it at the same time to be energy for the struggle toward new life. For many *North Americans* it marks a call by history and "development" to a contemplative or wisdom moment, a time of interiority, prayer and *waiting upon God* in a precisely theological faith and hope, that is, in a radical righting of the relationship with God and with one another. This means the cry indicates a time of painful knowledge and deep purification of national desire and resolve. It promises, however, the possibility of true liberation and transformation, a whole new view of what it means to be the *human* species on the planet earth.

All this is meant to show that the mystical tradition interpreted for today throws some light not only on our inner lives, but even on our life as a nation and on humanity in its present stage of development. We always speak as if the mystics' experience of God is the end of the life process, almost beyond our reach. I suspect their experience may be a beginning for us. The mystics not only give us paradigms from the past that enable us to interpret our present experience, but they also provide the materials to create new paradigms that unlock a way into the future and unveil the horizons to which contemplation, or the love-embrace of God's spirit, throws us open and makes us available as a people.

Signs of New Life, Transformation and a Cosmic Vision

In the midst of the signs of death, there are already signs of new life and new vision not accessible ten or fifteen years ago. We see them in the revolutions in the Philippines and Eastern Europe unfulfilled or tragic as these seem at times, in the Havels and the Chinese students of Tiananmen Square who have suffered the long dark night of the human spirit, in the energy of the poor who suffer the dark night of hunger, deprivation and abandonment and yet gather together in the basic ecclesial communities in faith and in hope, in the official dissolution of a policy of apartheid and the peaceful change to majority government in South Africa, in Oscar Romero, the Maryknoll women, the Jesuits and their women companions, the Trappists of Algeria and so many unnamed others who rise up in death within the people with the promise of victory for the oppressed in a voice stronger than anything they had in life.

We see signs of new vision in the passing of dictatorships, in the repudiation of communism and the claiming of freedom, precarious as this freedom has proved itself to be. We see signs in the fragile movement toward peace in Northern Ireland, in the decision for unity in Germany, in the fragile collaborative efforts between Russia and the United States, in the faltering peace negotiations between Israel and the Palestinians, in the consciousness of the West when faced with the starving refugees of Africa, and in the effort to solve international disputes by diplomacy. We see signs in the strength and respectability of the feminist movement in theology and life, in the commitment to justice and equality, and in communities who live together in harmony, genuine love and fidelity and thereby bear witness to peace and mutuality in a world where so many live isolated, lonely, disconnected and uncommitted. We see signs of life and vision in the dedication to financial, economic and social responsibility against staggering odds, in the dialogue among world religions, and in the growing awareness of the condition of the earth. Lastly, we perceive signs of hope in theology's recognition of the ill effects of having ignored as integral to the Christian faith the mystical dimension and kept contemplation confined in an airtight compartment of the Church's life for centuries. We see signs of life in human awareness and life-giving service on so many levels.

The price for this new insight and compassionate love, however, seems to be darkness, suffering and even death. Our gods have to die before we reach for the God who is beyond all our human images and projections and who waits over the brink of the known in the darkness. The signs of new life appearing among us are somehow the other side of an emptiness that paradoxically is not only bringing us closer to God but also purifying our desire and imagination and moving them toward transcendence of what has been.

John of the Cross holds out to us the promise of union with a God beyond all our inadequate images and finite gods, a union on the other side of this dark and empty time. In fact, the dark emptiness is already the beginning of this communion. The same light and love that cause the painful self-knowledge and empty questioning effect the transformation. Love will, if we accept it, answer the world's cry of desire and overtake our lives with tender communion, mutuality and an entirely different perspective which we of ourselves cannot produce by sheer determination and reason. The time of this Dark Night is in the end a hermeneutic of not only our immature or long-lost images of God but also of the Enlightenment's autonomous self!

In the very last stanza of *The Living Flame of Love*, John of the Cross sings of this transformation as *the awakening of God*:

> How gently and tenderly
> *You wake in my heart*
> Where in secret you dwell alone
> And in your sweet breathing,
> Filled with good and glory
> How tenderly you swell my heart with love. (LF III)

This awakening of God within the human heart is, of course, *human* awakening but because such a radical conversion of perspective and affectivity is engendered by the silent tenderness and inspiration of love, it is experienced as God's waking up and breathing love from the very core of a person to every thought, emotion, desire, action. When God "moves" in this way, John explains, everything in the universe is experienced as connected and moving together in harmony. All things disclose the beauty of their being and the root of their life. In consequence, every form of life is known and valued in and through God, the ground, source and center of not only the human but of everything in the universe (SC 15.25, 36.6, 39.11). The contemplative, therefore, sings without apology:

> My Beloved is the Mountains
> And lonely wooded valleys
> Strange islands
> And resounding rivers
> The whistling of lovestirring breezes
>
> The tranquil night
> At the time of the rising dawn,
> Silent music,
> Sounding solitude,
> The supper that refreshes and deepens love. (SC 14–15)

Now everything becomes the Beloved one and therefore part of the human person who is united with God and who now experiences herself as one species connected to every other form of life on the earth (SC poem, stanza 14 and 14.49, 24.6). This identity with the entire cosmic order within the contemplative and the discovery of the earth as a *living* organism are the foundation for an intimate and compassionate human presence to the earth and to one another as humans. It opens up the capacity for listening to what the earth is telling us. John writes of an immense, powerful voice which sounds in the soul, the voice of all the wonder of God heard in the voice of creation (SC 39.89, LF IV.1011).

> The soul becomes aware of Wisdom's wonderful harmony and sequence in the variety of her creatures and works. Each of them is endowed with a certain likeness to God and in its own way gives voice to what God is in it. So creatures will be for the soul a harmonious symphony of sublime music surpassing all concerts and melodies in the world. (SC 14/15.25)

The contemplative person stands, as it were, with the Creator of the Universe who awaits us in the future and calls us to completion by the desire, the dream, implanted not only within human *being*, but also within the earth and all its species as an organic whole.

If we Americans admit to an experience of God at all, we usually experience God through earthly realities, through the beauty of creation and the wonder of human love. A child, for example, is able to believe in God's love when she has been loved by her mother. The desire for God grows and develops imperceptibly in the ordinary experiences of life. This is the way it is meant to be. But in the contemplative experience of God "awakening" and filling human desire, the whole of created reality, the whole cosmic organism, is experienced as a part of Infinite Being. One's basic perspective changes. One "has God's view of things" (LF I.32). The contemplative truly knows and sees everyone, everything, the whole earth, from the divine perspective and with the love of God and, therefore, with the desire of God for the world (LF 4.25).

John writes at length in many places of this transformation of all the powers of the person. The mind no longer understands with the vigor of its own natural light but with the divine light. This is, in effect, the transformation of the mind through a new kind of knowledge, Holy Wisdom. The human capacity to love is changed because the mystic is so transformed by the unitive experience of God's love that she actually loves with the very love God has for us. Even the memory is changed in this union by the sure hope of a beckoning Future. John says the mind is God's mind, the will is God's will, the memory is God's memory and the person's delight and desire is God's delight and desire (LF II.34). All the powers and energies of the person move in love (SC 28.2-3, 8).

What is particularly significant is that for the contemplative person the old way of knowing and loving is gone. The process of transformation and conversion is really an irreversible evolution which amounts to a very radical reeducation and transformation of consciousness and human desire that cannot be controlled by short-sighted human governments or fearful Church authorities (SC 26.1317). This is the reason contemplation is so subversive and why, prior to the re-emergence of both popular and theological interest in it in the latter part of the twentieth century, it was so decisively muted for nearly three hundred years following the condemnation of quietism, as Joseph Chinnici so persuasively explains.[16] As long as contemplative transformation is looked upon solely as independent access to the divine, it will continue to be considered threatening rather than enlightening to the status quo. If, however, Ornstein and Erhlich are correct in suggesting the need for not just the refinement of the old mind but rather for a quantum leap in which our old minds are replaced by new ones, then contemplation assumes an importance religion, government, educators and leaders in the Churches have long denied it.

Conclusion

One wonders if there is a way in our extremely complex, sophisticated culture that education for contemplation, understood as a process of intentional consciousness evolution, can ever be seen by our struggling, violence racked society as a "new discipline" in which it is imperative that our people be literate. What if there were "schools" of contemplation or interiority all over the country, in business, in medicine, in education, in government? What if from pre-school to university *the art* of quiet reflection and listening, *the art* of prayer, *the art* of accessing the depth dimension of being human, without which we will never be fully human, were taught, nurtured and esteemed as central to all education? What if this manner of valuing the contemplative side of experience and development were seen as a response to and understanding of the darkness and fragmentation which afflict us as a nation? What if, in other words, the desire for God crying out among us were truly heard as we enter the twenty-first century?

I am suggesting that the call to contemplation be seen as integral to human selfunderstanding and an absolute imperative of American education. Most suppose it is impossible for many people to become contemplative, as if this were an esoteric

16. Joseph Chinnici's paper on "The Politics of Mysticism: Church, State and the Carmelite Tradition," was presented in 1990 at *Carmel 200* in Baltimore.

experience reserved for the few, a luxury for those who have leisure to be with God or simply consumer goods for a bored elite. But in the Carmelite tradition, the prayer that leads to the divine embrace of contemplative communion and transformation is not an obscure discipline, nor a complicated exercise, but a relationship developed day by day through fidelity to a presence that pervades every facet of our lives and whose image can be found etched in the length and breadth of the world.

The call is before us in both signs of death and signs of new life. We are summoned to recognize the shape of the desire for God asserting itself among us with more and more urgency. As North Americans we are greatly to be pitied if we cannot grasp our post-modern, post-enlightenment experience as an invitation to reliance on the God who truly is the mystery and energy pervading all things and who dwells darkly and secretly, as Karl Rahner writes, "in [the] nameless and pathless expanse of our consciousness" exposing to us the false visions of the present which afflict us while slowly revealing visions of hope for our future.

7

Impasse and Catastrophe

What the Virus Teaches

Susie Paulik Babka

In the dark times
Will there also be singing?
Yes, there will also be singing.
About the dark times.
—Bertolt Brecht, Motto to *Svendborg Poems*, 1939

On June 7, 2016, I was working on a paper scheduled for presentation at a conference in Puerto Rico, preoccupied by the problems that are also the privileges of academic research. My mother called, at what would have been one o'clock in the morning her time, so I knew that something was very wrong. In that flicker of a moment—the recognition that I was about to hear some bad news—I considered letting the call go to voicemail, briefly aware of the temptation to preserve life "before," and let the "before" be what it was for just a little while longer.

My father had been killed. An enthusiastic cyclist, he was with his group, "The Chain Gang," in late afternoon that bright summer day, nine riders single file, along a rural two-lane road. A white man in a pick-up truck deliberately accelerated and slammed into the back of the group as they started up a hill, killing five and seriously injuring the four who were cycling at the front of the line. None of the survivors remembers the incident, and after traumatic brain injuries, multiple surgeries, and rehabilitation, they continue to experience damage to their bodies to this day. News reports displayed pictures of their road bikes in tortured shapes and debris strewn over the road. Despite the fragile hope that my father's death was instantaneous, images of his body hurled into the air haunts my mind's assumptions, whether awake or dreaming, raw violence witnessed in my imagination, and the creeping horror of my father's familiar likeness, on his bike, in his neon yellow jacket, turned into its brutal opposite.

Then, the "after"—telling my children, making travel arrangements, the funeral home, the funeral Mass, seeing relatives and friends for the first time in years. The simulations of politeness, the conventions of custom, comforting and maddening at the same time: it was as though we were all conversing in foreign languages. But the actual "after" was still to come, in penetrating anger and chains of sleepless nights, in the confusion and fog of an ending that was not an ending. How do I reconcile my relationship with him without closure? How am I present to my mother's loss of her fifty-year marriage? Why am I crying during a car commercial? This, while also dealing with the city's prosecuting team, who were building a case against a man whose own pain had so twisted his judgment that he committed an unthinkable act. He is now in prison, convicted of second-degree murder and sentenced to five consecutive terms of five years each. Knowing how unjust is the system of incarceration in the United States, I am hardly consoled in this result, even while many who survive violent acts never see such a resolution. The anguish of those affected by his actions and his own distress are wounds that will never fully heal.

Such is the challenge of what Constance FitzGerald calls the "impasse." The night I learned of my father's death not only altered the course of events in the weeks following but profoundly altered how I view the world, my relationship with God, and how I am able to empathize with those who lose loved ones to violence. The impasse teaches the impermanence of any status quo. While humans have evolved to consider security of routine a source of survival, such precious "normalcy" masks underlying inequities and oppressions that will inevitably rise to the surface and slash a hole in the life to which we become accustomed. This slash is the impasse, deeply wrenching, but containing the possibility of transformation toward a higher truth. This begins in the way the impasse alters the imagination for the new. FitzGerald writes,

> The negative situation constitutes a reverse pressure on the imagination so that the imagination is the only way to move more deeply into the experience. It is this "imaginative shock," or striking awareness that our categories do not fit our experience, that throws the intuitive, unconscious self into gear in quest of what the possibilities really are.[1]

My father's violent death teaches this. He always kissed my mother whenever he left the house, but in a hurry to meet his fellow riders that afternoon, he only called a good-bye as he headed out the door. We all do this occasionally. They could not have known that this was their final good-bye, the last time my mother would hear his voice. We do not see the road ahead and cannot return to it, and such is the impasse.

On March 12, 2020, the University of San Diego, where I teach, ordered preparations for online teaching in response to the growing COVID-19 pandemic. Campus would be vacated in anticipation of Governor Newsom's statewide lockdown. While we were warned of this prospect, both students and faculty were caught in the whirlwind. Because USD had no online course system in place, we were given one week to learn how to conduct remote classes and for the students to pack and return home. The "before" and "after" was now suddenly fixed, not just for us, but for the country and the world. The COVID-19 pandemic will be remembered long after it dissipates, for the thousands of lives lost, the millions out of work, the dread that accompanies every ordinary activity during a health crisis.

1. Constance FitzGerald, "Impasse and Dark Night," in *Women's Spirituality: Resources and Development*, ed. Joann Wolski Conn (New York: Paulist Press, 1986), 289.

Anyone reading this has shared this experience. "Today our spirituality is rooted in experience and in story. . . . [It] must emerge from our concrete historical situation and because our time and place in history bring us face to face with profound societal impasse,"[2] FitzGerald writes in prescience. John of the Cross's "dark night" is the template for FitzGerald's contemporary interpretation of the experience of impasse, "which insinuates itself inescapably and uninvited into one's inner life and growth and into one's relationships."[3] The COVID-19 pandemic might be our common wound, our shared impasse, binding humanity in series of "befores" and "afters."

Except that this impasse is not proportionately shared. Disparities present well before the pandemic have intensified, with income and security gaps worsened to an inexcusable extent. The technologies and globalization on which world economies depend have produced a widening inequality, fertilizing the spread of new human pathogens[4] such as the novel coronavirus. To mitigate the virus's impact on those most at-risk, the healthy or asymptomatic must practice social responsibility. But the lockdowns and quarantines that drove the majority of the world's population out of public spaces are the very actions that exaggerate the depth and breadth of the social inequities and economic disparities that contributed to the pandemic's origin. It is perhaps the cruelest of circles ever witnessed in human history. Those with chronic conditions see an exacerbation of those conditions in the economic impact that comes with the lockdowns. Overwhelmed health care diverts toward treating COVID-19 patients, forsaking those who

2. Ibid., 287 and 299.

3. Ibid.

4. See Peter Turchin, "Modeling Periodic Waves of Integration in the Afro-Eurasian World-System," in *Globalization as Evolutionary Process: Modeling Global Change*, ed. George Modelski, Tessaleno Devezas, William R. Thompson (New York: Routledge, 2008), 161–89. Add the impact of factory farming to the list of conditions contributing to the origin and growth of a viral pandemic. For more on this, see Jonathan Safran Foer and Aaron S. Gross, "We Have to Wake Up: Factory Farms Are Breeding Grounds for Pandemics," *The Guardian* (April 20, 2020), https://www.theguardian.com/commentisfree/2020/apr/20/factory-farms-pandemic-risk-covid-animal-human-health.

need treatment for other illnesses. Signs of a coming health crisis went unheeded for years, as studies have shown that prevalence rates for chronic conditions are 15 percent higher for the bottom income quintile than the top income quintile.[5] Poverty precipitates chronic health problems, which leads to reduced income, which leads to more poverty.

Structural and systemic racism originates socio-economic inequality and produces the deficiencies in equitable access to proper health care; before the pandemic, the average lifespan for Blacks was six years less than that of whites.[6] That disparity has grown worse: COVID-19 mortality rates for people of color are significantly higher than for whites. As of July 30, 2020, if they had died of COVID-19 at the same rate as whites, about 17,000 Black, 3,000 Latinx, 500 Indigenous, and 50 Pacific Islander Americans would still be alive.[7] Structural racism led to living conditions (such as urban congestion from redlining practices) and the jobs that are either deemed "essential" without proper personal protection or eliminated altogether, while I, white and economically advantaged, comfortably work from home. FitzGerald observes, "On the other side of all our technology, we have come to poverty and dark night. We can find no escape from the world we have built, where the

5. Mark Stabile, Bénédicte Apouey, Isabelle Solal, "COVID-19, Inequality, and Gig Economy Workers," *Vox CEPR Policy Portal* (April 1, 2020), https://voxeu.org/article/covid-19-inequality-and-gig-economy-workers.

6. There are other significant disparities as well. For example, the mortality rate for babies born to Black mothers with a graduate degree is far worse than the mortality rate for babies born to white mothers with less than an eighth-grade education. Additionally, Black women are far less likely than white women to have breast cancer yet are 40 percent more likely to die from it. Niran S. Al-Agba, "How Structural Racism Affects Healthcare," *Medpage Today* (January 14, 2020), https://www.medpagetoday.com/blogs/kevinmd/84362.

7. APM Research (July 30, 2020), https://www.apmresearchlab.org/covid/deaths-by-race. In New York City, Black people die at twice the rate of whites; in Chicago, Black people comprise 50 percent of cases and 70 percent of deaths even though only 30 percent of the city's population is Black. See Anna North, "Every Aspect of the Coronavirus Pandemic Exposes America's Devastating Inequalities," *Vox* (April 10, 2020), https://www.vox.com/2020/4/10/21207520/coronavirus-deaths-economy-layoffs-inequality-covid-pandemic.

poor and oppressed cry out, where the earth and environment cry out."[8]

The Impasse

Within these disparities is the chasm of distance that creates a societal and systemic impasse of which FitzGerald speaks: "every normal manner of acting is brought to a standstill, and ironically, impasse is experienced not only in the problem itself but also in any solution rationally attempted."[9] While pandemics demand respect for the authority of scientists and the statistical data that supports taking actions such as stay-at-home orders, FitzGerald analyzes the Enlightenment's recourse to the rational and logical to address every implication of a crisis: "We Americans have lost faith and hope in human power and human reason. We are driven to interiority, to contemplation, to the desire for the experience of God's love by the poor and oppressed, by, in fact, the image of God scarred in the world and on the face of the earth."[10]

FitzGerald notes that the crises of Western prosperity lead to spiritual poverty as well as material poverty. Every plague and pandemic seen in human history has originated from and perpetuated both: the colonialism and slave trade that cemented the United States as a superpower are what laid the foundation for the spread of AIDS, Ebola, and COVID-19 viruses in recent times. These viruses teach that we do not control the basis of our economic security. Statistics and data do not explain this, and we cannot presume logic will answer every aspect of the impasse.

"Here is the strangeness of this strangeness," writes the philosopher Maurice Blanchot, "such an interruption . . . would be nevertheless a relation; at least if I take it upon myself not to reduce it, not to reconcile it, even by comprehending it, not to seek

8. FitzGerald, "Impasse and Dark Night," 299.

9. Ibid., 288.

10. Constance FitzGerald, "The Desire for God and the Transformative Power of Contemplation," in *Light Burdens, Heavy Blessings: Challenges of Church and Culture in the Post–Vatican II Era*, ed. Mary Heather MacKinnon, Moni McIntyre, and Mary Ellen Sheehan (Quincy, IL: Franciscan Press, 2000), 209.

to consider it as the 'faltering' mode of the unitary relation."[11] The impasse interrupts our secure routine and manifests the chasms between us. But this distance is nevertheless a relation, an interruption that cannot be comprehended by rational means. The failure of logic to deal fully with the impasse leaves it to the freedom of the imagination.

For the atheist Blanchot, God is neither an aspect of this relation nor this interruption; but for his close friend, the Jewish philosopher Emmanuel Levinas, there is a trace of the divine in the infinite difference between the before and after and between the self and Other. Levinas believes divinity shapes the impasse, between the benefits I enjoy in whiteness and the societal failures effected through systemic racism, between those who experience the COVID-19 pandemic as life and death and I who experience it within job security and a stable home. Personal experience of such impasse provides the divine opportunity for undoing white supremacy, and systems face impasse for the sort of transformative change that provides an opportunity for justice. Entering the collective impasse of the pandemic, seeing it as an opportunity to imagine and work toward a world of inclusion and equality, requires displacement of individualized fears and insecurities in favor of a wider scope of uncertainty, to identify in solidarity with those far more vulnerable. This means I must make myself more vulnerable than I am and acknowledge my complicity in an unjust status quo.

FitzGerald's description of impasse thus has both a societal or systemic aspect, a collective manifestation, as well as a personal aspect: the contemplative possibilities in the personal experience of impasse must necessarily result in the sort of compassionate society imagined through the fruits of spiritual vulnerability. The "negative situation" in which "our categories do not fit our experience" and we are within a void, or vacuum, of all expectation is the beginning of new life, "the experience of disintegration, of deprivation of worth," when the previously relied-upon concepts and support systems are gone.[12]

11. Maurice Blanchot, *The Infinite Conversation*, trans. Susan Hanson (Minneapolis: University of Minnesota Press, 1993), 68.

12. See FitzGerald, "Impasse and Dark Night," 289.

The way to traverse the difference within the personal and collective impasse is in openness to dismantle both the shelter of the ego and the shelter of the status quo. This openness, as an intentional vulnerability, means acknowledging that the impasse is infinitely beyond my capabilities: hence, the trace of divinity. I will never be able to enter the depth of another's suffering, but I can cultivate sensitivity to the impasse and openness to the displacing alterity of the Other. According to Levinas, being human, being a subject, refers to the Other as the primordial locus of responsibility, such that I share the burdens the Other suffers, which "qualifies alterity itself."[13] Any inclination to escape this responsibility ignores the meaning of being human in the world and fails the power of the imagination for vulnerability. This means that the constitution of being human is in openness to, and desire for, the very difference and uniqueness of the Other. The degree of openness constructs a "self." FitzGerald notes that this is the basis of prophetic hope: the vulnerability of the Other opens us to the infinite. For Levinas, this process begins with encountering the face of the Other, the seeing that is a summons to response, where the unknown becomes a palpable matter of experience, and where my responsibility in the practical trajectory of day-to-day life is evident.

The impasse will not take hold in us if we foolishly believe we are capable of certainty or security. Observes Dorothee Soelle, "Life that excludes and protects itself against death protects itself to death. . . . [O]nly life that opens itself to another, life that risks being wounded or killed, contains promise."[14] We pursue the illusion of certainty to escape the impasse. Modernity's notion of reason as an instrument of dominating power led to the

13. Levinas, *Totality and Infinity: An Essay in Exteriority*, trans. Alphonso Lingis (Pittsburgh, PA: Duquesne University Press, 2008), 256.

14. Dorothee Soelle, *The Window of Vulnerability: A Political Spirituality*, trans. Linda M. Maloney (Minneapolis, MN: Fortress Press, 1990), 7. Please do not assume I include these words as advice against protecting oneself from COVID-19; I also tell my daughter not to walk alone at night. But neither do I assume that protective gear and washing hands guarantees that I will not contract COVID-19, or that walking alone in the middle of the day guarantees personal safety.

identification of truth with certainty; claims to certainty became the way to justify acts that perpetrate the apparatus of authority. The inclination to control defends itself through violence. Defined as the refusal to be vulnerable, violence often masks fear of the unknown and the refusal to engage in any form of weakness or poverty. Violence against the stranger, the Other, rears from the misguided attempt to protect the ego-self at all costs. We do violence to the creative possibilities of the impasse when we escape the responsibility to be vulnerable, when we distract ourselves from the depth of the Other's pain. If the impasse is to have transformative possibilities, we must be willing to risk what Blanchot called the "consciousness of unhappiness," faithful to the "demands of grief."[15] For Levinas, such demands to be vulnerable are "the stripping of the skin exposed to wound and outrage. Opening is the vulnerability of a skin offered in wound and outrage beyond all that can show itself, beyond all that essence of being can expose itself to understanding and celebration."[16] For FitzGerald, these demands are the basis of prophetic hope, the catalyst of the possibility of justice.

Vulnerability to Proximate and Distant Others

The HIV/AIDS epidemic, which officially began in June 1981, became the leading cause of death in sub-Saharan Africa by the year 2000; today, numbers of deaths worldwide have been on the decline, due to the distribution of antiretroviral drugs. We must never forget, however, that such decline is a tenuous situation, and neither should we forget that the world has already lost at least thirty-two million to the virus. The Ebola outbreak between 2014 and 2016 threatened to become devastating on a similar scale, but it was contained to 11,325 deaths, until another outbreak occurred in the Democratic Republic of Congo in 2018 and 2019, which resulted in at least 2,271 deaths. These

15. Maurice Blanchot, *The Space of Literature*, trans. Ann Smock (Lincoln: University of Nebraska Press, 1989), 74.

16. Emmanuel Levinas, *Humanism of the Other*, trans. Nidra Poller (Urbana: University of Illinois Press, 2006), 63.

numbers, however, do not name the scope of the impasse, seen in the shattered families, the economic distress, and other forms of adversity that persist, conditions that made the COVID-19 pandemic possible.

Most of us in North America avoided the Ebola crisis. We mistakenly assume that we are insulated from the complex socioeconomic and cultural history that led to it. Those whose daily lives add *survival* to their own to-do lists, who live with death daily, are immeasurably Other to my routine. "They do not think of death," writes Blanchot, "having no other relation but with death."[17] This is how the majority of humanity lives: whether worlds away on the African continent or in my proximity, those with crude cardboard signs on street corners, Black youth dead by police brutality, those struggling to cross the Mexican-US border just twenty miles away. The weight of their struggle, and too often their failure to survive, rarely enters the landscape of my vulnerability.

How will I be infinitely responsible not only to the proximate Other but also to the distant Other, whom I will never physically meet? Or to the Other who is geographically proximate but worlds away in degree of difference between my whiteness and the experience I have never had: will the cop who just pulled me over deem my skin color a threat? How should I carry this distance? Cultivating the sort of sensitivity to vulnerability, to the interruption of the Other as impasse and relation, means being open to the suffering of Others who are distant, whether geographically, economically, culturally, or however alterity is described. The specific questions underlining the ethical "what must I do?" are not easily navigable; but the compass by which the prophets tell us to steer determines that our obligations to one another grow exponentially with the suffering that occurs in the world, no matter how far from my immediate experience.

If we explore this in terms of the doctrine of the incarnation—a belief that symbolizes human testimony to divine proximity—we see that "incarnation" refers to the dwelling of the infinite God in

17. Maurice Blanchot, *The Writing of the Disaster*, trans. Ann Smock (Lincoln: University of Nebraska Press, 1995), 40.

those who suffer. If the impasse widens our imagination, and if the imagination, as FitzGerald explains, "is the only way to move more deeply into the experience" of the negative situation, then cultivating vulnerability means that our perceptual awareness must be prepared for whatever it encounters, however disturbing to the shelter of the ego.

George Bataille writes that the receptive mind is an eye: "[E]xperience has an optical framework, in that one distinguishes within it a perceived object from a perceiving subject, the way a spectacle is different from a mirror."[18] Sensibility to vulnerability begins with the eye insofar as the face of the Other, the stranger, is the subject of ethics as an optics, according to Levinas. Hence the image makes possible a wide field that is outside the scope of ego-driven experience, beyond the nose of my perception, "outside the camp" as in Exodus 33:7, "Now Moses used to take the tent and pitch it outside the camp, far off from the camp; he called it the tent of meeting. And everyone who sought the LORD would go out to the tent of meeting, which was outside the camp."

Blanchot similarly notes that divine proximity is often understood through the metaphor of distance: "Peace, peace be to him that is far off, and to him that is near, says the Lord; and I will heal him (Isaiah 57:19)."[19] Similarly, Jesus declares divine proximity in distance in the parable of the Lost Son, which caps a series of parables on the art of losing, finding, and rejoicing. The son who has "traveled to a distant country" in an effort to spend the wealth he so brazenly demanded of his father—wealth that his father gave without so much as a word of caution or protest—is now destitute and has decided to return to his father so that he can at least eat, begins his journey home, rehearsing a little speech designed to fill his belly. My favorite line in the story refers to proximity in distance: "But *while he was still far off*, his father saw him and was filled with compassion; he ran and put his arms around him and

18. Georges Bataille, *Inner Experience*, trans. Stuart Kendall (Albany: SUNY Press, 2014), 125.

19. Maurice Blanchot, "Paix, paix au lointrain et au proche," cited by Kevin Hart, *The Dark Gaze: Maurice Blanchot and the Sacred* (Chicago: University of Chicago Press, 2004), 162.

kissed him" (Luke 15:20). Luke here uses the same phrase, "far off," found in Isaiah. The father does not bestow compassion on his wandering son because the son is proximate: rather, his compassion exudes while the son is "still far off." The son has not yet had a chance to deliver his little speech of recompense, and we are never sure in the story whether the son has actually learned anything about the unreasonable demands he made or the failures he accrued. For all we know, the son hocks the robe and ring his father lavishes on him and returns to the same wanton spending as before. But the son's action is not the focus of the story; the focus is on the father, who has watched from a distance, possibly for years, for evidence that his son is still alive: one who "was dead and has come to life; he was lost and has been found."

The Virus and the Problem of Catastrophic Suffering

"Catastrophic suffering" refers to the sort of suffering that is not in and of itself beneficial in any way to the growth or education of a human being. This is suffering that should not happen, suffering with no inherent purpose or end, suffering that is unjust and unnecessary. There is no purpose, goal, or relief within the experience of catastrophic suffering. Levinas called this "pain in its undiluted malignity, suffering for nothing. It renders impossible and odious every proposal and every thought that would explain it by the sins of those who have suffered or are dead."[20] There is simply no justification for such suffering; even if some good may result in the course of such suffering, even if some may survive and have the opportunity to reflect on it or ascribe meaning to it, this good is neither justification nor explanation for "why" it happens. This is suffering that is defined by its preponderance, not by its ability to educate or assist in meaning-making.

Indeed, *how* the problem of catastrophic suffering is addressed, how sensitive and attentive we are to the heart of the impasse, determines the contemporary relevance of theology. The ineq-

20. Emmanuel Levinas, "Useless Suffering," in *Entre-Nous: On Thinking-of-the-Other*, trans. Michael B. Smith and Barbara Harshav (New York: Columbia University Press, 1998), 98.

uities revealed in the COVID-19 pandemic manifest the "new kind of barbarism," as Theodor Adorno describes, that consistently sacrifices human lives and the health of the environment for the sake of power, wealth, and nationalism. This barbarism is obvious when we examine the colonial origins that underlie the string of genocides and pandemics that underscore Western history. The modern period represents the unqualified failure to recognize and name the atrocities as they festered and advanced, "and barbarism continues as long as the fundamental conditions that favored that relapse continue largely unchanged."[21] Pandemics are not anomalies in the course of modern history but result from systemic inequities. "All empires of humans are built on the destruction of the body,"[22] writes Ta-Nehisi Coates; "empire" is the illusion that there is, or can be erected, a bulwark to vulnerability. Protests after the horrific murders of George Floyd and Breonna Taylor reveal the atrocities on which white security depends. When the Trump administration sends federal troops to retaliate against protesters, "their own vulnerability becomes real—when the police decide that tactics intended for the ghetto should enjoy wider usage, when their armed society shoots down their children . . . they are shocked in a way that those of us who were born and bred to understand cause and effect can never be."[23]

In other words, modern society—modern Western society in particular, born of the Enlightenment—develops from what allows and promotes such atrocities. The Ebola epidemic grew in postcolonial distrust of the West, since colonial actions in medicine, military invasion, and control of the borders and resources of African nations decimated native societies and cultures. We often pin blame on leaders in such a way that we fail to see how even ordinary citizens share the burden of responsibility because we were silent and unquestioning when early stages of catastrophe cried out for recognition and witness.

21. Theodor Adorno, "Education after Auschwitz," in *Can One Live after Auschwitz? A Philosophical Reader*, ed. Rolf Tiedemann, trans. Rodney Livingstone, et al. (Stanford, CA: Stanford University Press, 2003), 19.

22. Ta-Nehisi Coates, *Between the World and Me* (New York: Spiegel and Grau/ Random House, 2015), 143.

23. Ibid., 107.

Why is it so difficult for persons and societies to acknowledge the impasse wrought by catastrophic suffering? Adorno calls us to face the depravity in human history and society squarely and soberly: "One must come to know the mechanisms that render people capable of such deeds, must reveal the mechanisms to them, and strive, by awakening a general awareness of those mechanisms, to prevent people from becoming so again. It is not the victims who are guilty. . . . Only those who have unreflectively vented their hate and aggression on them are guilty. The only education that has any sense at all is an education toward critical self-reflection."[24] Barbarism is obvious when we see the horrific daily headlines; it is not so obvious in the way we continue our banal business, when we switch channels to escape the disquieting truth that the barbarians are us. Those who benefit from North American society avoid confronting the horror that surrounds Western wealth, white supremacy, and concepts as nebulous as "national security." We who are comfortable do not like discomfort. Education for critical self-reflection, and the contemplation necessary for cultivating vulnerability, is our only hope to fashion a world without barbarism, in which catastrophic suffering is no longer tolerated.

Yet, the danger inherent in the typical processes of education—reading scholarly works, writing on them, delivering and hearing lectures—is in reifying the suffering, assuming that we could ever understand what it is like to experience the devastation of hunger or pandemic-related unemployment, die alone in an alley or in a refugee camp, simply because we have read about it or discussed it. This is where FitzGerald turns us toward the contemplative tradition, understood in the context of desire for the infinite God, manifested in the openness to and desire for the Other. "It is a cry for recognition of the connectedness of everything in the cosmos, and consequently, a desire for contemplation and transformation. . . . [R]esponsibility for the world, not just for individual well-being, moves us to contemplation."[25] Often more than we

24. Adorno, "Education after Auschwitz," 21.

25. FitzGerald, "The Desire for God," 209.

can bear, the responsibility to witness the suffering of others is what the Christian doctrine of the incarnation signifies: in Jesus, who suffers catastrophically as the victim of an oppressive regime that slaughtered thousands in its conquests, is also the God of compassion who participates in human suffering. Jesus' followers found divinity not in the Roman emperor but in a Jewish person without property or position, who died the death of a criminal; such is God suffering in resistance to the human empires that continue to slaughter. There is no God without such vulnerability and without such resistance.

The Suffering Other in Proximity

Casa Hogar Las Memorias is an HIV/AIDS hospice ten miles east of Tijuana, Mexico. The journey there winds through unpaved roads and barrios of homes patched with plastic tarp and corrugated tin in the community of La Morita. Although they depend entirely on donations and endure deterioration and loss daily, there is nothing somber at Casa Memorias; painted in bright colors and sprinkled with the giggles of caretakers' children, it feels more like entering a home than a care facility. Rooms are devoted to different levels of severity of illness, which means that sometimes the room housing the most critically ill is the most crowded.

Alberto arrived only a few days prior to my visit, and the only bed available in the critical room was near a door propped open for breeze. Without a screen, flies lazed in and out. Alberto was too weak to swat them away, so they pestered him. I could swat away flies and give him sips of water. But I had trouble understanding his Spanish, which was muffled by his weakness and mild dementia. From caramel skin stretched taut over his bones, his wide eyes pleaded to me to relieve him of his pain: the very thing that I could not do. I smiled stupidly and took his hand but his pain was too pervasive, too intense. I stood facing him, nodding as he cried, helpless as he fell from broken words into silence. He died two days later.

I have visited AIDS patients in other ministries, but none were so close to death; Blanchot describes this dying as "un-power" that wrests from the present, always a step over the edge, which rules out every conclusion and all ends: "it does not free nor does it shelter."[26] "In death, one can find an illusory refuge: the grave is as far as gravity can pull, it marks the end of the fall; the mortuary is the loophole in the impasse. But dying flees and pulls indefinitely, impossibly and intensively in the flight."[27] That night, at home, I searched for faith that God surpasses my failures to appreciate the extent of his suffering. The infinite God cannot be bound by my inability to do anything of service for him. My failure must guide through the field, the impasse, where my responsibility continues despite my limitations: precisely in my failure is an endless responsibility. Faith in the un-boundedness of God where catastrophic suffering occurs is the extent—perhaps the *only* extent—of the cross as "salvific." But how absurd to think that one dying like this could ever be salvific. Whatever "salvation" is, it must have something to do with the instinct of the early followers of Jesus that the divine dwells in these tents of meeting where there is only pain, heat, and flies.

Impasse in the Suffering of the Distant Other

In August 2014, I was listening to National Public Radio in my kitchen when I heard the story of Saah Exco, a young boy whose death by the Ebola virus was captured by photojournalist David Gilkey. Exco died in an alley in the densely populated township of West Point, in the capital city of Monrovia on the coast of Liberia, denied access to a clinic because it was not equipped to handle Ebola patients. He wandered into an alley and a crowd began to gather. Clothing was passed to him and he struggled, frail yet persistent, to dress himself. The crowd, anxious with dread over a virus as contagious as it is misunderstood, could only view his

26. Blanchot, *The Writing of the Disaster*, 48.
27. Ibid.

deterioration (including Gilkey, who admitted he was too paralyzed by fear to reach out to him), until his death.[28]

Primo Levi's poem introducing *Survival in Auschwitz* reminds me that I watch this little boy—"satisfied in my own living belly"—at a distance from his horror in every way possible; my color, my economic security, my geography might as well place me in another solar system, another galaxy apart from this scene. My distance is unspeakable: it is too far from this child's suffering. I "live safe in my warm house"; I "return in the evening to hot food and friendly faces."[29] I travel over this planet where Ebola and poverty cause immeasurable agony from the indifference of my computer, briefly engaged in concern, an interruption in workaday business. If I had actually been in that alley, I would have only watched in stupefied terror as well.

The cultural identity that has preserved communities in African nations beset by Western colonialism—an identity shaped by a rejection of Western individualism—has tragically been a factor in the rapid spread of the Ebola virus and subsequently predicts more devastation in the COVID-19 pandemic. In African cultures, it is unthinkable not to hold or otherwise touch a sick person in need of comfort. After someone has died, the act of washing, kissing, and caressing the body is ritually performed by those with high status in the family or in society. It is customary to spend hours preparing the body for the afterlife, from trimming nails to braiding hair. Actions that identify the life and value of persons and relationships are lethal in communities affected by the Ebola virus, and with the spread of COVID-19, measures such as social distancing jeopardize the very uniqueness of cultures in African

28. See Matthew Silver, "The 10-Year-Old Boy Has Died, Probably of Ebola," NPR (August 21, 2014), http://www.npr.org/blogs/goatsandsoda/2014/08/21/342216397/the-10-year-old-boy-has-died-probably-of-ebola. Gilkey, an investigative journalist with NPR since 2007, was killed by an IED in Afghanistan on June 5, 2016. We are indebted to journalists such as Gilkey who keep the suffering of the world proximate.

29. See Primo Levi, "If This Is a Man," in *Survival in Auschwitz*, trans. Stuart Woolf (Amazon Digital Services, 2013), preface.

nations. Mercy Amba Oduyoye writes, "To lose one's place in, or lose touch with, one's family is the worst possible misfortune."[30]

No one held Saah Exco while he died; no one cooled his feverish forehead; no one stroked his hair. We can only *approach* the catastrophe of his suffering, never comprehend it, by reminding ourselves of the complex history that led to it, and the attempt to recognize and address those complexities, layers that describe my distance from him—whether geographical, ethnic, or economic—will always be superseded by my failure to have any grasp of his suffering. Therein lies the infinite. I will not know the games he played when healthy, the way he looked at his mother or held his sister's hand. How do I explain that despite the chasm of difference and distance, I feel irrevocably changed by the photographer's heartbreaking narration of powerless witness?

Saah Exco's story is compelling because I am never to forget him. Levinas describes this as a relation with what is infinitely distant from my own reality, "yet without this distance destroying this relation and without this relation destroying this distance"[31]—a relation that depends on the distance that preserves his alterity and dignity. The bond with the Other, Levinas writes, "is not reducible to the representation of the other, but to his invocation" that is "irreducible to understanding."[32] Hence, it is not mere being that joins us, as though our shared human nature is enough, but the distance, the vulnerability, and the call to witness. The call, as Primo Levi writes, is to "Carve them into your hearts / At home, in the street / Going to bed, rising; / Repeat them to your children."[33] This invocation of the Other, which breaks through my complacency and is carved into my heart: this it is to be religious, writes Levinas, as "the essence of discourse is prayer."[34] The original meaning of "religion" is "to be bound," which seems to be Levinas' aim: "What distinguishes thought

30. Mercy Amba Oduyoye, *Beads and Strands: Reflections of an African Woman on Christianity in Africa* (Maryknoll, NY: Orbis Books, 2004), 47.

31. Levinas, *Totality and Infinity*, 49.

32. Emmanuel Levinas, "Is Ontology Fundamental?," in Smith and Harshav, eds., *Entre Nous*, 7.

33. Primo Levi, "If This Is a Man," preface.

34. Levinas, "Is Ontology Fundamental?," 7.

directed toward a thing from a bond with a person is that in the latter case a vocative is uttered: what is named is at the same time what is called."[35]

Considered further, I must ask whether my concern for his suffering is more precisely my desire to maintain him at arm's length, he and the virus, the poverty, the layers of colonial and postcolonial manipulations that have placed millions in the absurd situations of child soldiers and child brides. I can maintain Saah Exco at arm's length because he has died a world away, while hundreds of immigrant children from Mexico and Central America populate detention centers not an hour's drive from me. They may not be dying, but they are afraid and alone, awaiting deportation, caught within the web of our society's and our government's failure to provide refuge from the drug wars for which our society and our government, again in layers of colonial and postcolonial manipulation, are responsible. Because I benefit from this postcolonial economy and the worldview of white society, my responsibility is bound to that benefit. My responsibility is infinite to the distant Other because the benefits I enjoy are based on the illusion of distance.

The danger in keeping those who suffer catastrophically at either physical or intellectual arm's length is in their instrumental use for my own gain. Instrumentalization of the victims of catastrophic suffering refers to the possibility that I may take some perverse voyeuristic pleasure from the weight of the numbers of the dead, the gravity of their situation, the hopelessness of their stories. Adorno writes persuasively on this point: privileged distance runs the risk of turning victims themselves into works of art:

> When even genocide becomes cultural property in committed literature, it becomes easier to continue complying with the culture that gave rise to the murder. One characteristic of such literature is virtually ever-present: it shows us humanity blossoming in so-called extreme situations. . . . [T]his becomes a dreary metaphysics that affirms the horror . . . by virtue of the notion that the authenticity of the human being is manifested there.[36]

35. Ibid.

36. Adorno, "Commitment," in Tiedmann, ed., *Can One Live after Auschwitz?*, 252–53.

Adorno here refers to the way culture has a tendency to whitewash catastrophic suffering as somehow justifiable in the context of a medium that shows the "triumph of the human spirit"—trivializing terror into a neat package with beautiful people doing brave deeds. Bravery is abundant right now in the nurses and doctors who serve the sick and dying at risk of their own lives. But it is a "dreary metaphysics," indeed, if we consider that the manifestation of this courage is *why* catastrophic suffering occurs. Catastrophic suffering a world away does not occur to give my comfortable life gratitude and meaning; such an interpretation is the worst kind of theodicy.

Can there be discourse about Saah Exco in that alley without trivializing, instrumentalizing, or sentimentalizing him? His suffering surpasses my imagination, and his silence in death means he will never be able to represent himself, discuss his experience, or reflect on it. Saah Exco's dignity is in his alterity, and not in victimization by the history of colonialism and poverty: I must not define his life by his suffering, even though he suffers catastrophically and without purpose. His face interrupts my existence: his face demands something of me. In this impasse, I confront something infinite, something beyond my capabilities, something I will never understand or resolve. To paraphrase FitzGerald, will I see in the Ebola, AIDS, and COVID-19 viruses "the darkness of this empty time and barren space, personally and collectively, as the love and care of God in our lives desiring to purify our desire as persons and our national dream as a people?"[37] In this disturbance by Saah Exco's alterity, by his otherness, I am no longer free to be what I was. He must be more than a statistic, more than a symbol or theme: he must be he himself, and this very reality is beyond my comprehension, drawing me deeper into the ethical responsibility to say his name.

Constance FitzGerald is herself a prophet of the impasse, of the contemplation possible when the interruption of otherness and the unforeseen event reveals the impermanence of the status quo, whether the status quo conceals inequity and injustice or

37. FitzGerald, "The Desire for God," 213.

the security of the ego. In her writing and work, she witnesses to the suffering Other as the locus of the desire for God. She calls us to openness to ambiguity, uncertainty, and vulnerability to the unknown even in the "breakdown of what/whom we have staked our lives on" since it is only in the breakdown that "the depths of hunger and thirst that exist in the human person, the infinite capacity, can really be experienced."[38] In the impasse, in the breakdown, we may glimpse the infinite unbroken wholeness that generates hope and exposes desire: the fruits of envisioning a new world.

38. Constance FitzGerald, "From Impasse to Prophetic Hope: Crisis of Memory," *CTSA Proceedings* 64 (2009): 24.

8

Impasse and the Preferential Option for the Poor

Roberto S. Goizueta

> It is in this darkness, when there is nothing left in us that can please or comfort our own minds, when we seem to be useless and worthy of all contempt, when we seem to have failed, when we seem to be destroyed and devoured, it is then that the deep and secret selfishness that is too close for us to identify is stripped away from our souls. It is in this darkness that we find true liberty. It is in this abandonment that we are made strong. This is the night which empties us and makes us pure. Do not look for rest in any pleasure, because you were not created for pleasure: you were created for spiritual JOY. And if you do not know the difference between pleasure and spiritual joy you have not yet begun to live.
>
> —Thomas Merton, *New Seeds of Contemplation*, chap. 35

The Peruvian theologian Gustavo Gutiérrez has argued that the two principal, overarching themes in Scripture are (1) the universality and gratuity of God's love and (2) God's preferential love for the poor. At first blush, these appear to be mutually contradictory assertions. They are, in fact, however, mutually implicit; you can't have one without the other. To explain this integral relationship between God's universal, gratuitous love and God's preferential option for the poor Gutiérrez draws on the thought of the Christian mystics.[1] Even more explicitly, he presents a sustained, book-length reflection on the book of Job.[2] Gutiérrez thus outlines the intimate relationship between liberation theology and mystical theology (something too rarely acknowledged in the literatures of either liberation theology or contemporary spiritual theology). If Gutiérrez has incorporated the insights of the mystics into his theology of liberation, the Carmelite theologian Constance FitzGerald has consistently and systematically attended to the integral relationship between mystical theologies and the social concerns of liberation theologians. With her notion of "impasse," she approaches that relationship from the perspective of contemplation, while Gutiérrez does so from the perspective of social action.

This chapter will examine the gratuitous, universal, and preferential character of divine love by drawing on the thought of these two profound theologians. More specifically, I will suggest that FitzGerald's notion of "impasse" can mediate the integral unity of divine gratuity, universality, and preference to contemporary Christians. In the experience of impasse, the mystic and the revolutionary are revealed as one.

The Preferential Option for the Poor

Rooted in Scripture and the very nature of the Christian faith, the preferential option for the poor has been among the most influential theological concepts of the past fifty years. Articulated most systematically in the work of liberation theologians and other historically marginalized theological voices, the option for the poor has also become a key principle of Catholic social teaching. As such, the option for the poor has tended to be viewed as an ethical imperative, or a consequence of the Christian faith, i.e., Christians are obligated to put their faith into practice by prioritizing service to the poor. Likewise, in theology the option

1. See especially Gustavo Gutiérrez, *We Drink from Our Own Wells: The Spiritual Journey of a People* (Maryknoll, NY: Orbis Books, 2013).

2. Gustavo Gutiérrez, *On Job: God-Talk and the Suffering of the Innocent* (Maryknoll, NY: Orbis Books, 2013).

for the poor has often been viewed as a practical, ethical demand flowing from Christian belief (more specifically, from reading Scripture). In turn, theological reflection will itself be informed by the theologian's social praxis. Theological reflection thus takes place within a "hermeneutical circle," i.e., the ongoing interaction between reflection and social praxis.

Such an understanding of the preferential option for the poor, however, underestimates the radical, foundational character of this principle. This foundational character can only be properly appreciated when the option for the poor is viewed in its intrinsic relation to Gutiérrez's first scriptural principle, the gratuity and universality of God's love. It is this first principle that reveals the fundamental character of the option for the poor as not only an ethical mandate flowing from Christian faith but as a precondition of that very faith. The preferential option for the poor *defines* the very encounter with God in the person of Jesus Christ; without it, there can be no such encounter, no such relationship with Christ.

Of course, in making this argument, one must clarify what is meant by "preferential option," what is meant by "the poor," and what the relationship is between those two terms; what does it mean to make a preferential option *for* the poor? Finally, and most important, one must be able to articulate how and why the option for the poor is *intrinsic* to the encounter with God's love *as gratuitous and universal.* It is to these questions that I will now turn.

In his explanation of the option for the poor, Gutiérrez repeatedly stresses the word "preferential"; the option for the poor is not exclusive but preferential. Thus, love of the poor in no way excludes love of the non-poor. Christians are called to love *all* people. That love may need to take different forms, however, depending on historical circumstances. For instance, in a situation where African Americans are being enslaved, our preferential love for the poor (i.e., the slaves) will demand the liberation of the slaves. In that same situation, our love for the white masters will demand confrontation and a call to conversion, i.e., a love that the masters will not initially experience as love at all. In such a context of conflict and division, the *only* way to love *all* is to love the poor preferentially. *Not* to take sides out of a putative love for all sides would, in fact, be to side with the oppressors, who would benefit from our silence and inaction. In other words, to say that our love must be universal (like God's) is not to say that it must be neutral. Indeed, it can only be universal if it's *not* neutral.

As universal, God's love is also gratuitous. Indeed, its utter gratuity is what distinguishes God's love above all. Thus, Gutiérrez insists that divine preference must be viewed in the light of divine gratuity:

> We in Latin America are also convinced . . . that in the liberation process we are capable of creating our own idols for ourselves. For example, the idol of justice: it might seem strange to say this but justice can become an idol if it is not placed in the context of gratuity. . . . Gratuity is the framework for justice and gives it meaning in history. Social justice, no matter how important it is—and it is—can also be an idol, and we have to purify ourselves of this to affirm very clearly that only God suffices and to give justice itself the fullness of its meaning.[3]

If the universality of God's love becomes manifest in history in the form of God's preferential love for the poor, what is revealed above all is the character of God's love as sheer *gift*, as absolutely unmerited.

And what reveals the sheer gratuity of God's love is that the privileged recipients of the gift are "the poor," i.e., those who, in the eyes of the world, are *least* worthy of divine love. Gutiérrez's understanding of "poverty" is highly nuanced and is developed throughout the course of his writings. (Many of the polemics surrounding Gutiérrez's theology have been occasioned by superficial or simplistic interpretations of his notion of poverty.) He devotes the last chapter of his watershed *A Theology of Liberation* to an extended discussion of the term, focusing on a comparative analysis of the Matthean and Lukan Beatitudes.[4] It's not mere coincidence that the Peruvian theologian's articulation of a the-

3. Gustavo Gutiérrez, *The Density of the Present: Selected Writings* (Maryknoll, NY: Orbis Books, 1999), 141.

4. Gustavo Gutiérrez, *A Theology of Liberation: History, Politics, and Salvation* (Maryknoll, NY: Orbis Books, 2012), 162–73.

ology of liberation culminates in an analysis of "poverty"; one cannot understand the nature of Christian faith without a proper understanding of poverty.

Gutiérrez distinguishes between material poverty ("Blessed are you who are poor"; Luke 6:20) and spiritual poverty ("Blessed are the poor in spirit"; Matt 5:3) while insisting at all times that this distinction is not a separation. Indeed, any reduction of poverty to either its material or spiritual dimension distorts the Gospel. The reduction of poverty to its socioeconomic dimension can lead to a deracinated, ideological social activism not concerned with actual poor *persons* but with "the poor" as mere *objects* of social action. Conversely, the reduction of poverty to its spiritual dimension can lead to an ahistorical abstraction of Christian faith from its sociohistorical context and, hence, from the demands of Christian social praxis. The end result is the same: the real suffering and struggles of poor persons are ignored. The only proper understanding of poverty, therefore, is one that affirms the intrinsic, integral relationship between material poverty and spiritual poverty. More specifically, material (or socioeconomic) poverty mediates spiritual poverty, even as spiritual poverty furnishes the deepest meaning of material poverty.

The fundamental precondition for union with God is a radical, spiritual openness to and dependence on divine love. The "poor in spirit" are precisely those persons whose lives are characterized by such openness and dependence. Since we are embodied, sociohistorical beings, however, all aspects of our lives—including the spiritual—have a sociohistorical, material dimension (e.g., physical, cultural, political, economic). In the words of the great German theologian Karl Rahner, the human person is a "spirit in the world." Therefore, it would be difficult for someone to be "poor in spirit" who does not experience some form of material or physical deprivation (as difficult as it would be for "a camel to go through the eye of a needle").

Gutiérrez's most profound reflections on the meaning of poverty are found in his later book *On Job*. The central question of that book is, "How can we talk about a God who is love in the midst of innocent suffering?" Another way of phrasing the question (as posed now by the figure of Satan in the story) is, "Can human beings have a disinterested faith in God—that is, can they believe in God without looking for rewards or fearing punishment?" In this extraordinary, extended reflection on the book of Job, Gutiérrez lays out a topographic map of faith, inviting the reader to travel along the path from a "faith" that remains self-assured, self-interested, and conditional to a faith that emerges from the encounter with a God whose extravagant love is revealed only to those who plumb the depths of their radical poverty and contingency as creatures. The book of Job is a spiritual travelogue that delineates the path from faith-as-knowing to faith-as-unknowing. It is in the course of this spiritual travel that, Gutiérrez suggests, we will discover the connection between the universality and gratuity of God's love and God's preferential love for the poor. Or, rather, we will discover that connection retrospectively, after we've risked setting off and persisted on this spiritual journey.

In essence, what Job must contend with is the apparent contradiction between his religious beliefs and his experience. When Job is visited with the various afflictions, he is faced with two seemingly conflicting realities: (1) Job's *belief* that God is loving and just, yet (2) the suffering Job himself *experiences* is unloving and unjust. How will Job resolve the contradiction? One possible answer is to simply deny that the contradiction exists. He could do so in either of two ways: by rejecting God (the atheist's response) or by denying his own experience (the response of Job's religious friends, whose commitment to their religious "orthodoxy" precludes the possibility that Job may indeed be innocent). God's silence would not be a problem if not for Job's belief that God is all-loving, all-just, and all-powerful. Job, however, refuses to resolve the contradiction. He resists the temptation to resolve the contradiction by a premature recourse to theodicy, i.e., the attempt to *make sense* of the contradiction. Rather, he immerses himself in the very tension between his beliefs and his experience. In so doing, he struggles mightily with God, whom he questions angrily, and with himself, whom he wishes "had never been born." He stubbornly insists on being faithful *both* to God-as-love *and* to himself-as-innocent. In the midst of these struggles, Job hardly exhibits the "patience of Job." He's rebellious; he wants and demands answers! Yet Job does not despair; he continues to struggle even in the midst of the chaos. Hoping against all hope, he continues to reach out and cry out to a God who nevertheless remains silent. Here Job prefigures Christ's desperate (though not despairing) cry of abandonment on the cross: "*My God, my God* . . . why have you abandoned me?"

And here, in Job's own cry of abandonment, the language of contemplation becomes one with the language of prophecy. In his own desolation, Job shares in the desolation of the poor, i.e., those many other innocent sufferers:

> The question he asks of God ceases to be a purely personal one and takes concrete form in the suffering of the poor. The answer he seeks will not come except through commitment to them and by following the road—which God alone knows—that leads to wisdom. . . . Moreover, his line of argument will now change radically, as a result precisely of his realization that poverty and abandonment are not his lot alone. For he sees now that this poverty and abandonment are not something fated but are caused by the wicked, who nonetheless live serene and satisfied lives [Job 24:2-14]. . . . This time, Job's cry is not simply for himself, for he knows that he is part of the world of the poor.[5]

He thus acknowledges his solidarity with that world. Yet, despite this solidarity with the poor and commitment to justice, Job eventually realizes that "this kind of talk about God—talk that may be described as 'prophetic'—is inadequate. Job's thirst for understanding, which his trials have awakened and inflamed, is not satisfied."[6] Job continues to question God, but now in the name of all those persons who suffer innocently: "In the person of Job, alone here before God, are present all the innocent of this world who suffer unjustly and ask 'why?' of the God in whom they believe."[7]

Then—finally—God speaks. In this famous divine soliloquy, God does not answer Job's questions. Instead, God turns the

5. Gutiérrez, *On Job*, 34.
6. Ibid., 48.
7. Ibid., 68.

questions on their head and poses God's own questions to Job: "Where were you when I laid the foundations of the earth? Tell me, if you have understanding. Who determined its measurements—surely you know! Or who stretched the line upon it? On what were its bases sunk?" (Job 38:4-6). So much for tit-for-tat and "just rewards"! God "answers" Job by confronting him with the inherent irrationality of what Job (and his friends) consider reasonable and just. In the face of the utter gratuity of God's love, all our expectations fall short; whereas we demand that two plus two equal four, in God's eyes they add up to much, much more—beyond our capacity to fathom. While we demand our "just" deserts, God desires to give us much, much more than we deserve—if we will only leave behind our meager expectations. "The reason for believing 'for nothing,'" notes Gutiérrez, "is the free and gratuitous initiative taken by divine love."[8] It's not up to us to make sense of that love, which makes rain fall even on barren land and "desert, which is empty of human life" (Job 38:26). In the end, Job humbly repents by accepting and embracing his creatureliness before a God whose extravagant, unmerited, universal love is the very foundation of all that exists. Even the demands of justice can be properly understood only in the context of the gratuity that grounds those very demands.[9] For faith to be truly disinterested, its commitment to the poor is not an end in itself but the locus wherein is revealed and encountered God's gratuitous, universal love.

In the book of Job, according to Gutiérrez, the prophetic becomes the mystical. More precisely, it is in the innocent victim's cry of abandonment, when all hope of justice has been vanquished, that action finds its deepest, *theo*logical roots in contemplation. The struggle for justice has become futile—at least as determined by our calculations. It is then that the very terms of that struggle are called into question: the human victim's "why" must yield before the divine "why." Job's "where *are* you, God?" must yield

8. Ibid., 70–71.

9. Gutiérrez, *The Density of the Present*, 141.

to the Lord's "where were *you*, Job?" Before the Lord of the whirlwind, the very notion of divine justice withers. What is revealed is utter and sheer gratuity. If there is to be any justice (and the "if" remains stubbornly implicit in the Lord's soliloquy), then it will not and, even more ominously, *cannot* be anything we will initially recognize as such. By its very definition, God's love will not and cannot be recognized *as love*. We are thus stripped of all our expectations and preconceptions, leaving us with only two possible responses: despair or trust.

Both despair and trust are rooted in the same experience, that of *absolute isolation*. Despair is simply another word for suicide—whether a literal, physical suicide or, more common, the emotional, psychological, and spiritual suicide of someone who has become isolated from others, from God, and from their own interior lives (whether through apathy, through depression, or, perhaps, through innumerable forms of addiction). Trust, on the other hand, is the refusal to accept isolation even when there is no experience or evidence of an Other *in whom* to trust. Thus, the trust that is being asked of Job is an object-less trust. In the phrase made famous by the medieval German mystic Meister Eckhart, Job is being asked to "live without a why."[10] To live whylessly is the only way to participate in God's own love, which is itself "without a why." Here we have arrived at the terminus of the spiritual journey laid out in the book of Job. We have come a long way—from faith as calculus ("if, . . . then") to faith as object-less trust ("if, . . ."). This latter persists in crying out to a God who is silent. In so doing, such faith unites the believer to all those poor who, like Job and the crucified Christ, struggle for a justice defined not by human calculations but by sheer gratuity.

Impasse

Key to a proper understanding of the preferential option for the poor, then, is an appreciation of the intrinsic relationship between

10. For a discussion of Eckhart's notion of "living without why," see John M. Connolly, *Living without Why: Meister Eckhart's Critique of the Medieval Concept of Will* (New York: Oxford University Press, 2014).

the personal and social dimensions of liberation, the personal and social dimensions of the encounter with Christ. That is, the preferential option for the poor is not so much an ethical category as an epistemological, theological, and, indeed, *soteriological* category. Only when we are stripped of all our idols (including the idol of justice) and become one with the poor in their own desolation can we encounter the paradoxically salvific cry of the Crucified. As the Jesuit theologian Jon Sobrino has argued, there is "no salvation outside the poor."[11]

Constance FitzGerald's notion of "impasse" is an important contribution to our understanding of the preferential option for the poor precisely because impasse presupposes the intrinsic connection between the personal and the social as the locus of Christian faith, i.e., the "integration of contemplation and social commitment."[12] As Gutiérrez's notion of gratuity makes possible a contemplative grounding of the option for the poor, FitzGerald's notion of impasse makes possible a social contextualization of contemplative categories such as John of the Cross's "dark night of the soul" or Eckhart's "living without a why."

FitzGerald defines the reality of impasse as follows:

> By impasse, I mean that there is no way out of, no way around, no rational escape from, what imprisons one, no possibilities in the situation. In a true impasse, every normal manner of acting is brought to a standstill, and ironically, impasse is experienced not only in the problem itself but also in any solution rationally attempted. Every logical solution remains unsatisfying, at the very least. The whole life situation suffers a depletion, has the word *limits* written upon it. Dorothee Soelle describes it as "unavoidable suffering," an apt symbol of which is physical imprisonment, with its experience of being squeezed into a confined space. Any movement out, any next step, is canceled, and the most dangerous temptation is to give up, to quit, to surrender to cynicism

11. Jon Sobrino, *No Salvation Outside the Poor: Prophetic-Utopian Essays* (Maryknoll, NY: Orbis Books, 2015).

12. Constance FitzGerald, "Impasse and Dark Night," in *Living with Apocalypse: Spiritual Resources for Social Compassion*, ed. Tilden H. Edwards (San Francisco: Harper & Row, 1984), 93.

> and despair, in the face of the disappointment, disenchantment, hopelessness, and loss of meaning that encompass one.[13]

For FitzGerald, this experience of impasse is, first of all, a socio-historical, communal experience:

> the experience and story of women (poor women, black women, white women, exploited women, Asian women, Native American women, etc.); the experience of the poor and oppressed of the world; the experience of the aging; the experience of the fear of nuclear holocaust and the far-reaching evils of nuclear buildup for the sake of national security, power, and domination; the experience of the woundedness of the earth and the environment.[14]

Much as Mexican American theologian Nancy Pineda-Madrid and African American theologian M. Shawn Copeland have recently been examining human suffering as a social as well as personal reality by developing the notion of "social suffering," FitzGerald has retrieved the notion of the "dark night" in a contemporary context by examining its social dimensions through her notion of impasse.[15] FitzGerald views social action not only as the consequence of contemplation but as its context; there can be no authentic contemplation except in the context of solidarity with the experience of the poor. Likewise, the dark night has an inescapably social dimension. When we have reached an impasse, we literally cannot *move*. We are paralyzed emotionally, psychologically, spiritually, physically, and socially.

The experience of impasse thus reveals the social-structural dimension of the dark night. Impasse reveals how Job's "friends" are *themselves* caught in its paralyzing web. As FitzGerald notes, "Intrinsic to the experience of impasse is the impression and feeling of rejection and lack of assurance *from those on whom one*

13. Ibid., 94.
14. Ibid., 93.
15. See especially Nancy Pineda-Madrid, *Suffering and Salvation in Ciudad Juárez* (Minneapolis: Fortress Press, 2011) and M. Shawn Copeland, *Enfleshing Freedom: Body, Race, and Being* (Minneapolis: Fortress Press, 2009).

counts."[16] "At the deepest levels of impasse," she continues, "one sees the support systems on which one has depended pulled out from under one and asks if anything, if anyone, is trustworthy."[17] Consequently, the paralysis of impasse makes it impossible both to move and to *be* moved, since either possibility presupposes a fundamental trust in one's environment, i.e., in the social networks and structures that heretofore had lent their support.

It's at this point that the greatest danger lies, namely, that of denying and repressing the experience of impasse:

> The person caught in impasse must find a way to identify, face, live with, and express this suffering. If one cannot speak about one's affliction in anguish, anger, pain, lament—at least to the God within—one will be destroyed by it or swallowed up by apathy. Every attempt to humanize impasse must begin with this phenomenon of experienced, acknowledged powerlessness, which can then activate creative forces that enable one to overcome the feeling that one is without power.[18]

The greatest danger for the person caught in impasse is that the paralysis—the inability to move or be moved—will be denied and repressed. So painful is impasse that it leads to numbness and apathy, which is to say death. Indeed, the very social structures that have generated the paralysis must now, for their very survival, foster denial and repression. The interior death (i.e., apathy) that results from repression can then become externalized in various forms of self-destructive behavior, whether every conceivable kind of addiction, acts of self-harm, or even suicide. As sociologist Julie Phillips writes, "The data suggests that white and middle-aged Americans are the demographic groups most at risk for suicide. . . . In general, suicide rates among whites are about three times higher than among blacks and Latinos." On the same day that I write these words the *Washington Post* is carrying stories titled "Tech Addiction Is Real: We Psychologists Need to Take It Seriously" by Doreen Dodgen-Magee and "The

16. FitzGerald, "Impasse and Dark Night," 94–95; emphasis added.
17. Ibid., 95.
18. Ibid., 96.

Dangerous Shifting Cultural Narratives around Suicide" by Julie Phillips (*Washington Post*, March 21, 2019).

Thus, FitzGerald reminds us impasse is never a purely private, personal experience—any more than each one of us is ever an autonomous individual. Christ's own cry of abandonment was the consequence of a particular kind of life in the face of the "powers and principalities." Crucifixion was a *political* form of torture and capital punishment. Societal impasse can be repressed as easily as personal impasse; the power of oppressive political, cultural, racial, sexual, economic, and ecclesial structures to perpetuate societal impasse stems precisely from denial and repression. Where the reality of societal impasse is repressed—by, for instance, an ideology of "progress"—the victim will be held responsible for her or his suffering. This very self-victimization, fostered by social structures that repress the reality of societal impasse, is intrinsic to the experience of impasse. Of particular significance for FitzGerald here is the repression of *women's* experience of impasse as perpetuated by patriarchal social and even ecclesial structures: "The feminine experience of dark night, if we read it, interpret it, understand it, and live it through, is in itself a critique of religious consciousness and, therefore, ultimately of Christianity, with its roots in a sexist, patriarchal culture."[19]

This same impasse, when it is "lived through" rather than repressed, becomes both a critique of oppressive social structures and the privileged locus of conversion, of encounter with the Wounded and Risen Victim:

> The psychologists and the theologians, the poets and the mystics, assure us that impasse can be the condition for creative growth and transformation *if* the experience of impasse is fully appropriated within one's heart and flesh with consciousness and consent; *if* the limitations of one's humanity and human condition are squarely faced and the sorrow of finitude allowed to invade the human spirit with real, existential powerlessness; *if* the ego does not demand understanding in the name of control and predictability but is willing to admit the mystery of its own being and surrender itself to this mystery; *if* the path into the unknown,

19. Ibid., 107–8.

> into the uncontrolled and unpredictable margins of life, is freely taken when the path of deadly clarity fades. . . . It is precisely as broken, poor, and powerless that one opens oneself to the dark mystery of God in loving, peaceful waiting.[20]

In this terrifying unknown, we reach out in faith and trust *because we have no other option.*[21] Or, more precisely, the only other option is despair and suicide, in one of the many forms described above (e.g., the passive suicide of apathy or the more active forms of self-destruction). True faith—the faith of Christ on the cross—is born at that moment when one realizes one has no other option and, therefore, continues reaching out even in the void, at the moment when the Crucified cries out, "My God, my God, ..."

In the experience of impasse, contemplative receptivity grounds the preferential option for the poor. In the personal/societal experience of impasse, we confront the terrifying but ultimately liberating reality that we have no other choice; we have no choice but to stop demanding answers, for no answers will be forthcoming. Paradoxically, only at that point are we truly free; only when we have been stripped of all our idols are we free, because only then do we have nothing to lose. Like Job, we have no choice but to stop speaking and start listening. Even a putative option for "all" is revealed as simply another manifestation of the denial and repression of impasse, for it too represents a refusal to surrender, to "live without a why." Only God's preferential love for the poor, as experienced when we "live through" impasse, strips us of our need to make sense of divine love and justice. Only God's preferential love for the poor, as experienced when we continue to reach out in the void, places us in a position of absolute receptivity (as opposed to the mere passivity of apathy). As FitzGerald observes, "Impasse internalizes the option for the poor."[22]

At the same time, the option for the poor externalizes or, rather, historicizes impasse. Contemplative receptivity must never become an evasion of solidarity with the poor but is, on

20. Ibid., 96–97.
21. Ibid., 104.
22. Ibid., 113.

the contrary, its very source. Indeed, if not born from the crucible of contemplation, all our attempted solutions to societal impasse will inevitably fall short, precisely because they are *ours*:

> Is it by changing our religious language? By feminizing God, uncovering feminine images and attributes of God in the Scriptures? Is it by the desexualization of God and a move toward deism? Or is it by contemplation? . . . What our programs to eliminate sexist language in our theological, devotional, and liturgical life have shown us is that our solutions are unsatisfactory and confusing. We find impasse not only in the problems but even in the solutions. . . . Ultimately, therefore, impasse is a challenge to feminists to be mystics. . . . I believe there is no alternative for feminists except contemplation.[23]

In the light of Gutiérrez's claims concerning the two principal, overarching themes in Scripture, the experience of impasse thus affirms the intrinsic connection between these themes (i.e., between contemplation and action). In so doing, FitzGerald's concept of impasse brings to the fore the fundamentally *theological* character of the preferential option for the poor; in her words, "Impasse is a challenge to feminists [and all social activists] to be mystics."[24] It is precisely in the dark night of failed struggles for social justice in solidarity with the poor that we discover our deepest solidarity with the poor, as creatures kneeling before our Creator. Only when we ourselves "have no other option" can we even begin to identify with those millions of other women, men, and children for whom having no other option but to hope against all hope, to stand powerlessly before the God who alone empowers and liberates, is simply their daily bread. And only then can we begin to truly opt for the poor, because we can now begin to worship *their* God, the only God who will not be constrained by our expectations and presuppositions. We can begin to opt for the poor because the experience of impasse confronts us with the reality that *we* are not opting at all; *God* is opting and we have

23. Ibid., 110–12.
24. Ibid., 111.

no choice but to go along. Impasse thus strips us of the illusion that the preferential option for the poor is simply an ethical consequence of faith; it is, instead, an epistemological *precondition* of faith. It is then that we can begin to "live without a why."

The experience of impasse reveals the privileged social location of the outsider as the place where true solidarity is born, the place where we *all* identify with Job as he cries out to a silent God and with Jesus in his cry of abandonment on the cross. Yet impasse is also the place where Job's question, "Where are you, Lord?" is turned on its head by the divine query, "Where were you, Job?" Impasse is the place where Jesus' question, "Why have you abandoned me?" is answered by the angel's question to the women at the tomb, "Why do you seek the living among the dead?"

By literally changing the subject (from ourselves and our questions to God and God's questions), the experience of impasse unmasks the subtle temptation to turn our option for the poor itself into an idol.[25] Only when confronted by the sheer gratuity of divine love and, therefore, of creation can we avoid that temptation. Impasse strips us of our idols, including that of the "preferential option for the poor" itself. More precisely, in impasse the option for the poor finds its true roots in God's own option for the poor; it is no longer ours but God's. Finally, then, we are liberated to enter into solidarity with the outcasts, not out of duty, but out of gratitude. In impasse we discover our common powerlessness as the source of true empowerment, rooted in an encounter with a divine love that is universal and gratuitous. Through her extraordinary work in developing the notion of impasse, FitzGerald thus articulates the intrinsic relationship between God's preferential love for the poor and the utterly gratuitous, universal character of divine love.

25. See note 3 above for Gutiérrez's warning against the danger of idolizing even social justice.

9

Impasse and Climate Crisis

A Contemplative View

Margaret R. Pfeil

Writing in 2000, Connie FitzGerald reflected on her seminal 1984 essay, "Impasse and Dark Night," in which she extended John of the Cross's insights about the dark night to consider societal manifestations of impasse. She perceived a twofold experience of darkness "in our indissoluble connection or solidarity with the poor and marginalized, and in our own personal and societal failures."[1] Hubris lay at the root of this dual darkness, cutting off humans from our relationship, as subjects, with God and all other members of creation.

At the dawn of the new millennium, she mused, "I often feel that only if we are prepared for transformation by contemplation and thereby given a new kind of consciousness and imagination will humanity and the earth, with its various ecosystems,

1. Constance FitzGerald, "The Desire for God and the Transformative Power of Contemplation," in *Light Burdens, Heavy Blessings*, ed. Mary Heather MacKinnon, Moni McIntyre, and Mary Ellen Sheehan (Quincy, IL: Franciscan Press, 2000), 201–22 at 203.

survive."[2] Now twenty years later, FitzGerald's call for education in contemplative awareness as a spiritual discipline carries even greater urgency. Technologically driven human alienation has deepened, yielding the paradox of energy-intensive cultures of consumption persisting unabashedly even as the continent of Australia burns and low-lying homelands disappear into the sea.

FitzGerald's work points to the transformative potential of understanding anthropogenic climate crisis as planetary impasse. I wonder what it might mean to stand "with the Creator of the Universe who awaits us in the future and calls us to completion by the desire, the dream, implanted not only within human *being*, but also within the earth and all its species as an organic whole."[3]

By holding narrative accounts of contemplative responses to climate collapse in conversation with FitzGerald's commentaries on dark contemplation in the work of John of the Cross, the outlines of contemplative ecological education emerge: humble listening for God's desire expressed in and through all creation opens a path of liberation from the destructive grip of human hubris. FitzGerald shows the transformative power of Holy Wisdom quickening contemplative awareness and revealing the alternative vision available through Sophia's gifts, enabling humans to share humbly in God's infinite love of all creation.

Anthropogenic Climate Crisis: Signs of the Times

In "Impasse and Dark Night," FitzGerald asked, "What if by chance, our time in evolution is a dark-night time—a time of crisis and transition that must be understood if it is to be part of learning a new vision and harmony for the human species and the planet?"[4] She illuminated the *kind* of understanding emerging in dark contemplation, an evolution in consciousness beyond human rational capacities.

2. Ibid., 210.

3. Ibid., 220, emphasis in the original.

4. Constance FitzGerald, "Impasse and Dark Night," in *Living with Apocalypse: Spiritual Resources for Social Compassion*, ed. Tilden H. Edwards (San Francisco: Harper & Row, Publishers, 1984), 93–116, at 94.

"The external deserts in the world are growing, because the internal deserts have become so vast," Pope Francis writes in *Laudato Sì*.[5] The cry of the earth and the cry of the poor are one, and it is a cry within each of us. FitzGerald's work establishes the essential relationship between the inward roots of the climate crisis and its outward fruits manifested in the devastation of societies, cultures, human interrelationship, ecosystems, and the integrity of planet Earth.

> Today the whole world cries out with the desire of the mystics, "Where have you hidden and left me to my moaning?" . . . All cry out. Even the scarred earth itself cries out and rages against the devastation. Creation groans with its desire and its dream. . . . It is a cry for recognition of the connectedness of everything in the cosmos, and consequently, a desire for contemplation and transformation. . . . This universal cry is what makes contemplation different today. *The cry is within us.* My own personal cry is overcome by, engulfed in, the cry of the earth, and it is within me.[6]

The impasse of climate crisis becomes manifest in pervasive, systemic destruction and loss, impacting everything that supports life on planet Earth. "Five-hundred-year" floods occurring annually, all-consuming wildfires, intensifying hurricanes, and submerged homelands belie self-deceptive denial of climate emergency. Earth itself bears the wounds of impasse even as its human inhabitants cling to habits that accelerate global warming, speeding the death of all living things, as if all creation were not connected. Having lost a sense of our own creaturely subjectivity before God, humans fail to mourn the loss of life outside illusory bounds of self-interest.

5. Pope Francis, *Laudato Sì* (Encyclical Letter, 2015), paragraph 217, available at http://w2.vatican.va/content/francesco/en/encyclicals/documents/papa-francesco_20150524_enciclica-laudato-si.html, citing Benedict XVI, "Homily for the Solemn Inauguration of the Petrine Ministry" (April 24, 2005), AAS 97 (2005): 710. All references to *Laudato Sì* (LS) will use the relevant paragraph number and will be taken from this source.

6. FitzGerald, "Desire for God," 208–9, emphasis added.

Indigenous peoples, comprising less than 5 percent of the world's population, historically have contributed the least to climate change but are among those most affected by its consequences. They are disproportionately represented among the world's most marginalized, with few material resources to address the climate crisis.[7]

The Biloxi-Chitimacha-Choctaw indigenous people of Isle de Jean Charles, Louisiana, are recognized as the first climate refugees of the United States, grappling with the reality of relocation as their homeland steadily disappears into the sea. Likewise, the indigenous people of the Carteret Islands of Papua, New Guinea, are considered the world's first climate refugees. With global seas predicted to rise on average between .6 and 1.9 meters by the end of this century, the 2,700 inhabitants have already experienced the accompanying effects—from storm surge flooding, to salinization of their soil, to coastal erosion on these seven atolls with a maximum elevation of just 1.2 meters above sea level. Their land is expected to be uninhabitable by 2040.

Dynamics of Dark Night and Climate Impasse

The experiences of the Carteret Islanders and the Biloxi-Chitimacha-Choctaw people portend the climate impasse facing all inhabitants of Earth. FitzGerald's exploration of the dark night yields valuable insight into the contemplative process of educating human desire accordingly. At the point of impasse, FitzGerald observes, Sophia Wisdom's gifts of faith, hope, and love offer the soul profound liberation precisely as every aspect of one's life and prayer rebels against it. "Yet the only way the deprivation of the dark night will open into a radical change of consciousness and affectivity is by the

7. "Indigenous Peoples Disproportionately Impacted by Climate Change, Systematically Targeted for Defending Freedoms, Speakers Tell Permanent Forum," Economic and Social Council, Permanent Forum on Indigenous Issues, Seventeenth Session, Fifth and Sixth meetings, April 18, 2018, available at https://www.un.org/press/en/2018/hr5389.doc.html.

acceptance of this contemplative posture or vision whereby one actually passes over to the love perspective of Divine Wisdom."[8]

In the current climate crisis, the lack of mutuality between humans and the rest of God's creation in giving and receiving God's love characterizes the heart of the collective impasse. In her fine book, *Braiding Sweetgrass*, Robin Wall Kimmerer, a member of the Citizen Potawatomi Nation, recounts an exchange with her graduate students in a field biology course at the State University of New York. She invited them to articulate what they appreciate about nature, and they had much to say, at least initially.

> They professed without reservation that they loved the earth. And then I asked them, "Do you think that the earth loves you back?" No one was willing to answer that. It was as if I had brought a two-headed porcupine into the classroom. Unexpected. Prickly. They backed slowly away. Here was a room full of writers, passionately wallowing in unrequited love of nature.
>
> So I made it hypothetical and asked, "What do you suppose would happen if people believed this crazy notion that the earth loved them back?" The floodgates opened. They all wanted to talk at once. We were suddenly off the deep end, heading for world peace and perfect harmony.
>
> One student summed it up: "You wouldn't harm what gives you love."
>
> Knowing that you love the earth changes you, activates you to defend and protect and celebrate. But when you feel that the earth loves you in return, that feeling transforms the relationship from a one-way street into a sacred bond.[9]

8. Constance FitzGerald, "Transformation in Wisdom," in *Carmel and Contemplation: Transforming Human Consciousness*, ed. Kevin Culligan and Regis Jordan (Washington, DC: ICS Publications, 2000), 281–358, at 322; see John of the Cross, *The Ascent of Mount Carmel* 2.6.6 and *The Dark Night* 2.21.11-12 in *The Collected Works of John of the Cross*, trans. Kieran Cavanaugh and Otilio Rodriguez, rev. ed. (Washington, DC: ICS Publications, 1991). All references to the works of John of the Cross will be taken from this source.

9. Robin Wall Kimmerer, *Braiding Sweetgrass: Indigenous Wisdom, Scientific Knowledge, and the Teachings of Plants* (Minneapolis: Milkweed Editions, 2013), 124–25.

Allowing the land to shape communal identity deepens contemplative awareness of humans' sacred, inseparable bond with all creation. Daniel Scheid has written potently of the cosmic common good, in which humans perceive ourselves as "participants in a cosmic evolutionary development, as embedded in webs of ecological dependencies, as members of the ecosystems in which [we] live, as citizens of a greater Earthly and cosmic commons, as siblings in a 'universal family.'"[10]

Facing into the climate crisis, it is precisely through allowing God's love to draw us into mutual love relationships with all other members of God's creation that humans can grow authentically into who we were created to be—interdependent, vulnerable to the wounds of God's love, and responsive to the needs of the cosmic common good. To realize that we would not harm what gives us love, human self-interest requires purification. "For where there is true love of God," John of the Cross writes, "love of self and of one's own things finds no entry."[11] By renouncing selfishness and allowing ourselves to be loved in return by the rest of God's creation, we might then resist harming what gives us love.

This path of surrender unfolds by way of humble contrition (cf. Ps 51). Understanding humility as central to ecological conversion, Pope Francis asks, "What need does the earth have of us?"[12] His question turns anthropocentrism on its head, signaling a paradigmatic shift in theological anthropology that recognizes the human need to learn from the rest of God's creation about the inexhaustible depth of God's love, not just for humanity, but finally and totally for *all creation*.

As an ecological virtue, humility grounds and deepens contemplative awareness. The state of humility, André Louf writes, is abasement, "the condition in which one finds oneself flatly on the ground."[13] It is precisely when we have been leveled, with hearts

10. Daniel P. Scheid, *The Cosmic Common Good: Religious Grounds for Ecological Ethics* (New York: Oxford University Press, 2016), 43.

11. *Dark Night* 2.21.

12. LS 160.

13. André Louf, "Introduction," in *The Way of Humility*, trans. Lawrence Cunningham (Kalamazoo, MI: Cistercian Publications, 2007), 3–24, at 10.

broken, that the grace of God's love can break through to draw us closer to God. Humility and humiliation meet, encouraging interior surrender, as happens in dark contemplation.

The first sign of the dark night, John writes, is that "since these souls do not get satisfaction or consolation from the things of God, they do not get any from creatures either. Since God puts a soul in this dark night in order to dry up and purge its sensory appetite, he does not allow it to find sweetness or delight in anything."[14] One experiences the failure of rational, discursive analysis and communication in prayer as well as in the rest of life. "One's usual way of functioning, or relating, provides no satisfaction and does not work."[15] Paradoxically, John points to this experience as a sign of faith at work, as "the excessive light of faith bestowed on a soul is darkness for it; a brighter light will eclipse and suppress a dimmer one."[16]

In the current climate crisis, faith runs up against the idolatrous grip of what *Laudato Sì* calls the technocratic paradigm, a totalizing illusion of unlimited economic growth, driven by technological progress.[17] Theologian Daniel Castillo has astutely noted the dangerous implication of development theories that assume growth without end: This view "presupposes that economic growth is *necessary* for meeting the needs of present and future. Therefore, priority is placed on sustaining economic growth versus sustaining the resiliency capacity of the planet."[18] Human hubris threatens the survival of all creation. "Once we lose our humility," Pope Francis writes, "and become enthralled with the possibility of limitless mastery over everything, we inevitably end up harming society and the environment."[19]

14. *Dark Night* 1.9.2.

15. FitzGerald, "Impasse and Dark Night," 99.

16. *Ascent* 2.3.1.

17. LS 106; cf. Gilbert Rist, *The History of Development: From Western Origins to Global Faith*, 3rd ed. (New York: Zed, 2008).

18. Daniel Castillo, "Integral Ecology as a Liberationist Concept," *Theological Studies* 77, no. 2 (2016): 353–76 at 372–73, emphasis in the original.

19. LS 224. On the need for humble recognition of limits, see also paragraphs 11, 105, 177, 193, 204, 208, and 223.

Because creation is one, interconnected whole, the collective hubris of the technocratic paradigm affects all, even those members of the biotic community who have exercised no agency in creating it. "On the other side of all our technology," FitzGerald writes, "we have come to poverty and to dark night. We can find no escape from the world we have built, where the poor and oppressed cry out, where the earth and the environment cry out, and where the specter of nuclear waste already haunts future generations."[20]

These are signs of collective impasse. The technocratic paradigm, seen in the luminous darkness of faith, is collapsing along with Earth's climate, leaving humanity in contemplative unknowing:

> Thus, John explains, faith causes darkness in our very power to understand. Now it is at cross purposes with our ability to make *logical* sense out of life, death, and eternity, out of loss, rejection, and abandonment. Faith moves us into Mystery which is incomprehensible, unimaginable and uncontrollable. Only in some kind of searing loss, it seems, do we begin to know experientially that God is indeed *the* DARKNESS beyond all our concepts, images, experiences, feelings, and perceptions, and that, as John writes, no knowledge or feeling bears any resemblance to God.[21]

Anticipating the inevitability of losing the Carteret Islands to the sea, the government of Papua, New Guinea, organized two relocation efforts that failed due to lack of respect for indigenous participation in the planning process, a mistake emblematic of the technocratic paradigm.[22] "How much easier it would be to

20. FitzGerald, "Impasse and Dark Night," 105.

21. Constance FitzGerald, "A Discipleship of Equals: Voices from Tradition—Teresa of Avila and John of the Cross," in *A Discipleship of Equals: Towards a Christian Feminist Spirituality*, ed. Francis A. Eigo (Villanova: Villanova University Press, 1988), 88, referring to *Ascent* 2.3, emphasis in the original; see also FitzGerald, "Transformation in Wisdom," 322–23, and "Desolation as Dark Night," *The Way Supplement* 82 (Spring 1995): 104–5.

22. United Nations Development Programme, "Tulele Peisa: Equator Initiative Case Studies," (New York: Equator Initiative, 2016), 6, available at https://www.equatorinitiative.org/wp-content/uploads/2017/05/case_1473429470

bear the darkness were one not conscious of one's failures and mistakes," FitzGerald acknowledges. "The most confusing and damnable part of the dark night is the suspicion and fear that much of the darkness is of one's own making."[23]

Humble abasement before the devastating climate crisis carries with it an opportunity to hear Sophia Wisdom's invitation to interior surrender, and that entails further purification.[24] John's second sign of the dark night involves a profound sense of emptiness and dryness pervading one's whole life.[25] "Hope empties and withdraws the memory from all creature possessions, for as St. Paul says, hope is for that which is not possessed [Rom 8:24]. It withdraws the memory from what can be possessed and fixes it on what it hopes for."[26] FitzGerald highlights the searing purification of this dark night experience:

> When memory is "de-constructed" in the dark night, the past can no longer weave its thread of meaning through the person's lived experience into the future. . . . [T]he certainties on which we have built our lives are seriously undermined or taken away—not only in prayer, but also in and by life, and a profound disorientation results. . . . On a very fundamental level our selfhood—who we are—is threatened . . . leaving a person undone, silenced.[27]

Watching their lands and identity as a people gradually succumb to the sea as a direct result of the climate crisis not of their making, some of the Carteret Islanders have given voice to the isolation of impasse. "Abandoning one's land and thus the ancestors is a traumatic experience. Chief Paul Maeka from Han island in the Carterets explains: 'The hardest thing will be to lose our

---

.pdf; Volker Boege and Ursula Rakova, "Climate Change–Induced Relocation: Problems and Achievements—The Carterets Case," Toda Peace Institute, Policy Brief No. 33 (February 2019), 1–18, at 12.

23. FitzGerald, "Impasse and Dark Night," 103.

24. *Dark Night* 1.9.3.

25. FitzGerald, "Impasse and Dark Night," 101.

26. *Dark Night* 2.21.11.

27. Constance FitzGerald, "From Impasse to Prophetic Hope: Crisis of Memory," *CTSA Proceedings* 64 (2009): 21–42, at 23–24, referring to *Dark Night* 2.9.5; 2.9.7.

sacred places, our tambu places.' This is why there are still some people who do not want to leave, and why some people who do move suffer from mental health problems."[28] As a matrilineal culture, land transfers from mother to daughter among the Carteret people, and so the climate crisis impacts the women of the community in particular. Forced to seek out other lands and negotiate for their very survival, words cannot convey the meaning of their collective memory, a way of life woven inextricably with the land, sea, and surrounding biotic community.[29]

Though more than two dozen film crews have documented their plight, the Carteret Islanders have been left to devise their own relocation plan, with only modest support from nongovernmental and ecclesial organizations.[30] Ursula Rakova, leader of the Carteret people's relocation efforts, honestly names the impasse at hand: Watching their land disappear into the sea, they are paying the ultimate price for others' reckless destruction of Earth.

In such an experience of impasse, FitzGerald writes, "Any hope for new consciousness and a self-forfeiture driven by love stands opposed by a harsh reality: we humans serve our own interests, we hoard resources, we ravage the earth and other species."[31] Still, dark contemplation entails perseverance in hope as the deconstruction of memory and meaning gradually effects interior purification. God's love frees the person for more expansive reception of God: Love. It is the very limit situation of the dark night that offers ground for hope, which "can come into play only when we really are radically at the end, absolutely unable to find any further resources within ourselves to connect the memories, feelings, images, and experiences of life into a meaningful pattern or a promising future."[32]

Following Beverly Lanzetta's account of the purification of memory in the *via feminina*, FitzGerald relates the gradual deconstruction of body memory, social constraints, and past harms to

28. Boege and Rakova, "Climate Change–Induced Relocation," 8.
29. Cf. UN Development Programme, "Tulele Peisa."
30. Boege and Rakova, "Climate Change–Induced Relocation," 9.
31. FitzGerald, "From Impasse to Prophetic Hope," 37–38.
32. FitzGerald, "Discipleship of Equals," 88.

John of the Cross's dark-night purification of memory, the "purifying embrace of intimate divine love effecting woman's radical unsaying of 'all the images, understandings, and memories that do not name her' or her God."[33] Into the interior space freed by unsaying, hope can speak in the still voice of God's Spirit.[34]

Unsaying evokes the power of hope as an ecological virtue: to the contemplative heart, all creation bears hopeful witness to the Spirit's irrepressible joy. Through interior emptying that joins Jesus' kenosis, the humbled human heart can open to the truth of interconnection.[35] Stripped of the illusion of merely individual wholeness, the one experiencing the purifying dark night of memory becomes aware of the integrity of all creation in God, a wholeness much greater than the sum of its parts.[36] John of the Cross writes in *The Spiritual Canticle*, "In contemplation God teaches the soul very quietly and secretly, without its knowing how, without the sound of words, and without the help of any bodily or spiritual faculty, in silence and quietude, in darkness to all sensory and natural things." This can be called "knowing by unknowing."[37]

Ecologically, the process of unknowing passes by way of detachment, being stripped down to discover simplicity: Holding together the virtues of poverty and humility, St. Francis was thus freed to sing of the Sun, his brother, and the Moon, his sister, and all his relations.[38] His contemplative practice offers a hopeful guide for communal action in the current climate crisis. The throwaway culture, rooted in lustful and idolatrous desire to possess infinitely, can find transformation in the kenotic emptying of Jesus and dark night purification buoyed by hope: "When the

33. FitzGerald, "From Impasse to Prophetic Hope," 28.

34. Cf. LS 85.

35. FitzGerald, "From Impasse to Prophetic Hope," 29.

36. Cf. LS 141 and *Evangelii Gaudium* 237.

37. *The Spiritual Canticle* 39.12. See also Mary Frohlich, "Under the Sign of Jonah: Studying Spirituality in a Time of Ecosystemic Crisis," *Spiritus* 9, no. 1 (Spring 2009): 27–45, at 37.

38. See "The Salutation of the Virtues" and "Canticle of Brother Sun," in *Francis and Clare: The Complete Works*, ed. Regis J. Armstrong (New York: Paulist Press, 1982).

emptiness of the memory on the level of affectivity and imagination becomes a deep void of yearning, it is hope that opens up the possibility of being possessed by the infinite, unimaginable, incomprehensible Mystery of love that is so close."[39] Hope shifts the interior landscape from a disposition of grasping possessively to one of surrender into the truth of God's love ultimately holding all. Instead of despair born of fullness of self, humble hope takes root in the purified emptiness wrought by God's love.[40] "The selfhood that is lost," says FitzGerald, "will never be regained and therein lies its hope."[41]

In the impasse of the climate crisis, the dispossession of the Carteret people of their lands, sacred places, and communal identity in relationship with the rest of the surrounding biotic community evokes the kenotic meaning of Jesus' crucifixion, utter humility against despair, as it confronts the idolatrous consumption of throwaway cultures. What invitation might collective impasse hold for a world in which some are dispossessed of everything *because* others live in wasteful superabundance?

The rhythm of the dark night finds ready manifestation in the dynamic energy of God's creation, where ecosystemic health is marked by the continual renewal of life through death and new birth. The dark night "mediates the transfiguration of affectivity, and obstacles conceal within themselves untold, hidden energy, . . . life buried in its opposite: life concealed, life invisible, life unseen in death."[42] What might Earth have to teach its human inhabitants? This is a companion question to Pope Francis's query, "What need does the Earth have of us?" Both questions, born of humility, speak to the purifying freedom of prophetic hope, enabling "a person to reveal the vision of a different kind of future than the one we want to construct from our limited capacities. Such a person becomes a prophet when she shows the way; when

39. FitzGerald, "From Impasse to Prophetic Hope," 31–32.

40. See Thomas Merton, "Humility against Despair," in *New Seeds of Contemplation* (New York: New Directions Books, 1961), 180–90.

41. FitzGerald, "From Impasse to Prophetic Hope," 31.

42. FitzGerald, "Impasse and Dark Night," 102.

she is willing to stand on the horizon so that all can see this future, God's future."[43]

Teresa Shiki, of the Shuar indigenous people in the western Amazon, engages in contemplative ecological education, passing on lessons in humble listening from her grandmother as an act of prophetic hope:

> [S]he learned to listen to plants, to hear what they offered to humans. *Every tree is a living person, with speech. . . . [Y]ou cannot listen to "one" tree; there is no one tree living alone. . . . [L]isten and live from within the tree, hold it close. Only with the tree's energy can we replenish our own spirits and have hope of survival. Only in wordless relationship to the tree can we receive this energy.*[44]

Shiki's prophetic witness resists a common temptation of impasse to succumb to hopelessness and abandonment of relational ties that once were anchoring, a third sign of the dark night.[45] FitzGerald emphasizes, however, that desire is not destroyed: "Rather, right in this situation of unassuaged emptiness and apparent deadness of desire, in the very area of life in which one is most involved and therefore most vulnerable, desire is being purified, transformed, and carried into deeper, more integrated passion."[46] On the other side of the death of one's previous understanding of life, hope, and God is a new interior freedom, a new vision of life in God. Precisely through what and who we love, God purifies and transforms the soul.[47]

Broken open, the heart and soul seek and encounter God's love in new ways and in the rest of creation. "[T]he true mystic," FitzGerald writes, "is enthralled by the diversity and beauty, the unfailing harmony and interconnectedness of the entire creation. All this is the work of Sophia ('the Word') by whom they were

43. FitzGerald, "From Impasse to Prophetic Hope," 35.

44. David George Haskell, *The Songs of Trees: Stories from Nature's Great Connectors* (New York: Penguin Books, 2017), 27, emphasis in the original.

45. *Dark Night* 1.9.8. See also *Ascent* 2.13.4.

46. FitzGerald, "Impasse and Dark Night," 102.

47. FitzGerald, "Discipleship of Equals," 84. See *Dark Night* 2.21.11.

created. Everyone and every living thing are clothed with the image of Sophia as we see in 'The Spiritual Canticle' poem where the lovesick bride questions the created world."[48] There, John of the Cross writes: "Where have You hidden, Beloved, and left me moaning? . . . O woods and thickets planted by the hand of my Beloved! O green meadow, coated, bright, with flowers, tell me, has he passed by you?"[49] In the very brokenness that compels the human soul to search for love, grace works to reveal God's love from within and in all.

John comments on *The Spiritual Canticle*, stanza 4: "Only the hand of God, her Beloved, was able to create this diversity and grandeur. . . . This reflection on creatures, this observing that they are things made by the very hand of God, her Beloved, strongly awakens the soul to love [God]."[50] FitzGerald has embraced appreciatively the work of Hein Blommestijn, Jos Huls, and Kees Waaijman as they explore the Franciscan undertone of this passage:

> [A]ll of created reality is put on display to bear witness to God's creative presence which has passed through them and left his tracks in them. By reflecting on the beauty and excellence of the creation we discover the hand of the Creator. We "see" him in the creatures who by their very existence witness to the creative love of "the Lover, God." By this splendid spectacle we humans, too, are moved to love.[51]

In *The Spiritual Canticle*, the soul looks for the Beloved among creation. Seeking "that invisible beauty which caused this visible beauty,"[52] and finding only a trace of the Beloved, she must turn inward, another aspect of the inner purification wrought by the Spirit. There within, the soul experiences God's love, an interior *beholding* in God's desire that sparks a new kind of conscious

48. FitzGerald, "Transformation in Wisdom," 293.

49. *Spiritual Canticle* 1 and 4.

50. *Spiritual Canticle Commentary* 4.3.

51. Hein Blommestijn, Jos Huls, and Kees Waaijman, *The Footprints of Love: John of the Cross as Guide in the Wilderness*, trans. John Vriend (Leuven: Peeters, 2000), 137.

52. *Spiritual Canticle Commentary* 6.1.

participation in God's beholding of *all* life, desiring its flourishing with God's desire. "From within this mystical experience we discover the face of God in the whole creation. . . . In the goodness and beauty of creation the 'wisdom' and love of the Creator lights up."[53] Tenderly beheld by and beholding all in God's love, the contemplative desires to cooperate with God's creative healing of the earth instead of harming it.

David George Haskell recounts that tropical biologists working in the Yasuní Biosphere Reserve have recently begun exploring the tree crowns, where they have discovered that an estimated half of the known species live exclusively.[54] "Species unknown to and undescribed by Western science are all around. . . . This forest is the place where biological hubris dies: we live in profound ignorance of the lives of our cousins."[55] Contemplative humans come to know these other living beings relationally, part of one whole in which all life shares. The indigenous Waorani living in the Yasuní decline to give individual names to other members of the biotic community. Rather, they describe plants and trees in relation to their surrounding ecological context.[56] Theirs is an understanding rooted in interrelationship as subjects, not objects.

In and through all of God's creation Sophia Wisdom draws humanity to God. John of the Cross identifies the consummation of the journey through the dark night as *"union with Divine Wisdom."*[57] In an essay published in 2000, FitzGerald described her own process of coming to insight:

> Initially, when I hinted at the subversive character of Sophia, it was because I thought transformation in Wisdom radically changed desire, consciousness, and ultimately, behavior, personal and societal. Now, I realize the experience of Sophia may be subversive, above all, because it affects how we understand the very

53. Blommestijn, Huls, and Waaijman, *The Footprints of Love*, 137–38.
54. Haskell, *The Songs of Trees*, 9.
55. Ibid., 10.
56. Ibid., 15.
57. FitzGerald, "Transformation in Wisdom," 288, emphasis in the original; cf. *Ascent*, 1.2.4.

> nature of God, and our understanding of God is what affects the character and quality of our human living.[58]

When Wall Kimmerer invited her students to consider what it might mean to let the Earth and its inhabitants love them mutually, as subjects, it was an invitation to the decentering and unsaying that mark humility, a prompt to listen to the subtle signs of Sophia in the rhythms of creation, to learn about the Beloved and to be transformed as lovers. "Sophia is secret; she dwells in secret and has an affinity for darkness. . . . Sophia is loving knowledge of God, both the teacher and what is learned. Sophia is on the side of continual learning."[59] As humans seek to discover as much as possible about a beloved person when falling in love, Sophia Wisdom opens space in the heart so that humans can come to know God's creation as revelatory, drawing us in and through what and who we love, into Love, God. In this way, FitzGerald indicates, Sophia educates human desire over the course of the soul's journey, effecting "a gradual transference of desire to Jesus Christ, the Beloved!"[60]

The human learning required in the Anthropocene both springs from and nurtures the mutual love relationship of all members of creation. The collective impasse of climate change presents humanity with an opportunity to move through and past self-knowledge to the necessary implication of creaturely interdependence: reciprocity in love with all God's creation. "The deepening presence of Holy Wisdom pervading one's whole life and environment gradually educates desire and in that process eventually fulfills it."[61]

Sophia's secret, silent music resounds in all creation, John sings in *The Spiritual Canticle*:

> My Beloved, the mountains,
> and lonely wooded valleys,
> strange islands,
> and resounding rivers,

58. FitzGerald, "Transformation in Wisdom," 284.
59. Ibid., 288.
60. Ibid., 291.
61. Ibid., 292.

the whistling of love-stirring breezes,

the tranquil night
at the time of the rising dawn,
silent music,
sounding solitude,
the supper that refreshes, deepens love.[62]

Commenting synthetically, FitzGerald offers this insight: "[I]n the last part of both *The Spiritual Canticle* and *The Living Flame*, one of the astounding graces of transformation in wisdom, or union with the divine, is that one actually *experiences* the harmony, mutuality, and diversity of all creation *moving in God* in a unified, interdependent connectedness and enjoys this as a mirror or image of Sophia-God."[63] In the process, John writes, all members of creation become "for the soul a harmonious symphony of sublime music surpassing all concerts and melodies of the world."[64]

The contemplative holds all the joy and pain of that symphony together as one whole. Awakened, the soul transformed in Sophia Wisdom desires to go "deep into the thicket" with Jesus crucified:

> [I]t will be a singular comfort and happiness for her to enter all the afflictions and trials of the world and everything, however difficult and painful, that might be a means to this knowledge, even the anguish and agony of death, all in order to see herself further within her God. . . . Suffering is the means of her penetrating further, deep into the thicket of the delectable wisdom of God.[65]

In the interconnectedness of God's creation, as in Jesus' cross, suffering and joy meet. In the experience of awakening, FitzGerald writes, "one *sees and knows* it is a delusion to perceive ourselves as separate from the earth, from one another, and from all other species of life, superior and unaccountable to the earth and other forms of life. The vision of Divine Sophia enables contemplative

62. *Spiritual Canticle* 14 and 15.

63. FitzGerald, "Transformation in Wisdom," 297, commenting on *Spiritual Canticle Commentary* 14, 15.10, and 25; 36.6-7; 39.11; *Living Flame of Love* 4.4-7, emphasis in the original. See also "Desire for God," 219.

64. *Spiritual Canticle Commentary* 14 and 15.25.

65. *Spiritual Canticle* 36.11-12; cf. *Living Flame of Love* 4.

people to be keepers of the earth and of beauty because they experience the connectedness of it all in *the* Beauty."[66] Likewise, the vulnerability and suffering of Earth and all our relations, understood contemplatively, become part of one's experience of God, suffering Sophia, Jesus crucified.

The Carteret Islanders, following the wisdom of their Council of Elders, ultimately rejected the government's relocation plans and formed their own nonprofit, Tulele Peisa, which means "sailing the waves on our own" in the Halia language. Seeking creative approaches to relocation, Tulele Peisa embraces the values of "active promotion of community self-reliance, environmental awareness and sustainability, and cultural survival."[67] With little financial support and significant governmental obstacles, they built an indigenous climate response plan that received the United Nations Development Programme's 2014 Equator Prize.

Ursula Rakova, executive director of Tulele Peisa, faces into the climate impasse: "I love my islands, we live by the sea and they provide for us every day, but we have to move now."[68] Going deep into the thicket, she is well aware that while her community is suffering the first and most drastic effects of the climate crisis, this reality encompasses the whole, interconnected planet, all our relations.

Conclusion

FitzGerald's realization that Sophia Wisdom subverts and transforms human understanding of God in a life-changing way provides an important hermeneutical key in relating the dark night experience to the collective impasse of climate crisis. In and through Sophia Wisdom, each and every member of creation

66. FitzGerald, "Transformation in Wisdom," 337, emphasis in the original.

67. UN Development Programme, "Tulele Peisa," 6.

68. Mark Bowling, " 'We Have to Move Now,' Islanders Watch as Their Home Disappears into the Sea," *Catholic Leader* (April 20, 2016), available at http://catholicleader.com.au/news/we-have-to-move-now-islanders-watch-as-their-home-disappears-in-the-sea.

becomes revelatory of God's infinite love. Each is a subject, loved by God and made for interrelationship.

Learning to listen for the still voice of Sophia Wisdom through the dark night experience, contemplatives may discover in the climate crisis an opportunity to go deep into the thicket. Humbled, stripped, and interiorly freed, those drawn in contemplative prayer become available to cooperate with Jesus' Spirit in the creative, communal, and relational work of transformation, beginning where our relations are most vulnerable and surrendering to God's gentle beholding of all in love.

10

Transformation in Wisdom

The Subversive Character and Educative Power of Sophia in Contemplation

Constance Fitzgerald, OCD

Introduction

We need a spirituality for our time, an in-between time some have called it. Who is the God who will accompany us, if as some suggest there looms on the horizon for the inhabitants of this earth an era demanding a change of consciousness more radical than we can imagine?[1] Or what kind of spirituality will address our

1. For example, Brian Swimme, a mathematical cosmologist, and Thomas Berry, a historian of cultures, suggest that we stand between two great eras: "the Cenozoic era" which began sixty-seven million years ago and is now in its terminal phase due to a distorted aspect of the myth of progress, and "the Ecozoic era" whose central commitment believes "that the universe is a communion of subjects rather than a collection of objects" (*The Universe Story* [San Francisco: Harper, 1992], 241–43). Cultural theorist, Rene Girard, according to Gil Bailie, writes in terms of "the disintegration of conventional culture, a process that is irreversible and one that constitutes humanity's moment of truth. . . . Coming to grips with the depths of the crisis (the greatest anthropological challenge in history precipitating a major epochal shift) is a daunting task, but it is also one that is full of promise, and the price to be paid for shrinking from it is too

experience if, indeed, the tremendous emergence of the feminine in culture, visible in so many different ways, truly heralds the end of the fundamental masculine dominance of the "Western mind," as Richard Tarnas proposes.[2] Some suggest that it is at great transitions such as this, when there are such insoluble problems, such a radical breakdown of structures, and so many confusing questions, that a new religious tradition rises up.[3]

Must we begin again then or can we build a new conceptual house for faith by gathering up what Ray Hart calls "the debris" around us and using it to make something new?[4] More precisely, are the traditions and language of mysticism, muted and suspect in the public life for centuries and yet coming to life again in our time, capable of giving radical direction to our search for a meaningful God and a new way of living in the universe?[5] Can the

---

horrendous to seriously contemplate" (*Violence Unveiled* [New York: Crossroad, 1995], 5, 13).

2. Richard Tarnas, *The Passion of the Western Mind* (New York: Harmony Books, 1991), 441. Tarnas sees this masculine dominance as beginning "four millennia ago with the great patriarchal nomadic conquests in Greece and the Levant over ancient matriarchal cultures, and [being] visible in the West's patriarchal religion from Judaism, its rationalist philosophy from Greece, its objectivist science from modern Europe."

3. Swimme and Berry, 255.

4. Ray L. Hart, *Unfinished Man and the Imagination* (New York: The Seabury Press, 1968), 26–36.

5. We need to understand the history that makes us the inheritors of a long period of what historian Joseph Chinnici, calls "muted mysticism." When the sixteenth- and seventeenth-century debates over the role of mystical prayer in the context of the early modern Church and state finally culminated in the condemnation of quietism in 1699, the language of mysticism and the whole tradition of contemplative prayer were muffled and privatized. In these debates carried on in Spain, England, France and Italy, as political and social as they were religious, some questioned the advisability of mystical prayer for the common, unlearned people, particularly women. They feared the influence of interior inspiration on the obedience of the people and the effect of trust in experience and personal discernment on the order of the prevailing system, civil and ecclesiastical. "Feared by authority in both Church and state, confined by 'reason' to the cell of the 'irrational,' and removed from the marketplace by the forces of capitalism, mysticism after 1700 lost its place in the communal consciousness. Now cloistered, contemplative prayer ceased to be available to all, and the highest reaches of

mystical or contemplative tradition, specifically the teaching of a sixteenth century *man*, John of the Cross, ground us in our passage from one age to another and deal with our questions about God, about the Earth and about the Universe? The experience of the western mystics is, undoubtedly, confined in part by the language and culture of western civilization and particularly of their own specific time in history. But if we decode their contemplative teaching, will it point us into the future and push us to envision and even experience a new mysticism, truly new and appropriate to our time and yet in continuity with our past?[6]

If, as I continue to believe, mystics live on the frontiers of human consciousness and address us from the farthest edges of the human spirit, we should not be surprised to find in the mysticism of John of the Cross some extremely important and yet hitherto undecoded clues about a God-image capable of supporting our crossing into a new era of life on our planet earth. This raises the specific question of whether the teaching of John of the Cross, which delineates with such clarity the critical, central function of "Divine Wisdom" in human transformation and communion with God, validates and even enlarges upon the extensive

---

holiness eluded the aspirations of the baptized. Now privatized, contemplation lost its connection with political and social change; its practitioners became irrelevant. It is this history, also, which we inherit, and the mutation of our true mystical tradition accounts in large measure for the contemporary groping for a stable spiritual center" (Joseph Chinnici, "The Politics of Mysticism, Church State and the Carmelite Tradition," delivered during the Bicentennial Symposium of Baltimore Carmel: *Contemplation and American Culture,* Baltimore, 1990).

6. I am conscious of how "the master narratives" of Western culture and theology are, as Elisabeth Schüssler Fiorenza believes, "always implicated in and collude with the production and maintenance of systems of knowledge that either foster exploitation and oppression or contribute to a praxis and vision of liberation." Furthermore, I am specifically aware of how some interpretations of John of the Cross' works have contributed to oppression and isolation and I have no wish to surrender to what Schüssler Fiorenza calls "a hermeneutics of undiscriminating acceptance of. . . tradition" in this study (*Jesus: Miriam's Child, Sophia's Prophet* [New York: Continuum, 1994], 5, 12). However, I do continue to ask if the tradition of mysticism as we find it in John of the Cross (and other mystics) can function for the liberation and transformation of people.

research and theological investigations of feminist thinkers and theologians regarding the feminine God gestalt, Sophia?

These questions and assumptions motivate this study of Wisdom in John of the Cross, which will examine, first of all, the transformation of the person in Wisdom (Sophia), a transformation of human desire and consciousness that is in its unfolding a process of education for contemplation; second, the subversive and therefore emancipatory character of the experience of Sophia in contemplation; third, what this experience and process of transformation suggests regarding the feminine God-image Sophia; fourth, what implications this has regarding education for contemplation.[7] Furthermore, because the members of the Carmelite Forum have been attempting to guide students in reading and interpreting the classic Carmelite texts, I will attempt to include in this interpretation of John of the Cross actual texts from his writings as an integral part of this article in the hope that these texts will be educative rather than tedious and will not interrupt the flow of my thought. It is my desire that others will grasp and develop implications from this study of Divine Wisdom in John of the Cross, if indeed there are any implications of value to contemporary spirituality, which I am only able to hint at or may not even see.

I will frequently be using Sophia instead of Wisdom because feminists prefer the Greek *sophia* which is *chokmah* in Hebrew and *sapientia* in Latin—all feminine grammatical gender. This in itself is not significant since feminine grammatical gender cannot be equated with actual gender. Nevertheless, the biblical depiction of wisdom in pre-Christian Judaism is invariably female suggesting to us a person rather than a concept or an attribute. Biblical wisdom is treated, not as an it, but as a summoning "I": sister, mother, spouse, female beloved, teacher, chef and hostess, preacher, judge, liberator, establisher of justice and numerous other female roles.[8]

7. These areas may prove to be important for the emergence in spirituality of a new experiential cosmic gestalt.

8. See Elisabeth Schüssler Fiorenza, *In Memory of Her* (New York: Crossroad, 1983), 133; and *Jesus: Miriam's Child*, 135–39. In the latter treatment, Schüssler

Influenced by feminist scholars, I have been working for a number of years with wisdom in John of the Cross. As I have searched and analyzed his many wisdom texts and tried to interface them with contemporary studies and the tradition of wisdom in Jewish theology and in the Christian Scriptures,[9] I have discovered considerable potential for spirituality today.

I now find myself asking if possibly this *is the time*, the age, for Sophia: God experienced in feminine categories from the ground up. Until now the masculinity of the Western intellectual and spiritual tradition has been pervasive and fundamental as has been the masculinity of the Western man's [*sic*] God.[10] Perhaps in a time when this long dominant masculinity has become so apparent to us and when the feminine principle is welling up with such powerful energy, Sophia is a God image capable of moving with humanity into the next evolutionary era when the universe will be experienced not as a collection of objects for human use and mastery but rather as an intimate, interconnected and diverse communion of subjects.[11] If "the evolutionary imperative for the masculine is to see through and overcome its hubris and one-sidedness . . . [and] to choose [to transcend itself and] enter into a fundamentally new relationship of mutuality with the feminine

---

Fiorenza has an interesting development of the gender question. See also Elizabeth A. Johnson, *She Who Is* (New York: Crossroad, 1992), 87, whose lucid theological writing on Sophia has greatly inspired and influenced my own work with Sophia in John of the Cross. See also "Redeeming the Name of Christ," in *Freeing Theology*, ed. Catherine LaCugna (San Francisco: Harper, 1993) and Roland E. Murphy, *The Tree of Life: An Exploration of Wisdom Biblical Literature* (New York: Doubleday, 1990), 133–49, for a treatment of "Lady Wisdom." The endnotes and bibliographies in the works cited above provide evidence of the very extensive research available on Sophia.

9. I have decided, with considerable hesitation, to use *Christian Scriptures* for what we have traditionally called the New Testament. Some scholars also propose Christian Testament or Second Testament as possibilities. Because I realize New Testament is considered by some scholars to be offensive to Jews, I am making this change. However, my concern is that those who read this for spirituality and prayer may be unfamiliar with this discussion.

10. Tarnas, 441–45. When I am using or building on Tarnas' thought, I use his capitalization of "Western."

11. Swimme and Berry, 243.

in all its forms,"[12] then this embrace of the feminine may well reveal Sophia-God.[13]

This means the experience of Wisdom in transformation or contemplation according to John of the Cross is so subversive it could change the content of our theological discourse, as Elizabeth Johnson suggests in her groundbreaking, scholarly study, *She Who Is*. Initially, when I hinted at the subversive character of Sophia, it was because I thought transformation in Wisdom radically changed desire, consciousness and ultimately behavior, personal and societal. Now, I realize the experience of Sophia may be subversive, above all, because it affects how we understand the very nature of God and our understanding of God is what affects the character and quality of our human living.

For John of the Cross the experience of contemplative union reveals and supports an experience of God as Sophia. He moved in the milieu of Sophia-Wisdom from the beginning of *The Ascent of Mount Carmel* to the end of *The Living Flame of Love* and kept the tradition of Sophia alive, waiting there for our discovery. When the tradition of contemplation or mysticism was finally decisively muffled by the condemnation of quietism in 1699, ending two centuries of struggle and debate, so, perhaps, was the opportunity to develop this strong experience of Sophia.[14] In fact, the marginalizing of the language of mysticism has a symbolic affinity not only with the disparagement of Sophia but also with the marginalization of women and the neglect of the Spirit. Have no doubt that the muting of contemplation was/is directly related to the place of women in society, the role of conscience in religion and politics,

12. Tarnas, 444.

13. I realize the danger of this language since God is for John of the Cross and for us incomprehensible, beyond all our images and forms. Nevertheless, even the mystics express their ineffable experiences in images and the human person and theology will always symbolize God in some specific anthropomorphic image or images, which in turn affect human self-understanding.

14. Augustine Baker, *Sancta Sophia or Directions for the Prayer of Contemplation* (Douay: John Patte & Thomas Fievet, 1657), introductory letters and preface, give some feel for this debate. This volume is in the archives of the Carmelite Monastery, Baltimore.

the fear of direct inspiration by the Spirit, and the transformative and therefore seditious character of contemplative prayer.[15]

John of the Cross and Wisdom

To understand the contemporary significance of Sophia and attempt to interpret adequately the meaning of Wisdom in John of the Cross, one has to have some knowledge of the complex background and extensive research related to wisdom. In the light of contemporary scholarship, particularly feminist studies, one has to examine not only possible influences on John from pre-Christian Judaism and the Christian Scriptures, but also from early Church writers and the mystical tradition as it developed through the centuries with particular emphasis on Christology and Trinitarian theology. One cannot make even a cursory study of these ancient and contemporary sources without coming up with questions that both challenge and confuse the religious imagination.

Mindful of this very complex backdrop and aware of the limitations of my own knowledge, I will attempt to contribute to contemporary studies of Wisdom or Sophia by concentrating on John of the Cross. When one begins to examine his major writings, one is awed by the extent and significance of the presence of Sophia who appears absolutely fundamental to John's understanding and description of contemplative experience. Although at times wisdom seems to be either an attribute or even a gift of God, Wisdom is basically a way of naming and symbolizing God's very self. Wisdom is primarily "Divine Wisdom" and Divine Wisdom is identified with Jesus Christ, the Word, the Son of God. Moreover, the entire process of human transformation is seen in terms of Wisdom, as evidenced, for example, by John's description of "the subject of [the] stanzas" of the poem, *The Spiritual Canticle*, as "mystical Wisdom which comes through love" (C prologue, 2).[16]

15. Although I have realized for a long time the relationship between the cloistering of contemplation, the role of women and the seditious character of contemplative prayer, nevertheless, Joseph Chinnici has added new historical dimensions to this understanding.

16. Most references to John of the Cross are inserted in text. The abbreviations for his works are as follows: A=*The Ascent of Mount Carmel*, N=*The Dark Night*,

Pre-Christian Judaism

Many contemporary scholars believe that the development and biblical depiction of the figure of Sophia in Jewish wisdom theology was influenced by an extra-biblical figure of a female deity. While some endorse the Mesopotamian goddess Ishtar or the Canaanite goddess of love, Astarte, others prefer the Egyptian goddess Ma'at who represented law, order, and justice. More attractive to many scholars, however, is the theory that the figure of Jewish Sophia has been greatly influenced by the Hellenized form of the Egyptian goddess Isis. Personified Wisdom was the response of orthodox Judaism to the threat of the Isis cult which was experienced as a temptation to the Jews to doubt and even turn from their traditional faith. While defending monotheism, Jewish wisdom theology was not afraid of the goddess but rather transferred the characteristics of mighty Isis to the figure of personified Wisdom in a creative effort to counteract the influence of this popular deity. Using goddess language and imagery drawn from wider religious thought and worship, they presented Jewish worshippers with an attractive as possible alternative to the cult and philosophies prevalent in the ancient near East at the time.[17] Divine Sophia is therefore, according to Fiorenza, Israel's saving and gracious God "in the language and gestalt of the goddess." With the exception of Yahweh, Sophia was, Elizabeth Johnson concludes, the most carefully limned God-image in pre-Christian Judaism; far more common and extensive than Word, Spirit, Torah or Shekinah.[18]

C=*The Spiritual Canticle*, F=*The Living Flame of Love*, CW=*The Collected Works of John of the Cross*. Although I have made some changes in the text for inclusivity, most quotations are from Kieran Kavanaugh and Otilio Rodriguez, *The Collected Works of John of the Cross* (Washington, DC: ICS Publications, 1991). I have used italics in quotations for emphasis.

17. For further clarification and development, investigate Johnson, *She Who Is*, 92–93, and James Dunne, *Christology in the Making* (Philadelphia: Westminster Press, 1980), 170f. I draw closely on these writings. See Johnson above and "Jesus the Wisdom of God: A Biblical Basis for Non-Androcentric Christology," *Ephemerides Theologicae Lovaniensis* (December 1985): 269–71, and Schüssler Fiorenza, *Jesus: Miriam's Child*, 135–36, for a comparison of texts regarding Isis and Sophia.

18. Johnson, *She Who Is*, 87; "Jesus, the Wisdom of God," 264.

It would be helpful to bear this development in mind if we are threatened by talk about a Sophia-God. The Jews did not sacrifice their belief in a monotheistic God; they brought to the fore a feminine God/dess metaphor important for their age and used it to speak of the God of Israel![19]

Later, the writers of the Christian Scriptures took this very God-image, this figure of personified Wisdom, and applied it to Jesus to show his continuity with the God of Israel in a manner that influenced the whole development of the doctrine of the Incarnation. The way this figure of Wisdom appeared in the literature of pre-Christian Judaism affected Christology, tradition, and John of the Cross. The problem here is, of course, the intervening tradition and what sources regarding Sophia-Wisdom from this cumulative tradition were influential in John's education and study and ultimately in his contemplative experience and writings.[20]

John of the Cross and Sophia in the Old Testament[21]

While how much John or his contemporaries knew about the origins of personified Wisdom in Jewish thought and theology could be the subject of an historical study, an analysis of his major writings reveals the radical influence of the wisdom texts of the Old Testament in shaping not only his understanding of Sophia but also his expression of religious experience. Particularly important

19. Sandra Schneiders, "Feminist Spirituality," in *The New Dictionary of Catholic Spirituality*, ed. Michael Glazier (Collegeville, MN: Liturgical Press, 1988), 397–99, has a concise, lucid treatment of "The Rediscovery of the Goddess."

20. While I see it as a deficiency in this study, the limits of this article prevent me from dealing with any adequacy with the presence of Sophia-Wisdom in the development of spirituality from the time of the early Church up to sixteenth century Spain, but future study in this area is important for a more comprehensive understanding of John's use of Divine Wisdom.

21. I am using Old Testament for the first testament of the Christian Bible especially since the book of Wisdom is not part of the *Jewish Scriptures*, the Jewish Bible as it is used today among Jews. For a good explanation, see Sandra M. Schneiders, *The Revelatory Text* (San Francisco: Harper, 1991), 6. Besides, "Old" need not mean superseded but rather revered, venerable and valuable.

in John's writings for defining who Sophia is and what she does are the books of Proverbs (chap. 8) and Wisdom (chaps. 7–9), and to some extent Sirach, to which he repeatedly returns throughout his three major works.[22] From these sources the specific view of Wisdom we find in these texts arises. To summarize very briefly:

1. Sophia has a divine origin, that is, Sophia is the spotless mirror of the power of God, the image of God's goodness, the brightness of the eternal light.
2. Sophia has a unique role in creation. God creates through Sophia.
3. Sophia moves and re-creates, more active than all active things, touching, enlivening, penetrating and energizing everywhere. The touch of Wisdom is important.
4. Sophia calls to all to come to her, to choose her.
5. Sophia dwells on the earth and delights to be with humankind in the world making them friends of God.
6. Sophia works gently, with order and harmony, taking account of created capacity and progressive development.
7. Sophia is secret; she dwells in secret and has an affinity for darkness.
8. Sophia eats at a common table with humankind in this world: "Come eat my bread and drink the wine I have mixed for you."
9. Sophia is loving, nurturing and compassionate. Sophia is, in fact, a Lover: "My Beloved to Me . . . "
10. Sophia is loving knowledge of God, both teacher and what is learned. Sophia is on the side of continual learning.

22. Not only Proverbs chap. 8 and Wisdom chaps. 7–9, but also Wisdom 6:13-15; 8:1 & 31; 18:14-15; Baruch 3:23, 31; Ecclesiasticus 51:25 & 29; Song of Songs; Psalm 76:19-20; Job 37:16; Genesis 1:31 are used by John of the Cross in a wisdom context.

Out of his own distinctive configuration of Jewish wisdom literature, which one would expect research in John of the Cross' writings to refine and make more precise over time, emerge some of the most basic principles of his teaching. It fashions an understanding of *who Jesus is*, who God is and how this God functions in the dynamic of human purification and transformation. It suggests the place of Sophia in human suffering and hints at how the beloved of Sophia sees the world and functions in it. I want to tease apart this configuration in what follows though not necessarily in the order I have enumerated them.

Sophia Dwells on Earth and Calls to All to Desire Her and Come to Her

John begins *The Ascent of Mount Carmel* by describing the journey to God as a dark night and the completion or goal of that journey through the darkness as *union with Divine Wisdom*:

> When this third night (God's communication to the spirit . . .) has passed, a union with the bride, who is the Sophia of God, then follows. (A 1.2.3)[23]

In actuality, Divine Sophia figures prominently throughout the first book of *The Ascent*. She takes her stand on the heights, along the highways of this world, at the very crossroads of the human enterprise, calling to the path of transformation and communion the children of this earth. She highlights human desire and pities those whose primary focus of desire and meaning is askew. She challenges those who are unfree, consumed by the possessive desire for what can never completely satisfy. She calls them "little ones" because they become as small as that which they crave, while the lasting affection and reassurance they unconsciously search for in their choices are present and available in Sophia. Therefore, Sophia says, desire me.

23. There is an interesting gender change in this passage in the revised 1991 translation of *The Complete Works of John of the Cross* where Kieran Kavanaugh equates *bride* rather than bridegroom with divine Wisdom.

> O people, I cry to you, my voice is directed to all that live. Be attentive, little ones, to cunning and sagacity; and you ignorant, be careful. Listen, because I speak of great things. Riches and glory are mine, high riches and justice. The fruit you will find in me is better than gold and precious stones; and my generations . . . are better than choice silver. I walk along the paths of justice, in the midst of the paths of judgement, to enrich those who love me and fill their treasures completely [Prv. 8:4-6, 8-21]. (A 1.4.8)

It is important to note at this point that at the beginning of *The Ascent*, when John begins to set in place his core teaching on the education of human desire, he uses specifically *Sophia* texts, showing some of the same connections between the Sophia of the Old Testament and Sophia-Jesus in the Christian Scriptures that contemporary scholars are indicating.[24]

The presence of Jewish Sophia with humankind (Prv. 8:31; Wis. 24:1-12) provides the context for one of John's most basic and yet most misunderstood and difficult principles, one that appears to be at odds with his mystical experience of the harmonious presence of Sophia in all of creation. At first reading, the text seems to insist that only God is worthy of our desire and that this earth, people, human ability, human love are worthless, nothing. Yet, it must be carefully noted that it is *only in comparison with* Divine Wisdom that they pale into insignificance; *only when preferred* to Sophia do they become idols, addictive and obsessive in character.[25]

> Oh, if [people] but knew what a treasure of divine light this blindness caused by our affections and [desires] deprives them of . . . They must not rely on their sharp intellects or upon their gifts received from God as to believe that their attachments or

24. See for example, *Ascent* 1.7.3-4 in connection with *Ascent* 1.4.8 and 13.3-4.

25. "All creatures of heaven and earth are nothing when compared to God" or " . . . all the being of creatures compared to the infinite being of God is nothing and . . . therefore, anyone attached to creatures is nothing in the sight of God (A 1.4.3-4)." *Ascent* 1.4 is a pivotal chapter on this subject but *Ascent* 1.6-12 delineates the destructive effects of addictive desire which weaken, weary, torment, blind and defile.

> [desires] will not blind, darken, and cause them to grow gradually worse . . . Solomon [wise man] . . . Although in the beginning he was truly restrained, *this rush after his desires,* and failure to deny them gradually blinded and darkened his intellect so that finally *the powerful light of God's Wisdom was extinguished.* (A 1.8.6)

For John of the Cross desire has a central and defining role in our lives. He assumes first of all, that we are inescapably driven and motivated by our desires; secondly, if our desires are addictive and unfree, they weaken, weary, torment, blind and demean us; and thirdly, the desire for Divine Wisdom (who is Jesus Christ) has to become greater than the desire for everyone and everything else that gives us pleasure.

> A love of pleasure, and attachment to it, usually fires the will toward the enjoyment of things that give pleasure. A more intense enkindling of another, better love (love of the soul's Bridegroom) is necessary for the vanquishing of the [desires] and the denial of this pleasure. (A 1.14.2)

What is indicated here is a decisive, preferential choice of the heart for God,[26] a conscious shift in terms of one's focus of meaning, which ever so slowly redirects and claims desire. The love of Divine Wisdom as it grows and develops in life experience actually *educates human desire,* that is, effects a gradual transference of desire to Jesus Christ, Beloved Sophia! John writes with profound insight about the agony and ecstasy of the journey of human desire and explains for us what kind of affective education is carried on by Divine Sophia over a lifetime. Contemplation, which is the concern of this volume, comes by the very gradual adherence of our desire to God, which truly illuminates human perception and understanding. *We educate people to contemplation, therefore, by consciously guiding the complex education of human desire as it is being influenced and effected by Beloved Sophia in each one's life situation.*

26. A key text for understanding and interpreting John is indicated here, one to which I will return later: "Have a habitual desire to imitate Christ in all your deeds by bringing your life into conformity with his. You must then study his life in order to know how to imitate him" (A 1.13.3).

For it is Divine Sophia, herself, who sets the stage by her presence and invitation for the long and difficult life-passage, first of all, from a possessive, confining, unfree desire for pleasure, safety and reassurance to a desire and passion for God transcending that consuming concern for oneself and one's own interests, where human desire is transformed and fulfilled in the deep communion of love; and secondly, from a myopic, self-centered, isolated, non-nurturing presence to others and to reality to a Wisdom surpassing the knowledge we learn and accumulate through education and culture.

As in *The Ascent*, so at the very beginning of the commentary on *The Spiritual Canticle*, in the context of an Old Testament wisdom text, we see the underlining of the cost and significance of the self-transcendence required to pursue the desire for divine Sophia:

> Sophia is bright and never fades and is easily seen by them that love her and found by them that seek her. She goes out before them that covet her that she might first show herself to them. Those who awake early in the morning to seek her shall not labor but will find her seated at the door of their house (Wis. 6:13-15). *This passage indicates that when the soul has departed from the house of her own will and the bed of her own satisfaction, she will find outside divine Wisdom, the Son of God, her Spouse.* (C 3.3)

Those who decide to commit their lives to God frequently fail to realize that this very decision will activate an uncomfortable self-knowledge. Nevertheless, there is reason for encouragement when one realizes that *in the painful self-searching* that a choice for Divine Wisdom stimulates, content is being put into our relationship with Beloved Sophia and our desire for God is growing.[27] It

27. In other words, the experience of one's self, painful as this can be, is an experience of God or stimulates the desire for God: "The soul has made known the manner of preparing oneself to begin this journey: to pursue delights and satisfactions no longer, and to overcome temptations and difficulties through fortitude. *This is the practice of self-knowledge, the first requirement for advancing to the knowledge of God*" (C 4.1), that is, the initial step on the path to contemplation. See Karl Rahner, "Experience of Self and Experience of God," *Theological Investigations*, vol. 13 (New York: Crossroads, 1983), 122–32. Rahner's work, here and elsewhere, shows a striking familiarity with John of the Cross and Teresa

is the deepening presence of Holy Wisdom pervading one's whole life and environment which gradually educates desire and in that process eventually fulfills it. In other words, Wisdom is not only the teacher but also what is learned, not only the educator of desire, but also the love perception and fulfillment itself!

Sophia Moves, Touches, Re-creates, Energizes Gently, Always with Order

A fundamental dynamic of this transformation of desire is inspired by the first verse of the eighth chapter of the Book of Wisdom and an understanding of this dynamic allays some of our anxiety about purification. Even though Divine Wisdom is always active, re-creating, touching, energizing powerfully from one end of the earth to the other, and the all-pervading effectiveness of Wisdom in the world is reiterated again and again, still Sophia touches gently, with order, with careful respect for the human maturation process.[28] Moreover, if we understand the human spirit as the crowning point of evolution at the present time, or if aware of the incalculable limitations of our knowledge of the evolving universe, we yet dare, as some do, to consider the human spirit as the cosmos come to full consciousness, then in the gentle, energizing touch of Divine Sophia resides an equal, correlating respect for the gradual, evolutionary process of the earth.

This means that Wisdom moves from within the person and teaches through the human processes of knowing and loving, so that step by step over a lifetime, in the experience of human relationships and human love, in the experience of the created universe, of one's task in this world, and even of one's deepest self, human desire gathers strength and passion and moves toward God. In other words, we gradually see the dedication of all our desire or affectivity by a hunger for God. Divine Sophia is so at

---

of Avila. Elizabeth Johnson also deals with the self in relation to Rahner in *She Who Is*, 65–67.

28. See *Ascent* 2.17.1-5 for this important dynamic and its relationship to wisdom. This is a very important text in interpreting John of the Cross because he gives here his epistemology, or the way he understands the whole process of acquiring knowledge.

home on the pathways of this world and so delights in dwelling with the children of earth that a person grows and is transformed, not by a leap over or denial of life, not by suppression of desire, but through the experience of the sensual and sexual, the physical and material, through life and life's loves, through what one cherishes and what gives one delight, security and support.[29] Sophia is so subtle and so patient, *so indwelling human experience,* that only looking back can one say: Sophia, the fashioner of all, taught me everything I know (A 3.2.12; Wis 7:22).[30]

Within this epistemological framework we are able to understand the progressive character of the schema of the nights: active night of sense, passive night of sense, active night of spirit and passive night of spirit. The dark night is in actuality a *gradual* purification and transformation of desire and consciousness with a corresponding *developing* experience of Divine Sophia who is loving knowledge.

Sophia Creates with Harmony and Order

Contrary to what many readers initially believe about the mystic's feelings for the world, relationships and human love, the true mystic is enthralled by the diversity and beauty, the unfailing harmony and interconnectedness of the entire creation. All this is the work of Sophia ("the Word") by whom they were created. Everyone and every living thing is clothed with the image of Sophia, as we see in *The Spiritual Canticle* poem where the lovesick bride questions the created world:

> O woods and thickets
> planted by the hand of my Beloved!
> O green meadow,
> coated, bright, with flowers,
> tell me, has he passed by you?

29. See my earlier work on the dark night: Constance FitzGerald, "Impasse and Dark Night," in *Living with Apocalypse*, ed. Tilden Edwards (San Francisco: Harper and Row, 1984), 97, and Michael Buckley, "Atheism and Contemplation," *Theological Studies* 40 (1979): 696, which I cite there.

30. Wisdom 7:13-22.

Creatures then respond:

> Pouring out a thousand graces,
> he passed these groves in haste;
> And having looked at them,
> with his image alone,
> clothed them in beauty. (C 4-5)

The commentary explains:

> Only the hand of God, her Beloved, was able to create this diversity and grandeur. . . . This reflection on creatures, this observing that they are things made by the very hand of God, her Beloved, *strongly awakens the soul to love [God]*. (C 4.3)

Far from being an obstacle, delight and immersion in the wonder of the universe propels desire on its way toward God. The genuine mystic has frequently been prophetic in transcending the hierarchical dualism[31] of his or her time in contemplative "knowing." In every living thing, therefore, the mystic sees a *trace* of God's passing through which one can track down God's *image* or presence in the world:[32]

> God created all things with remarkable ease and brevity, and in them left some trace of Who [God] is, not only in giving all things being from nothing, but even by endowing them with

31. Elizabeth Johnson, *Women, Earth, and Creator Spirit* (New York: Paulist Press, 1993), 10–11, explains "hierarchical dualism" as the dominant form of western rationality, a major taproot connecting the exploitation of the earth and the treatment of women. "This is a pattern of thought and action that (1) divides reality into two separate spheres, and (2) assigns a higher value to one of them. In terms of the three basic relations that shape an ecological ethic, this results in a view in which humanity is detached from and more important than nature; man is separate from and more valuable than woman; God is disconnected from the world, utterly . . . transcendent over it . . . Hierarchical dualism delivers a two tiered vision of reality that privileges the elite half of a pair and subordinates the other, which is thought to have no intrinsic value of its own but exists only to be of use to the higher." See pp. 10–22.

32. See *The Spiritual Canticle* st. 4-6 with the corresponding commentary.

> innumerable graces and qualities, making them beautiful in a wonderful order and unfailing dependence on one another. *All of this [God] did through [God's] own Sophia, the Word, [the] only begotten Son by Whom [God] created them.* (C 5.1)
>
> And she says "he passed" because creatures are like a trace of God's passing. Through them one can track down [God's] grandeur, might, wisdom, and other divine attributes. (C 5.3)[33]

The *image* of Jesus-Sophia, developmental and transformative in character, is central to John's theology and whenever we encounter "image" (i.e., trace, sketch, imprinting, mirror) in his writings, we can be certain we are in the sphere of wisdom Christology.[34] John of the Cross follows St. Paul in teaching that this image is Jesus-Sophia and that it is in Jesus-Sophia, the Son, the splendor of God's glory, that God "looked at" all creation, that is, created everything and made all complete and whole by the imprinting of Sophia.

> and having looked at them,
> with his image alone,
> clothed them in beauty.
>
> St. Paul says: *the Son of God is the splendor of [God's] glory and the image of [God's] substance* (Heb. 1:3). It should be known that only with this figure, [the] Son, did God look at all things, that is, [God] communicated to them their natural being and many natural graces and gifts, and made them complete and perfect, as is said in Genesis: *God looked at all things that [God] made, and they were very good* (Gn. 1:31). To look and behold that they were very good was to make them very good in the Word, [God's] Son. (C 5.4)[35]

33. The influence of Sophia as she appears in Proverbs 8:22-30 is apparent in this section of *The Spiritual Canticle*: "The Lord begot me . . . When [God] established the earth I was there . . . " See also Wisdom 7:24-27.

34. For a contemporary treatment of image of God, see Elizabeth Johnson, *She Who Is*, 69–75.

35. Hebrews 1:2 is significant here: "In this the final age [God] has spoken to us thru [the] Son whom [God] has made heir of all things and thru whom [God] first created the universe."

To look at and experience the beauty, gifts and sacredness of the earth, therefore, is to behold and experience Divine Sophia who, looking back, marvelously energizes human desire:

> The soul, *wounded with love through a trace of the beauty of her Beloved, which she has known through creatures* and anxious to see that invisible beauty which caused this visible beauty, declares . . . who has the power to heal me?
>
> Since creatures gave the soul signs of her Beloved and showed within themselves traces of [her Beloved's] beauty and excellence, *love grew in her and, consequently, sorrow at [her Beloved's] absence. The more the soul knows of God the more the desire and anxiety to see [God] increase.* (C 6.1-2)

If this experience of the creative presence and image of Jesus-Sophia in the world strongly awakens the person to love and causes desire for God to grow, what can we say about the experience of Sophia in human relationships?

> All who are free,
> tell me a thousand graceful things of you;
> all wound me more
> and leave me dying
> of, ah, I-don't-know-what beyond their stammering. (C 7)

The commentary continues:

> In this stanza she asserts that she is wounded with love because of another higher knowledge she receives of the Beloved through rational creatures. . . . She also asserts she is not merely wounded but is dying of love . . . due to an admirable immensity these creatures disclose to her, yet do not completely disclose. Because this immensity is indescribable, she calls it an "I-don't-know-what." And because of it the soul is dying of love. (C 7.1)

Desire for Beloved Sophia is enkindled and gathers even more passion and momentum by nothing so much as human friendship and love, even when one is captivated by a powerful infatuation and thus largely unconscious that the power and attraction experienced come from the image or trace of Sophia within the loved one. John of the Cross' incarnational position, like Karl Rahner's, insists that created mediations do not destroy the immediate relationship of the graced person to God. Rather, they make it possible and attest to its authenticity in everyday life.[36] This means that human desire is moved toward Divine Sophia and gathers strength through what/whom we cherish and it is purified and transformed through not only the joys and ecstasies but also the sorrows, losses and disappointments of human relationships (C 7.1-9, 8.1).

While this stance found in *The Spiritual Canticle* (st. 3-7) is not always easy to reconcile with the teaching on desire in the first book of *The Ascent* where all desires are potential idols, still for the mystic the experience of this world is an experience of God! While every desire has the latent possibility of focusing on an idol, love of God and human love are not in competition. The totality of creation—ourselves, our relationships, our world—is a milieu of prayer, and content is put into our relationship with Beloved Sophia in the very experience of it. This is how our desire or affectivity is educated. To express this another way, to experience Divine Sophia in this manner sketches color and depth into one's own slowly developing, inner image of Sophia-Christ.

I will return to this later and to what it means to be a friend and prophet of Sophia possessing the perspective and desire of Divine Sophia in and for the world. It is sufficient to indicate here that in the last part of both *The Spiritual Canticle* and *The Living Flame*, one of the astounding graces of transformation in wisdom, or union with the divine, is that one actually *experiences* the harmony, mutuality and diversity of all creation *moving in God* in a unified, interdependent connectedness and enjoys this as a mirror or image of Sophia-God. This is so true that the universe itself and all it nurtures with life become for the person a harmonious symphony surpassing the most wonderful melodies one has ever heard (C 14/15.10 & 25; 36.6-7; 39.11; F 4.4-7).

36. Harvey Egan, *What Are They Saying about Mysticism?* (New York: Paulist Press, 1982), 106.

Sophia Delights to Be with the Children of Earth and Makes Them Friends of God

Sophia is not, therefore, distant or removed from human affairs nor from this world. She is involved in and concerned with the lessons and significance of human experience. By the gates, at the approaches of the city she waits, her delight and concern with the children of the earth. Again and again we are assured of her undiscriminating delight:

> the Father of lights [Jas. 1:17] . . . is not closefisted but diffuses himself abundantly, as the sun does its rays, without being a respecter of persons, wherever there is room—always showing himself gladly along the highways and byways—does not hesitate or consider it of little import to find his delights with the children of [earth] at a common table in the world [Prv. 8:31]. (F I.15)

This text is complex since it draws on the book of Proverbs for its strong wisdom content but does so in the context of the Letter of James and the Acts of the Apostles. Here Sophia's delight to be with humanity is associated with the doctrine of the indwelling of the Trinity and in the process Sophia's presence and delight is transferred to the Father thereby masculinizing Sophia. The commentary continues:

> And it should not be held as incredible in a soul now examined, purged, and tried in the fire of tribulations, trials and many kinds of temptations, and found faithful in love, that the promise of the Son of God be fulfilled, the promise that the Most Blessed Trinity will come and dwell within anyone who loves him (Jn. 14:23). The Blessed Trinity inhabits the soul by divinely illuminating its intellect with the Wisdom of the Son, delighting its will in the Holy Spirit, and by absorbing it powerfully and mightily in the delightful embrace of the Father's sweetness. (F I.15)
>
> And this is what happens, in an indescribable way, at the time this flame of love rises up within the soul. Since the soul is completely purged in its substance and faculties (memory, intellect and will), the divine substance which, because of its purity, as the Wise Man says, *touches everywhere profoundly, subtly, and sublimely* (Wis. 7:24), absorbs the soul in itself with its divine flame. *And in that*

> *immersion of the soul in Wisdom,* the Holy Spirit sets in motion the glorious flickerings of his flame. (F I.17)

Sophia delights precisely in dwelling with the human person and rejoicing in her delight and happiness. John's central emphasis on a relationship of mutual indwelling is rooted in this truth.

> . . . The Son of God finds delight in the soul in these her delights, and is sustained in her, that is, he dwells in her as in a place that pleases him. This, I believe, is what he meant through what Solomon said in Proverbs: *"My delights are with the children of [earth]" [Prv. 8:31], that is, when their delight is to be with me, Who am the Son of God.* (C 17.10)

Sophia desires human presence and companionship. From the very beginning of *The Ascent of Mount Carmel* through the concluding stanzas of *The Spiritual Canticle* to the end of *The Living Flame of Love,* these writings never swerve from this framework in which union with Divine Wisdom through a mutual likeness effected by the companionship of love is the promise and the goal. Sophia is so desirous of this mutual transfiguration that she is actually *called the spouse* of the soul. This central role of Wisdom is explicit in the first book of *The Ascent* in a text already quoted:

> When this third night . . . has passed, a union with the Spouse, Who is the Sophia of God, then follows . . . love is perfect when the transformation of the soul in God is achieved. (A 1.2.4)

And in one of the last stanzas of the *Spiritual Canticle* we hear the plea:

> Transform me into the beauty of divine Sophia and make me resemble the one who is the Word, the Son of God. (C 36.7)

Jesus Christ Is Divine Wisdom: John of the Cross and the Christian Scriptures

It is clear that for John of the Cross, as for St. Paul and the writers of the Gospels of Matthew and John, Jesus Christ *is* divine

Wisdom (Sophia), the Word, the Son of God. In the unitive experience of Jesus-Sophia the person is transformed and, in this Jesus, the entire creation is touched and gathered into the tender, unifying embrace of Sophia-God who pervades and connects the entire cosmos and every form of life in it.

This means John of the Cross appropriates not only some of the understandings of Sophia in the Old Testament, but he seems to be completely at home with the identification of Jesus with divine Sophia that some of the writers of the Christian Scriptures make: *Jesus is Sophia incarnate*.[37] In Jesus, therefore, we find the incarnation of a feminine gestalt of God. To underpin his own cohesive Christology John uses most of the significant Wisdom texts of the Christian Scriptures currently being analyzed by contemporary scholars and he does this in a context that frequently reveals his knowledge of their connection with the wisdom texts of the Old Testament. The tradition of personified Wisdom, which played a foundational role in the development of Christology in the early church, seems to have been singularly important to him since some of his most profound Christological assertions are couched in its terms. The recognition of the central, critical function of Wisdom is therefore basic to understanding John's Christology. Elizabeth Johnson clarifies precisely what this means when she writes:

> Whoever espouses a wisdom Christology is asserting that Sophia in all her fullness was in Jesus so that in his historicity he embodies divine mystery in creative and saving involvement with the world. In Augustine's words, "But she was sent in one way that she might be with human beings; and she has been sent in another way that she herself might be a human being."[38]

I have met numerous religious people in recent years who, because of their own spiritual experience, feel a great affinity for the writings of John of the Cross but do not want to deal with the dominant place of Christ in his teaching. One cannot begin to explore the transformative function of Sophia in John, however,

37. See, e.g., Dunne, *Christology*, 177–209; Johnson, *Jesus, the Wisdom of God*, 276–89.

38. *Redeeming the Name*, 127.

without simultaneously probing *the role of Jesus Christ* in the process of Christian transformation, or vice versa.[39] John appropriates as his own the words of the Book of Wisdom together with those of Paul the Apostle to accent the centrality and complete sufficiency of Jesus, Sophia incarnate.

> If you desire me to answer with a word of comfort, [God says] behold my Son, subject to me and to others out of love for me, and you will see how much he answers. If you desire me to declare some secret truths or events to you, fix your eyes on him, and you will discern hidden in him the most secret mysteries, and wisdom, and the wonders of God, as My Apostle proclaims: In the Son of God are hidden all the treasures of wisdom and knowledge of God (Col. 2:3). These treasures of wisdom and knowledge will be far more sublime, delightful, and advantageous than what you want to know.[40] The Apostle, therefore, gloried, affirming that he had acted as though he knew no other than Jesus Christ and him crucified (1 Cor. 2:2). And if you should seek other divine or corporeal visions and revelations, behold him, become human, and you will encounter more than you imagine, because the Apostle also says: In Christ all the fullness of divinity dwells bodily. (Col. 2:9, A 2.22.6)[41]

In investigating Sophia-Wisdom, one discovers just how cohesive and all-pervasive John's wisdom Christology really is. Furthermore, it is rooted in the whole Christological development beginning with the Christian Scriptures and early Church writers.[42]

To see the significance of John's understanding of Jesus as Sophia and his use of a wisdom Christology, we must examine briefly how and why the writers of the Christian Scriptures, par-

39. To witness a feminist theologian underlining the importance of Jesus for personal spirituality, see Sandra M. Schneiders, "The Resurrection of Jesus and Christian Spirituality," in *Christian Resources of Hope*, ed. Maureen Junker-Kenny (Dublin: Columba Press, 1995), 81–114.

40. John comments again on this same text in *The Spiritual Canticle* 37.4.

41. Compare with Wisdom 7:6 and Colossians 2:2-3, & 9; see also *Flame* 3.17.

42. Feminist writers suggest this is not necessarily positive for feminist emancipation. See, for example, Schüssler Fiorenza, *Jesus: Miriam's Child*, 131–62.

ticularly Paul, Matthew and John, understood Jesus in Wisdom categories and what this meant for them and for the tradition.[43] Elizabeth Johnson tells us that first century Christians, "in the process of giving expression to their experience of the saving significance of Jesus of Nazareth and to his ultimate origin in God's gracious goodness," turned to Jewish theology and Hellenistic culture for elements of interpretation. One of the very first they put to use was the Jewish figure of personified Wisdom, that female figure of the late Old Testament and intertestamental literature whose words, characteristics and functions they quickly shifted to Jesus. They therefore interpreted Jesus within the framework of the tradition of personified Wisdom.[44]

Through the feminine Sophia God image, New Testament writers linked the man Jesus to Yahweh of Israel thereby showing the intrinsic continuity between their Yahwistic faith and Christianity and revealing how, in Jesus Christ, all that Yahweh is was present in their midst. Johnson writes:

> What Judaism said of Sophia, Christian hymn-makers and epistle writers now came to say of Jesus: he is the image of the invisible God (Col. 1:15), the radiant light of God's glory (Heb. 1:3); he is the firstborn of all creation (Col. 1:15), the one thru whom all things were made (1 Cor. 8:6). Likewise, the way in which Judaism characterized Sophia in her dealings with human beings, Christian gospel writers now came to portray Jesus: he calls out to the heavy burdened to come to him and find rest (Mt. 11:28-30); he makes people friends of God and gifts those who love him with life (Jn. 15:15; 17:2). As the trajectory of wisdom Christology passages in the New Testament shows, the identification of Jesus with Sophia was so closely made that Jesus is presented not only as a wisdom teacher, not only as a child and envoy of Sophia, but more significantly as Sophia herself: Biblical scholarship in recent decades has been lifting this tradition from the footnotes of scripture studies into more central consideration. Regarding NT Christology James Dunne concludes, "Jesus is the exhaustive embodiment of divine

43. This study limps, as was said before, as long as we do not understand the precise theological trajectory of Wisdom Christology to which John was heir.

44. "Jesus, The Wisdom of God," 261.

wisdom"; M. Jack Suggs argues that for Matthew, "Jesus is Sophia incarnate"; according to Raymond Brown's analysis, "in John, Jesus is personified Wisdom"; this early use of Wisdom categories had profound theological consequences. It enabled the fledgling Christian communities to attribute cosmic significance to the Crucified Jesus, relating him to the creation and governance of the world, and was an essential step in the development of incarnation Christology.[45]

The Role of Jesus in Our Lives

In John's anthropology the human person is seen as an "infinite" capacity for God (F 3.19-22).[46] As long as the great "caverns" of the mind, heart, memory and imagination are filled with human knowledge, loves, dreams and memories that seem to promise to satisfy completely, the person is unable to even feel or imagine the depths of the capacity that is there. Only when one becomes aware of their emptiness, in the face of the experience of the fragility and breakdown of what or whom we have staked our lives on, the limitation and failure of our life project and life love, the shattering of our dreams and meanings, can the depths of thirst and hunger that exist in the human person, the infinite capacity, really be felt.

The mind is a deep cavern whose emptiness is a thirst for God. The mind thirsts, often unknowingly, for the waters of God's Wisdom to satisfy and complete human knowing. The will is a great cavern whose affective emptiness is a hunger for the ultimate, unconditional reassurance and fulfillment of love. The memory is a cavern, too, and its obsession with the past, its suffering over losses, its confusion with and need to organize images, become a deep void of yearning for the possession of God.

45. Ibid. See also John Dunne, *Christology*, 164–66 and all of chaps. 6 and 7 for an excellent treatment which includes the scriptural texts.

46. While an *infinite* human capacity for God can be questioned, John explains in *Flame* 3.22 that "the capacity of these caverns (intellect, memory, will) is deep because the object of this capacity, namely God, is profound and infinite. Thus, in a *certain fashion their capacity is infinite, their thirst is infinite, their hunger is also deep and infinite, and their languishing and suffering are infinite death.*"

Few people understand that John is actually addressing this infinite capacity when he urges them at the end of the first book of *The Ascent* to have an on-going desire to pattern their lives on Christ's.

> Have a habitual desire to imitate Christ in all your deeds by bringing your life into conformity with his. You must then study his life in order to know how to imitate him and behave in all things as He would behave. (A 1.13.3)[47]

This means only one thing: *desire to know* Jesus Christ. Human desire is educated by an immersion in the Jesus of the Gospels. However, if you channel your desire toward knowing Jesus Christ, this person who has become in his life, death and resurrection the Sophia of God, the one you will learn to know is loving Sophia who will slowly and secretly redirect and claim your desire and subvert your life. Desire is educated, therefore, by the companionship, the friendship, of Jesus-Sophia. This dynamic underlies John's whole philosophy of prayer and indicates how a conscious decision of the heart for Christ takes place, how a shift in the focus of desire and meaning *begins* in our lives.

But often the human person is not satisfied with the day to day fidelity to this companionship, nor to its slow, unpretentious, mysterious development. Too many people educated in our culture live with a consuming desire for novelty, excitement, change, new pleasures, visions, and extraordinary experiences. We have only to reflect on the way Americans flocked to Medjugorje before the war in Bosnia or the way people in our country search for unusual spiritual experience at the sites of reported apparitions. But John, appropriating both St. Paul and the Book of Wisdom in a Christological passage quoted previously, affirms that we do not need unusual new revelations, visions, or secret truths. We have everything we desire in the Gospel and the unitive companionship of the human Jesus in whom dwells for us the nearness and fullness, the compassionate kindness, of Sophia-God embracing

47. This is a fundamental text regarding affective purification. It interprets all that precedes it in book 1 of *The Ascent*.

and energizing from within the totality of the human situation. Jesus-Sophia is the "sole Word" spoken by the "mouth of God."[48]

> Those who now desire to question God or receive some vision or revelation are guilty not only of foolish behavior but also of offending him by not fixing their eyes entirely on Christ and by living with the desire for some other novelty.
>
> God would answer as follows: If I have already told you all things in my Word, my Son, and if I have no other word, what answer or revelation can I now make that would surpass this? Fasten your eyes on him alone, because in him I have spoken and revealed all, and in him you shall discover even more than you ask for and desire. You are making an appeal for locutions and revelations that are incomplete, but if you turn your eyes to him you will find them complete. For he is my entire locution and response, vision and revelation, which I have already spoken, answered, manifested, and revealed to you, by giving him to you as a brother, companion, master, ransom, and reward. Since that day when I descended upon him with my Spirit on Mount Tabor proclaiming: "This is my beloved Son in whom I am well pleased, hear him" (Mt. 17:5), I have relinquished these methods of answering and teaching and presented them to him . . . behold him well, for in him you will uncover all these revelations already made, and many more.
>
> Thus we must be guided humanly and visibly in all by the law [Gospel] of Christ, who is human, and that of his Church and his ministers, . . . One should not believe anything coming in a supernatural way, and believe only the teaching of Christ who is human. (A 2.22.5,7)

This long text is particularly enlightening since John places it within the context of Sirach 24 where Sophia speaks of herself:

> Wisdom praises herself and tells of her glory in the midst of the people. In the assembly of the Most High she opens her mouth, and in the presence of his hosts she tells of her glory: *I came forth from the mouth of the Most High,* and covered the earth like a mist (Sir. 24:1-3).

48. See *Ascent* 2.22.3. Although in this part of the text Sophia is subsumed in the Word, the Logos, nevertheless by using "the mouth of God" symbolism, an allusion to Sirach 24, it distinctly shows the connection made between the two.

In accenting the complete sufficiency and unlimited potential of Christ as Divine Sophia, John of the Cross validates new possibilities for appropriating in our time the inexhaustible meaning of Jesus. If Jesus is Sophia incarnate, then new possibilities for studying his life do open before us. And what will we unlock if *in contemplative prayer* we experience again the life, death and resurrection—the meaning—of Jesus in the light of Sophia, thereby transforming for our time the symbol of Christ and reclaiming Christ and Christological doctrine in a new way?[49]

Image of Jesus Christ and Growth in Wisdom

This walking with the historical Jesus is how Sophia becomes a life-giving, indwelling image and one's primary focus of affective and cognitive meaning. This image is unique for each person as a basis for relationship, direction, love, purification and transformation. In fact, a gradual transference of desire occurs as the presence of loving Sophia takes shape within, influencing motivation and affecting imagination.[50] While it is the intimacy of prayer which above all shapes this image, nevertheless study, theological reflection, art, music and a myriad of other life experiences contribute to this Christic patterning. We have already seen how in *The Spiritual Canticle* (st. 3-7) the experience of oneself, others and the whole creation slowly roughs in and sketches color and depth into one's developing, inner image of Jesus-Sophia.

A principle fundamental to John's wisdom Christology is operative here: love will never reach the fullness of its possibilities, human desire will never stop yearning and aching, until the lovers are so alike that one is transfigured in the love and goodness of the other. This means an imprint of Jesus-Sophia transformative of the human person is, in a mysterious way, totally harmonious with human development, gradually etched within the human

49. See Schüssler Fiorenza, *Jesus: Miriam's Child*, 162.

50. In *Canticle* 12, John develops at length this inner image as a faith experience which has intellectual, volitional and emotional components. There is a sketch of faith in the mind giving meaning to a person's life (C 12.6), a sketch of love in the will effecting commitment to the beloved and a sketch of hope in the memory producing trust and a sense of belongingness (C 12.7).

personality. As I know Jesus-Sophia, this knowledge subverts my life, shows me to myself as in a mirror and redirects and purifies my desire.

If I look long enough at one who truly loves me, I become what I see in the other's eyes. I am transfigured. The image of the loved one, the eyes of the beloved are burnt into my heart and seen with my inner eye. This image is not impersonal! Rather, it is relational. We see this with remarkable clarity in *The Spiritual Canticle* poem:

> Reveal your presence,
> and may the vision of your beauty be my death;
> for the sickness of love
> is not cured
> except by *your very presence and image.*
>
> O spring like crystal!
> If only, on your silvered over face,
> you would suddenly form
> the eyes I have desired,
> which I bear sketched deep within my heart. (C 11-12)

This is not difficult to understand when we reflect on how, when we love someone very much, we carry the image of that loved one within where he or she is always present with us influencing motivation. John explains:

> The soul experiences within herself a certain sketch of love . . . and she desires the completion of the sketch of this image, the image of her Bridegroom, the Word, the Son of God, who as St. Paul says, "is the splendor of [God's] glory and the image of [God's] substance" (Heb. 1:3); for this is the image . . . into which the soul desires to be transformed through love. (C 11.11-12)[51]

51. There is such an interplay of wisdom symbolism here: crystal, face, sketch, mirror, eyes, seeing, knowing and being known, being carried away by the beauty one beholds and therefore, being changed and made beautiful like the beauty one sees.

In wonderfully graphic imagery along the same line of wisdom symbolism, the commentary continues:

> [The person] feels that she is like wax in which an impression, though being made, is not yet complete. She knows, too, that she is like a sketch or the first draft of a drawing and calls out to the one who did this sketch to finish the painting and image. (C.12.1)

Because this is a fundamental experience, and not just a concept, it is important to understand the educative and transformative function of this Wisdom image and its affective power over desire. Through this image the whole creative aspect of Old Testament Sophia is brought to human transformation. If it is not valued relative to spiritual growth, the tender, careful, nurturing creativity of Sophia will be thwarted and we will "damage or lose the sublime image that God [is] painting within [us]."[52]

At first the developing image of Jesus-Sophia is a strength and consolation motivating one toward a generous, self-giving life influenced by the Jesus of the Gospels and sensitizing one to this Sophia presence in the world energizing and connecting all of reality—the likeness within recognizing and catching the reflection of the outer likeness.[53] In fact, the presence of this tracing in human relationships, throughout the beauty and wonder of the created universe, in human culture and in all that human creativity is able to achieve, causes desire for God to grow by leaps and bounds.

52. In *Flame* 3.41-45, John castigates those spiritual directors who do not understand the secret, loving wisdom of contemplative prayer, that is "the sublime anointings and shadings of the Holy Spirit," and therefore damage or destroy by poor direction the image God is painting within the human person. "Who will succeed," he says, "in repairing that delicate painting of the Holy Spirit once it is marred by a coarse hand." Without an understanding of the essential role of the developing pattern of Jesus-Sophia in a person's spiritual growth, one can "lose the sublime image that God [is] painting within."

53. We can note an intersection here with John M. Staudenmaier's interpretation of the dynamic of the Second Week of the Exercises of St. Ignatius which "inculcates a form of personal intimacy with Jesus that opens out to intimacy with the larger world, an intimacy of affective engagement that leads to action in the world." See "To Fall in Love with the World," *Studies in the Spirituality of Jesuits* (May 1994): 1–28.

Dark Night and the Continuing Role of Secret Sophia[54]

As the intimacy with Christ matures, however, this presence, within and without, begins to make deeper claims and there is a shift in the way Sophia operates within the depths of human personality. Romance departs, and I see myself, my relationships, my community, and my world clearly in the mirror of loving Sophia.[55] This is almost more than one can endure. Now we experience Sophia as a teacher, that is, one who is always on the side of continual learning, even though not everything we learn from Sophia is comforting.[56]

In time, the presence of Sophia becomes afflictive. The image becomes too threatening. Jesus-Sophia subverts my own self-image and this marks the first level of subversion. I cannot accept the claims of Sophia upon me nor can I accept Wisdom as a life vision in an unconditional commitment; this vision is too revolutionary and seditious. Sophia turns life upside-down, challenges my most deeply held beliefs and values, undermines what I have learned, claims whom and what I possess, and highlights the limitations and oppressive character of what I depend on most for satisfaction and assurance.

This brings us to the relationship between the presence of loving Wisdom and the dark night.[57] John says very explicitly that

54. This section on the dark night was first published in part in *Ignatian Prayer, The Way Supplement*, 1995, as "Desolation and Dark Night: The Transformative Influence of Wisdom in John of the Cross." I intended the title to have been "The Transformative Influence of Wisdom in the Dark Night" since I do not deal with Ignatian spiritual desolation there, and never intended to do so.

55. Teresa of Avila writes about this kind of experience in *The Book of Her Life*. See, for example, Kieran Kavanaugh and Otilio Rodriguez, trans. *The Collected Works of St. Teresa of Avila*, vol. 1 (Washington, DC: ICS Publications, 1976), chap. 40.10, 280–81.

56. See *Ascent* 2.17 and note 24 to understand John's teaching on knowledge and Sophia's role in this process.

57. When I wrote "Impasse and Dark Night" in *Living with Apocalypse*, later reprinted in *Women's Spirituality*, ed. Joanne Wolski Conn (New York: Paulist Press, 1984), I did not directly address the significance of Jesus-Sophia in the dark night. This Christological way of experiencing the dark night is a neces-

dark night, infused contemplation, *is* the loving Wisdom of God.[58] *Dark Night = inflow of God = infused contemplation = loving Wisdom.*

> This dark night is an inflow of God into the soul, which purges it of its habitual ignorances and imperfections, natural and spiritual, and which contemplatives call infused contemplation or mystical theology. Through this contemplation, God teaches the soul secretly and instructs it in the perfection of love without its doing anything nor understanding how this happens.
>
> Insofar as infused contemplation is loving Wisdom of God, it produces two principal effects in the soul: it prepares the soul for union with God through love by purging and illumining it. Hence the same loving Wisdom that purges and illumines the blessed spirits, urges and illumines the souls here on earth. (N 2.5.1)

> Why, if it is a divine light . . . does the soul call it a dark night? In answer to this, there are two reasons why this divine Wisdom is not only night and darkness for the soul but also affliction and torment. First, because of the height of the divine Wisdom that exceeds the abilities of the soul; and on this account the Wisdom is dark for the soul. Second, because of the soul's baseness and impurity; and on this account it is painful, afflictive, and also dark for the soul. (N 2.5.2)[59]

Contemplation = mystical theology = secret Wisdom = ray of darkness.

---

sary complement to the impasse experience, just as the impasse experience I describe is a part of my development here.

58. See *Dark Night* 2.5.1-2; 2.17; *Ascent* 2.8.6 to study in context the equivalencies that John sets up.

59. Another relevant text is *Dark Night* 1.10.6 where infused contemplation is, according to Kieran Kavanaugh, mentioned for the first time and equated with "dark and secret contemplation" and "secret and peaceful and loving inflow of God." "Such persons should not mind if the operations of their faculties are being lost to them; they should desire rather that this be done quickly so they may be no obstacle to the operation of the infused contemplation God is bestowing, so they may receive it with more peaceful plenitude and make room in the spirit for the enkindling and burning of love which this dark and secret contemplation bears and communicates to the soul. For contemplation is nothing else than a peaceful and loving inflow of God, which, if not hampered, fires the soul in the spirit of love."

> Contemplation, consequently, by which the intellect has a higher knowledge of God, is called mystical theology, meaning the secret Wisdom of God. For this Wisdom is secret to the very intellect that receives it. St. Dionysius on this account refers to contemplation as a ray of darkness. The prophet Baruch declares of this wisdom: "There is no one who knows its way or can think of its paths" (Bar. 3:23). To reach union with God the soul must obviously blind itself to all the paths along which it can travel. (A 2.8.6)[60]

It follows that if Jesus Christ *is* Divine Wisdom (Sophia), then *dark contemplation is the presence of Jesus Christ as Wisdom* and dark night is the time when the image of Jesus-Sophia takes on all the marks of crucifixion: violence, suffering, isolation, failure, marginality, rejection, abandonment, hopelessness, meaninglessness, death. The image of the Crucified One,[61] reflective of a seemingly silent, incomprehensible God, functions in the dark night as *incomprehensible, secret, hidden* and yet *loving* Sophia. And this is the second level of subversion: not only has my self-image been subverted, but now too the image of Christ and of God. Therefore, when John says that the dark night is an inflow of God, *this inflow of God is very precisely in terms of secret Wisdom who is Jesus Crucified,* a secret, unitive, loving knowledge indicative of more intimate relationship (N 1.10.6; N 2.17; N 2.5.1-2). Dark night is not primarily *some thing,* an impersonal darkness like a difficult situation or distressful psychological condition, but *someone,* a presence leaving an indelible imprint on the human spirit and consequently on one's entire life.

This imprint is the touch of the hand of God marking, wounding, challenging, shaping, purifying, transforming human personality.

> You have wounded me in order to cure me, O divine Hand, and you have put to death in me what made me lifeless, deprived me

60. See also *Dark Night* 2.17 for an extensive and very beautiful treatment of secret mystical Wisdom and dark contemplation.

61. In *Ascent* 2.7.8-9 we see how Christ Crucified is seen as the pattern or mirror of the dark night. The whole context of this chapter is important because it shows Jesus dying as the unitive image.

> of God's life in which I now see myself live. You granted me this liberality of your generous grace, which you used in contacting me with the touch of the splendor of your glory and the figure of your substance, which is your only begotten Son, through whom, being your substance (Heb. 1:3), you touch lightly from one end to the other (Wis. 8:1). And your only begotten Son, O merciful hand of the Father, is the delicate touch by which you touched me with the force of your cautery and wounded me. (F 2.16)[62]

In the mirror of *this* broken, ambiguous image of suffering Wisdom, we see the miseries and hypocrisies of our lives.[63] This Crucified image is living knowledge of human darkness, violence, limitation, oppression, and sinfulness that overpowers our shallow self-confidence and sense of direction, questions what we think we know about God, raises doubts about what we have accomplished, and undercuts our entire affective life.[64]

In fact, this Crucified presence subverts and contradicts our whole individualistic perception of reality, that is, the way we experience not only other people, not only the loved one and loved community, but also the victims and scapegoats of our society, and even other species, the earth itself and the cosmos (DN 2.8.4). This image of crucifixion is the language of God (Word) opening and teaching the human mind and heart, calling us in our confusion and emptiness to pass over into the perspective of loving Sophia by an identification or profound unitive relationship with Jesus Crucified.

At this point in life and prayer development, the images of the poor, the victimized, the oppressed, the exploited, and the suffering

62. See also *Flame* 2.17 and Wisdom 7:24 and 8.

63. *Dark Night* 2.5.5: "This divine and dark light causes deep immersion of the mind in the knowledge and feeling of one's own miseries and evils; it brings all these miseries into relief so that the soul sees clearly that of itself it will never possess anything else."

64. This is what I have called the purification of desire in *Impasse and Dark Night*. This purification takes place in one's life situation and therefore is mediated through one's central human relationships and life project.

take on a clarity and significance that is overpowering. They are clearly a suffering extension of the inner imprinting of Jesus-Sophia, and they make a claim. They are the darkness of humanity; they are *our* darkness. In the image of Crucified Sophia, our violence is unveiled.[65] Just as personal darkness is exposed in the mirror of suffering Sophia, so is the collective darkness and violence of humanity. The "poor" are recognized and embraced to the degree that this identification with suffering Sophia has taken place in the inner darkness. This is a major internal connection Sophia effects with "the world." Having subverted our images of ourselves and of God, Sophia now subverts our relationship to the world and this is the third level of subversion. Here, *now*, in the dark night, the Crucifixion is recognized finally for what it is: the total, irrevocable unveiling of our cultural violence. Consciousness is the issue, but a love-consciousness born when this unitive relationship with Crucified Sophia takes hold in darkness and in deprivation of one's deepest affective resources, thereby redeeming or redirecting affectivity and transforming human desire. For so long, year after year, in meditation, in theological reflection, in liturgy, in suffering, during the dramatic liturgy of Good Friday, we have looked at the Crucified One, but only now do we realize *that Christ is looking back* with all the pain of the world in his eyes.

In other words, in the secret, painful, unitive relationship with dark Sophia, a new kind of *participatory love-knowledge* begins to take over human desire and consciousness and to express itself, not only in the gradual repudiation of all kinds of personal and socio-cultural violence and oppression, but also in an entry, *albeit still dark and unfinished,* into the experience of mutuality, communion, connectedness, and kinship with the earth that marks transformed or mystical consciousness.[66] Richard Tarnas sug-

65. This is the powerful title of Gil Bailie's groundbreaking work mentioned at the beginning of this study.

66. As I have suggested in "Impasse and Dark Night," 97, "transfiguration does not happen at the end of the road; it is in the making now. If we could see the underside of this death, we would realize it is already resurrection." Furthermore, as Sandra Schneiders suggests in "Feminist Spirituality," 400: For feminist spirituality groping to claim and understand Sophia, the personal is

gests that a "subtler understanding of human knowledge," a participatory way of knowing that moves beyond the hierarchical dualism[67] characteristic of the Cartesian-Kantian paradigm, has been emerging in philosophy for over a century. Common to all its thinkers—Goethe, Schiller, Schelling, Coleridge, Hegel, and Rudolf Steiner—is an essential conviction that the relation of the human mind to the universe is ultimately not dualistic but *participatory*.[68]

> In its own depths the imagination directly contacts the creative process of nature, realizes the process within itself, and brings nature's reality to conscious expression.
>
> Then the world speaks its meaning through human consciousness. Then human language itself can be recognized as rooted in a deeper reality, as reflecting the universe's unfolding meaning. Through the human intellect, in all its personal individuality, contingency and struggle, the world's evolving thought-content achieves conscious articulation . . . the world's truth achieves its existence when it comes to birth in the human mind. As the plant at a certain stage brings forth its blossom, so does the universe bring forth new stages of human knowledge. And as Hegel emphasized, the evolution of human knowledge is the evolution of the world's self-revelation.[69]

I quote at length because this view of an emerging, different epistemological perspective, a "participatory epistemology," to which I will return later in dealing with transformation or the awakening of God, is strikingly similar, not only to the experience

---

always political; personal transformation is the only possible basis for societal transformation. In this context, it is important to note that the presence of loving Wisdom in John of the Cross is not an esoteric, condescending or world-transcending presence, but an affirmation of and solidarity with the human, with the body, with the earth, in all its fragility and poverty. Sophia is at home on the streets of the world. Where Sophia is, we hear the call: "Come all who are burdened . . . Come eat and drink you who have no money . . . Come all who are thirsty."

67. Description given in note no. 30 above.

68. Tarnas, 433–45. I draw on his thought in the following section.

69. Tarnas, 434–35.

of contemplative consciousness in John of the Cross and other mystics, but also to the new paradigm of connectedness and communion emerging in various other disciplines and numerous other writers. Without necessarily realizing the relationship to contemplative consciousness and transformation in Suffering Wisdom, some of these trailblazers in religious thinking challenge humanity to accept the limitation and death (dark night) that will usher in the next great epoch or evolutionary era when the long-alienated modern mind will break through to discover its intimate relationship with nature and the larger cosmos. Then the universe will be experienced, as Thomas Berry suggests, as an intimate, interconnected, and diverse communion of subjects rather than a collection of objects or victims existing only for human use or domination.[70]

Integral to and one with this rising participatory way of knowing and understanding life on earth is the tremendous emergence of the feminine in our culture rising out of the unitive energies at work in the universe and heralding the end of the fundamentally masculine dominance of the Western mind. It appears that we are truly at a highly critical stage of purification, closely associated with the emerging numinosity of Sophia, in which the masculine (in all of us) must voluntarily transcend itself in its own dark night of death, which will fit it to enter into a fundamentally new and reconciling relationship of mutuality with the feminine in all its forms.[71]

As we observe the twentieth century's massive deterioration of so many structures, suggesting the necessary deconstruction or death prior to new birth, we see this participatory vision struggling to break through on so many levels and in so many disciplines. Experienced, first, in the bald exposure of so much violence and evil in our time; second, in increasing oneness with the suffering, this vision appears to be reflective of a deep and powerful pro-

70. Among these trailblazers in religious thinking is Thomas Berry, *The Dream of the Earth* (San Francisco: Sierra Club Books, 1988); see also Swimme and Berry, *The Universe Story*, 243: "Existence itself is derived from and sustained by this intimacy of each being with every other being."

71. Tarnas, 444.

cess impelled by forces beyond the merely human. This is where the personal experience of dark Crucified Sophia intersects and resonates with the current state of the collective "soul" because the human spirit in the dark night does follow a numinous paradigmatic path unfolding from within on a trajectory that leads to transformation. This means the unitive relationship with Suffering Sophia can be so deep and, consequently, the solidarity with "the other" so profound that not only does the contemplative person in this dark night carry and bring to consciousness the collective longings and pain of humanity and the energies of the cosmos, but also brings *to them* in her very being and desire this participatory love-knowledge which Jesus-Sophia gives and is.

This contribution of Sophia mysticism to a broader transformation must not be overlooked by those in other disciplines: namely, feminists, ecologists, creationists, geologians, scientists, philosophers or theologians. Above all, it must not be overlooked by educators. Those who teach the next generation need to understand and believe in the transformative character of the contemplative process inasmuch as this process is integral not only to fully developed humanity, but also to the new form of human existence struggling to be born, therefore, to the continued evolutionary thrust of the earth and the universe. Teachers need to know how to educate for contemplation and transformation if the earth is to be nurtured, if the people are to be delivered from the scapegoating oppression of all kinds of violence, and if humanity is to fill its role in ushering in the next era of life on earth. This may be the *most* basic challenge of religion today: not sexual mores or bioethics, or commitment to justice, not dogmatic orthodoxy, not even option for the poor and oppressed or solidarity with women, but education for a transformative contemplation, which would radically affect human motivation, consciousness, desire, and, ultimately, every other area of human life and endeavor. As if to verify this at the end of his extremely significant book, *Violence Unveiled*, Gil Bailie moves from contemporary versions of crucifixion, wrenching accounts of the Buchenwald death camp, and the rape and murder of a young girl on La Cruz during the massacre at El Mozote, El Salvador, to the Gospel (Matt. 22:37-39):

> The Jesus of Matthew's Gospel did not say the greatest commandment was to *believe* in God and love humanity. He did not say that we should be nice to one another because that's the way God would like us to behave. He said the first and most essential thing is to *love God* with a paramount love. It is the most hackneyed notion in the world, but once or twice in a lifetime its dulling familiarity vanishes, and one feels for a moment the unfathomable significance and centrality of Jesus' suggestion for breaking the grip of sin and death: *to love* God. Partly due to humanists' romantic idea of basic benevolence and partly to the rationalistic "where-there's-a-will-there's-a-way" spirit of the Enlightenment, the modern world came to believe it could fulfill the requirements of the second commandment without having to bother with the first. We moderns came to believe, in effect, that by itself the second commandment was a civilizing force sufficient to the task at hand. The creaking and groaning, indeed, the shouting and shooting, that we now hear all around us is coming from the collapse of that assumption.[72]

This makes it critical to realize that the dark night is the time in contemplative prayer development to seek, not the consolation and escape of other images, experiences, practices, relationships, or spiritual experiences, but "the living image of Christ Crucified within" (A 3.35.5) and stand open to this purifying, transforming image of suffering Sophia *which is actually experienced as "no image" or "nothing"* but which nonetheless acknowledges, reflects, and even accepts our personal and societal darkness, violence, disgrace, failure, injustice, selfishness. This soul-experience is not easy to grasp because to all appearances Christ recedes from consciousness and loses significance, God is beyond reach, belief is threatened, and atheism is logical. This experience has nothing to do with imagining or "seeing" the Crucified Christ (A 2.12.3-6), but with staying in the hidden, dark mystery of Suffering Sophia with an incredibly simple faith-attentiveness that does not even perceive or feel the participatory love-knowledge secret Sophia-Jesus is (A 2.14.8).[73]

72. Bailie, 272.

73. John says in *Ascent* 2.12.3: "The soul will have to empty itself of these images and leave this sense in darkness if it is to reach divine union. For these im-

It is only in the context of this dark experience that we are able to make any sense out of the difficult and complex directives, found in the second and third books of *The Ascent*, to cease clinging to images and to reject visions and revelations:

> When individuals have finished purifying and voiding themselves of all forms and apprehensible images, they will abide in this pure and simple light, and be perfectly transformed into it. . . . If individuals would eliminate these impediments and veils and live in pure nakedness and poverty of spirit . . . their *soul in its simplicity and purity would then be immediately transformed into simple and pure Sophia, the Son of God.* (A 2.15.4)

> . . . since these imaginative apprehensions, visions, and other forms and species are presented through some image or particular idea, individuals should neither feed upon nor encumber themselves with them. . . . The reason is that being apprehended these forms are always represented as we said in some limited mode or manner. But God's Wisdom to which the intellect must be united has neither mode nor manner, neither does it have limits nor does it pertain to distinct and particular knowledge, because it is totally pure and simple. That the two extremes, *the soul and the divine Wisdom,* may be united, they will have to come to accord *by means of a certain likeness.* As a result the soul must also be pure and simple, unlimited and unattached to any particular knowledge, and unmodified by the boundaries of form, species, and image. *Since God cannot be encompassed by any image, form or particular knowledge,* the soul in order to be united with God the

---

ages, just as the corporeal objects of the exterior senses, cannot be an adequate, proximate means to God." In *The Collected Works of St. John,* 186, Kavanaugh adds a note: "Having in mind . . . a contemplative simplification of prayer, John stresses communion in living faith rather than discursive reflection. These passages do not advise one to turn away from Jesus Christ but insist on the simple gaze of faith and personal communion rather than on imaginative representation. John's teaching is in harmony with St. Teresa of Avila's. Strongly asserting that one must never turn from the humanity of Christ, she nonetheless admits that it is common for contemplative souls to be unable to engage in discursive thought about the mysteries of Christ's life. Communion with the Person, however, 'dwelling on his mysteries with a simple gaze,' is another matter and 'will not impede the most sublime prayer' (*Interior Castle* 6.7.6-7, 11-12; *Way of Perfection* 34.11)."

> soul should not be limited by any particular form or knowledge. (A 2.16.6-7)[74]

By and large, most of us are ill-equipped to understand the contemplative process of identification with the Crucified Sophia whereby our desire and consciousness are being transformed. The image of secret Sophia teaching, nurturing, and purifying, unlike clearly defined images of the past, blocks out or makes ineffective other images life-giving until now. When, therefore, in the second book of *The Dark Night* we read that a person is no longer able to pray or communicate as before, that in fact, one feels abandoned and rejected, we learn that *in experience* darkness eclipses other images in one's life as sources of satisfaction and ultimate assurance: the loved one, the beloved community, images of oneself as successful and loved, but above all, life-long images of God and Christ.

This teaching is important today for two very different reasons. First, we must not decide to do away with human images by sheer will power, most of all the image of Jesus Christ, until contemplative development undermines them. Second, lacking the tools of contemplative interpretation and hindered by the marginalization of Divine Sophia and ignorance of how her secret touch marks one's life, contemplatives at this stage, instead of understanding this positive unveiling of darkness, begin to feel alienated from Jesus Christ.[75] In an effort to understand their experience and rescue their

74. In this context, *Ascent* 1.8 (chapter heading) and 4-5 are instructive also: "No creature or knowledge the mind can understand can serve it as a means of union with God. . . . Everything the intellect can understand, the will enjoy, the imagination picture is most unlike and disproportionate to God . . . the intellect will be unable through its ideas to understand anything like God, the will unable to experience a delight and sweetness resembling God, and the memory unable to place in the imagination remembrances and images representing him." See also *Ascent* 1.9.4: "Union with God in this life, and direct communication with [God], demands that we be united with the darkness in which, as Solomon said [I Kgs. 8:12], God promised to dwell."

75. This experience may be further complicated by contemporary developments and questions in Christology particularly those regarding the divinity of Jesus.

God from oblivion, it is not uncommon for them to speak of their God experience in terms of God present in others or of a kind of "cosmic" power or presence. This "vague presence" is actually understandable when one considers the secret Mystery that Crucified Sophia really is in the dark night. Not only the awareness of our own darkness and deficiency, therefore, but the dark beginning of a whole new consciousness of God without the clearly defined parameters of the past characterizes "the union of love" that is being activated. This is the blackest time of night when the last delicate shading of the image of Christ, crucified and abandoned, is being sketched within the human heart and flesh in total darkness and silence. As *The Spiritual Canticle* expresses it:

> The soul cannot see herself in the beauty of God unless she is transformed into the Sophia of God . . . and made to resemble the one who is the Word, the Son of God . . . [but] the gate entering into these riches of Sophia is the cross. (C 36.7-8,13)

Deeper Level of Night

When the invisible, silent God of an abandoned Jesus seems to draw us into lonely introspection where prayer and relationships as we have known them are painful or gone; when loss, failure and hopelessness loom large; when all supports drop from one's consciousness and life's deepest meanings and symbol systems are empty and stale; when our inherited language and images no longer reveal the divine, then a dark Wisdom is operative, nurturing the human person with love and confirming values less highly prized in our society.[76]

The second book of *The Dark Night* throws a stark light on the experience by showing *the whole person* deprived totally in her or

76. I first began developing the interpretation of "the dark night of the spirit" set forth in this section in "A Discipleship of Equals: Voices from Tradition—Teresa of Avila and John of the Cross," in *A Discipleship of Equals: Toward a Christian Feminist Spirituality*, ed. Francis A. Eigo (Villanova: Villanova University Press, 1988), 63–97. I have included it in *The Way* article and here because the Villanova volume has been unavailable almost from the time of its publication.

his imaginative powers, intellectual intuitions, and human sensibilities, that is, in all one's human powers:

> God divests the faculties, affections and senses, both spiritual and sensory, interior and exterior. God leaves the intellect in darkness, the will in aridity, the memory in emptiness and the affections in supreme affliction, bitterness and anguish by depriving the soul of the feeling and satisfaction it previously enjoyed from spiritual blessings. . . . For this privation is one of the conditions required that *the spiritual form, [the image] which is the union of love,* may be introduced into the spirit and united with it. The Lord works all this in the soul by means of a pure and dark contemplation. (N 2.3.3)

As long as one cannot receive and hold the imprinting of the image, or "spiritual form," as this text reads, there is suffering. If one keeps a death grip on one's affective life and fulfillment as it has been experienced in the past and clings tenaciously to one's previous experience of life and perception of Christ/God, one is unable to *completely* "hold" the contradictory presence of Crucified Sophia (N 2.8.2.2, 9.1). This means one's habitual way of understanding, long in use and characteristic of conventional wisdom,[77] has to go, wrenched from us either by the circumstances of life or finally in death. Likewise, one's habitual way of feeling and experiencing love has to go so that one can *experience the transforming touches* of divine love (N 2.9.3 & 9.4). Finally, one's habitual way of harboring memories has to be refined with the effect that the memory will feel alien to all familiar things, a stranger to one's own life, as it were (N 2.9.5 & 9.6).

Such a drastic subversion of the human powers can only be understood when we remember what was said earlier in the context of John's anthropology. As long as the great "caverns" of the mind, heart, will, memory, and imagination are filled with human knowledge, loves, dreams, and memories that seem to satisfy

77. That Jesus as the Sophia of God subverts conventional wisdom is persuasively suggested by Marcus J. Borg, *Jesus a New Vision* (San Francisco: Harper, 1987), chap. 6: "Jesus as Sage: Challenge to Conventional Wisdom," and *Meeting Jesus Again for the First Time* (San Francisco: Harper, 1994), 84–84, 106, 134.

completely, the person will never realize the depths of the capacity that is there. It is only when we actually *feel* their emptiness and darkness, that we thirst and hunger and yearn for these caverns to be filled with God.

> . . . when these caverns of the faculties are not emptied, purged and cleansed of every affection for creatures, they do not feel the vast emptiness of their infinite capacity. (F 3.18)

The powers of the human person—John calls them intellect, memory, and will—are central to his anthropology. The purification process is centered on them in the darker experiences of night with an almost frightening specificity about this experience of the self.

But what precisely can it mean to say *the intellect* is emptied and left in darkness? Perhaps we are warned that the time does come when our philosophy of life, our theology, our carefully constructed meanings fall apart before our eyes. All we have accumulated intellectually that has given us "God," "faith," and security loses its significance. Nothing makes any sense. The mind, while *full* on one level of a lifetime of knowledge, is in total darkness on another, the level of meaning. We feel as if we have been duped and succumb to silence, afraid to shock others by the depth of our cynicism and unbelief (N 2.9.3; 5.3-5; A 2.4&8).

To understand this symbolic, intuitive language of dark contemplation is very difficult (IIDN 17). Suffering Sophia, called by John "living knowledge," is so potent, so contradictory, so immanent and yet so transcendent, that this presence really obscures what has been learned in life and consequently darkens and confuses our understanding.

> When this divine light of contemplation strikes a soul not yet illumined, it causes spiritual darkness, for it not only surpasses the act of natural understanding but it also deprives the soul of this act and darkens it. (N 2.5.3)

A dark Wisdom is operative here, confirming values little prized by the masculine mind of Western society. Divine Sophia defies the supremacy of linear logic and rational explanation; she rejects the pyramid of hierarchical dualism by resisting our dichotomies (e.g., between self and others, matter and spirit, body and soul, passion/desire and reason, feeling and thinking, masculine and feminine, humanity and the earth, success and failure, sacred and profane) and withstanding the compartmentalized, objective mind-set to which we have been educated and out of which much of our society lives and operates. In a word, Wisdom undermines the need to control life in tidy segments (F 3.38-39).

Our minds stumble, also, over the concept of emptiness in *the memory* because we know human memory is *full* of experience. But now the imagination can no longer connect life's memories to create meaning and hope. We can speak of emptiness in the memory, not because one remembers nothing, but because all the memory holds, which once provided motivation and security, which engendered trust and promise for the future, seems now an illusion and a mockery. Memories do not mean what one thought they did. The memory is indeed empty, possessing nothing but the scattered remains of cherished experiences and the crushing remembrance of personal failure and defeat.

> . . . persons feel so unclean and wretched that it seems God is against them and they are against God. . . . [There is a] a deep immersion of the mind in the knowledge and feeling of one's miseries and evils; it brings all these miseries into relief so that the soul sees clearly that of itself it will never possess anything else . . . the soul at the sight of its miseries feels that it is melting away and being undone by a cruel spiritual death. (N 2.5.5 & 6)[78]

Doubts, imaginings, and fears tear the person to pieces and fill one's affections and energies with indescribable anguish and lethargy.

This kind of clarity about one's miseries generates the overwhelming feeling of being rejected and abandoned not only by one's friends but particularly by God. In fact, abandonment and the betrayal of trust are the hallmark of this dark experience.

78. See also *Dark Night* 2.10.2; *Flame* 1.22 & 23. No. 23 is on the will.

However it happens, what or whom one cherishes most in life is cut off, taken away. The worst thing about this "purification of *the will*" is that the loved one, the very focus of one's love and desire, becomes the cause of one's agony.[79] There is nothing so destructive of affirmation and worth as rejection by one who has loved you and on whom you have counted with complete assurance. It leaves one unable to grasp anything affectively. The seeming destruction of mutuality, with its deep frustration of desire, leaves one without any strength of purpose, bereft of motivation and prone to bitterness. A transcendence in which one is not at home and against which one rebels is forced upon the person.

Alternative Vision: Faith, Hope and Love

We face a challenge in this night to throw into gear the kind of radical faith, hope and love that can endure the death dealing "touch of God's hand," the imprint, which is emptying out our isolated self-sufficiency, on the one hand, and our unfree dependence and fear of transformation and change, on the other. Activated by Sophia's dark presence, the *theological* virtues are our only option, presenting a very uncomfortable alternative vision. Because initially we do not *feel* faith, hope and love, maintaining this basic *contemplative posture* in our prayer and life is extremely difficult. It must overcome an anger, fear and rebellion that want to refuse these theological *gifts* rather than be left with "nothing." Yet the only way the deprivation of the dark night will open into a radical change of consciousness and affectivity is by the *acceptance* of this contemplative posture or vision whereby one actually passes over to the love perspective of Divine Wisdom (A 2.6.6, N 2.21.11-12).

This seems so contradictory, however, because *faith* causes darkness in our very power to understand. Now, in this dark period, it is at cross purposes with our ability to make logical sense out of life, death or eternity. In fact, as Denis Turner suggests in

79. See *Dark Night* 2.7 on "straits of the will"; *Dark Night* 2.9.3 and 7; *Ascent* 3.16 and 35.5; *Flame* 1.23.

The Darkness of God, Negativity in Christian Mysticism, we are actually dispossessed intellectually by faith of any power to construct a meaningful world or a meaningful God.[80] When Jesus Christ recedes from consciousness, it is faith that moves us into the Mystery that is unimaginable, incomprehensible and uncontrollable. While we do not set out to empty the mind, imagination or memory, prayer development and life exacts this of us and then faith becomes an opening into a realm of significance far beyond human understanding.[81]

> Faith darkens and empties the intellect of all its natural understanding and thereby prepares it for union with the Divine Wisdom, [who is the Word the Son of God]. (N 2.21.11)

The hopelessness and emptiness of the dark night is precisely the condition that makes *hope* in the strictly theological sense possible. Hope comes into play when we are really radically at the end, unable to find any further resources to connect the memories, feelings, images and experiences of life in a meaningful pattern, an independent identity of one's own, or a promising future. Then hope, transvaluing the past and forfeiting the struggle to press meaning out of loss, becomes a free, trustful commitment to the impossible which cannot be built out of what one possesses.[82]

> Hope empties and withdraws the memory from all creature possessions, for as St. Paul says, hope is for what is not possessed [Rom. 8:24]. It withdraws the memory from what can be possessed and fixes it on that for which it hopes. Hence, only hope in God prepares the memory perfectly for union with God. (N 2.21.11)

80. Denis Turner, *The Darkness of God: Negativity in Christian Mysticism* (Cambridge: Cambridge University Press, 1995), 246.

81. For a description of faith see *Ascent* 2.3, 4.1-3, 8, 9; *Dark Night* 2.16.8.2.

82. Karl Rahner has helped me interpret John's thought on hope and on the theological virtues. See "On the Theology of Hope," in *Theological Investigations*, vol. 10 (New York: Herder and Herder, 1973), 242–53, and "Theology of Death," in *Theological Investigations*, vol. 13 (New York: Crossroads, 1983), 169–86.

Estrangement and abandonment administer the final test of love. Theological *love* prevents us from forcing the loved one into the constraints of our needs and so takes the beloved as he or she is. In the face of seeming rejection and affective loss, theological love will not in the end surrender to hate or violence nor forfeit belief in one's own worth and lovability. Overcoming the will to die, this love lives honestly with the pain of its own woundedness and longing. It continues to serve others, often with great effectiveness, in spite of intense affective deprivation and loss. This is a profound possession of the self, which frees the will from its own *possessive* desire and readies the person for transformation, as John explains:

> Charity also empties and annihilates the affections and appetites of the will of whatever is not God and centers them on God alone. Thus charity prepares the will and unites it with God through love. (N 2.21.11).

The contemplative posture of faith, hope and love slowly repatterns or transforms desire and consciousness and prepares the human person for the participatory love-knowledge Divine Wisdom is and gives (N 2.21.12). However, even though secret Wisdom is the beginning of a new, more symbolic and integrated way of knowing and valuing, a deeper mutuality and connectedness that subverts our usual understanding of life and reality and expected experiences of satisfaction, nevertheless, Sophia is imperceptible, hidden from our view as a focus of meaning and motivation. She functions, on the one hand, when the image of Christ who has accompanied us thus far recedes from consciousness and cannot be recaptured for motivation and meaning. On the other hand, the subversive dynamic of beloved Sophia is set in motion when human suffering, loss and emptiness have reached such a pitch of consciousness, are such a reflection of Jesus silenced, rejected, abused, dismissed and abandoned that the capacity of the human person is hollowed out for deeper knowing, deeper mutuality, a Wisdom presence and vision in the world (N 2.17).

Then the image of Jesus-Sophia Dying, the image of all that is dying within and without, reaches completion.

> [This is] the real imitation [imprinting] of the perfect life of the Son of God . . . [through which God] will bring her to the high perfection of union with the Son of God, her spouse, and transformation in him through love. (C 1.10)[83]

Ever so slowly Divine Sophia actually shows herself in the soul and in the world transforming and completing human knowing and loving, fulfilling human desire.

> When this . . . night (God's communication to the spirit, which usually occurs in extreme darkness of soul) has passed, a union with the Spouse, *Who is the Sophia of God,* then follows [and] love is . . . perfect when the transformation of the soul in God is achieved. (A 1.2.4)

> Loving knowledge [Divine Wisdom] is given in the beginning through interior purgation and suffering, afterwards in the delight of love. (F 3.34)

> First, we can understand that *the very loving light and Sophia into which the soul will be transformed* is that which in the beginning purges and prepares it, just as the fire which transforms the wood by incorporating it into itself is that which was first preparing it for this transformation. (N 2.10.3)

Transformation and Images of Fruition

What does it mean to be united with and transformed in Sophia? What does the person see and know as a result? And how will a person who becomes such a friend and companion, the Beloved of Sophia, live and function in the world? While the text does not speak specifically of the image of the risen Jesus to indicate the completion of the image of Christ, the symbols of fruition it uses

83. Elizabeth Johnson reminds us of a long-standing tradition of interpretation concerning martyrs, a tradition which Vatican II continues: "Martyrdom 'transforms' a disciple into an intense image of Christ, *imago Christi,* for the martyr 'perfects that image even to the shedding of blood'" (*She Who Is,* 74; *Lumen Gentium* 42).

to describe the experience of transformation do indicate the reality of passing from death to life, from old to new, from present to future. Two of these, *the touch of God* and *the awakening of God,* help us to probe these questions about transformation in Wisdom.

The Touch of Sophia-God

First of all, in an experience of loving communion and total mutuality,[84] the person is touched and marked with an "image of fruition" that now heals and affirms rather than wounds and oppresses (F 3.81). With this symbol of the touch of God, a distinctly Wisdom image found in *The Living Flame,*[85] we see the mysterious evolution from the imprinting of dying Crucified Sophia to the image or all-pervading presence of a Sophia-God who gently touches the totality of a person's life with acceptance and gathers up the scattered fragments of alienation, loneliness, longing, loss and failure into a meaningful whole. Life is no longer seen in painful, confusing, segmented parts.

> You have wounded me [with your touch] in order to cure me, O divine Hand, and you have put to death in me what made me lifeless, deprived me of God's life in which I now see myself live. . . . [You] touch [with] the splendor of your glory and the figure of your substance, [Heb. 1:3], which is your only begotten Son, through whom, being your substance, you touch mightily from one end to the other (Wis. 8:1). And your only begotten Son, O merciful hand of the Father, is the delicate touch by which you touched me with the force of your cautery and wounded me. . . . [Now] then, [through] the delicate touch, the Word, the Son of God, . . . you subtly penetrate the substance of my soul and lightly touching it all, absorb it entirely in yourself in divine ways of delights and sweetnesses. (F 2.16-17)[86]

84. See, for example, *Flame* 3.79.

85. The "touch of divinity" is found also in *The Ascent* (e.g. A 2.26.5-10 and A 2.32) and *The Dark Night*.

86. See *Flame* 3.81. Touch is also an important symbol of desire in *The Spiritual Canticle*. Here in *Flame,* the Word, the Son of God is a touch of the divine hand. Note the comparison at the end of *Flame* 2.17 between the touch or

> O sweet cautery,
> O delightful wound!
> O gentle hand! O delicate touch
> that tastes of eternal life
> and pays every debt!
> In killing you changed death to life. (F 2)

John indicates that now the *glorious* image of Sophia-Jesus has been sketched within: a touch of affirmation, a seal of divinity on a person's life and being (F 2.8). This touch is gentle, adjusting to human readiness, for although Wisdom reaches from one end of the universe to the other, pervading everything, she shows herself in order to exalt and affirm those she loves (Wis. 8:1) and this is a continuing and deepening subversion of the self-image, this time on the side of exaltation. Ultimately, Sophia-Beloved is the presence of a God who not only delights to be with us but whose only desire is to exalt us, delight us, affirm us and make us an equal.

> Since God's purpose in granting these communications is *to exalt the soul,* God does not weary and restrict it, but enlarges and delights it; God does not blacken and convert it to ashes, . . . but brightens and enriches it. (F 2.3)

> If anything pleases [God], it is the exaltation of the soul. Since there is no way by which [God] can exalt her more than by making her equal to [the Divine], God is pleased only with her love. . . . Since the soul in this state possesses perfect love, she is called the Bride of the Son of God, which signifies equality with him. In this equality of friendship the possessions of both are held in common. (C 28.1)[87]

While there is a time to see our miseries and hypocrisies in the mirror of secret, suffering Wisdom and to recognize our suffering lives as a reflection of Jesus rejected, abused and dismissed, the time does come to see one's own beauty in the mirror of

---

tracing within and the withdrawal from the touch or trace of creatures. This is to accent the touch of Sophia-Jesus "compared with" all other touches and is an allusion to *Ascent* 1.4.

87. See *Canticle* 39.6: " . . . equals and companions of God."

the glorified Jesus-Sophia and to experience oneself so loved, so cherished, so affirmed—"a union of love"—that one realizes God deals with one now as with "a Queen," that is, an equal.[88] Over and over again John accents the exaltation, affirmation, delight, sweetness and equality of love:

> Let us rejoice, Beloved,
> and let us go forth
> to behold
> ourselves in your beauty,
> to the mountains and to the hills,
> to where the pure water flows
> and further, deep into the thicket. (C 36)[89]

The person is only able to see herself in the mirror of God's beauty because she has been transformed in Divine Sophia, has received the imprint of the *total* life of Jesus Christ in whom she experiences herself in possession of everything worthwhile on earth and in heaven (C 36.8). As in the dark night, Sophia is full of subversive, creative power, the source of newness and radical self-valuation.[90]

> When you looked at me
> your eyes imprinted your grace in me;
> for this you loved me ardently;
> and thus my eyes deserved
> to adore what they beheld in you.

88. *Flame* 4.13 brings together the Wisdom image of Christ or Word with the experience of equality: " . . . there *the face of the Word,* full of graces, . . . *shines on the queen,* which is the soul, and clothes it in such fashion that, transformed in these attributes of the heavenly king, it is aware of having become a queen." See also *Canticle* 30.6.

89. See commentary *Canticle* 36.5 on this stanza for equality emphasis and extravagant expression of mutuality. See also *Canticle* 32.6; 24.5; 38.3-6. This equality is taken to even greater lengths when God becomes the person's slave and prisoner, subject to her desires (*Canticle* 27.1; 32.1).

90. Susan Cady, Marian Ronan, Hal Taussig, *Sophia, The Future of Feminist Spirituality* (San Francisco: Harper and Row, 1986), 84, suggest that "by identifying with the one who took a playful part in creation, women can imagine new and larger arenas in which their creativity can flourish" in the world.

> Do not despise me;
> for if, before, you found me dark,
> now truly you can look at me
> since you have looked
> and left in me grace and beauty. (C 32-33)

> By this look of love God made her gracious and pleasing to himself [*sic*]. And . . . from this grace and value she received from him, she merited his love *and a value within herself*. (C 32.2)

A value, an appreciation, within herself! If anything marks transformation in Sophia, it is self-acceptance and self-appreciation. In the latter part of both *The Spiritual Canticle* and *The Living Flame*, one can trace a thrilling affirmation of the gifts of the person that undercuts any temptation to false humility.[91] When a person is transformed in divine Sophia, therefore, her view of herself is radically altered. She moves from self-doubt, loneliness, powerlessness, inferiority and subordination to see the completed inner image and to claim her own inner truth, her own inner voice, that is, to claim Wisdom: the creative power to bring into being new ways of thinking, new ideas and priorities, new visions, new ways of living and being together with others on the earth in cooperation and mutuality.[92] In other words,

> . . . the experience is not only within her but overflows and becomes manifest outside of her, and those capable of recognizing it are aware of her experience. . . . This causes awe and respect in others. (C 17.7)

She moves, as well, from domination, control, anxiety, competition and exploitation to receive Wisdom in mindless, playful joy and delight. For the transformed person there is, therefore, not only validation of the inmost self but a fundamental revision of previously held beliefs and a radical questioning of deeply entrenched societal systems.

91. There are many texts that could be cited. See, for example, *Canticle* 30.2-3; 14/15.29; 33.6-9; 16.1 & 8-9; 32.2; 36.5; 24.2-4; 17.5-7.

92. See Cady, Ronan, and Taussig, 84.

But the glorious presence or imprinting of Divine Sophia effects even more. When Sophia-Beloved transforms and exalts a person, every wound of the past, every hurt and bitterness, becomes a wound of love. In fact, the person becomes "completely healthy in love" (F 2.7).[93] Can we even imagine all our wounds, sufferings, obsessions and sins being energized for love, becoming a power for love? The force and weight of our mistakes and failures flipped over to reveal sheer love? Can we imagine feeling a love commensurate with all our life sufferings and losses? The healing promised here is indescribable and it is theological in character rather than simply psychological. This is the other side of the dark night revealing the Resurrected One whose wounds shine brightly forever as wounds of love, and this is the image the transformed person bears sketched within. In the mirror of this Sophia-Jesus, risen from the dead, every wound is seen to be and therefore given back as a wound of love, given back, in fact, as a capacity to see and an empowerment to touch tenderly the mysterious imprinting of divinity present in every person. Furthermore, these wounds of love have been in the making for a very long time. Here the text sings of the person so healed:

> The soul feels its ardor strengthen and increase and its love become so refined in this ardor that seemingly there are seas of loving fire within it, reaching to the heights and depths of the earthly and heavenly spheres, imbuing all with love. It seems to it that the entire universe is a sea of love in which it is engulfed, for conscious of the living point or center of love within itself, it is unable to catch sight of the boundaries of this love. . . . For the soul is converted into an immense fire of love which emanates from the enkindled point at the heart of the [human] spirit. (F 2.10-11)

What must be understood here is that the contemplative person "no longer goes about in search of her own gain" or self-fulfillment, nor does she occupy herself with matters foreign to God's concerns, since now she has traded her former selfcentered

93. Examine *Flame* 2.7-8 to see what "completely healthy" in love means.

manner of dealing with life for a love and service of the Beloved One which embraces the universe. All the powers of the person move in love (C 28.23, 8).

> Now I occupy my soul
> and all my energy in his service;
> I no longer tend the herd,
> nor have I any other work
> now that my every act is love. (C 28)

As Pierre Teilhard de Chardin has also insisted in *The Divine Milieu,* nothing in the universe is a more powerful energy than love. This is what Sophia-God makes use of to bring creation to completion (C 27.8).

> These acts of love are so precious that they are more valuable for the world than any acts that could be done without this love. (F I.3)

Furthermore, this love overflows of necessity and is therefore effective in the service of the world (C 36.4). And few of us would dispute the need for this kind of effective love as a resource for humanity today.

The Awakening of Sophia-God

We have here such a radical change of desire and consciousness that John, in the final stanza of his last major poem, *The Living Flame of Love,* writes about *the awakening of God,* a second image of fruition. It is the symbol of the dark night itself that gives the clue and direction for one of the most dynamic and all-embracing images of the transforming presence of the risen Christ, Divine Sophia. After the silence and suffering of a long dark night, secret Wisdom awakens:

> How gently and lovingly
> you wake in my heart,
> where in secret you dwell alone;
> and in your sweet breathing,
> filled with good and glory,
> how tenderly you swell my heart with love. (F 4)

The awakening of God in the fourth stanza of *The Living Flame* is one of the most significant wisdom sections in John's writings. It is an ode to the fullness of the presence of Divine Sophia in a life and therefore in the world. It shows how profound was John's conscious dependence on the Book of Wisdom for an understanding of *who* the glorified Jesus is for us, how progressively subversive Wisdom really is and who the friend of Wisdom becomes in the world. We read again the description of Sophia influencing John here:

> Wisdom is more mobile than any motion; because of her pureness she pervades and penetrates all things. For she is a breath of the power of God and a pure emanation of the glory of the Almighty. . . . For she is a reflection of eternal light, a spotless mirror of the working of God, and an image of God's goodness. Although she is but one, she can do all things; and while remaining in herself, she renews all things; in every generation she passes into holy souls and makes them friends of God and prophets. . . . She reaches mightily from one end of the earth to the other and orders all things well. (Wis. 7:24-28; 8:1; F 4.6)

The awakening of God within the human heart is, obviously, human awakening to what is. However, since such a fundamental transformation of knowledge, such a radical conversion of perspective and desire, such a drastic expansion of imagination are experienced, it is perceived as God's waking up (seeing) and gently breathing love from the very core of a person to every thought, emotion, desire, action.

> For since it is the soul that is renewed and moved by God so that it might [have] supernatural sight, and since that divine life and the being and harmony of every creature in that life, with its movements in God, is revealed to it with such newness, it seems to the soul that it is God who moves. . . . "For Wisdom is more moveable than all moveable things" [Wis. 7:24]. And this is not because she moves but because she is the principle and root of all movement. *Remaining in herself the same . . . she renews all things* [Wis. 7:27]. Thus . . . Wisdom is more active than all active things. We then ought to say that in this movement it is the soul

> that is moved and awakened from the sleep of natural vision to supernatural vision [i.e., God's vision]. . . . And [thus] the soul sees what God is in [God's very self] and what God is in . . . creatures in only one view. . . . God effects this awakening and view given to the soul [by] remov[ing] some of the many veils and curtains hanging in front of it so that it might get a glimmer of [God] as [God] is. And then that countenance of God, full of graces, becomes partially and vaguely discernible, for not all the veils are removed. (F 4.6-7)

The person then "knows" with a deeper kind of participatory love-knowledge, for when Divine Sophia, the Beloved, the Word "awakens" and "moves" in this way, altering permanently and radically one's vision of reality, then absolutely everyone and everything in the universe is experienced as indissolubly and harmoniously interconnected and part of an energizing Mystery that binds everything together. In the Lover of Divine Sophia we see a remarkable instance of the earth, the cosmos, becoming truly conscious of itself as it really is, every species connected to every other, seeing itself for the first time, as it were, in the eyes of the person transformed in Sophia. For such a person, the face of the awakening God is filled with the gifts and graces of all creatures, the entire creation. The grace, the beauty of every form and species of life is seen in the inner mirror of Wisdom and is, therefore, known in a new way and valued for itself in God.

To see a "trace" of God's passing in the beauty of creatures and the wonder of the earth is one way of knowing and experiencing God. We learn to love God through this experience: finding God in all things! To see and possess the beauty of the created universe and everyone and everything in it *in God* is quite another vision.[94] Some of John's most frequently quoted lines of poetry express this vision:

94. This vision is familiar to the mystics. See, e.g., St. Teresa's experience in *The Book of Her Life*, 40.9-10, *Collected Works*, 1, 280–81: "Once while I was in prayer I was shown quickly, without my seeing any form—but it was a totally clear representation—how all things are seen in God and how [God] holds them all in himself [*sic*]. . . . Let us say that the Divinity is like a very clear diamond, much greater than all the world; or like a mirror, as I said referring to the soul in

> My Beloved, the mountains,
> and lonely wooded valleys,
> strange islands,
> and resounding rivers,
> the whistling of love-stirring breezes.
>
> the tranquil night
> at the time of the rising dawn,
> silent music,
> sounding solitude,
> the supper that refreshes and deepens love. (C 14-15)

These mountains—my Beloved is this to me! These valleys—my Beloved is this to me! Strange islands and resounding rivers that drown our dark desires and fill everything with peace—God is this to me! The Beloved becomes everything and yet everything becomes the "Beloved" one, the Sophia of God, and therefore integrally part of the beloved friend of Wisdom who now experiences herself connected to every other form of life on the earth (C 14/15.4-9; 24.6).[95] In this unearned, gratuitous awakening of consciousness, the participatory love-driven knowledge initially experienced secretly and painfully in the dark night now explodes into an undeniable, conscious insight and passionate love for "the world." This identification with the entire cosmic order and the discovery of the earth as a living organism is the mystical basis for an intimate and compassionate human presence to other humans, to the earth and to all living things.

First of all, then, the capacity for hearing the cry of the poor and suffering of the earth breaks open into a nearly incomprehensible desire to "enter all the afflictions and sorrows of the world" (C 36.11) in order to enter even more deeply into the Divine Wisdom

---

that other vision, except that it is a mirror in so sublime a way that I wouldn't know how to exaggerate this. And we could say that everything we do is visible in this diamond since it is of such a kind that it contains all things within itself; there is nothing that escapes its magnitude. It was a frightening experience for me to see in so short a time so many things joined together in this diamond."

95. Dichotomies are reconciled and cease to exist when the self is no longer defined by opposition and separation but by relationship and connectedness.

in which all are rooted and connected. Because it brings together delight and suffering, happiness and death, *The Spiritual Canticle* 36.11-13 is a mysterious text, difficult to interpret, showing a distinctly different experience from the identification with "the poor" in the dark night. Since the experiences described in these texts are never disembodied, no matter how lofty they seem to be, one has to think that the person transformed in Divine Wisdom is to the rational mind a confusing and wonderful paradox, propelled *to run* with joy into the thicket of the poor and suffering, seeing there *already* the resurrected face of Beloved Sophia.[96]

> And in exchange, it will be a singular comfort and happiness for her to enter all the afflictions and trials of the world, and everything that might be a means to this, however difficult and painful, even the anguish and agony of death, all in order to see herself further within her God. (C 36.11)

> *Suffering is the means of her penetrating further, deep into the thicket of this delectable Wisdom of God.* The purest suffering brings with it the purest and most intimate knowing, and consequently the purest and highest joy, because it is a knowing from further within. (C 36.12)

> Oh! If we could but now fully understand how a soul cannot reach the thicket and wisdom and riches of God, which are of many kinds, without entering the thicket of many kinds of suffering, finding in this her delight and consolation; and how a soul with an authentic desire for *Divine Wisdom wants suffering first in order to enter this Wisdom by the thicket of the cross.* Accordingly, St. Paul admonished the Ephesians not to grow weak in their tribulations and be strong and rooted in charity in order to comprehend with all the saints what is the breadth and height and depth, and to know also the supereminent charity of the knowledge of Christ,

96. I am reminded of an impressive report made some years ago by representatives of the Leadership Conference of Women Religious after attending a conference with religious of Latin America. The LCWR representatives were deeply moved by the joy, the sense of resurrection, that emanated from the religious of Central America who lived and worked with the poor and oppressed and in many cases lived under death sentences because of their ministry.

> in order to be filled with the fullness of God [Eph. 3:13, 17-19]. *The gate entering into these riches of [God's] Wisdom is the cross,* which is narrow, and few desire to enter by it, but many desire the delights obtained from entering there. (C 36.13)

One suspects the Beloved of Sophia has a whole new slant on suffering and identification with the poor and marginalized. Sophia is so related to the world, to the people, that the friend of Sophia will experience herself immersed in and connected to the suffering with the compassion of Sophia. She will value life and health everywhere; value food for bodies as well as education and love for mind and soul; value justice and affirmation and equality. This means that in the transformed person, Sophia's compassionate presence will be productive and deeply subversive.

Second, and related to the first, the capacity for listening to what the earth is telling us opens up. The text speaks, in fact, of an immense, powerful voice that sounds in the soul: the voice of creation in all the magnitude of its struggles and wonders.

> What a person knows and experiences of God in this awakening is entirely beyond words. Since this awakening is the communication of God's excellence to the substance of the soul, . . . an immense, powerful voice sounds in it, the voice of a multitude of excellences . . . infinite in number. The soul is established in them . . . [and it sees God whose] countenance [is] filled with the graces of all creatures, awesome in power and glory, and with the voice of a multitude of excellences. (F 4.10-11)[97]

In actuality, compassionate presence and subversive identification with the marginal experienced in the dark night take on broader and even more effective cosmic significance here. In other words, Sophia awakens not only in a person's individual self, not only in one's sisters and brothers, not only in the poor and marginalized, but Spirit-Sophia awakens simultaneously in all of matter to be enjoyed in the immensity of all that is. The person transformed in Sophia experiences the sacred community of the earth, the

97. See also *Canticle* 39.8-9,11; 14/15.4 & 9-11 for more on this voice.

entire earth with all its energies and diversity and all its species awakening and coming to life—all a part of each, and all a part of her—each with a value and a wisdom of its own, all moving in a wonderful harmony and each giving voice to what Creator-Sophia is in it.

> In the nocturnal tranquility and silence and in that knowledge of the divine light the soul becomes aware of Wisdom's wonderful harmony and sequence in the variety of her creatures and works. Each of them is endowed with a certain likeness of God and in its own way gives voice to what God is in it. So creatures will be for the soul a harmonious symphony of sublime music surpassing all concerts and melodies of the world. (C 14/15.25)

To know oneself, the human, one with the immensity of all that is, is an ecstatic experience in which to rest and rejoice, and even to suffer. Because historically until very recently we have been deprived of the language of contemplation or mysticism in ordinary life and religious education, American spirituality is not at home with words like resting, tasting, ecstasy, being, delight, joy, Lover/Beloved, nor are Americans, therefore, at home with "the languages of the multitude of beings" inhabiting the earth in such a highly differentiated unity.[98] Our culture has had far too much to do with achieving mastery over the earth, other earth species and one another, to be mindful that there is a contemplative time for resting and delighting in the exquisite harmony of

98. Here John of the Cross' teaching intersects with Brian Swimme's and Thomas Berry's thinking in *The Universe Story*, 258. They suggest we need an earth-centered language, one enjoyed, until now, only by the mystics and poets: "Beyond any spoken or written language are the languages of the multitude of beings, each of which has its own language given to it generally, in the world of the living, by genetic coding. Yet each individual being has extensive creativity in the use of language. Humans are becoming more sensitive to the nonhuman languages of the surrounding world. We are learning mountain language . . . This capacity for understanding and communicating in these languages, until now enjoyed only by our poets and mystics, is of immense significance since so much of life is lived in association with the other beings of the universe. . . . A more symbolic language is needed to enter into the subjective depth of things."

all that is and for understanding and communicating in the nonhuman languages of mountain, river, tree, wolf, stars. The person transformed in Beloved Sophia hears the new, more symbolic languages needed to enter into the subjective depths of things.

We need this experience, enhancing self-appreciation and yet relativizing self-importance, if we are to move toward an understanding of the connectedness of the cosmos that will save the earth and all its life. It is Divine Sophia, the glorified Christ, who shows us the unbreakable connection between creator and creatures, between heaven and earth, between one another, for Sophia pervades, connects and energizes the entire cosmos. It is not that Sophia-Jesus reconnects us to the earth and to one another. Rather, in the experience of awakening, one *sees and knows* it is a delusion to perceive ourselves as separate from the earth, from one another, and from all other species of life, superior and unaccountable to the earth and to other forms of life. The vision of Divine Sophia enables contemplative people to be keepers of the earth and of beauty because they experience the connectedness of it all in *the* Beauty.

John of the Cross could not have expressed this experience as twentieth century writers like Thomas Berry, Brian Swimme, Elizabeth Johnson and Sallie McFague do:

> Even as a species we are not separate and isolated, but in all our uniqueness . . . [w]e belong, from the cells of our bodies to the finest creations of our minds, to the intricate, constantly changing cosmos.[99]

Nevertheless, within the framework of a Sophia-God, this sixteenth century mystic does describe this experience of the reality of the universe in a way we are only beginning to understand and express.

99. Elizabeth Johnson, *Women, Earth, and Creator Spirit* (New York: Paulist Press, 1993), 32, with note: Sallie McFague, *Models of God: Theology for an Ecological, Nuclear Age* (Philadelphia: Fortress 1987), 7–8. Johnson proposes a model of kinship "that traces an organic connection between human beings and the earth."

> This is the third gift the Beloved will bestow on the soul. Since many plants and animals are nurtured in it, the "grove" refers to God, for God nurtures and gives being to all creatures rooted and living in God. Through this gift God shows himself [*sic*] to her and reveals himself as Creator.
>
> By the "living beauty" of this grove, for which she asks the Bridegroom here, she intends to beg for the grace, wisdom, and beauty which every earthly and heavenly creature not only has from God but also manifests in its wise, well-ordered, gracious, and harmonious relationship to other creatures. Thus we find this accord among the lower creatures and among the higher, and we find it as well in the relationship between the higher and lower. The knowledge of this harmony fascinates and delights the soul. (C 39.11)

Implications

The Mystic Vision

In actuality, John had a vision of kinship with the earth whose evolutionary truth and meaning he could not have begun to fathom with his sixteenth-century cosmology and world view.[100] Yet it welled up from the ageless roots of his being, from the Source of all life, from the Wisdom of the Universe itself—all the collective energies of the cosmos, all the reserves of life in the earth coalescing and reaching for consciousness in this sixteenth-century mystic. His wisdom vision was far ahead of his time—in a sense, ahead of himself. Yet he looked over the edges of human consciousness and dwelt there. And his life, dedicated to the companionship of Sophia-Jesus, not only endured the darkness of a dying time but actually called forth the *unitive* energies of the cosmos and gave them sanctuary within himself. The universe spoke its meaning in him.[101]

100. According to Kieran Kavanaugh, *Collected Works of St. John*, 709, John seemed to have accepted the Copernican theory. The University of Salamanca, where John studied, was the first to accept and teach the Copernican system but by the time the first edition of John's works appeared, Copernicus' work was on the Index of Forbidden Books.

101. Tarnas, 435.

If indeed matter, alive with energy stretching back through galactic ages to the Big Bang, does somehow evolve to spirit, as Teilhard de Chardin said some years ago and others are suggesting now, if the human spirit is the cosmos come to full consciousness, then the mystic transformed in Divine Sophia is the human spirit itself at the fullest consciousness possible to the human species at any one time in history.[102] This means that transformation in Divine Sophia is not something completely new and extraordinary added to the universe from outside by a God distant from the cosmos; rather, this transformation is the most advanced evolutionary possibility and expression, the cutting edge of evolution, the full flowering of the earth and of the cosmic energies within the human. As such, the mystic is a prophecy and a promise. And the wisdom language of the mystic is a code to be broken by us for our time and situation when the survival of the earth hangs on humanity's total, unwavering appropriation of a new vision of the cosmos and even a new vision of God.

In John's writings we gain some idea of the frontiers to which Sophia brings us. Sophia is the key for understanding the place of the mystic at the forefront of the earth's evolutionary process, the cosmos come to full consciousness. If, as Thomas Berry and Brian Swimme believe, the next stage in the development of the universe will require, above everything else, the insight of shamanic powers, then Sophia may be the God we need to make us mystics.[103]

The Prophet of Sophia and Contemplative Transformation

Transformation in Loving Sophia actually changes the mind, the imagination, the memory, the heart, the desires, the will, through a painful process of death and thereby advances human knowing and loving with a vision of the universe that places Sophia in intimate, dynamic, energizing, life-giving relationship to the whole

102. For one careful analysis of the evolution of human consciousness see Johnson, *Women, Earth, and Creator Spirit*, 37–38. I have drawn on her development aware that recent discoveries in outer space raise questions about the beginning of the Universe as well as the evolution of human life and consciousness. Another theory may in time replace the one Johnson describes.

103. See Swimme and Berry, 238.

evolutionary process. The mystic's human powers, the "deep caverns of feeling," united with and transfigured in Sophia, take on the Divine Energy at the heart of the universe (C 26.5-9; 28.3-5).

The person no longer knows and understands with the vigor of her own natural light but with the divine light. This is, in effect, the transformation of the mind through a new kind of loving knowledge: Sophia. The memory, too, is changed in this union by an experience of ultimate assurance. Obsession with the past gives way to a new possession and sense of belongingness, and this conversion of memory releases creativity. The human capacity to love is also changed by the experience of God's love, as has been said above. The mystic is transformed by love and therefore loves with the love God has for us. The imprinting ("I live now not I but Christ lives in me.") is so complete that the mind is God's mind, the will is God's will, the memory is the eternal memory of God and its delight and desire are God's delight and desire (F 2.34). The person becomes, therefore, "like the shadow of God" in the world: in other words, the prophet of Sophia (F 3.78).

These are realities almost impossible to comprehend or even believe in with our postmodern consciousness but what is significant is that for the friend and prophet of Divine Sophia the conventional way of knowing and loving is gone (C 26.13-17). The process of contemplative transformation is, moreover, not only an irreversible maturation but also a very radical re-education of human desire and consciousness. This is why Sophia-Wisdom is so subversive and perhaps this is one reason why her presence and power have been so confined and muted in the history of Christianity.

Those who have become friends and intimates of Wisdom, the shadow of God in the world, whose consciousness, imaginations, hearts, desires, are radically expanded by the awakening of God, by the drink of Loving Sophia, truly touch the interiority of everything living and understand the community of which we are all a part. These prophets embody the desire of Sophia-Christ for the world. They threaten the security of our way. They stand, as it were, on the side of the creative Wisdom of God actively calling us to re-creation and continual learning, to sensitivity, to beauty and wonder, to responsibility for one another and for the earth, to participative living and teaching, to connectedness and community, to justice in coherence with the harmony and order of everything on earth, over against selfish detachment, isolated individualism, self-concerned competition, domination and oppression of others.

Participatory Love Knowledge

It should be clear now why the Wisdom of the mystic can be called a *participatory* way of knowing and loving that moves beyond the paradigm of hierarchical dualism that has been, in the past, part of the philosophical underpinning for our lives. There is a thrilling intersection between the love-knowledge of the contemplative and the participatory epistemology Richard Tarnas believes has been slowly surfacing in philosophy. The experience of the person transformed in Sophia validates the emerging conviction that the relation of the human mind to the cosmos is ultimately not dualistic but participatory. This throws additional light on Tarnas' previously quoted words:

> In its own depths the imagination directly contacts the creative process of nature [the universe], realizes the process within itself, and brings nature's reality [of the cosmos] to conscious expression.
>
> Then the world speaks its meaning through human consciousness. Then human language itself can be recognized as rooted in a deeper reality, as reflecting the universe's unfolding meaning. Through the human intellect, in all its personal individuality, contingency and struggle, the world's evolving thought-content achieves conscious articulation, . . . the world's truth achieves its existence when it comes to birth in the human mind. As the plant at a certain stage brings forth its blossom, so does the universe bring forth new stages of human knowledge. And as Hegel emphasized, the evolution of human knowledge is the evolution of the world's self-revelation.[104]

104. Tarnas, 434–45.

This understanding is strikingly similar to the new paradigm proposed by Thomas Berry, the "geologian" and historian of cultures, and written about by many others, particularly women. While we do witness the frightening breakdown of many structures—cultural, philosophical, scientific, religious, moral, artistic, social, political, atomic, ecological—we see, also, this new participatory world view breaking through on so many levels, in so many disciplines, reflective of a deeper, powerful process impelled by forces beyond the merely human.[105]

Sophia God Image

In this world view presently crying out for paradigmatic significance, Sophia may well be a God image that corresponds and resonates with the current state of the evolving collective psyche of the Earth. It seems to me that Sophia is one clear, significant God gestalt retrieved from the tradition and emerging out of a long, dark night of broken God symbols.[106] Spiritual directors

105. Tarnas clarifies that this participatory epistemology is not a "regression to naive participation mystique but . . . the dialectical synthesis of the long evolution from the primordial undifferentiated consciousness through the dualistic alienation. It incorporates the postmodern understanding of knowledge but goes beyond it" (434–35).

106. Tarnas writes with incisive clarity about the progression in history from one paradigm to another, about the birth and death of paradigms and why one paradigm is perceived at one time as a liberation and then at another as a constriction and prison. "For the birth of every new paradigm is also a conception in a new conceptual matrix, which begins the process of gestation, growth, crisis, and revolution all over again. Each paradigm is a stage in an unfolding evolutionary sequence, and when the paradigm has fulfilled its purpose, when it has been developed and exploited to its fullest extent, then it loses its numinosity, it ceases to be libidinally charged, it becomes felt as oppressive, limiting, opaque, something to be overcome—while the new paradigm that is emerging is felt as a liberating birth into a new, luminously intelligible universe. . . . As the inner gestalt changes in the cultural mind, new empirical evidence just happens to appear, pertinent writings from the past suddenly are unearthed, appropriate epistemological justifications are formulated, supportive sociological changes coincidentally take place . . . new psychological predispositions and metaphysical assumptions emerge from the collective mind, from within many individual minds simultaneously" (438–39).

find that people, both women and men, are actually experiencing Sophia and her emancipatory and transformative potential in their prayer, theologically confusing as this may sometimes seem to them. We may see Jesus more and more taking on the marks of Sophia, and this is probably what will save Jesus for some people. This is where *the tradition of Wisdom* in mysticism, so long muted and marginalized but embodied with such prophetic power in John of the Cross' writings, will reassure us and enable theology to speak anew about Jesus Christ.[107] The mysticism of John of the Cross supports a Sophia-God image, and a Sophia-God image, before everything else, subverts the way we understand God. It has the potential, therefore, to transform not only our consciousness and desire but most of all to change radically our theological discourse.

Feminist Consciousness and New Relationship of Mutuality

Just as there was a correlation in the past between the muting of contemplation, the suppression of Sophia, the exploitation of the earth, and the marginalization of women, so now is the emergence of feminist consciousness in so many cultures and disciplines directly connected to both the Sophia-God image and the participatory or contemplative way of knowing and understanding human life, as was already indicated in relation to the dark night. The emergence of women's voices and influence is part of an enormous epochal shift taking place in human consciousness and rising out of the unitive energies at work in the universe. As far back as the sixteenth century, a mystic like John, educated by lifelong companionship with Divine Sophia, experienced the

107. See Tarnas, 438, and Johnson, "Redeeming the Name," 116: "Is the Christological tradition hopelessly patriarchal or are there marginalized impulses that can be released to shape a Christology of healing and liberation? With critical analysis and alternative possibilities in view, theology then speaks anew about Jesus the Christ." Moreover, John of the Cross is not the only one in the tradition who was prophetic for a future time concerning Wisdom. He stands in a long line of church writers and mystics. See, for example, Sophia Barbara Moore's recent treatment of wisdom and Louis de Montfort in "Wisdom, A Hidden Treasure," *Christian Spirituality Bulletin* 3 (Spring 1995): 18–23.

movement of this marginalized feminine toward reconciliation and mutuality. Even the major symbolism of his poetry, Lover/Beloved, is testimony to this experienced mutuality and as such is prophetic for our time, for Who is Lover, who Beloved, who masculine, who feminine?[108]

It is not by accident, therefore, that Sophia-God, bearing the marks of the feminine, comes to the forefront at a time when many believe the dominant and pervasive masculinity of the Western intellectual and spiritual tradition is dying. Actually, the mystical language of John was a promise of this and a validation for us now of its rightness and inevitability.

Feminists have long been conscious of the darkness of this dying time as they have struggled to find meaning in the experience of impasse in their God images, in their churches and theology, in their institutional lives, in their social and political lives. Richard Tarnas, however, emphasizes that the crisis of modern man [*sic*] is essentially not a feminine but a masculine crisis whose transforming resolution is actually occurring within the tremendous emergence of the feminine in our culture and in the struggles surrounding it. The dominance of the masculine (in all of us) is not only dying (dark night), but, touched by the increasing numinosity of Holy Sophia, is truly at a highly critical stage of awakening and is slowly entering, as Tarnas writes,

> into a fundamentally new relationship of mutuality with the feminine in all its forms. The feminine then becomes not that which must be controlled, denied and exploited, but rather fully

108. Sandra Schneiders writing in *Women and the Word: The Gender of God in the New Testament and the Spirituality of Women* (New York: Paulist Press, 1986) on the Song of Songs, which influenced John so profoundly, says: "As Phyllis Trible has explained, this celebration of human sexual love is completely devoid of patriarchal overtones. In fact scholars continue to be unable to distinguish precisely between the discourse of the woman and the man. . . . Although the androcentric imagination of commentators has always assumed that the male lover is God and the female Israel, the Church, or the soul, there is nothing in the Canticle itself to suggest this. God might just as plausibly be represented by the woman as by the man" (34f.). Schneiders's essay provides a powerful underpinning for this entire study.

> acknowledged, respected, and responded to for itself. It is recognized not as the objectified "other," but rather source, goal, and immanent presence.[109]

In the concluding paragraphs of *The Passion of the Western Mind*, Tarnas responds to the question often asked: Is this not just a passing fad, the last gasp of the Enlightenment? Why have we become so aware of the pervasive masculinity of our culture and spiritual tradition only now when for almost every previous generation it was nearly invisible?

> I believe this is occurring now because, as Hegel suggested, a civilization cannot become conscious of itself, cannot recognize its own significance, until it is so mature that it is approaching its own death. Today we are experiencing something that looks very much like the death of modern man. . . . Perhaps, the end of "man" himself is at hand. But man is not a goal. Man is something that must be overcome—and fulfilled in the embrace of the feminine. . . . And their synthesis leads to something beyond itself: It brings an unexpected opening to a larger reality that cannot be grasped before it arrives, because this new reality is itself a creative act.[110]

Perhaps now when the dominance and effects of the isolated masculine have become so apparent and when the feminine is welling up with such powerful energy, Sophia is a God-presence capable of moving with humanity into the next epoch of life on earth. When we have passed through this night, says the mystic, we will be united with and transfigured in Divine Sophia, she who is the Word, the Christ. In this union, the evolutionary imperative of the earth, which is before us now, will come to full consciousness in the human spirit. We need a Sophia-God for this, a God who, while touching and embracing tenderly both man and woman, truly transcends patriarchy and is able, therefore, to sustain this cultural death and new synthesis and give life and meaning to them.

109. Tarnas, 444 with 435, 442.
110. Tarnas, 445.

Conclusion

It is no wonder that now when the human species' manipulation of the earth and the long oppression and neglect of the feminine truly threaten the survival of life on earth, when we are conscious of so many insoluble problems coming to a head in our age, when so much is breaking apart in violence and hatred, we may finally be ready and open to the experience of Sophia-God, that is, to the mystical experience and to a kind of love-knowledge as yet uncommon in human consciousness today.

At a time when philosophy is shifting radically and theology is searching for a meaningful God, when the age of technology, with all its magnificent achievements, has yet exploited the earth as an object for domination, and when a new participative epistemology is beginning to operate, a mystic like John provides some of the most precious materials for the new conceptual house of faith we are trying to build for ourselves. He "knew" that "all thinking must begin with [belief in that] cosmic genetical relatedness" that the mystic transformed in the mirror of Sophia experiences.[111]

I believe we have held up John of the Cross as if he were the end of the process of transformation. The wisdom of this mystic is more like a beginning in that his insight and experience point toward and even usher in an age yet unborn. He had the magnificent contemplative experience of mutuality and connectedness, of being part of and kin to all creation in Beloved Sophia who secretly deconstructed the pyramid of hierarchical dualism that philosophically supported his life.[112] Now, at the end of the twentieth century, there is a significance to his experience that only we can name and understand this way as his insight, once

111. Brian Swimme cited by Sallie McFague, "Imaging a Theology of Nature: The World as God's Body," in *Liberating Life: Contemporary Approaches to Ecological Theology*, ed. Charles Birch (Maryknoll, NY: Orbis Books, 1990), 225.

112. See Johnson, *Women, Earth*, 28, 60, 63. John could only write with the philosophical assumptions and language of sixteenth century Spain. Nevertheless, his experience, I believe, surpassed in significant ways the philosophical paradigms of his time. So we struggle with his language, even while we resonate with the experience described.

so prophetic and almost unimaginable, actually takes shape in postmodern consciousness.

Most importantly, this means John's vision is not just a goal to be repeated but rather one example of life-long companionship with Sophia. His vision is only one segment of a sequence of irreversible transformations in space and time into which we need to enter on our own, thereby creating another segment, our own piece,[113] in the evolution of cosmic consciousness. We must be ready to surrender to the process of transformation ahead of us; eager, or at least willing, to appropriate the patterns of Beloved Sophia and move with the earth toward greater variety and intensity and depth of expression and to ever more intimate bonding with woman, with man, with every species of life that exists.

One thing is certain: In this movement of transformation, the mystical intuition does not allow the suppression of Divine Sophia's personal engagement in the developmental process of the earth. Furthermore, since Spirit-Sophia is the unceasing, dynamic flow of divine power that sustains and pervades and embraces the universe, bringing forth life and energy at every moment, the prophet of Sophia cannot transcend the human or the cosmos, and contemplation is more starkly necessary than ever before.

We are faced with a question repeatedly raised through the centuries by the contemplative tradition and repeatedly muted, suppressed or ignored by the churches and society: is it time for a public contemplation, public education for contemplative prayer, that is, the integration into public life and education of a societal understanding of the contemplative process of transformation[114] rather than a contemplative life largely hidden in the cloisters, hermitages and ashrams of the world, muted by those who fear,

113. While I am conscious of having done a new critical reading of John of the Cross in retrieving wisdom, I believe that there is another creative step in interpretation that must be taken in contemporary spirituality.

114. The desire for this pervades our society. See, e.g., Michael Crichton, *Travel* (New York: Ballantine Books, 1988) for the account of an unusual life-long search for contemplative experience. Crichton concludes his book: "We need the insights of the mystic every bit as much as we need the insight of the scientist" (375).

however unconsciously, not only Divine Sophia but the evolutionary power of mystical transformation? And what would we have to do to achieve this if we believed it? What would educators in our schools and colleges do? What would business leaders meeting to discuss how to break the cycle of violence and bolster the economic vitality of our cities do? What agenda would politicians pursue? What would women's groups do? Where would Church leaders put their energies? What would each one of us do if we believed in the enormous power of contemplative transformation, transformation in Beloved Sophia?

11

Contemplative Transformation in Sophia-Wisdom

A Way of Decolonizing Faith and Society

Alex Mikulich

> "Do not conform yourself to this age but be transformed by the renewal of your mind, that you may discern what is the will of God, what is good, pleasing and perfect."
> —Romans 12:2

> "O my body, makes of me always a man who questions!"
> —Franz Fanon

> "What is even more significant today is that many of our societal experiences open into profound impasse, for which we are not educated, particularly as Americans."
> —Constance FitzGerald, OCD

This chapter celebrates Carmelite mystic Constance FitzGerald's education for contemplative transformation as a way of being that nurtures the conditions of the possibility of decolonizing faith and society. In her now classic essay "Impasse and Dark Night," she called our attention to the profound impasse we face personally and societally. By "societal impasse," FitzGerald discerned the "signs of the times," indeed of an epoch, in which citizens of a dominant nation—the United States—"can find no escape from the world we have built, where the poor and oppressed cry out, where the earth and the environment cry out, and where the specter of nuclear waste haunts future generations."[1]

FitzGerald's prophetic insight endures three decades later. She poses a contemplative and critical way of framing this chapter in terms of three interrelated and fundamental crises of our time: ecological, socioeconomic, and spiritual-cultural. In the midst of a culture of climate-change denial and a fossil-fuel-based economy, it seems nearly impossible to even begin to adequately address the ecological crisis that threatens the very life of the planet. As the global neo-liberal economic way of life threatens the planet, it simultaneously spawns a socio-economic crisis in which the wealth of society is directed to the richest while the most vulnerable bear ever-increasing and death-dealing burdens. These ecological and economic crises are fundamentally intertwined with three spiritual-cultural divides: disconnections between persons and nature, between individuals and others, and between society and authentic ecological development—that is the full thriving of human and planetary biodiversity. The profound disconnection between the imperative for infinite growth of current economic logic and the finite resources of the earth threaten all of life as we know it. People who are oppressed everywhere and planetary biodiversity seem only to cry out more.

In the midst of this predicament, FitzGerald explains, logical solutions rooted in Western rationality, however attractive they may be, do not yield or facilitate transformation. FitzGerald's analysis of Western epistemology and patriarchy, I contend, finds deep resonance in decoloniality and its relentless questioning and critique of the "darker side of Western modernity,"[2] that is, the Colonial Matrix of Power (CMP).

1. Constance FitzGerald, "Impasse and Dark Night," in *Living with Apocalypse: Spiritual Resources for Social Compassion*, ed. Tilden Edwards (San Francisco: Harper & Row, 1984), 105.

2. Walter Mignolo, *The Darker Side of Western Modernity: Global Futures, Decolonial Options* (Durham: Duke University Press, 2011), 16.

Constance FitzGerald's public education for contemplation and transformation, I argue, grounds a spirituality to create the conditions of the possibility of decolonizing faith and society. In decolonial terms, FitzGerald's questioning and critique of modernity, in particular, offers a way of undoing the Eurocentric totalizing claims of modernity/coloniality. The problem of those totalizing claims is that "*knowledge itself is an integral part of imperial processes of appropriation.*"[3] An incessant critique of modernity's epistemological rules is necessary. Epistemic disobedience means disobeying the rules of the game set by modernity/coloniality.

Disobeying the rules of the game is a condition of the possibility of de-linking from modernity's hegemony and setting the conditions for authentic liberation. Far more profound than resistance to the colonial matrix of power, FitzGerald's contemplative praxis, drawing on the life-giving well of Sophia-Wisdom, underscores the need for un-learning the untruths in which we are humanly, spiritually, and morally deformed every day through white settler coloniality. Her acoustic ethic suggests reexisting on other grounds than modernity/coloniality that create the conditions for the possibility whereby women, peoples of colors, and the *damned of the earth*[4] may fully thrive through ways of living that give life to planetary biodiversity.

I proceed in three steps. Since FitzGerald does not explicitly name decoloniality, my first section frames her social analysis of impasse within a larger decolonial praxis. I find convergence between FitzGerald's critique of modernity with decolonial praxis. Drawing on my own experience of dwelling in colonized New England, my second part elucidates how quotidian white settler common sense reinforces the global culture and structures of American settler colonialism. White settler colonialism underscores the need for unlearning the totalizing claims of modernity/coloniality.[5] My final section turns to contemplative transformation in

3. Ibid., 205.

4. Frantz Fanon's *The Wretched of the Earth* is an enduring decolonial text that names modernity/coloniality's despised peoples *les damnés de la terre*.

5. Madina V. Tlostanova and Walter D. Mignolo, *Learning to Unlearn: Decolonial Reflections from Eurasia and the Americas* (Columbus: Ohio State University Press, 2012).

Sophia-Wisdom. FitzGerald's praxis, centered in Sophia-Wisdom and framed within decoloniality, I suggest, offers a way of unlearning modernity's totalizing claims, relearning our pasts, and co-sensing communal futures whereby all people and planetary biodiversity may fully thrive.

Part 1: The Problem of Societal Impasse and Modernity/Coloniality

Interestingly, at roughly the same time (mid-1980s) Anibal Quijano was conceiving the Colonial Matrix of Power (CMP), Constance FitzGerald began to articulate a Carmelite conception of a societal dark night. Both begin their respective social analyses with the concrete historical situation in which people live, and, importantly, invite a spirituality that returns to that situation in order to respond to it. Both interpret modernity to be a time full of multiple social, political, economic, religious, and environmental crises.

While Western modernity celebrates itself through a rhetoric of incessant progress and secular salvation its "underside," or "hidden agenda," reveals the "*dispensability* (or expendability) *of human life*" as Western economic practices and "knowledge justified racism and the inferiority of human lives that were naturally considered dispensable."[6] The CMP is the logic that "generates, reproduces, modifies, and maintains" interconnected, historical hierarchies of race, class, labor, gender/sex, heterosexuality/homosexuality, spiritual/religious, aesthetic, epistemic, linguistic, and the "modern subject" as "the idea of Man" that "became the model for the Human and for Humanity."[7]

In his original formulation of the colonial matrix, Quijano described four interrelated domains of management and control: of the economy, of authority, of gender and sexuality, and of knowledge and subjectivity.[8] These four domains of management

6. Mignolo, *Darker Side*, 6.

7. Ibid., 17–19.

8. Ibid., 8–9. See also Anibal Quijano, "Coloniality and Modernity/Rationality," in *Globalization and the Decolonial Option*, ed. Walter Mignolo and Arturo Escobar (London and New York: Routledge, 2010), 22–32.

and control of world order are supported by two legs of racial and patriarchal foundations of knowledge. Both Quijano and Walter Mignolo contend that the original racial and patriarchal foundation of the matrix is Western Christian theology. Christian theology constructed the "blood" distinction between Christians, Moors, and Jews.[9] While the initial conquest of the so-called New World configured race as "blood," eventually the key marker of race became skin as a way for Western imperialists to justify antiblackness through the Atlantic slave trade.

Coloniality is the ongoing oppressive side of modernity. Everyone is within the matrix. Each hierarchical domain is interconnected with all others—the matrix cannot be observed from some universal perspective outside of it. The CMP is continually renewed through quotidian living in local contexts in relationship to larger state systems of domination, what Mignolo names global or imperial designs.[10] There is no outside perspective. If there is an unobserved universal observer that outside viewer will "either be the God of Christian theology or the Subject of Secular Reason."[11]

I find an uncanny resemblance between decoloniality and FitzGerald's interpretation of societal impasse. The problem of impasse, FitzGerald finds, is far more than personal, because its historical roots are global in scope. Both decoloniality and FitzGerald find interwoven roots of global domination in Western epistemology, patriarchy, and racism. Our dominant nation, she contends, exacerbates the problem of impasse because it only teaches us "illusion, minimization, repression, denial, [and] apathy," through the "social, economic, and political forces of our time."[12]

FitzGerald's critique of our national lust for domination, and how this lust itself is an illusion that exacerbates impasse, is especially poignant since the 2016 election of a white nationalist

9. See also Willie James Jennings, *The Christian Imagination: Theology and the Origins of Race* (New Haven: Yale University Press, 2010).

10. Walter Mignolo, *Local Histories/Global Designs: Coloniality, Subaltern Knowledges, and Border Thinking*, rev. ed. (Princeton, NJ: Princeton University Press, 2012).

11. Mignolo, *Darker Side*, 16.

12. FitzGerald, "Impasse and Dark Night," 105.

president. The president's minimization of suffering inflicted on migrants, women, people of color, and people who are disabled feeds on a white electorate that celebrates this administration's cruelty.[13] Reports of sexual assault by officers of the US Customs and Border Protection,[14] abuse of children in detention, separation of children from their parents,[15] as well as the president's repeated racist attacks[16] on four women of color and the Americans whom they represent in Congress are only the most recent manifestations of the dynamic of oppression and impasse that FitzGerald describes. Patriarchal, egotistical reason, left to itself, leads to more destruction and is unrecognized by the president, his party, and his followers.

In other words, FitzGerald's description of impasse itself provides an analysis of the "signs of the times" and the CMP. Her critique of Christianity and modernity begins with a critique of a patriarchal system that visualizes God, and implicitly the church, in exclusively male terms that are destructive. An exclusively male image of God is experienced as unsatisfying "because it serves to reinforce male domination, a patriarchal value system, and an entire male world view."[17]

The problem is the (il)logic of Western rationality only leads to more oppression. The oppressive side of desire shows up in the "national projection of our shadow on others." If we refuse to

13. Joan Walsh, "A Weekend of Trumpian Cruelty: Remember That Is the point," *The Nation* (July 15, 2019), available online at https://www.thenation.com/article/trump-pence-ice-raids-cruelty-is-the-point/.

14. Jacob Soboroff and Julia Ainsley, "Migrant Children Describe Sex Assault, Retaliation by Border Agents," *NBC News* (July 9, 2019), available online at https://www.nbcnews.com/politics/immigration/migrant-kids-overcrowded-arizona-border-station-allege-sex-assault-retaliation-n1027886.

15. National Network for Immigrant and Refugee Rights, "Separation of Families at the Border—Overview and Update" (January 17, 2019), available online at https://www.nnirr.org/drupal/family-separation-at-border.

16. Laura King, "Trump Renews Attack on Minority Congresswomen; Congressman Offers Sharp Rebuke," *Los Angeles Times* (July 21, 2019), available online at https://www.latimes.com/politics/story/2019-07-21/trump-renews-attack-on-minority-congresswomen.

17. FitzGerald, "Impasse and Dark Night," 108.

read the signs of dark night and impasse, and "avoid appropriating the impasse, we see cold reason, devoid of imagination, heading with deadly logic toward violence, hardness in the face of misery, a sense of inevitability, war, and death."[18] Rational planning cannot extricate us from impasse.

Impasse is a limit situation in which there is "no way out, no way around, no rational escape from what imprisons one, no possibilities in the situation."[19] Ironically, FitzGerald explains, impasse is experienced, both personally and societally, as the problem itself in the attempt to respond rationally. Logical solutions provide no way out and feel dissatisfying. She notices how the "whole life situation suffers a depletion" in which suffering seems to take over one's entire life. Impasse may feel like physical and spiritual imprisonment. The most dangerous temptation is giving in to despair "in the face of disappointment, disenchantment, hopelessness, and loss of meaning that encompass one."[20] Unsurprisingly, such attitudes may "engender a sense of failure," enforcing the assumption, often incorrect, that an individual or a group is culpable for their own predicament.

At deeper levels of impasse, moreover, there seems to be a complete loss of the support systems on which we previously relied. Powerlessness takes over as we lose trust and do not know to whom to turn. For people caught in the experience of impasse and imprisonment there seems only to be disintegration of the self and self-worth, both personally and societally.

As Americans "we are not educated for impasse, for the experience of human limitation that will not yield to hard work, studies, statistics, and rational analysis. We stand helpless before the insurmountable problems of our world."[21] Perhaps worse, we dare not engage impasse, as we will not let impasse come to full consciousness. It is too destructive of individual and US national self-esteem.

18. Ibid.,107.
19. Ibid., 94.
20. Ibid.
21. Ibid., 105.

The problem religiously, spiritually, and morally is that collectively we do not allow ourselves to be totally challenged by anyone who is oppressed or "by the unjust, unequal situation of women in a patriarchal, sexist culture; by those tortured and imprisoned and murdered in the name of national security; by the possibility of the destruction of humanity."[22]

The problem of impasse is captured in the epigraph from Saint Paul's letter to the Romans: "Do not conform yourself to this age but be transformed by the renewal of your mind, that you may discern what is the will of God, what is good and pleasing and perfect" (Rom 12:2; NABRE). Perhaps Saint Paul's admonition seems fairly straightforward to North American people of faith who pride themselves on being independent. The call appears relatively uncomplicated. Our individualist mind-set assumes it does not address more complex biblical and moral issues like love of neighbor.

Saint Paul, however, highlights a problem that precisely concerns larger social and moral issues where we dwell, sense, think, and act. The question of the composition of our time and place may have everything to do with our capacity to even begin to *not* conform to "this age." Walter Wink explains that there are two interchangeable terms for "age" or "time" that are used in biblical texts: *kosmos* and *aiðn*. Wink finds that *kosmos* denotes a spatial concept of time as "system," while *aiðn* indicates a temporal "epoch." Maintaining the similarity and distinction of the terms is important for grasping the full meaning of biblical texts.

In his exegesis of Saint Paul, Paul uses the word *aiðn*, translated as "Domination Epoch," to mark "the intolerable extension of oppression from generation to generation, and century to century, presided over by Satan, the god of the Domination Epoch."[23] Wink translates the first phrase of Romans 12:2 as "Do not be conformed to this Domination Epoch." Wink warns that liberation becomes nearly impossible if we conform to the Domination

22. Ibid., 106.

23. Walter Wink, *Engaging the Powers: Discernment and Resistance in a World of Domination* (Minneapolis: Fortress Press, 1992), 59-60.

Epoch. Saint Paul clarifies this difficulty when he warns: "If you think you are wise in the ways of the Domination Epoch, you should become fools so that you may become wise. For the wisdom of the System [*kosmos*] is foolishness to God" (1 Cor 3:18).

How wise are white settler people of faith to the current Domination Epoch? How do I/we even begin to discern what is good and pleasing to God when our entire socialization system conforms to the CMP rather than the life, death, ministry, and memory of Jesus Christ?

Part 2: Dwelling in Colonizing New England

We overprivileged white settler beneficiaries of the CMP tend not to have a way to name the system. I am constantly (re)learning how multiple gender, sexual, racial, and other hierarchies are sedimented in how I live and view the world even as I advocate with and for other ways of being.

The deeper problem is that the CMP is being reconstituted, often unconsciously, every day *where and how* we live. I became recently sensitized to this quotidian process through disorientation to my surroundings. I moved from southern Louisiana to the Berkshire mountains in western Massachusetts. Since I have moved many times, I am familiar with a certain experience of disorientation, even vertigo, in adjusting to a new place. My disorientation is partially due to the fact that my partner and I left behind a home that we enjoyed. Conversely, my experience of discombobulation is exacerbated by temporarily living in a rental space where we don't feel connected to the space because it is impermanent. Our sense of self is intertwined with possessing the domicile we call home.

The sensory experience of a legally owned property as an extension of self is one critical manifestation of the history and culture of white settler common sense.[24] In his elucidation of white settler common sense, Mark Rivkin explores "the ways the

24. Mark Rivkin, *Settler Common Sense: Queerness and Everyday Colonialism in the American Renaissance* (Minneapolis: University of Minnesota Press, 2014), xv.

macrological dynamics and institutionalized frameworks of settlement—the exertion of control by nonnatives over Native peoples and lands—give rise to certain modes of feeling."[25] My sense of personhood in an owned home and disorientation in temporary housing are generated in no small way by the institutionalized relations of settlement rooted in American history, law, and public policy. American history, law, and public policy, as integral pieces of the CMP, form our modes of everyday feeling. They also "generate forms of affect through which they become imbued with a sensation of everyday certainty."[26] This highlights how everyday affect among nonnatives normalize "settler presence, privilege, and power, taking up terms and technologies of settler governance as something like a phenomenological surround that serves as the animating context for nonnatives' engagement with the social environment."[27] In other words, the CMP deforms our entire way of being. Now I recognize that the assumption of ownership, so critical economically, culturally, and socially in North American culture, disconnects us from the history of how colonization decimated First Peoples.

While I was looking forward to returning to the bucolic environs of the Berkshire mountains, I am struck by white settler common sense in the sign on the highway that reads: "Welcome to the Berkshires: America's Premier Cultural Resort." That is one of many regional signals that convey white settler insouciance. My vertigo is intensified by the local language of multiculturalism that celebrates a collective intention to assimilate everyone as it reinscribes white settler colonialism.

I am writing this essay on ancestral lands of Mohican, Mohawk, and Pocumtuck peoples. A common assumption in the Berkshires is that the colonial period is past. In other words, we don't perceive how coloniality endures here. How do we white colonial settlers recall that "under the crust of that portion of the Earth called the United States of America . . . are interred the

25. Ibid.
26. Ibid.
27. Ibid.

bones, villages, fields, and sacred objects of American Indians"?[28] Coloniality endures in how we white settlers forget the bones, villages, fields, and sacred objects of the Mohican and how they survive through more than fifteen hundred tribal members in western Massachusetts today.

For example, Dorothy Davids, a member of the People of the Waters That Are Never Still—also known as the Mohican tribe—described the Mohican way of life in her 2004 booklet *A Brief History of the Mohican Nation Stockbridge-Munsee Band*. She remembers how her tribe arrived long before white colonists, settling along the Mahicannituck River where they encountered Henry Hudson in 1609.[29] Colonialists renamed that river the Hudson. Davids tells the story of her people after Hudson arrived: the Mohican were decimated by European diseases, by conflicts over the fur trade, through fighting for the American revolution, through Christianization and expulsion by colonizers in the eighteenth century. Davids and half of the tribe live on reservation land in Wisconsin.

There is little indication of the Mohicans along the contemporary rendering of the Mohawk Trail, whose presence goes back thousands of years. That white settler colonists in the Berkshires have continually forgotten and mischaracterized indigenous people in order to promote tourism is documented in David Quay's 2004 senior thesis at Williams College.[30] Quay focused his study on "The Pageant of the Mohawk Trail," which was enacted four times in June 1914 by white actors in North Adams Hoosac Valley Park to publicize the completion of the Mohawk Trail motor touring route.[31] He found that settlers did not know anything about People of the Waters That Are Never Still. He describes

28. Roxanne Dunbar-Ortiz, *An Indigenous Peoples' History of the United States* (Boston, MA: Beacon Press, 2014), 1.

29. Elodie Reed, "Whose Homeland Is the Mohawk Trail?," *The Berkshire Eagle* (May 3, 2019), available online at https://www.berkshireeagle.com/stories/whose-homeland-is-the-mohawk-trail,572346.

30. David Quay, "Mohawks, Model Ts, and Monuments" (senior thesis, Williams College, Williamstown, MA, 2004). Available online at http://citeseerx.ist.psu.edu/viewdoc/download?doi=10.1.1.121.5840&rep=rep1&type=pdf.

31. Ibid., 7.

how the play enacted a romantic narrative of the Mohawk Trail "as an inevitable progression from primitive Indian wilderness through Anglo pioneer simplicity to modern Anglo American civilization."[32] The storytelling never included any Mohican. After the play's 1700s episode, once "early settlers" arrived on the scene, First Peoples disappeared entirely. The pageant erased the Mohican, their history, and the history of European-led conflict that decimated First Peoples.

The forgotten history of the Mohican illuminates a deeper complexity of ongoing white settler colonialism. White settler colonialism should not be reduced to a white/Black binary or to an inclusionary multiculturalism. As Jodi Byrd illustrates, when "the remediation of the colonization of American Indians is framed through discourses of racialization that can be redressed by further inclusion into the nation-state, there is significant failure to grapple with the fact that such discourses further re-inscribe the original colonial injury."[33] Byrd exposes how assumptions of racialization along a white/Black binary become conflated with indigeneity in a way that "masks the territoriality of conquest by assigning colonization to the racialized body, which is then policed by its degrees from whiteness." She laments how this form of domination erases "Indian national assertions of sovereignty, self-determination, and land rights," which "disappear into U.S. territoriality as indigenous identity becomes a racial identity and citizens of colonized indigenous nations become internal ethnic minorities within the colonizing nation-state."[34] In other words, white settler Americans' "orientation to the reconciliation of Indigenous nationhood with state sovereignty is still *colonial* insofar as it remains structurally committed to the dispossession of Indigenous peoples of our lands and self-determining authority."[35]

Even as white settler common sense appears inclusive, it reinforces the original colonial wound—stolen land and the era-

32. Ibid.

33. Jodi Byrd, *The Transit of Empire: Indigenous Critiques of Colonialism* (Minneapolis: University of Minnesota Press, 2011), xxiii.

34. Ibid., xxiv.

35. Glen Sean Coulthard, *Red Skin, White Masks: Rejecting the Colonial Politics of Recognition* (Minneapolis: University of Minnesota Press, 2014), 151.

sure of First Peoples. We white settlers, who now assume to be indigenous,[36] tend not to perceive a different consciousness. The assumption of a single consciousness is striking in its forgetfulness of how First Peoples' entire way of life and spirituality was rooted in this land for at least ten thousand years before arrival of English Puritans in 1621. Historians Colin Calloway and Neal Salisbury explain that "legacies of colonial invasion—dispossession, racism, and ethnocide—are inextricably linked to loss of land, loss of political sovereignty, and loss of control of telling of native histories."[37] Or, as Patrick Wolfe demonstrates in his study of genocide of First Peoples, the white settler logic of elimination "destroys to replace."[38]

Part 3: Learning to Unlearn Modernity/Coloniality: Engaging Impasse and Transformation in Sophia-Wisdom

An epigraph above quotes Frantz Fanon's prayer that closes his *Black Skin/White Masks*. It reads: "Oh my body, make of me always a man who questions!" Fanon's prayer conveys his sensing bodily the existential geo-political predicament of the *damnés de la terre*. Fanon's bodily prayer is thinking geo-politically. In the geo-political context of French colonized Algeria, Fanon enacts bodily epistemic disobedience, whereby his sensing "created the conditions to link border epistemology with immigrant consciousness and, consequently, delink from territorial and imperial epistemology grounded on theological (Renaissance) and egological (Enlightenment) politics of knowledge."[39]

36. Walter Mignolo offers a decolonial critique of "indigenous" in "Coloniality Is Far from Over, and So Must Be Decoloniality," *Afterall: A Journal of Art, Context and Enquiry* 43 (Spring–Summer 2017): 38–45.

37. Colin G. Calloway and Neal Salisbury, "Introduction: Decolonizing New England Indian History," Colonial Society of Massachusetts, Volume 71: Reinterpreting New England Indians and the Colonial Experience (2003), 14.

38. Patrick Wolfe, "Settler Colonialism and the Elimination of the Native," *Journal of Genocide Research* 8, no. 4 (December 2006): 388.

39. Walter Mignolo, "Geopolitics of Sensing and Knowing: On (De)coloniality, Border Thinking, and Epistemic Disobedience," in *Confero* 1, no. 1 (2013): 129–50, here 132–33.

In contrast to Fanon's bodily sensing the geo- and political-historical predicament of *les damnés de la terre,* modernity's theo- and ego-politics of knowledge are grounded in suppressing bodily sensing. It is through this suppression of bodily sensing that European modernity claims universality of knowledge and "hides coloniality and prevents pluriversal, dialogic, and epistemically democratic systems of thought from unfolding."[40] Fanon's prayer is a bodily way of practicing epistemic disobedience, the first step in learning how to unlearn modernity/coloniality.

How do white colonial settlers in North America even begin to sense our geo-political and historical situation? This is an enduring problem of white settler colonialism because white American settlers actively suppress the violence on which the nation was built. Perhaps, however, there is nothing that prevents a white body from recognizing how coloniality works in other non-Western European bodies. Maybe, but it is extremely difficult. As Mignolo observes, "that would be rational and intellectual but not experiential."[41] He continues: "For a white European body to think decolonially means to give; to give in a parallel way that a body of color formed in colonial histories has to give if that body wants to inhabit postmodern and poststructuralist theories."[42]

What would it mean for a white colonial settler body "to give" in a way that inhabits—dwells within—a disobedient, decolonial way of being in the world? Intellectual questioning does not necessarily involve bodily sensing like Frantz Fanon questioning with his entire body or W.E.B. Du Bois sensing double-consciousness bodily, socially, intellectually, morally, and spiritually.[43]

Decolonial dwelling, Mignolo argues, demands an *aesthesis,* which involves one's entire way of being in the world, including sensing and feeling with and for other human beings. Nelson Maldanado-Torres describes decolonial aesthesis as embodied subjects "who can not only reflect about but also mold, shape, and

40. Mignolo, *Darker Side*, 82.

41. Mignolo, "Geopolitics of Sensing," 145.

42. Ibid.

43. W.E.B. Du Bois, *The Souls of Black Folk* (New York: Barnes and Noble Classic, 2003 [1903]), see especially chapter 1, "Of Our Spiritual Strivings."

reshape subjectivity, space, and time."[44] Mignolo describes the aesthesis of decoloniality as "disobedient conservatism," that is, the "energy that engenders dignified anger and decolonial healing."[45]

The main goals of decolonial aesthesis as disobedient conservatism include (1) delinking from modernity in order to re-exist and (2) relinking with the "legacies one wants to preserve in order to engage in modes of existence with which one wants to engage."[46] Re-existing on terms that are disobedient to modernity means discerning how to live life in one's local context "instead of giving our time and bodies to corporations, our attention and intelligence to mainstream media, our energy to banks, which are constantly harassing us to obtain credits to pay high interest."[47] Mignolo argues, however, that this is not a call to delinquency. Rather, disobedient conservatism entails Gandhian-like civil disobedience in order that people deemed "untouchable" may re-exist and thrive on their own terms.

Re-existing means that Indigenous people relink with and conserve their own memories and legacies and live in ways that conserve the life and energy of the entire community and the earth itself. For example, Madina Tlostanova and Mignolo highlight the creation of the Amawtay Wasi, Universidad Intercultural de los Pueblos y Naciones Indigenas del El Salvador in the 1970s. Indigenous communities realized that they could and should not merely replicate a Western university because "it was not possible to go very far thinking with the tools of the master, so to speak."[48] Instead, Amawtay Wasi was born from the idea that they needed their own educational institutions just like their ancestors. They do not reject Western science and knowledge. Rather, it facilitates

44. Nelson Maldonado-Torres, "Outline of Ten Theses on Coloniality and Decoloniality," (Frantz Fanon Foundation), available online at http://fondation-frantzfanon.com/outline-of-ten-theses-on-coloniality-and-decoloniality/.

45. Walter Mignolo, "Coloniality Is Far from Over, and So Must be Decoloniality" in *Afterall: A Journal of Art, Context, and Enquiry* 43, (Spring/Summer 2017): 38–45, here 40–41.

46. Ibid.

47. Ibid., 41.

48. Tlostanova and Mignolo, *Learning to Unlearn*, 226.

ways of recovering, remembering, and relearning Indigenous ways of living.

The praxis at the core of Amawtay Wasi is *vincularidad. Vincularidad* is analogous to the Western concept of "relational ontology." The Western notion of relational ontology, however, misses the meaning of *vincularidad. Vincularidad* is best translated as "co-relational," but that too misses its cosmological vision. Co-relationality is at the center of the whole of the life-giving energies of the universe and "emerges from the correlations between 'complementarity,' 'reciprocity,' 'correspondence,' and 'proportionality.' "[49] *Vincularidad* correlates all dimensions of existence including the agro-ecological, the four elements or life-energies (*Pachamama*) of air, fire, land, and water, and interrelate four nodes of knowledge and doing including interculturality, cosmovision, ecology, and technoscience. Facilitating a lived understanding of *vincularidad*, of course, would entail giving oneself with and for the Indigenous peoples who co-create Amawtay Wasi.

An Indigenous praxis analogous to *vincularidad* in the northeast of the United States is the "Common Pot."[50] In her remapping of Native spaces in the northeast, Lisa Brooks focuses attention on *Wlôgan*, which "is that which feeds and nourishes. It is the wigwam that feeds the family, the village that feeds the community, the networks that sustain the village."[51] The "pot" is made from birch trees, the clay of the earth, and is the *Wlôgan* or "dish" of interconnected social and ecological interrelationships. Women play a central role in facilitating co-creative relationships in the Common Pot. "All our relations" are evoked in the Common Pot and the closely related Abenaki word *wlidôgawôgan* proclaims "thanks to all our relations." The Common Pot interrelates the whole of existence, including the divine, as the pot is "our mother" who "is Sky Women's body, the network of relations that must nourish and reproduce" life itself.[52]

49. Ibid., 232.

50. Lisa Brooks, *The Common Pot: The Recovery of Native Space in the Northeast* (Minneapolis: University of Minnesota Press, 2008), 3–4 and 253–54.

51. Ibid., 4.

52. Ibid., 4 and 253–54.

Returning to Constance FitzGerald, I contend that her contemplative, acoustic ethic of listening and hearing the cries of the earth and the *damnés* is a decolonial aesthesis that facilitates a way of developing co-relational, mutual, ethical relationships with Indigenous peoples and the Common Pot. Her praxis bodily co-senses a geo-political and historical shift away from modernity to a spirituality that nurtures the conditions of the possibility of decoloniality. Recall that the Christian mystics whom FitzGerald draws on, Saint Teresa of Avila and John of the Cross, lived simultaneously within the growing Spanish Empire, what modernity terms the "Age of Exploration."

FitzGerald situates their witness to Sophia-Wisdom within the Western theological and societal muting of contemplation and mysticism. She finds that Saint John of the Cross was being moved in the "milieu of Sophia-Wisdom" from the beginning of *The Ascent of Mount Carmel* to the end of *The Living Flame of Love* and keeping Her tradition alive for us to discover. Precisely at the time of colonization, the Church and society were marginalizing women, condemning the language of mysticism, disparaging the feminine image of God, and neglecting the Spirit. When the traditions of contemplation and mysticism were "muffled by the condemnation of quietism in 1699, ending two centuries of struggle and debate, so, perhaps, was the opportunity to develop the strong experience of Sophia."[53] In terms of decoloniality, the traditions of John of the Cross, Teresa of Avila, and Sophia-Wisdom dwell within the cracks of Western imperialism. It is precisely at these interstices, argues Mignolo, where marginalized peoples are delinking from modernity and re-existing on their own terms.[54]

FitzGerald enacts epistemic disobedience. Her contemplative reading of the "signs of the times" and societal impasse is a way of living Saint Paul's admonition to *not* conform herself to the Domination Epoch in which we struggle to be human and witness to

53. Constance FitzGerald, "Transformation in Wisdom: The Subversive Character and Educative Power of Sophia in Contemplation," in *Carmel and Contemplation: Transforming Human Consciousness*, ed. Kevin Culligan and Regis Jordan (Washington, DC: Institute of Carmelite Studies Publications, 2000), 284.

54. Tlostanova and Mignolo, *Learning to Unlearn*, 218.

Sophia-Wisdom. Most important, FitzGerald's retrieval of Sophia-Wisdom nurtures a decolonial aesthesis of re-existing on other grounds than modernity/coloniality that create the conditions of the possibility for all peoples and the earth itself to thrive.

Paradoxically, as FitzGerald explains, impasse itself may provide the conditions of the possibility of bodily co-sensing the cries of the earth and the *damnés* everywhere. That means embracing impasse, however, and dying to false images of self and society. Left to our own devices, we are unable to free ourselves of our attachments to wealth, privilege, and power. In the face of this challenge, she continues, we need the kind of radical faith, hope, and love that "can endure the death-dealing 'touch of God's hand,'" the only touch that facilitates an "emptying out of our isolated self-sufficiency, on the one hand, and our unfree dependence and fear of transformation and change, on the other."[55] We need to bring personal and societal impasse to prayer and the presence of Sophia-Wisdom. That is the only way "society will be freed, healed, changed, brought to paradoxical new visions, therefore, for community on this planet earth."[56] FitzGerald warns that the indwelling of Sophia-Wisdom involves death, "dying in order to see how to be and to act on behalf of God in the world."[57] Impasse itself may provide the conditions of the possibility of transformation "if the limitations of one's own humanity and human condition are squarely faced and the sorrow of finitude allowed to invade the human spirit with real, existential powerlessness."[58]

It is in times of impasse, when we do not feel faith, hope, and love, precisely when it is most difficult to do so, that we need to maintain a contemplative posture of acceptance in our prayer and life. This seems so contradictory, says FitzGerald, because it is faith itself that "causes darkness in our power to understand."[59]

55. FitzGerald, "Transformation in Wisdom," 322.

56. FitzGerald, "Impasse and Dark Night," 107.

57. Ibid.

58. Constance FitzGerald, "Impasse and Dark Night," in *Women's Spirituality: Resources for Christian Development*, ed. Joanne Wolski Conn (Mahwah, NJ: Paulist Press, 1986), 410–50.

59. FitzGerald, "Transformation in Wisdom," 323.

She reminds us that dark night "is not primarily *something,*" like an abstract, impersonal darkness causing "a distressful psychological condition." Rather, dark night "is *someone,* a presence leaving an indelible imprint on the human spirit and consequently on one's entire life."[60] That someone is the indwelling Jesus-Sophia who transforms all of the destructive values we settlers possess. In her elucidation of dark night in John of the Cross, FitzGerald describes three levels that the indwelling Jesus-Sophia subverts: (1) our self-image; (2) our image of God and Christ; and (3) our relationship to the world including "unveiling our cultural violence."[61] Ultimately, Sophia-Jesus draws us away "from domination, control, anxiety, competition, and exploitation to receive Wisdom in mindless, playful joy, and delight."[62]

Sophia-Jesus transforms us and the universe beyond our wildest imagination. Sophia-Jesus engenders the preservation of all of life and facilitates a way of being in which we relearn with Her and oppressed peoples everywhere how to co-create and coexist on grounds of the Common Pot of creation. Sophia-Jesus draws us ever more deeply into intimate interdependence and interconnection with all oppressed peoples and the most vulnerable creatures of the earth. She builds our capacity for hearing the cry of the poor and suffering of the earth "that breaks open into a nearly incomprehensible desire to 'enter all the afflictions and sorrows of the world.'"[63] This includes hearing the cries and wisdom of First Peoples, including remembering those buried underneath our feet, and re-learning the legacies they desire to enkindle with and for the Common Pot. Sophia-Jesus draws one and all into a participatory-love knowledge that nurtures mutual relationship and creates the conditions of the possibility of an epochal shift of human consciousness.[64] She tenderly connects all creatures to experience:

60. Ibid., 310.
61. Ibid., 312.
62. Ibid., 329.
63. Ibid., 334.
64. Ibid., 343.

the sacred community of the earth, the entire earth with all its energies and diversity and species, awakening and coming to life—all a part of each, and all a part of her—each possessing a value and wisdom all its own, all moving in a wonderful harmony and each giving voice to what Creator-Sophia is in it.[65]

65. Ibid., 336.

12

Toward a Spirituality for Racial Justice

The Transformation of Consciousness and the "Souls of White Folks"

Bryan N. Massingale

> Every white person in this country—I do not care what he says or what she says—knows one thing . . . : They know that they would not like to be black here. If they know that, they know everything they need to know. And whatever else they may say is a lie.[1]

As I write this essay, I am haunted by the long series of tragic killings of unarmed African Americans—especially Black young men—by police officers, security guards, and neighborhood vigilantes that are occurring with terrible frequency in the United States. An advocacy group, the Malcolm X Grassroots Movement, documented over 313 such extrajudicial killings of African American men in 2012 alone—a rate of one such death every

1. James Baldwin, "Speech at the University of California Berkeley" (1979). Online at https://www.youtube.com/watch?v=PQejcZc4uFM.

twenty-eight hours.[2] The scope of this tragic reality continues unabated even to the present. The "Mapping Police Violence" project notes that although only 13 percent of the US population, in 2015, 36 percent of unarmed persons killed by police were Black—a rate that is five times that of unarmed whites.[3] Among the most recent and notorious of these killings are those of Trayvon Martin (Sanford, FL), Michael Brown (Ferguson, MO), Eric Garner (Staten Island, NY), Tamir Rice (Cleveland, OH), Breonna Taylor (Louisville, KY), and Ahmaud Arbery (Brunswick, GA). Though each death has unique circumstances, there is a disturbing pattern here, one eloquently expressed by *New York Times* columnist, Charles M. Blow:

> There is an eerie echo in it all—a sense of tragedy too often repeated. And yet the sheer morbid, wrenching rhythm of it belies a larger phenomenon, one obscured by its vastness, one that can be seen only when one steps back and looks from a distance and with data: *The criminalization of black and brown bodies—particularly male ones*—from the moment they are first introduced to the institutions and power structures with which they must interact.[4]

This pervasive criminalization of dark-skinned bodies disturbs me. Especially troubling is that this ascription or stereotype is not necessarily deliberate or conscious. One researcher, studying the propensity of police officers to use deadly force more often in situations involving Black people, rejects the conclusion that such officers must be either intentional bigots or completely unbiased. Rather,

2. Malcolm X Grassroots Movement, *Operation Ghetto Storm: 2012 Report on the Extrajudicial Killings of 313 Black People by Police, Security Guards and Vigilantes* (April 2013). Available at www.mxgm.org.

3. Mapping Police Violence, https://mappingpoliceviolence.org/unarmed. In 2019, Black people were 24 percent of those killed by police, despite again being only 13 percent of the population. It should be noted that there is no official record of or source for these statistics, as police departments are not required to record or report the rate of unarmed killings of civilians.

4. Charles M. Blow, "Michael Brown and Black Men," *New York Times* (August 13, 2014), http://www.nytimes.com/2014/08/14/opinion/charles-blow-michael-brown-and-black-men.html.

she notes something much more complex at work: "Racial stereotypes operate at a subconscious level to influence a police officer's decision to use deadly force. The police officer may not consciously decide to use deadly force because of the suspect's race, but the suspect's race nonetheless influences the officer[, altering] the officer's perception of danger, threat, and resistance to authority."[5] The Malcolm X Grassroots Movement concurs, concluding that these deaths are the effects of a pervasive social "conditioning."[6]

Other scholars also note the endemic social conditioning at work in US racism in general and its role in the killings of African Americans. African American sociologist Noel Cazenave examines what he calls "the pervasive, disproportionate, and persistent police and vigilante killings of African Americans."[7] Cazenave makes a direct connection between such killings and the long history of callous disregard for Black life in the United States. He thus understands these events as part of a broader cultural phenomenon. He writes:

> I became increasingly convinced that [such killings] are acts of racial terrorism that the perpetrators see, in their own perverted way, as a form of morality enforcement that serves the same function as lynchings and the Ku Klux Klan during earlier periods of U.S. history, especially in the South. Building on Michelle Alexander's reference to mass incarceration as "the New Jim Crow," I surmised, as other African Americans have, that we might best think of such lethal terrorism as the new, 21st-century version of lynchings. Like the old ones, these "new lynchings" send a message that it is so-called "white" people who are in control and that "black" people had better stay in our place and behave as "white" men with guns would have us behave. Finally, I concluded that the underlying premise behind these new lynchings is that we African Americans have no rights, and that "white"

5. Cynthia Ann Lee, "But I Thought He Had a Gun: Race and Police Use of Deadly Force," *Hastings Race and Poverty Law School Journal* (2004).

6. Malcolm X Grassroots Movement, *op. cit.*

7. Noel A. Cazenave, *Killing African Americans: Police and Vigilante Violence as a Racial Control Mechanism* (New York: Routledge, 2018), xv.

> men, whether in uniform or not, have the right to kill "black" people as they please.[8]

In response to these police and vigilante killings, over 450 US Catholic theologians published a moral analysis in 2014. In the "Statement of Catholic Theologians on Racial Justice," they called for extensive reforms in the practice of policing such as an end to the militarization of police departments, honing guidelines for the use of lethal force, better police recruitment and training, the use of body cameras by police officers, and the establishment of publicly accountable police review boards. Yet, while the statement reaffirmed the US bishops' teaching on the sin of racism and called for deeper scholarship on racial justice, it did not note that the social sinful practices and patterns they rightly decried are rooted in and reflective of "pervasive social conditioning," that is, the manifestations of a much deeper cultural ethos. This cultural ethos, which I name as White supremacy, went unnamed and unexamined.[9]

But if Cazenave is right, and I believe that he is, the reforms that the Catholic theologians espoused will prove limited and even ineffective. For an ethos of White supremacy is what is at play here, and without a proactive concern with it, new forms of injustice will emerge that reflect this deeper cultural malformation. In other words, what theologians and ethicists call "social sin" is itself but a symptom, an expression of a deeper, more fundamental ethical disorder.

In other words, it is too easy to focus our moral concern on rogue police officers, security guards, or neighborhood vigilantes. I contend that these individual actors are influenced by and

8. Cazenave, *Killing African Americans*, xii. Note the resonance of his conclusion with the judgment reached in the infamous US Supreme Court decision, *Dred Scott v. Sanford* (1857), where the justices declared that persons of African descent were such "a subordinate and inferior class of beings" that they "had no rights that the white man was bound to respect."

9. "Statement of Catholic Theologians on Racial Justice" (December 8, 2014), available online at https://catholicmoraltheology.com/statement-of-catholic-theologians-on-racial-justice/. I note that I am one of the signatories of this statement.

products of an underlying cultural formation system. That is, they are not "aberrations" but representatives of something normal and typical in US and Western society. They are the products of a collective consciousness that they have absorbed through a "pervasive socialization."

This, then, is what I want to examine in this essay, not only the reality of social injustice—specifically the killings of unarmed African Americans and especially Black men. Rather, I also seek to highlight "culturally legitimated" unjust social situations[10] and how cultural formation facilitates not only the commission of but also blindness and/or indifference to social injustice. If this is the case, then how do we move beyond such a malformation—indeed, a soul sickness? What can help us address and redress such a fundamental deformation in and warping of the human spirit?

To reflect on such questions, I examine the formative effects of culture, especially as it expresses or comprises the "soul" of a people. This leads us to understand White supremacy as a cultural phenomenon, one that reflects the "soul" of white people. The thoughts of the noted African American intellectual W.E.B. Du Bois give us excellent insight into the workings of White supremacy in his classic essay, "The Souls of White Folks." Next, I turn to the thoughts of Carmelite scholar Constance FitzGerald, who provides interpretations of classical concepts of Christian spirituality that can address and redress such fundamental malformations in the human spirit as it evolves into higher forms of consciousness. Finally, I discuss the work that remains in using FitzGerald's insights for racial justice advocacy, noting their resonance with the convictions of contemporary activists who strive to contend with what Pope John Paul II rightly called "one of the most persistent and destructive evils of the nation."[11]

10. Gregory Baum, *Essays in Critical Theology* (Kansas City, MO: Sheed and Ward, 1994), 196.

11. John Paul II, "Homily," (St. Louis, MO: January 27, 1999), http://www.vatican.va/content/john-paul-ii/en/travels/1999/documents/hf_jp-ii_hom_27011999_stlouis.html.

The Culture of White Supremacy

In my work, I strive to account for both the reality of undeniable major progress in race relations in the United States—especially as symbolized in the election of the first person of African descent as its president—with the equally undeniable reality of the continuing persistence of racial disparities and resentments. What, I wonder, is the underlying constant that endures despite external changes in social institutions? What is the link that unites African enslavement, Jim Crow segregation, and the so-called "new Jim Crow," also known as "James Crow, Jr. Esquire"?[12]

My insight is to look beneath the visible personal and institutional manifestations of racism and to understand racism as a "culture." Using Canadian philosopher Bernard Lonergan's understanding that "a culture is a set of meanings and values that informs a community's way of life,"[13] I posit that culture is more fundamental than social institutions, policies, and customs. Culture expresses the meaning of society and the significance of the ways in which we order our communities. The pivotal insight that I take from Lonergan is that "culture stands to social order as soul to body";[14] that is to say, culture is the spirit that animates social institutions and customs, makes them intelligible, and expresses their meaning. This cultural "set of meanings and values" could endure despite changes in social institutions. Left unchallenged and unnoted, this set of underlying values simply adapts new social forms and expressions.

Moreover, I note that cultures—the sets of meanings and values that inform a people's way of life—are also systems of identity formation. Cultures shape a human group's behavior and consciousness; they condition thoughts, values, actions, and awareness. They provide the matrix of meaning for answering the questions of who we are and what we stand for.

12. Michelle Alexander, *The New Jim Crow: Mass Incarceration in the Age of Colorblindness* (New York: The New Press, 2010).

13. Bernard Lonergan, *A Second Collection*, ed. William F. J. Ryan and Bernard J. Terrell (Philadelphia: Westminster Press, 1974), 232.

14. Ibid., 102. I discuss this in greater depth in *Racial Justice and the Catholic Church* (Maryknoll, NY: Orbis Books, 2010), 13–19.

Thus, I argue for a more cultural and systemic understanding of racism. I contend that racism is a deeply entrenched symbol system of meanings and values attached to skin color that provides group identity, shapes personal consciousness, and justifies the existence of race-based economic, social, and political disparities. The specific disparities and race-based injustices change over time; the underlying symbol system, left unchallenged, assumes shifting social forms and expressions that nonetheless reflect the underlying set of meanings and values. As important as these functions are, however, "racism" does more. As a "culture," racism is also *formative*. Racism is a symbol system, a culture operating on a preconscious level, a learned and communal frame of reference that shapes identity, consciousness, and behavior—the way social groups and their members understand their place and worth. Race, in the Western world, tells us who we are both as individuals and as social collectives.[15]

More specifically, I argue that the culture of racism is more accurately understood as a worldview of White supremacy. This move is inspired by my deep engagement with the tradition of Black radical social thought (a.k.a. Africana critical theory),[16] especially thinkers such as Malcolm X, James Baldwin, Audre Lorde, Charles Mills, and Ta-Nehisi Coates. As the acclaimed essayist Ta-Nehisi Coates observes: "Black [radicals] have always perceived something unmentionable about America that integrationists dare not acknowledge—that white supremacy is not merely the work of hotheaded demagogues, or a matter of false consciousness, but a force so fundamental to America that it is

15. Gary L. Chamberlain, "A Model to Confront Racism," *Theology Today* 32 (January 1976): 355.

16. Reiland Rabaka defines Africana critical theory as Black-centered social and political reflection that results in "theory critical of domination and discrimination in continental and diasporan African life-worlds and lived experiences" and grounds "radical political practice geared toward social transformation and human liberation in the modern moment." See his "Malcolm X and/as Critical Theory: Philosophy, Radical Politics, and the African American Search for Social Justice," *Journal of Black Studies* 33 (2002): 146.

difficult to imagine the country without it."[17] Elsewhere, Coates describes White supremacy as "an age-old system in America which holds that whites should always be ensured that they will not sink to a certain level. And that level is the level occupied by black people."[18]

Because White supremacy is a culture, it often operates below the level of conscious awareness, present in individuals more as an inchoate feeling or intuitive conviction. Put more directly, White supremacy describes the nonrational, instinctual, existential, and visceral conviction that this nation—particularly its public spaces and institutions—belongs to white people in a way that it does not and ought not belong to "others." Therefore, people of color, and especially Black people, are present in white spaces only because of either *white permission and toleration* (e.g., in limited numbers to meet the requirements of decency or "diversity"), or *nonwhite fraud* (e.g., illegal immigrants, undeserving beneficiaries of affirmative action, and the "birther" allegations that a Black man functioned as an illegitimate president). Consequently, white permission or toleration can be withdrawn when white discomfort is triggered and people of color can be removed from public spaces "by any means necessary" (e.g., family separation and deportation polices or calling the police when Black people are sleeping in college dorms, picnicking in public parks, waiting for friends at Starbucks, or otherwise engaged in actions or present in places that make white people uncomfortable).

White supremacy is a culture, that is, "the set of meanings and values," that animates and informs our nation's social institutions, policies, and customs. It is a way of life, a way of being in the world. It can be expressed benevolently and paternalistically or harshly and brutally. It is a constant and consistent feature in

17. Ta-Nehisi Coates, "The Case for Reparations," *The Atlantic* (June 2014), available online at https://www.theatlantic.com/magazine/archive/2014/06/the-case-for-reparations/361631/.

18. Bill Moyers, "White Supremacy Is Alive and Well: Ta-Nehisi Coates and the Case for Reparations," *Salon* (May 22, 2014), http://www.salon.com/2014/05/22/white_supremacy_is_alive_and_well_ta_nehesi_coates_and_the_case_for_reparations_partner/.

our national life that assumes different historical expressions. Moreover, like all cultures, it is *formative*. It socializes people into a way of being, often in ways that escape conscious awareness. White supremacy finds expression in external realities such as employment practices, literature, music, art, and social life but is much more than the sum of these realities. It is the set of values that informs the visible patterns of social life. White supremacy expresses the "soul" of a people.

These thoughts are consistent with the deepest understanding of Martin Luther King Jr.'s ministry of social activism. King described his ministry as a quest "to redeem the soul of the nation."[19] He viewed his mission as the "transformation of society, not simply social change."[20] While challenging segregation laws and exclusionary social practices were necessary strategies, King believed that these were insufficient. Such laws and customs were merely the external signs of a much deeper reality. His guiding insight was that communities, as well as individuals, have "souls," that is, deeply held values and beliefs that motivate their collective social practices. He was convinced that without deep soul work, without what he called a "revolution in values," racism would simply mutate and take different forms and expression. Racial justice thus requires the spiritual transformation of the nation's racial consciousness.[21]

The Soul Sickness of White Folks

What, then, is the set of meanings and values that inform the social practices of the culture of White supremacy? What is pervasive socialization that forms the collective and personal consciousness of white people in visceral and preconscious ways?

19. Martin Luther King Jr., "A Testament of Hope," in *A Testament of Hope: The Essential Writings of Martin Luther King, Jr.*, ed. James Melvin Washington (San Francisco: Harper and Row, 1986), 318.

20. Cited in Hilda Raye Tompkins, *To Redeem the Soul of America: The Leadership Challenges Martin Luther King, Jr., Faced and Managed as Leader of a Social Movement* (PhD diss., University of Georgia, 2009).

21. King, "The Meaning of Integration," in *A Testament of Hope*.

What is the "soul" of white culture? These are complex questions that elude definitive responses. Yet reflecting on them is essential for understanding the "soul sickness" of White supremacy that FitzGerald's interpretations of spirituality can help us address.

The noted African American intellectual W.E.B. Du Bois provides an incisive articulation in his classic essay, "The Souls of White Folk." He wrote this analysis in 1920 as he reflected on the causes of the First World War and its implications for race relations both nationally and internationally.[22]

He begins by stating that he speaks from intimate experience, as a member of a race with deep knowledge born of long familiarity "with the ways of white people." He then asserts what he sees as the key to understanding values that inform this people's way of life: "the assumption that of all the hues of God whiteness alone is inherently and obviously better than brownness or tan." He then voices the white consciousness this assumption gives birth to, a Whiteness or frame of reference that looks with pity and condescension on all who are not white:

> *My poor, un-white thing! Weep not nor rage. I know, too well, that the curse of God lies heavy on you. Why? That is not for me to say, but be brave! Do your work in your lowly sphere, praying the good Lord that into heaven above, where all is love, you may, one day, be born—white!*

Note that Whiteness is more than a sense of condescension or pity grounded in racial superiority. It is also an attitude of entitlement, an awareness that Whiteness should be served: "Do your work in your lowly sphere." But there is more. Whiteness describes a conviction of ownership, indeed, a belief in "the ownership of the earth forever and ever. Amen." Furthermore, this presumption of dominance, entitlement, and superiority is

22. W.E.B. Du Bois, "The Souls of White Folk," chapter 2 of his monograph, *Darkwater: Voices from within the Veil* (New York: Harcourt, Brace and Company, 1920). I am working with an online version of this essay: https://medium.com/religion-bites/the-souls-of-white-folk-by-w-e-b-du-bois-354f91ca08ef; all citations are from this source.

asserted as being of divine origin and plan. "Un-whiteness" is a divine curse; thus Whiteness is a divine blessing. Indeed, God's love will be most manifest if in the afterlife all who are not white would be born again as white. Thus, Du Bois declares that the right to earthly dominance, dominion, and domination becomes, in effect, "the doctrine of the divine right of white people to steal."

The religious nature—the sacralization—of this stance of racial dominance is not only implicitly present in unspoken thoughts or the prayer formula of "forever and ever. Amen." Du Bois asserts it explicitly in his examination of white Christianity. He judges this religion to be "a miserable failure," rooted in self-deception and hypocrisy as to its faithfulness to the example of Christ. Thus, it instills both delusion and moral blindness in the minds and souls of white people.

From this divinely conferred superiority, dominance, and entitlement flow several pernicious consequences. First, *a belief that nonwhite lives are expendable*, that is, of worth and importance only as they relate to white material ends and comfort. It follows, then, that such lives may be taken with impunity when they become a threat to white well-being. Du Bois states the grim result: "Kill the nigger." Nonwhite lives simply count less than white lives. In short, White supremacy = blackness unloved.

The second is that *the goods, lands, and material wealth of nonwhite peoples exist for the benefit of white people* and can be seized by any means they deem fit. Du Bois asserts that this justifies European colonial expansion and domination: "It was this competition for the labor of yellow, brown, and black folks that was the cause of the World War. Other causes have been glibly given and other contributing causes there doubtless were, but they were subsidiary and subordinate to this vast quest of the dark world's wealth and toil."

A third consequence follows from the second, although it is rarely examined in discussions of white consciousness: *even the lives of fellow whites are expendable if they interfere with or infringe on the right to own, control, and benefit from the goods of the nonwhite world.* The mentality that justifies the violent subjugation of nonwhite peoples for the sake of white material gain in turn justifies violence on white people who become obstacles to avaricious acquisition:

> Each nation felt its deep interests involved. But how? Not, surely, in the death of Ferdinand the Warlike; not, surely, in the old, half-forgotten *revanche* for Alsace-Lorraine; not even in the neutrality of Belgium. No! *But in the possession of land overseas, in the right to colonies, the chance to levy endless tribute on the darker world*—on coolies in China, on starving peasants in India, on black savages in Africa, on dying South Sea Islanders, on Indians of the Amazon—all this and nothing more.

This belief in a divinely conferred right to acquire and control the wealth of the nonwhite peoples, Du Bois avows, is the deepest reason for the massive loss of life that Europeans visited upon each other in the world war: "Let me say this again and emphasize it and leave no room for mistaken meaning: The World War was primarily the jealous and avaricious struggle for the largest share in exploiting darker races." A fundamental cause of "The Great War," for Du Bois, was competition over the spoils of nonwhite colonies, lands, and peoples.

Thus, the belief in racial superiority and the quest for material dominance leads to the annihilation of other white people. White consciousness is thus deeply anxious, marked by a fear and suspicion not only of nonwhites but of *all*. (Note that the white "god" that confers racial superiority in the end cannot provide a sense of security.)

Hence, Du Bois understands Whiteness as a consciousness marked by racial superiority, dominance, and entitlement. Condescension, avarice, acquisition, and competition are among its core components. Whiteness becomes not only a skin color but a social status; Du Bois suggests one becomes "more white" through the number of goods one possesses or controls. Note also that White supremacy is inherently violent. Violence is essential for both seizing and maintaining possession of one's goods, and thus of one's status as "white." Violence is necessary for protecting one's goods both from the nonwhites who would retake what was theirs and from other whites who seek to increase their status as "white." All of this is sustained and justified by a corrupt deformation of Christianity, a peculiar form of religious belief predicated on a white deity who created and ordained human societies as grossly unequal and warlike.

But note that this white culture—that is, the white "soul"—is riddled with anxiety and fear. It is afraid of not only nonwhites but also fellow whites who are competitors for material comfort and social deference. It is also anxious as it is founded on a lie; at the core of this consciousness is a profound self-deception. It is a worldview of delusion. Its understanding of self and others is divorced from reality. Such Du Bois and many other Black scholars declare are the souls of white folks: "This is Europe."[23]

This, then, is the "pervasive conditioning" that marks the "souls of white folks." There are many ways to understand racism, namely, as a political issue, as a sociological phenomenon, as a cultural divide. But at its deepest level, White supremacy is a soul sickness. It is a profound warping of the human spirit that enables human beings to create communities of cold, callous, and even violent indifference to their darker sisters and brothers. Stripped to its core, White supremacy is that disturbing interior disease, that malformed consciousness, which enables white people to not care for those who don't look like them, even if only through a nonconscious withholding of sympathy, empathy, and concern. As one scholar succinctly sums up, "The real meaning of race comes down largely to this: *Is this someone I should care about?*"[24]

The Insights of Constance FitzGerald

Constance FitzGerald's contributions lie in offering new understandings of classic Carmelite spiritual pioneers, especially John of the Cross, so as to show their relevance to the concerns of contemporary women and men. One of her earliest and enduring efforts was the interpretation of the "dark night of the soul" in

23. Du Bois's conviction that white consciousness rests upon a delusion bordering on madness is one also espoused by thinkers such as James Baldwin (cf. his masterful essay, "The Fire Next Time") and Frantz Fanon (cf. his classic work, *Black Skins, White Masks*).

24. Paul L. Wachtel, *Race in the Mind of America: Breaking the Vicious Circle between Blacks and Whites* (New York: Routledge, 1999).

terms of "impasse."[25] The dark night refers to a process of interior purification, inner transformation, and intense spiritual growth that both marks and stems from a more or less prolonged crisis, breakdown, and failure. In her seminal essay, FitzGerald posits that the tradition's understanding of the interior desolation and purification that accompanies spiritual growth could be understood as a time of crisis when one's typical—meaning rational, analytical, "left-brained"—approaches to resolving life situations are not only no longer useful but indeed failed and counterproductive. She writes: "By impasse, I mean that there is no way out of, no way around, no rational escape from, what imprisons one, no possibilities in the situation. . . . [I]mpasse is experienced not only in the problem itself but also in any solution rationally attempted."[26] Moreover, she underscores the universality of this radically transformative and shattering experience by declaring, "Every God relationship, every significant human love, every marriage, every ministry, every relationship between a person and a community, and *perhaps every human group* and every nation will come to this point of impasse, with its intrinsic demands for and promise of a new vision, a new experience of God, a quieter, deeper, freer, more committed love."[27]

I call attention to two moves in FitzGerald's reinterpretation of dark night as impasse. The first is her conviction that the dark night is not only a personal reality but also collective. Dark night understood as impasse allows us to ascribe this phenomenon to human communities, to the "souls" of social groups, and to relationships between genders and racial groups. Our Carmelite author maintains, "The 'no way out' trials of our personal lives are but a part of the far more frightening situations of national and international impasse that have been formed by the social, economic, and political forces of our time."[28] Societies and nations can be plagued by the consequences of unchecked egoism that

25. Constance FitzGerald, "Impasse and Dark Night," in *Living with Apocalypse: Spiritual Resources for Social Compassion*, ed. Tilden H. Edwards (San Francisco: Harper and Row, 1984), 93–116.

26. Ibid., 94.

27. Ibid., 98; emphasis added.

28. Ibid., 105.

lead to intractable social conflicts that appear to be insolvable and without resolution. What FitzGerald calls "societal failures" are the "dark night" writ large: "The poor and the marginalized are our darkness. . . . In 'the poor' our violence is unveiled."[29]

The second is her belief that the way out of personal and societal impasse requires the abandonment of one's former consciousness with its dependence on rational analysis, oppressive institutions, and false identities. The way forward lies in the cultivation of "intuitive, symbolic, unconventional" responses that facilitate new ways of being—"new minds, new intuitions, new wills, and passionate new desires"—that lead beyond impasse.[30] FitzGerald declares that through contemplation, "our society will be freed, healed, changed, brought to paradoxical new visions, and freed for nonviolent, selfless, liberating action, freed, therefore, for community on this planet earth."[31]

What is noteworthy to highlight is FitzGerald's conviction that social crises and political divisions are also spiritual turning points. Successfully navigating them requires responses beyond technical reason or social policy; these are dead ends that only reinforce human hopelessness. A world of justice demands interior conversion and spiritual evolution.

Since her seminal essay on impasse, FitzGerald's works and wisdom have moved beyond the project of describing social impasse to advancing visions of what lies beyond group impasse and unjust human relationships. Perhaps the most concise presentation of her efforts is articulated in her 2017 address to the Leadership Conference of Women Religious:

> We have spent many years interpreting the darkness and liminality, analyzing and understanding the transitions and purifications, and grieving over the losses—in our personal lives, in the lives of

29. Constance FitzGerald, "The Desire for God and the Transformative Power of Contemplation," in *Light Burdens, Heavy Blessings: Challenges of Church and Culture in the Post Vatican II Era*, ed. Mary Heather MacKinnon, Moni McIntyre, and Mary Ellen Sheehan (Quincy, IL: Franciscan Press), 210.

30. FitzGerald, "Impasse and Dark Night," 95; "Desire for God and Transformative Power of Contemplation," 214.

31. FitzGerald, "Impasse and Dark Night," 107.

> our communities, and in society, politics, and culture—and that is not over, I know—but now is the time . . . to live into and decidedly influence a new evolutionary stage of consciousness: communion—in every fiber of our beings.[32]

Here, FitzGerald calls on women religious—and indeed all people of goodwill—to be at the forefront of an evolutionary advance in human consciousness, a consciousness marked by the values of mutuality, relationality, communion, and interconnectedness. This band of evolutionary trailblazers would be comprised of those who manifest the fruits of contemplative transformation. But FitzGerald is clear that the consequences of this transformation, what in an earlier work she described as the "contemplative healing of desire,"[33] extend far beyond the individual and the personal. Rather, in and through "the spiritual generativity" of such individuals "a new evolutionary direction is being given to humanity"; as she says in another recent essay, at the deepest levels of contemplative purification, "the human person is being changed radically" as contemplatives become "the carriers of the evolution of human consciousness for the rest of humanity."[34]

Thus, she summons contemplative believers—women and men, vowed and secular, Christian and beyond[35]—to live out of

32. Constance FitzGerald, "2017 LCWR Outstanding Leadership Award Acceptance Remarks," online at https://lcwr.org/sites/default/files/calendar/attachments/lcwr_outstanding_leadership_award_acceptance_-_constance_fitzgerald_ocd_0.pdf.

33. FitzGerald, "Desire for God and the Transformative Power of Contemplation."

34. Constance FitzGerald, "From Impasse to Prophetic Hope," *CTSA Proceedings* 64 (2009): 39–40.

35. The interreligious dimensions of contemplative growth and human evolutionary change are hinted at in a series of lectures FitzGerald gave with Brian McDermott, SJ, "Christ Consciousness: Carmelite and Ignatian Spiritualities in Dialogue, Part 4" (October 16, 2017), available online at https://www.youtube.com/watch?v=Cieha45-kZk. In this same lecture, FitzGerald elaborates on the societal, even cosmic, implications of contemplatives' communal transformation into Christ consciousness: "They have made their own evolutionary contribution toward laying down *permanent structural capabilities* for creative communion and cutting deep cosmic tendencies and possibilities for transforming love and service into the universe" (my emphasis).

and decidedly influence a new evolutionary stage of human consciousness; indeed, a new way of being human. This evolutionary leap in the human species, through contemplative growth into the "relational identity" of the Godhead, has inevitable and even explosive consequences and implications for political and social life:[36] FitzGerald declares, "Contemplation is not a validation of things as they are . . . but a constant questioning and restlessness that waits for and believes in the coming of a transformed vision of God . . . a new and integrating spirituality *capable of creating a new politics and generating new social structures.*"[37]

FitzGerald avows that this evolutionary leap in the human spirit, through a radical contemplative healing and refashioning of the human spirit, is essential not only for individual salvation but also for the well-being—indeed, the survival—of human communities and humanity itself:

> The very bleakness, disunity, suspicion, deceit, cruelty, violence, cowardliness, and lack of compassion in our own country and far beyond demand this of us. The degrading condition of our earth home and the increasing extinction of other species demand this of us. The multitudes of poor, starving, suffering, displaced, migrant, violated, murdered people—women and children—clinging to our souls demand this of us. A massive unconscious resistance to interdependence is at work fighting against the new stage of cosmic consciousness that is struggling to emerge. Certainly, a sign that something—a new epoch—is already strengthening on the invisible level of spirit! We don't know how long this emergence will take, nor how far-reaching the opposition, disturbance and turbulence will be, but what vast energy fields of communion and interdependence would be created on this earth, in our cosmos, if our consciousness were more closely aligned with the consciousness of Jesus Christ, if his relational identity were more nearly ours, if we could share more explicitly in the all-embracing, pulsing dynamic of Trinitarian life! This union, this gift, is the goal of contemplative prayer . . . and it isn't only for

36. FitzGerald describes contemplation as "a time bomb [that] will explode in new abilities and new energy" ("Impasse and Dark Night," 114).

37. Ibid., emphasis added.

> "eternal life," as you know so well. It is the heart of all engagement. Wherever, whenever these experiences of deep communion happen, the transformation of humanity and the evolution of human consciousness are more assured.[38]

Thus, in her most recent work, FitzGerald advances a visionary manifesto for societal transformation and epochal human development. The contemplative journey from impasse to full Christ consciousness, she avows, is the only way to redress the profound social distresses and divisions that stem from warped human consciousness and deformed human desires. She writes: "A transformation of consciousness frees the person to place on the currents of human consciousness not violence, greed and hatred, but love, compassion and prophetic hope for a transformed community."[39]

Contemplative transformation, then, becomes the antidote to White supremacy's soul sickness, with its tragic consequences of brutal violence and callous indifference. FitzGerald movingly declares, "Profound contemplative union—the fullness of Christ consciousness—changes individuals radically. . . . In them humanity is opened to new possibilities, new vision, a vast unimaginable future."[40] Such human beings, freed from the shackles that imprison and constrict the human spirit, become "prophets of hope" as they summon humanity to evolve into God's future: a world marked by truth rather than delusion and justice rather than greed.

Healing the Soul Sickness as Essential for Racial Justice

For some time, I have been haunted by an insight attributed to Albert Einstein: "No problem can be solved at the level of consciousness that created it." This insight expresses a conviction

38. FitzGerald, "2017 LCWR Address."

39. See "Carmelite Spirituality," at https://www.baltimorecarmel.org/carmelite-spirituality/.

40. Constance FitzGerald, "John of the Cross and Prayer," in *Prayer in the Catholic Tradition: A Handbook of Pastoral Approaches*, ed. Robert J. Wicks (Cincinnati, OH: Franciscan Media, 2016).

that I and many other racial justice advocates have been coming to, namely, that White supremacy is a culturally entrenched evil that cannot be adequately addressed through social and political change alone. The "souls of white folks" constantly resist and are seemingly impervious to rational, analytical, and discursive appeals. The challenge that confronts racial justice activists is acutely and perceptively described by the famed racial justice advocate and scholar Michelle Alexander. In discussing her decision to move beyond the legal profession to engage the study of theology, she writes:

> But I also know that there is something much greater at stake in justice work than we often acknowledge. Solving the crises we face isn't simply a matter of having the right facts, graphs, policy analyses, or funding. And I no longer believe we can "win" justice simply by filing lawsuits, flexing our political muscles or boosting voter turnout. Yes, we absolutely must do that work, but none of it—not even working for some form of political revolution—will ever be enough on its own. *Without a moral or spiritual awakening, we will remain forever trapped in political games fueled by fear, greed, and the hunger for power*. . . . [White supremacy] is not simply a legal problem, or a political problem, or a policy problem. *At its core, America's journey from slavery to Jim Crow to mass incarceration raises profound moral and spiritual questions about who we are, individually and collectively, who we aim to become, and what we are willing to do now.*[41]

Though she seems unaware of this, Alexander is echoing insights articulated almost a half-century earlier by another visionary African American racial justice activist, Vincent Harding, who wrote:

> *I have felt a renewed urgency to emphasize the role of religion and spirituality in our freedom struggle.* I have also become increasingly dissatisfied with any analysis of the external forces opposing our

41. "Michelle Alexander Explains Her Transition from Law to Religion," *Faithfully Magazine* (September 19, 2016), online at https://faithfullymagazine.com/michelle-alexander-new-jim-crow-author-explains-transition-law-religion/; emphases added.

> liberation which sees only racism and capitalism at work in the world. . . . I have long sensed that these were necessary but insufficient definitions of the malaise that has grasped the white mainstream of America. *Beneath such distortions of human community lies a deeper illness, a lack of attunement, a loss of sense of self, an unspoken fear. I have yet no satisfactory name for this ailment of the spirit,* but I am now more certain than ever that it has been at work throughout the history of our black and white—and red—encounters in this land, and that *there will be no hope for a truly just society on these shores until we address the issue of the human spirit and its role in our struggles for political transformation.*[42]

The convergence of these scholars, advocates, and activists around viewing White supremacy as a spiritual crisis and the necessity of spiritual transformation is truly remarkable. Note that neither Du Bois, Coates, King, Alexander, Harding, nor I advocate abandoning strategies of social change and political engagement. As a theologian, I would say that doing so would indicate an anti-incarnational worldview and a specious form of docetic spirituality. We need social and economic analysis, as well as political struggle and cultural engagement, in the quest for racial justice and equality.

But what we are saying is that while these approaches are necessary and essential, they alone cannot save us. Moreover, we all contend that absent a spiritual (r)evolution, they will prove short-lived, ineffective, and at times counterproductive—magnifying instead of eliminating the savage and brutal conditions they aim to redress. We need new ways of thinking, living, praying, loving, and being. The struggle against the massive weight of White supremacy demands attention to the realm of the Spirit. The seismic social, economic, and interpersonal shifts that a genuinely equal and just society demands are otherwise too far-reaching, indeed too threatening. And as such, they are anathema to an already anxious and fear-ridden white consciousness.

42. Vincent Harding, *There Is a River: The Black Struggle for Freedom in America* (New York: Harcourt Brace and Company, 1981), xxiii; emphases added.

Seen in this light, this essay can be understood as the beginning of a dialogue between classical Christian spirituality and the Black radical tradition. FitzGerald's insights into the spiritual crisis underlying societal impasses and the contemplative healing of malformed consciousness find strong resonance with racial justice advocates. Much work remains, however, concerning how to translate FitzGerald's visionary insights into a societal register. Her vision, while thrilling and intuitively attractive, raises nagging questions: How does contemplation and the transformation it promises "create a new politics and generate new social structures"? How do contemplatives engage in social and political struggle? How does contemplation become present on the massive scale needed to heal the sickness in white souls and affect the course of human evolution? What supports are needed for white people to engage in the radical dying to the too small selves and gods that support a false identity and then to embrace the unknown, terrifying, and yet longed for liberation of spirit? Finally, and more pointedly, why is it that so many white religious and spiritual formation programs have failed to produce the vanguard of contemplative white persons with a consciousness freed from the soul sickness of White supremacy? These are the urgent questions that mark the frontiers that await those who would build on FitzGerald's seminal vision.

What is clear is that her intuitions resonate with the "souls of Black folks" who agree that White supremacy is a demonic reality and spiritual distortion that cannot be legislated or litigated out of existence. It is also clear that until there is a massive embrace of transformed consciousness, tragic racial disparities and divisions will continue to plague our national and global communities. And the "sheer morbid, wrenching rhythm" of killing, grief, and lament will not only continue in African American communities but also continue to fall on deaf white ears and impervious white souls.

13

Passion in the Carmelite Tradition

Edith Stein

Constance FitzGerald, OCD

The Carmelite tradition transmits a legacy of profound passion. While the *Carmelite Rule* (1206) cautions moderation in everything, in all the major texts and personalities of the tradition beginning with its basic Elijahn myth in the *Institution of the First Monks* and moving through the life and writings of Teresa of Avila, John of the Cross, Therese of Lisieux, Edith Stein and others, one encounters magnificent passion bordering on excess.[1] The way the Carmelite prayer tradition helps and educates is by showing

1. For me three questions form a background for this essay. First, where do we really find passion or excess in the Carmelite tradition? Second, how does the passion of the Carmelite tradition meet the hunger of our own time for spirituality and even mystical experience, the thirst for the divine and for community? Third, how does the Carmelite tradition move out from the familiar, from an enclosure of language and esotericism into new social and cultural situations? I am deeply indebted to Leah Hargis, OCD, for formatting the notes for me and helping me with the Edith Stein sources which she knows extremely well. My discussions with her were invaluable. This article will appear in the forthcoming volume *Carmelite Prayer: Essays by the Carmelite Forum*, ed. Keith J. Egan (Mahwah, NJ: Paulist Press, 2003).

us how passion for God matures, that is, how desire grows in ardor, how communion and being God's partner in love comes about in our lives.

In *Webster's Dictionary* passion is defined, first of all, as suffering or agony (from the Latin to suffer) and secondarily, as compelling emotion, specifically, enthusiasm, strong love and desire. Taken together these meanings show the complexity and richness of my understanding of the word passion as I use it in this essay.[2]

The ardor of their desire to love and be transformed in love and the intensity of their experience of, reflection on and appropriation of human suffering is precisely what characterizes those marked by the Carmelite ethos. In fact, nothing is so expressive of the passion we find in the Carmelite prayer tradition as this simultaneous intertwining emphasis on love and suffering which we see elegantly portrayed, for example, in the poetry of John of the Cross and more simply demonstrated in the writings of Therese of Lisieux. John sings:

> O living flame of love
> that tenderly wounds my soul in its deepest center! Since now you are not oppressive,
> now consummate! if it be your will:
> tear through the veil of this sweet encounter.[3]

When Therese, in her turn, writes that, "she had but one desire, that of being taken to the summit of the mountain of love,"[4] she is echoing the aspiration of Carmel through eight hundred years.

> Love, how well our heart is made for that! . . . Sometimes, I seek for another word to express love, but on this earth of exile words

2. *Webster's Twentieth Century Unabridged Dictionary*, 2nd ed., s.v. "passion." It is instructive to note synonyms for passion such as: ardor, rapture, vehemence, zeal, devotion, pathos and attachment.

3. John of the Cross, "Living Flame of Love," in *Collected Works of St. John of the Cross*, trans. Kieran Kavanaugh and Otilio Rodriguez (Washington, DC: ICS, 1973), 578.

4. Therese to Sr. Agnes of Jesus, 30–31 August 1890, *Saint Therese of Lisieux: General Correspondence*, volume 1, trans. John Clark (Washington, DC: ICS, 1982), no. 110.

are powerless to express all the soul's vibrations, so we have to keep to this one word: (love!).[5]

If we study *The Story of a Soul* we are not only awed by the magnitude of Therese's love, but also perplexed by the way she seems actively to pursue suffering, unable to learn the borderline between acceptance of the human condition and actually precipitating suffering. This is a danger she poses to those who do not read her work critically, who do not interpret her text. In this she is probably as "dangerous" as her Carmelite mentor, John of the Cross, who realizing that "love consists not in feeling great things but in having great detachment and in suffering for the Beloved" seems to counsel us to deny all human desires and choose what is most difficult, that is, make ourselves suffer.[6]

Edith Stein, the actual focus of this study, in her turn attempts to fathom the significance of this attitude toward suffering in John and in her own Carmelite life in an essay written around 1934 in which she explores "the burden of the cross."[7] I suspect, moreover, that this is so important to her that in her last written and unfinished work, *The Science of the Cross,* composed during the year before her death in the gas chambers of Auschwitz in August 1942, she uses her own philosophical theory of empathy, initially developed in her doctoral dissertation, as a hermeneutic to trace the inner experience and processes of prayer John goes through in his life and writing to reach his convictions about love and suffering. By means of this profound, original analysis she, herself, connects with and lays claim to his meanings which empower and energize her life, motivation and ultimately her death. One conclusion stands out: the more important loving becomes for John, Therese and finally also Edith, the more significant or

5. Thérèse, *General Correspondence,* Thérèse to Marie Guerin, 27–29 July 1890, no. 109.

6. John of the Cross, *The Sayings of Light and Love, The Collected Works of Saint John of the Cross,* rev. ed., trans. Kieran Kavanaugh and Otilio Rodriguez (Washington, DC: ICS Publications, 1991), no. 115, 93.

7. Edith Stein, "Love of the Cross: Some Thoughts for the Feast of St. John of the Cross," in *The Hidden Life: Hagiographic Essays, Meditations, Spiritual Texts,* ed. L. Gelber and Michael Linssen, OCD, trans. Waltraut Stein (Washington, DC: ICS Publications,1992), vol. 4, *The Collected Works of Edith Stein,* 91.

"desirous" suffering is. It is an expression of their passion; it becomes a proof of love, a medium of solidarity and a threshold to depth and transformation.

We, on the other hand, in the repudiation of a spirituality which seemed to stress an excessive and sometimes unhealthy self-sacrifice and love of suffering, have perhaps lost passion as evidenced by a certain spiritual fatigue, softness and malaise. Modernity, with its often one-sided emphasis on the development and realization of the autonomous self without adequate concern for the common good or multipersonal community, has left us bereft of passion, and herein, I suggest, lies a radical call to self-transcendence.[8] Our passionless, "so-what" society needs a new language of selflessness or of the Cross that describes and supports the loss of possessive selfhood. Such a forfeiture is indispensable in the contemporary quest for the transforming love, universal communion and cosmic consciousness that seem today beyond the achievement of human ability.

This is why I want to concentrate on Edith Stein, a victim of the Holocaust who literally disappeared with six million other people into the hell "where God died." I intend, first, to follow in some measure the mysterious faith/prayer process whereby the rejections, exclusions and marginalization she experienced were transmuted into the Way of the Cross. Second, I hope to discover how her understanding of atonement and expiation together with her convictions about community shaped this entrance into and appropriation of the mystery of the Cross. Third, I desire thereby to see how the energy of her powerful love and singular perception of suffering, particularly as this was mediated to her through her mentor, John of the Cross, seeps into and enlarges or distinctly marks the passion of the Carmelite tradition and in so

8. I am aware that some have difficulty with a call to "self-transcendence." They see it as a denial of the human, of the need for a strong, well-developed sense of self. This is especially threatening and even unfair for women, many of whom have come so belatedly into full selfhood. Nevertheless, the summons to a cosmic consciousness is so urgent and the spiritual experience of some women so compelling that I think we must speak of self-transcendence until we have another word that expresses the real radicality of the challenge today.

doing possibly points to a meaningful spirituality of selflessness, solidarity and communion that pierces through the limitation of accustomed boundaries.

Edith Stein—Passion for Greatness

In sharp contrast to the obvious revelatory character of both Therese of Lisieux's and Teresa of Avila's writing, Edith Stein did not leave us a personal journal or autobiographical account of her prayer or spiritual experience. While her letters and autobiography certainly provide insight into her inner life, yet she bore witness to her desire for anonymity by keeping secret the depth of her soul life. We are left to discover the footprints of her soul from her more "objective" writings, her intellectual passion and her life. Her message, however, is not less powerful for this reason since in studying her spiritual writings, one cannot doubt that she knew whereof she spoke.

From her youth, long before Edith became a Catholic, we see in her a raw passion for greatness that could only be assuaged by the absorption of self into an overwhelming plan beyond her own personal life.[9] She could not really know what a step-by-step immersion in anonymity and sacrifice would ultimately cost her nor imagine where the final focus of her love and devotion would be directed. Nevertheless, her employment of a phenomenological methodology to observe her own passionate behavior, emotion and absolute convictions concerning "German-ness" provides us with an entry point for tracking, in depth, a movement of displacement that began in a total, extreme, chilling dedication to the German State and evolved into complete, unconditional commitment to God and the Cross in radical solidarity with her own Jewish People.

In 1917 when she was 25 years old, Edith looked back on her experience of her country's "mobilization day" for World War I. At that time it became crystal clear to her that her individual life

9. See Patricia Hampl, *I Could Tell You Stories: Sojourns in the Land of Memory* (New York: W.W. Norton, 1999), 104–5.

with its private affairs and concerns had ceased and that, by her own free desire, all that she had and was belonged to the state, to be used up completely in the service of "the fatherland." She agonized continually because she could not find "the right place in which [she] could live up to this conviction."[10]

This woman, who struggled in young adulthood to give her life in passionate self-forgetfulness to an ultimate cause in the German state, who could not bear being at any one person's disposition, even the great Edmund Husserl's,[11] would by 1935 write that the real content of her life, of the Carmelite vocation, was "to stand before the face of God . . . looking up [in prayer] into the face of the Eternal," believing that a fountain of grace would bubble up over everything, without her knowing precisely where it would go and without those whom it would reach ever knowing from whence it came.[12] By 1938, on the eve of her departure from her cherished "fatherland" to escape the extreme exclusionary policies of Nazi Germany and guarantee the safety of her community in Cologne, in a poem entitled *I Will Remain with You,* Edith wrote with simple poignancy: "Heaven is my glorious homeland [now]."[13] She revealed, moreover, the completeness of the displacement of her extravagant desire and capacity for dedication by the very manner in which she explains "the highest stage of personal life" in *The Science of the Cross*:

> . . . When [the soul] has reached [this inmost sphere] God will work everything in the soul, itself will have to do no more than to receive. Yet its share of freedom is expressed in just this receiving. Beyond this, however, freedom is involved even far more decisively, for in this state [mystical marriage] God works everything only because the soul surrenders itself to God perfectly. This surrender is itself the highest achievement of its freedom. St. John [of the Cross] describes the mystical marriage as the voluntary

10. Edith Stein to Roman Ingarden, 3 & 9 February 1917, *Self-Portrait in Letters: 1916– 1942,* trans. Josephine Koeppel (Washington, DC: ICS Publications, 1993), vol. 5, *The Collected Works of Edith Stein,* nos. 6, 7.

11. Stein, *Self-Portrait in Letters,* Edith to Roman, 19 February 1918, no. 19.

12. Stein, "On the History and Spirit of Carmel," *The Hidden Life,* 1–6.

13. Stein, "I Will Remain With You . . . " *The Hidden Life,* 135.

> mutual surrender of God and the soul [in love] and attributes to the soul at this stage of perfection so great a power that it can dispose not only of itself, but even of God.[14]

Marginalization and Anonymity

Her passion notwithstanding, mutual surrender did not come easily to Edith Stein. She learned slowly in her experience, undoubtedly by the revisioning of her own life, that this union with God is "bought by the Cross, accomplished on the Cross, and sealed with the Cross for all eternity."[15] Little of what this truly brilliant Jewish woman philosopher aspired to or was capable of reached fulfillment.

Caught in the confluence of personalities, an inflexible German, male, academic structure and pervasive anti-Semitism, she was effectively marginalized as an intellectual not only because she was a woman, but specifically because she was a single woman. Although she attempted several times over a period of years to follow her *summa cum laude* doctorate in philosophy with a normal university appointment, no one, not even her mentor Husserl, would put his life on the line to sponsor her second thesis to obtain habilitation, that is, the license to lecture necessary for a university position.[16] Limited, therefore, in what she was allowed to do as a woman and a Jew, she spent her professional career, following her conversion to Catholicism, at a Dominican teachers' college for women and as a well-known and sought after lecturer, principally in Germany, Austria and Switzerland. Her competency included theory of pedagogy, women's education, equality of sexes' abilities for professions and scholarship, and broad work with Thomistic themes.

14. Edith Stein, *The Science of the Cross: A Study of St. John of the Cross*, trans. Hilda Graef (Chicago: Henry Regnery Co., 1960), 122.

15. Stein, *Science of the Cross*, 207.

16. Edith Stein, *Life in a Jewish Family: Her Unfinished Autobiographical Account*, trans. Josephine Koeppel (Washington, DC: ICS Publications, 1986), vol. 1, *The Collected Works of Edith Stein*, note 86, 185. And Edith to Fritz Kaufmann, 8 November 1919, *Self-Portrait in Letters*, no. 31.

Edith's recurring doubts about her ability as a scholar must undoubtedly be traced in large part to her cumulative experience in the academic arena. In 1932 she wrote to Sr. Adelgundis Jaegerschmid expressing the inadequacy she felt as a scholar created by her ten-year exclusion from the continuity of academic work and her isolation from the contemporary intellectual scene.[17] Her very next extant letter, written to a Thomist scholar who had found fault with her translation of Thomas Aquinas, again cited her deficiency and lack of resources.[18] Even more poignant is the correspondence with Hedwig Conrad-Martius in which Edith admitted to her own limitations in philosophizing and to the fear she had lost connection with technical thoroughness and was generally incompetent to function in the world of academia, that is, in the classroom, the lecture hall or as a philosopher.[19] She asked, nevertheless, for a radical critique of her writings in the hope that Hedwig might mediate for Edith the meaning of her life's task and assure her that she was not overreaching her own capabilities in the philosophical work she had undertaken.[20] But running through all her doubts was the realization that anything she could now accomplish would be far more fragmentary that she had dreamed.[21] Her losses were irreversible and would never be recouped. What remains significant in terms of her spiritual evolution is the fact that throughout this especially ambiguous, bleak time she delivered some of her most effective lectures verifying the presence of a hidden power not her own.

With her conversion to Catholicism in 1922 Edith was isolated on another level by the serious separation it created, first of all, between her and some of her close friends with whom she had felt

17. Edith to Sr. Adelgundis Jaegerschmid, 9 June 1932, *Self-Portrait in Letters*, no. 116.

18. Stein, *Self-Portrait in Letters*, Edith to P. Petrus Wintrath, 12 June 1932, no. 117.

19. Stein, *Self-Portrait in Letters*, Edith to Hedwig Conrad-Martius, 13 November 1932, no. 126.

20. Stein, *Self-Portrait in Letters*, Edith to Hedwig, 24 February 1933, no. 135.

21. Stein, *Self-Portrait in Letters*, Edith to Hedwig, 5 April 1933, no. 139.

there existed an unshakable bond.[22] Even more distressing was the deep misunderstanding between her and her family, particularly her dearly loved and greatly admired mother whose youngest child she was. Seen by her family initially as a rejection of her Jewishness and later as an effort to save herself from the fate of the Jews in Nazi Germany by entering Carmel, Edith's conversion and vocation effected further alienation in her life. With the rise to power of Hitler's National Socialism in 1933, her marginalization became even more acute. The "fatherland" pronounced her an outcast, specifically because she was a Jew—something unimaginable to Edith at the time of World War I when she had described what being German meant to her.[23]

It is ironic that her very Germanness and Jewishness, along with her intellectual life, the once thought solid parts of her identity, would be so challenged and so thoroughly stretched. A displacement and even forfeiture of identity, which she was helpless to protest effectively, was forced upon her. One supposes she was attempting to deal with all these various facets of exclusion, personal and social, when, prior to her entering Carmel, she gathered together the memories of her family experience, intellectual life and cultural milieu in *Life in a Jewish Family*. Not only was she attempting, as a phenomenologist, to educate German youth to see the similarities between the lives of assimilated, German Jews and their own, thereby making hatred of Jews (other I's) impossible, she was also, in accordance with her own philosophical convictions about human solidarity, freely taking her stand with her own persecuted people and publicly recognizing herself as one of them, an outcast. This autobiographical self re-creation as a Jew was, as Rachel Felday Brenner rightly suggests, absolutely essential to Edith's evolving self-understanding prior to entering Carmel.[24] It was the expression of a solidarity that drew meaning from her

22. Stein, *Self-Portrait in Letters*, Edith to Fritz Kaufmann, 13 September 1925, no. 38a.

23. Stein, *Self-Portrait in Letters*, Edith to Roman Ingarden, 9 February 1917, no. 7.

24. Rachel Felday Brenner, *Writing as Resistance: Four Women Confronting the Holocaust* (University Park: Pennsylvania State University Press, 1996), 80–84.

phenomenological understanding of the devoted individual who is a "carrier" of the communal life insofar as her personal being is faithful to a particular community and remains steadfastly planted within it even if she has been excluded from or, in fact, excludes herself from the communal life.[25] Whereas Edith's family and friends believed she was distancing herself from the Jewish community, and the state was attempting to ostracize her from her Germanness, she was, in fact, more deeply associating herself with both. In her Carmelite life of prayer this perception would expand into a desire to bear the burden of the cross in communion and expiation and would reach its "logical" consummation in her final words as she left Carmel for the extermination camp: "Rosa, come, let us go for our people."[26]

Prayer Development and the Mystery of the Cross

But how did the path of the outcast become the Way of the Cross? If we try to follow the intimate trail of her spirit, the pathway of her prayer, it leads to the Cross so that no one can doubt that the passion and death of Jesus became her inner mystery and the suffering and destruction of her people the preoccupation of her Carmelite life. Her spiritual writings provide ample evidence that she understood clearly by experience and education how growth in prayer works. She had learned well the tradition of contemplation from her Carmelite teachers, John of the Cross and Teresa of Avila, but she also comprehended the process as a phenomenologist, as a scholar. In *The Science of the Cross*, after describing faith and meditation with amazing clarity, she explained:

> St. John [of the Cross] also knows a higher form of meditation: a naturally lively and highly gifted mind may deeply penetrate into the truths of faith, consider them in all their aspects, con-

25. Edith Stein, *Philosophy of Psychology and the Humanities*, ed. and trans. Marianne Sawicki (Washington, DC: ICS Publications, 2000), vol. 7, *The Collected Works of Edith Stein*, 273–83.

26. This statement was supposedly the last one made by Edith Stein to her sister Rosa upon their arrest and departure from Echt Carmel and is widely quoted. There is no reliable source for this quotation.

> verse about them with itself, develop them to their intellectual conclusions and discover their inner connections. This activity will become even more lively, easy and fruitful if the Holy Spirit inspires the human mind and raises it above itself. Then it will feel to be in the hands of a higher power enlightening it, so that it seems no longer to be active itself, but to be instructed by divine revelation. Anything the spirit has acquired by meditation in one of these forms becomes its permanent possession. . . . Through its constant occupation with God, the spirit—and this means here not only the understanding but also the heart—becomes familiar with him [*sic*], it knows and loves him. This knowledge and love have become part of its being; the relation between God and man [*sic*] at this stage may be compared with that between two people who have lived together for a long time and are on most intimate terms.[27]

I believe Edith learned to pray in Speyer. Following her conversion to Catholicism she resided there with the Dominican Sisters who ran St. Magdalena's training institute for women teachers. During the eight years she taught there she lived like an enclosed nun dedicating herself to prayer and rarely going out except to lecture. She immersed herself totally in Christ through daily Eucharist, the Liturgy of the Hours, theological study and the intimacy of silent prayer, thereby learning "how to go about living at the Lord's hand."[28] Meditating on the gospels, she grew to know Jesus and discovered what God wanted of her by "learn[ing] from him [*sic*] eye to eye."[29] At the end of this period she wrote to a friend:

> God leads each of us on an individual way. . . . We can do very little ourselves, compared to what is done to us. But that little bit we must do. Primarily this consists before all else of persevering in prayer to find the right way.[30]

27. Stein, *Science of the Cross*, 85–86, see also 137.

28. Stein, *Self-Portrait in Letters*, Edith to Sr. Adelgundis Jaegerschmid, 28 April 1931, no. 89.

29. Stein, *Self-Portrait in Letters*, Edith to Rose Magold, 20 August 1931, no. 103.

30. Stein, *Self-Portrait in Letters*, Edith to Anneliese Lichtenberger, 17 August 1931, no. 102.

In the same year, 1931, in an essay on St. Elizabeth of Hungary, she painted what was likely a mirror image of her own soul:

> Mighty was the tug of war in the soul of the child Elizabeth. It set her on fire, and the flame of the love of God flared up, breaking through every cloak and barrier. Then this human child placed herself in the hands of the divine Creator. Her will became pliant material for the divine will, and, guided by this will, it could set about taming and curtailing her nature to channel the inner form. Her will could also find an outer form suitable to its inner one and a form into which she could grow without losing her natural direction. And so she rose to that perfected humanity, the pure consequence of a nature freed and clarified by the power of grace.[31]

During these years, her spiritual guide described her as

> . . . filled with grace, rich in the love of God and men [*sic*], filled with the spirit of the scriptures and the liturgy, from which she draws, in which she prays and meditates, and by which she lives.[32]

Later Edith, anonymously bearing witness to her own growth, would acknowledge that "no human eye can see what God does in the soul during hours of inner prayer. It is grace upon grace."[33]

Inasmuch as consulting human experience is an identifying mark of phenomenology, we must assume Edith consciously brought into her prayer all her physical, emotional and intellectual experiences of exclusion along with the increasing suffering of her people. Then her own precise, internalized understanding of the science of "empathy," so fundamental to her own identity, had to lead her so to follow in her meditation the suffering (emotional and mental) of Jesus that her spirit quite literally connected or "ported" to a transcendent source of energy, of "motivation,"

31. Stein, "The Spirit of St. Elizabeth as It Informed Her Life," *The Hidden Life*, 28.

32. Hilda C. Graef, *The Scholar and the Cross: The Life and Writings of Edith Stein* (London: Longmans, Green and Company, 1955), 100.

33. Stein, "On the History and Spirit of Carmel," *The Hidden Life*, 6.

beyond herself in the passion and death of Jesus.[34] "Before you hangs the Savior on the Cross. . . . The arms of the Crucified are spread out to draw you to his heart. He wants your life in order to give you his. . . . Look at the Cross. . . . Look at the Crucified," she wrote.[35] Edith's commentary on John of the Cross' dark night communicates the power of the energy she received:

> . . . Faith offers [the soul] Christ, poor, humble, crucified, forsaken on the Cross even by his divine Father. In the poverty and desolation the soul recognizes its own. Aridity, distaste and pain are the "purely spiritual Cross" presented to it. If it accepts this, the soul will find that the yoke is sweet and the burden light; the Cross will become its staff by which it quickly mounts upward. For Christ accomplished his greatest work, the reconciliation and union of mankind [*sic*] with God, in the utmost humiliation and annihilation on the Cross. When the soul realizes this, it will begin to understand that it, too, must be led to union with God through annihilation, a "living crucifixion. . . . " As, in the desolation of his death, Jesus surrendered himself into the hands of the invisable and incomprehensible God, so the soul must enter the midnight darkness of faith, which is the only way to God.[36]

For the realist phenomenologist there was no way to experience *as her own* Jesus' physical death, the material body broken, the blood poured out—this would come for her—but from the quality of Jesus' attitudes of loving surrender for others, of giving up his life freely in complete selflessness, of loving his friends, his

34. I was greatly assisted toward a more thorough comprehension of phenomenology as Edith understood it by a lengthy conversation with Dr. Marianne Sawicki in the spring of 2000. She introduced the notion of "porting" and defined "motivation," "demand" and "value" as Edith would have understood them. This paragraph and the one that follows have been influenced by Dr. Sawicki's explanations.

35. Stein, "Elevation of the Cross, September 14, 1939: Ave Crux, Spes Unica!" *The Hidden Life*, 94–6. Edith Stein would have understood those contemporary Christologies which see the suffering Christ as "the paradigmatic locus of divine involvement in the pain of the world." See Elizabeth A. Johnson, *She Who Is* (New York: Crossroad, 1992), 263.

36. Stein, *Science of the Cross*, 89.

people, even to death, of prizing truth and fidelity to his mission to the end above his own safety, of absorbing violence and evil while refusing to hate, of forgiving his killers and sending back love, she assimilated an intrinsic infinity of meaning. From his suffering her spirit accessed a profound explosion of energy in the realm of significance that could never be spent down. When Edith encountered such meaning in prayer, as a phenomenologist she "owed" it reception. Her attitude toward such "value" became non-optional. It tugged at her and demanded to be let in. She willingly, therefore, opened the gates of her inner spirit, the vestibule to the spiritual realm—like letting down the drawbridge into a castle—to soak up suffering from the Jewish Jesus by connecting or "porting" to his feelings and attitudes which empowered her toward love and impelled her "to take up the burden of the Cross," in what she called "expiation."[37] This is how Edith Stein, the philosopher, the Carmelite, became a passionate "lover of the Cross."

Community

To comprehend better, however, both the complexity and congruence of her passion for the Cross and the resulting inner movement toward expiation, we need to stress how integrally they grew out of the soil of an already existing sensibility that pervades her philosophical work and can be traced back to her early schooling at the University of Breslau (1911–1913). At that time she admitted to a feeling for the solidarity not only of all humankind but also of smaller social groupings.[38] The singular attention Edith gave to the study of the essence of community and mutual communication between human beings in her doctoral dissertation, *On the Problem of Empathy* (1916), and in *Individual and Community* (1920) was an expression of and enlargement upon this initial intuition. But community solidarity was far more than just a major theoretical concern for her, as her friend, Roman Ingarden,

37. Stein, "Love of the Cross," *The Hidden Life*, 92.
38. Stein, *Life in a Jewish Family*, 190.

points out. Belonging to a community was a personal necessity; solidarity a requisite for her life.[39]

But precisely what convictions about community were so foundational in Edith's thought that they remained a bedrock influencing her spiritual experience and development as a Carmelite? First, she believed that the very essence of community is the union of free persons who are connected on the deep level of their innermost personal lives and, therefore, have a vital influence on each other. Each one feels responsible for herself and for the community. Second, a community like a person can be said to have a spirit, a character, a soul. Third, some community members are "carriers" of the communal life. Their personal being is so totally given to the community that they are its "core" from which its spirit or character or soul is shaped and which guarantees its enduring reality. The further their devotion extends the more secure are the values and outward face of the community. Fourth, some individuals with higher sensitivity, often these carriers of community, function as the open eyes with which their community (or communities) looks at the world.[40]

Grasping Edith's prophetic perception concerning the truly faithful person who is a carrier of the communal life and a shaper of its spirit, and realizing the different communities to which she passionately belonged, we are in a better position to understand the manner in which four particular experiences were unfolding simultaneously in her prayer life: first, a typically Carmelite intimacy with "the Crucified" was constantly maturing; second, as their oppression mounted, a more profound identification with the Jewish people was developing that paralleled her growing communion with Christ; third, some kind of responsibility for the violence of the German Nazi state pressed in upon her; fourth, she was integrating her long held philosophical convictions about human community with both a theological understanding and

39. Mary Catherine Baseheart, *Person in the World: Introduction to the Philosophy of Edith Stein* (Dordrecht, The Netherlands: Kluwer Academic Publishers, 1997), vol. 27, *Contributions to Phenomenology*, 69.

40. Baseheart, *Person in the World*, 62–66. See also Stein, *Philosophy of Psychology and the Humanities*, 278–79.

experience of the "body of Christ" and the "prayer of the church." As these four realities coalesced in her life, a deep unitive experience of solidarity took hold of her.[41]

Expiation

From the perspective of Carmelite prayer growth, this development was to be expected. In her specific time and place in history, however, she named it the desire for "voluntary expiatory suffering" or the willingness to commit herself to "the works of expiation" which, she observed, only served to bind her even more closely in love to Christ in a powerful exchange of energy, meaning and direction.[42] Some of Edith's most passionate spiritual writing is expressed in the language of expiation.

What many find difficult to interpret today is not that Edith voluntarily desired to share the suffering of her people in intimate union with the Crucified—Oscar Romero, for example, and numerous others have done that in our own time—but that she did so depending on the theological categories of sacrifice, satisfaction, substitution and expiation. These classical salvation theories have a long history in theology.[43] Particularly since the early Middle Ages, it has been said that Christ, the God-man, offered through the sacrifice of his death infinite satisfaction and expiation to his Father and that in our place he atoned for the limitless offense inflicted on God through human sin. Even if Augustine's hypothesis on sacrifice, satisfaction and substitution and Anselm's lucid interpretation of salvation in terms of satisfaction and substitution, especially in their vulgarized forms which penetrated the public consciousness of the Church, appear extravagant to us inasmuch as they seem to contradict New Testament statements and no longer fit with the way we postmoderns

41. Stein, "Love of the Cross," *The Hidden Life*, 93.

42. Stein, "Love of the Cross," 92.

43. I have drawn in this paragraph from the excellent synthesis of Roger Haight, *Jesus: Symbol of God* (Maryknoll, NY: Orbis Books, 1999), 223–43 and also Raymund Schwager, *Must There Be Scapegoats? Violence and Redemption in the Bible* (New York: Crossroad, 2000), 206.

think about God and Christ, in the 1930s and 1940s before and after Edith entered Carmel, substitution and satisfaction were operative, viable theological constructs in soteriology and expiation profoundly influential and inspiring in the spiritual life of Carmelites.

Clearly, however, Edith's evident appropriation of an attitude of expiation/atonement—she differentiated between the two—was not only a function of Carmelite devotion nor simply a consequence of a Christian theological theory of salvation. It was also rooted in her Jewish origins and her scholarly work. Pivotal for Edith's self-understanding as a Carmelite nun was her birth on the Day of Atonement, the highest of the Jewish festivals "when the High Priest used to enter the Holy of Holies to offer the sacrifice of atonement for his own sins and the sins of all the people," after which the scapegoat was driven out into the desert with the sins of all upon his head.[44] Not through mere nostalgia, but with passionate purpose and identification did Edith repeatedly refer in her spiritual writings to the significance of this scapegoat ritual and the offering of expiation for sin.[45] Furthermore, as long as she lived she celebrated Yom Kippur each year by fasting throughout the entire day. Thus she could not fail to see the scapegoat mechanism in operation as the violence and hatred within the Nazi soul was projected upon her people. Such sin demanded an offering of expiation!

Even as an academic, as far back as 1921, prior to her conversion, Edith pursued the topic of expiation in a very technical essay, *On the State*, in which she analyzed the distinction between legal guilt or crime, which demands punishment, and moral guilt or sin, which requires atonement or expiation. Expiation, she explained, is born of contrition which has its effects "in the soul." Expiation is, accordingly, carried out interiorly, as is atonement, but expiation is characterized by the free taking upon oneself of a quite definite suffering or punishment to "offset" or balance a

44. Stein, *Life in a Jewish Family*, 71.

45. See, for example, Stein, "The Prayer of the Church," and "The Marriage of the Lamb," *The Hidden Life*, 12 and 97–98.

concrete sin (*peccatum actuale*). Atonement, on the other hand, is directed against the sinful state of the soul and not a specific sin.[46]

Edith's powerful reflections on suffering and the Cross written during the last years of her life are clearly marked by the distinctions in this very early study. For her, therefore, it was "logical" that the extreme violence of Hitler's Germany had to be balanced or blotted out by a greater measure of suffering freely borne in expiation. This is apparent in a meditation inspired by John of the Cross' love of suffering. He was the guide of Edith's desire, the person whose life and teaching undoubtedly had the most profound influence of all on her desire for voluntary expiatory suffering.[47] Edith's words bear the mark of John's passion for the way of the cross:

> The entire sum of human failures . . . must be blotted out by a corresponding measure of expiation. The way of the cross is this expiation. . . . Typical of those who submit to the suffering inflicted on them and experience his blessing by bearing it is Simon of Cyrene . . . Christ the head effects expiation in these members of his Mystical Body who put themselves body and soul at his disposal for carrying out his work of salvation. . . . The meaning of the way of the cross is to carry this burden [of sin] out of the world [like the scapegoat and like Jesus].[48]

Edith Stein was concerned about the body of Christ, her own people, the human community, and as an authentic carrier of the communal life, she was squarely, and some would say audaciously, placing herself in the battle going on between good and evil in that community, striving to shape its spirit. Is it blasphemous to suggest that, in a prophetic critique of the idolatrous and barba-

46. Edith Stein, "Eine Untersuchung uber den Staat," *Jahrbuch fur Philosophie und phanomenologische Forschung* 7 (1925): footnote, 103–8. (Reprinted Tubingen: Niemeyer, 1970).

47. Edith spent her retreat for her "clothing" in the Carmelite habit with *The Ascent of Mount Carmel*, her retreat for first profession with *The Dark Night*. *The Science of the Cross* is her study of John's complete works. She referred several times in her letters to her ongoing reading of and meditation on John's writings.

48. Stein, "Love of the Cross," *The Hidden Life*, 91–92.

rous plans of her own German people, she, like Jesus in his death, wanted to absorb the evil energy of hate and violence of the Nazi regime, throw down the drawbridge to receive the evil abroad in the world and carry it out into the desert to its death in her own body, like Jesus, on the shoulders of a love that could not be spent down? Even though she knew it would kill her? Like a scapegoat, in a collective transfer of energy to a victim, she desired to soak up the violence of the German state, ultimately of humankind, and thereby be a cause of harmony and peace, to surrender herself like Jesus so that men and women could be freed from their hate by unloading their wickedness on her.[49] Only love could bear the freight of such suffering, and yet she yearned to give back in love more than was being taken away in hate.[50]

I believe Edith knew God needs no human expiation or atonement, but rather human persons must be extricated from their own prison if they are to be capable of opening their hearts to God's freely offered love and thereby be liberated from their resentment. Her theology, on some issues, manifests such a surprisingly close affinity with the thought of German theologian Raymund Schwager that his theology actually throws light on hers. Writing some thirty-seven years after Edith's death, Schwager insists, in his analysis of violence and redemption in the Bible, that it is not God who must be appeased, but humans who must be delivered from their hatred, resentment and will to kill.[51]

49. It is worthwhile noting that Roger Haight points to Raymund Schwager's soteriology as one theological view of "how Jesus saves." Schwager employs the anthropological theory of Rene Girard regarding violence as a hermeneutical framework for interpreting the manner in which the death of Jesus mediates God's salvation. Haight, *Jesus: Symbol of God*, 349; see also Schwager, *Must There Be Scapegoats?*, 212, and 190–214.

50. See Roger Haight's explanation of Anselm's theory of satisfaction in *Jesus: Symbol of God*, 229: "Satisfaction presupposes injury done. It consists not in rendering to God what is owed God . . . but in making up to God for an injury done and repairing damage. . . . This means going beyond restitution. . . . It entails that one 'give back more than one takes away.'" Edith uses Anselm's exact words in *Cur Deus Homo*.

51. Schwager, *Must There Be Scapegoats?*, 209.

We must remember that Edith's personalist phenomenology was built upon the certainty that no human being is a mere individual; we all tap into a kind of energy from other persons and especially from the common reservoir of the community.[52] Because we are all connected in a vast network, whether we send love or hate along the energy currents is critical for the healing and evolution of human consciousness.[53] If we take into account Edith's strong assertion of woman's superior destiny to be educator and empathic redeemer of humanity, that is, to bring true humanity in herself and then in others to more mature development,[54] her words in 1939 for the feast of the Exaltation of the Cross, the day vows are renewed in Carmel, pierce our hearts in all their poignant passion and strong critique of immediate consciousness:

> Will you remain faithful to the Crucified? . . . The world is in flames, the battle between Christ and the Antichrist has broken into the open. If you decide for Christ, it could cost you your life. . . . Before you hangs the Savior on the cross . . . obedient to death. . . . Your Savior hangs naked and destitute before you. . . . Do not be concerned with your own body. . . . The Savior hangs before you with a pierced heart. . . . It is the loving heart of your Savior that invites you to follow. . . . From the open heart gushes [his] blood. This extinguishes the flames of hell. Make your heart free . . . then the flood of divine love will be poured [concretely ported, hardwired] into your heart until it overflows and becomes fruitful to all the ends of the earth. . . . If you are nuptially bound to him . . . your being is precious blood.
>
> Bound to him, you are omnipresent as he is. You can be at all fronts wherever there is grief, in the power of the cross. Your compassionate love takes you everywhere, this love from the

52. Marianne Sawicki, "Edith Stein and the Prospects for Jewish-Catholic Dialogue" (Comments prepared for the panel discussion at Holy Cross College, 20 October 1999), 3.

53. Stein, *Self-Portrait in Letters*, Edith to Erna Stein, 6 July 1918, no. 24.

54. See Brenner, *Writing As Resistance*, 164–73. In words closer to Augustine we could say the real sacrifice of her life in an inner act of total devotion was motivated by an overwhelming desire to make visible or bring closer to fulfillment humankind's unity through Christ in God. See Haight, *Jesus: Symbol of God*, 224–25.

> divine heart. Its precious blood is poured everywhere soothing, healing, saving.[55]

"Your being is precious blood." We are stunned by such a forfeiture of selfhood, such a transparent premonition of her physical death and so profound a consciousness of her vocation to carry compassionate love, the fruit of mature contemplative prayer, out of the very circumscribed space of the cloister into the depths of the abyss, "to walk on the dirty and rough paths of this earth . . . and [to] cry with the children of this world,"[56] to be, in fact, a carrier of helpless compassionate divinity into the bowels of hell and to answer the conspiracy of hatred with an outpouring of love. The cross revealed to her that God is to be found in the midst of pain and violence, with Christ and with crucified people; so would she be and thus could she write:

> The more powerfully God woos the soul and the more completely it surrenders to him [*sic*], the darker will be the night and the more painful the death.[57]

Solidarity

Edith Stein could not intellectually unravel the scandal of suffering and human violence, the mystery of the cross, any more than we can. As her union with God deepened, she could only enter more and more radically and even joyfully into solidarity with the Crucified Christ and those who suffer after the pattern confirmed by John of the Cross toward the end of the *Spiritual Canticle*:

> . . . it will be a singular comfort and happiness for her [the one united to God] to enter all the afflictions and trials of the world, and everything that might be a means to this, however difficult

55. Stein, "Elevation of the Cross, September 14, 1939: Ave Crux, Spes Unica!" *The Hidden Life*, 94–96.

56. Stein, "Love of the Cross," *The Hidden Life*, 93.

57. Stein, *Science of the Cross*, 207.

> and painful, even the anguish and agony of death, all in order to see herself further within her God.[58]

Clearly, during the nine years Edith lived in Carmel, what carrying the cross really meant for her evolved in tandem with Germany's escalating hatred of the Jews. Even before she entered Carmel, however, she sensed their fate would also be hers. This premonition is not altogether surprising, but what is profoundly disturbing, at first reading, is her interpretation of the Jewish oppression.[59]

> I talked with the Savior [she remembers] and told him I knew that it was His Cross that was now being placed upon the Jewish people; that most of them did not understand this, but that those who did, would have to take it up willingly in the name of all. I would do that. He should only show me how. At the end of the service I was certain that I had been heard. But what this carrying of the cross would consist in, that I did not yet know.[60]

What reading do we give to Edith's experience? As early as 1933, she seemed to grasp by a kind of prophetic intuition that both in Jesus' death on the Cross and in the Nazis' torturous, evil repression of the Jews we see the same unmitigated violence and hatred of "the other," the same sin, we see the same projection of violence onto a scapegoat, the same sins of the many placed upon the innocent.

The Jews were not sinless as Jesus was—they were human, they were not flawless—but in their innocence as a collective racial scapegoat, they were like Jesus in bearing the sins of the many. Like Jesus they were, Edith may have been suggesting,

58. John of the Cross, SC 36.11–13. I have described this kind of spiritual maturity in my essay, "Transformation in Wisdom: The Subversive Character and Educative Power of Sophia in Contemplation," in *Carmel and Contemplation* (Washington, DC: ICS Publications, 2000), 334–35.

59. Sawicki, "Edith Stein and the Prospects for Jewish-Catholic Dialogue," 4.

60. Stein, "How I Came to the Cologne Carmel," 18 December 1938, in *Edith Stein: Selected Writings with Comments, Reminiscences and Translations of Her Prayers and Poems by Her Niece*, trans. Susanne M. Batzdorff (Springfield, IL: Templegate Publishers, 1990), 17.

dying for all because all had already turned against them, rejected them, concretely transferring to them their resentment against God and their will to kill.[61] In this sense, the gas chamber was like the Cross in that the same burden of hatred and exclusion was placed upon the Jews as had been placed upon Jesus. What had killed Jesus, Marianne Sawicki suggests, also killed the Jews: hatred of humanity.[62] In both cases, in fact, we detect the rejection of the full, overflowing humanity of the Jew Jesus and by implication the presence of the divine in every human person. Manifested in the extermination of the Jews and all Jewishness from the human gene pool was also, therefore, the real hatred and ultimate rejection of God. Edith apparently recognized this deep-seated human resentment against God that showed itself in the repudiation of the reality of Incarnation and God-likeness in which every kind of degradation becomes possible.

In the last analysis, what the systematic dehumanization and death of the Jews signified for Edith was the abhorrence and denial of humanity's fundamental, intrinsic, unbreakable interconnectedness, solidarity and communion in God beneath all socially constructed differences. This amounted to a radical rejection of the life-long pillars of her intellectual and spiritual life. I am convinced that the pronounced orientation of her spirituality toward voluntary expiation in identification with Jesus Crucified must be interpreted in terms of solidarity and its central significance as "a value" coming out of her particular work as a phenomenologist and her prayer development as a Carmelite. Here, I believe, we find the contemporary key for accessing her passionate language of expiation and intentional suffering.

Conclusion: Contemplative Conviction and Prophetic Vision

Edith was one of those persons, whom she herself described in 1920, who with special sensitivity serves as the open eyes with which the community looks at the world. She knew even then that

61. Although the application to the Jews is mine, I am clearly indebted to Schwager's interpretation of Jesus' suffering and death in *Must There Be Scapegoats?*, 205–14.

62. Sawicki, "Edith Stein and the Prospects for Jewish-Catholic Dialogue," 4.

when the failure of the masses stands in the way of the receptivity of a true vision of values, it is crucial for those who possess eyes open to the world of spiritual values not to be closed in on or concerned about themselves, but rather turned outward to permit the wealth of their inner life to become visible in the community, even if the community at large is not receptive or succumbs to collective delusion.[63]

Twenty years later, having been educated by Carmelite tradition, life and prayer, her early insight matured into a prophetic, contemplative conviction. Thus she explained only a year and a half before her death:

> The deeper a soul is bound to God . . . [The silent working of the Holy Spirit made them into friends of God.] the stronger will be its influence on the form of the church. Conversely, the more an era is engulfed in sin and estrangement from God the more it needs souls united to God. . . . The greatest figures of prophecy and sanctity step forth from the darkest night. But for the most part the formative stream of the mystical life remains invisible. Certainly the decisive turning points in world history are substantially co-determined by souls whom no history ever mentions. . . . Hidden souls do not live in isolation, but are a part of the living nexus and have a position in a great divine order, we speak of an invisible church. Their impact and affinity can remain hidden from themselves and others for their entire earthly lives. But it is also possible for some of this to become visible in the external world. . . . [e.g., Mary, Joseph, Anna, Zechariah, Elizabeth, etc.] all of these had behind them a solitary life with God and were prepared for their special tasks before they found themselves together in those awesome encounters and events and, in retrospect, could understand how the paths left behind led to this climax.[64]

Edith was a carrier of the communal life and consciousness of Carmel, of the Jews, of the Church, of the Germans, of humanity, into the belly of hell. Her voluntary going—"Rosa, come, let

63. Baseheart, *Person in the World*, 62.
64. Stein, "The Hidden Life and Epiphany," *The Hidden Life*, 109–11.

us go for our people"—signaled her deliberate desire to stand in the face of communal blindness for an unbreakable love and solidarity, for a defiance of the conspiracy of hatred, of exclusion and marginalization, of reprisal, of evil for evil. Ultimately, she witnessed, like Jesus, to God's salvation to humanity in overflowing love. She took the mystical stream of the church, its deepest life, beyond the confinement of cloister and the boundaries of Carmel into the horror of Auschwitz. Words from her last letter on the way to the gas chamber—"So far I have been able to pray gloriously"[65]—epitomize with peaceful simplicity an earlier expression of her belief:

> When the mystical stream breaks through traditional forms, it does so because the Spirit that blows where it will is living in it, this Spirit that has created all traditional forms and must ever create new ones. . . . [Then the carriers of the mystical stream] can do nothing but radiate to other hearts the divine love that fills them and so participate in the perfection of all into unity in God which was and is Jesus' great desire.[66]

I sense that in her life as an intellectual, in her death in the Holocaust as a voluntary scapegoat, Edith broke through the traditional form of the Carmelite nun, a stone rejected and yet destined to become, in the twenty-first century, a cornerstone in Carmel. This is why we dare not minimize the extent of the influence of her passionate intellectual life upon her equally passionate contemplative prayer life nor the radicality of her total involvement in the social situation.

Neither may we spiritualize the brutality and anonymity of her death: one among six million, stripped naked, violated at the very least by the eyes of the guards, herded into the gas chamber, murdered, reduced to smoke billowing into Polish skies, with only vague memories of her peace and care of the women and children remaining. With an unspeakable, fathomless forfeiture of

65. Stein, *Self-Portrait in Letters,* Edith to Mother Ambrosia Antonia Engelmann of Echt Carmel, 6 August 1942, no. 342.

66. Stein, "The Prayer of the Church," *The Hidden Life,* 14–16.

possessive selfhood, she took the life of Carmel, of the Carmelite nun, to a new frontier far beyond the familiar.

If, as many pray, our civilization with its dying totalitarian systems, its holocausts, its destruction of life, its mass tortures, rapes and murders, its rampant ethnic hatred, its oppression of the poor and marginal, its response to terrorism, even its struggle over the death penalty, is the last long gasp of a vengeful society, it will be because people like Edith have dismantled hatred by refusing to imitate evil with corresponding vengeance and have injected love into the energy current connecting humankind and everything living in the universe in a vast network of interdependence. Edith Stein offers a key to the passion of the Carmelite prayer tradition today. She is an inspiration and teacher in fashioning a healthy, though demanding, contemporary Carmelite spirituality of selflessness and cosmic communion that makes a place for a very real, inescapable dispossession of selfhood in the service of love and solidarity.

The way Edith described John of the Cross at the end of *The Science of the Cross*, after following him through his life and writings, I want to apply to her because it summarizes and completes this study:

> [Her] soul had, indeed, attained to perfect detachment, to simplicity and silence in union with God. But this was the fruit of an interior purification in which a richly gifted nature burdened itself with the cross and surrendered itself to God to be crucified, a most powerful and lively spirit made [herself] a prisoner, an impassioned fiery heart found peace in radical resignation. The accounts of the witnesses confirm this result.[67]

67. Stein, *Science of the Cross*, 223.

14

Grace in a Violent World

Constance FitzGerald's Reading of Edith Stein

Andrew Prevot

In her scholarship and vowed religious life, Constance FitzGerald, OCD, not only bears faithful witness to the Carmelite contemplative tradition of Sts. Teresa of Avila, John of the Cross, Thérèse of Lisieux, and Edith Stein (whose religious name is Teresa Benedicta of the Cross). She also demonstrates this tradition's profound significance amid the crises of our modern or postmodern age. These crises are precipitated by a dehumanizing yet all-too-human form of self-interested subjectivity that wants to exert control through instrumental reason, that promotes individualism and exaggerated ideas of personal autonomy, that oppresses the poor and racially marginalized, that exalts the masculine over the feminine, that jeopardizes the ecological conditions of life, and that idolatrously exchanges the gracious God of classical mystical theology—the divine Sophia revealed most fully in Christ and in Christian practices of prayer—for idols of worldly knowledge and power. FitzGerald perceives a prolonged spiritual immaturity precisely there where Immanuel Kant and other moderns would locate their supposed spiritual maturity, namely, in the cultural pretense of an absolute self-certainty, self-possession, or self-validation.[1] I have analyzed this epochal problem in terms of interrelated crises of secularity, metaphysics, and violence.[2] FitzGerald treats it under the polyvalent category of "impasse." But by whatever name we call it, FitzGerald and I fundamentally agree that this age suffers from a host of theoretical and practical maladies that only a deep reabsorption of ancient streams of spiritual wisdom can thoroughly address.

What Is the Relationship between Impasse and Dark Night?

FitzGerald's work becomes most provocative when it closely links the experience of impasse with that of the contemplative dark night. This is a startling connection. It stops me in my tracks. Does FitzGerald mean to suggest that the traumas, blockages, and contradictions of this world from which there appears to be "no way out"[3]—that is, the impasses of modernity writ large and of its individual participants—are, like John of the Cross's dark night, purgative operations of a hidden divine love? Does she ask us to think, not only that God is compassionately present as a solidaristic co-sufferer and liberator with those burdened by impasses (as Elizabeth Johnson argues),[4] but also that the impasses themselves are God's loving acts of transformation, the painful instruments by which God is unmaking and remaking each person and the world?

Some passages seem to support such a startling conclusion. After approvingly citing Dorothee Soelle's claim that "all extreme suffering" involves "the experience of being forsaken by God" and

1. Immanuel Kant, "An Answer to the Question, 'What Is Enlightenment?,'" in *Kant: Political Writings*, ed. Hans Reiss, trans. H. B. Nisbet (New York: Cambridge University Press, 1991), 54–60.

2. Andrew Prevot, *Thinking Prayer: Theology and Spirituality amid the Crises of Modernity* (Notre Dame, IN: University of Notre Dame Press, 2015).

3. Constance FitzGerald, "Impasse and Dark Night" (1984), in *Women's Spirituality: Resources for Christian Development*, ed. Joann Wolski Conn, 2nd ed. (Mahwah, NJ: Paulist Press, 1996), 410–35, at 411.

4. Elizabeth A. Johnson, *She Who Is: The Mystery of God in Feminist Theological Discourse* (New York: Crossroad, 2007), 246–72.

"forsaken by everyone," FitzGerald says, "Yet it is the experience of this abandonment and rejection that is transforming the human person in love."[5] Does extreme suffering always have the capacity to transform one in love? In another text, FitzGerald writes:

> When the invisible, mute God of an abandoned Jesus seems to draw us into lonely introspection where prayer and relationships, as we have known them, are painful or gone; when loss, failure and hopelessness loom large; when all supports drop from one's consciousness and life's deepest meanings and symbol systems are empty and stale; when our inherited language and images no longer reveal the divine, then a dark Wisdom is operative, nurturing the human person with love and confirming values little prized in our society.[6]

Does this grammatical construction—"when" an impasse experience happens, "then" the love of God is operative—encourage one to believe that any and all impasse experiences, however painful or traumatizing, have the theological meaning of John of the Cross's contemplative dark night, such that it would be right to view them as disguised instruments of divine love that are doing God's healing, purifying work?

Drawing on traditions of modern philosophical romanticism and idealism ("Goethe, Schiller, Schelling, Coleridge, Hegel, and Rudolf Steiner"), as well as the thought of the Jesuit evolutionary theorist Teilhard de Chardin, FitzGerald contends that impasses may be vehicles not only for personal growth but also for social evolution.[7] She suggests that "as Americans we are not educated for impasse. . . . We cannot bear to let ourselves be totally challenged

5. FitzGerald, "Impasse and Dark Night," 421. See also Dorothee Soelle, *Suffering* (Philadelphia: Fortress Press, 1975), 85.

6. FitzGerald, "Desolation as Dark Night: The Transformative Influence of Wisdom in John of the Cross," *The Way Supplement* 82 (Spring 1995): 96–108, at 103.

7. FitzGerald, "Transformation in Wisdom: The Subversive Character and Educative Power of Sophia in Contemplation," in *Carmel and Contemplation: Transforming Human Consciousness*, ed. Kevin Culligan and Regis Jordan (Washington, DC: ICS, 2000), 281–358, at 313 and 339.

by the poor, the elderly, the unemployed, refugees, the oppressed; by the unjust, unequal situation of women in a patriarchal, sexist culture; by those tortured and imprisoned and murdered in the name of national security; by the possibility of the destruction of humanity [in nuclear war]." After listing these impasses that Americans refuse to face, she asks: "Is it possible these insoluble crises are signs of passage or transition in our national development and in the evolution of humanity?"[8] There is a danger here of suggesting, as Hegel does more directly, that the negations of history are productive means by which the absolute Spirit gradually actualizes itself. Such a dialectical, evolutionary logic urges one to "accept" (FitzGerald's word) tragic events as steps on a path toward more holistic consciousness and to see them as "the necessary deconstruction or death prior to new birth."[9]

One cannot object to FitzGerald's effort to take seriously "our concrete historical situation"[10] and to exhort her fellow Christian scholars to become "contemplative theologians willing to be stretched beyond [them]selves toward a new epiphany of the Holy, incomprehensible Mystery."[11] Yet it seems important to pursue this task of a socially conscious mystical theology without immediately identifying every impasse with the contemplative dark night, since "John says very explicitly that Dark Night, infused contemplation, *is* the loving Wisdom of God" and since presumably we do not want to tell an abuse victim, a slave, a rejected refugee, a woman afflicted by patriarchal oppression, a Jewish person in the hell of Auschwitz, and other sufferers that all of their pain is *actually*, despite any contrary views they may have of it, an experience of Sophia's loving, purgative grace and that their task, as persons aspiring to greater spiritual maturity, is simply to surrender themselves to this pain and let it do its secret, salvific work.

8. FitzGerald, "Impasse and Dark Night," 423.

9. FitzGerald, "Transformation in Wisdom," 313, 314, and 316.

10. FitzGerald, "Impasse and Dark Night," 422.

11. FitzGerald, "From Impasse to Prophetic Hope: Crisis of Memory," *CTSA Proceedings* 64 (2009): 21–42, at 42.

I do not believe that FitzGerald wants to make such a claim. I contend, rather, that FitzGerald wants to argue more subtly and credibly that some experiences of impasse can become occasions for a contemplative deepening of relationships with God and with others. Her point is not to divinize the violence of the world that produces many horrific impasse situations but to suggest that even in the midst of such violence, and precisely as our last and greatest hope against it, there are countless possibilities for a radically transformative union with God and with others that are simply awaiting our free consent. Violence is not grace. But the sort of grace that can overcome violence is available in its midst, in the lives of those suffering from it. The love of God has the power to reach not only those in contexts of communal joy but also even those in prisons of loneliness and despair, such as the terrible site of John's incarceration in Toledo, which informed his mystical poetry, and other similar places of quiet agony in our world. FitzGerald wants us to acknowledge that receiving this grace ultimately involves a costly form of discipleship. In the final analysis, the experience of its full reception is one with Christ's experience of dying and being reborn. Yet the cruciform aspects in FitzGerald's proposed spirituality do not imply that she condones the world's cruel systems of crucifixion. On the contrary, she is seeking the deepest conditions of their abolition. When well understood, FitzGerald's interpretation of the Carmelite tradition points toward the extraordinary possibility of being perfectly at the disposal of Sophia's compassion in a world that desperately needs it.

Surrender to God, not the World—and Do So out of Strength, not Weakness

Two questions may help us better understand and appreciate the nuances of FitzGerald's challenging contemplative-theological perspective. The first is the question of precisely to whom, or to what, we are called to surrender. Crucially, FitzGerald answers this by saying that we are called to surrender ourselves completely only to the loving God who creates and redeems us, who opposes violence and injustice, and who does not want anyone to suffer unnecessarily. This is not a sadistic pseudo-deity but rather a tender, merciful, and holy mystery who wants all creatures to flourish and to be free. FitzGerald's work honors the God of liberation theologians, political theologians, feminist theologians, womanist theologians, and eco-theologians, the God who demands prophetic resistance against structures of oppression and those complicit in them.[12] FitzGerald does not ask us to surrender to the possibly horrific events of history simply as a matter of course. In the end, she does not advance a fatalistic ontology but rather a theology of cruciform spiritual transformation, and these are importantly quite different.

The second key question is under what precise conditions FitzGerald believes such a total surrender to God, such a passage through the contemplative dark night, is conceivable, discernible, or advisable. A very partial answer would be: at a certain stage of spiritual development and strength. John's ascent and Teresa's inward journey do not begin by throwing one unprepared into an experience of utter desolation, suspension of faculties, total loss of self, and terrifying God-forsakenness. These profound trials and purifications come relatively late on the contemplative spiritual path. The Carmelite tradition presupposes as the audience for its advanced mystical teachings persons who "have begun to walk along the road of virtue" and have already received "consolations [that] arise from the virtuous work" they do.[13] These are persons already formed in relationship with God and with others, who are seeking greater perfection in love. Therefore, to suggest that anyone who suffers an impasse is in the grips of a contemplative dark night could be rather misleading. Many impasse sufferers are not in the sort of spiritual or psychological place at which it would

12. FitzGerald, "Impasse and Dark Night," 412–13 and 426–27; "Transformation in Wisdom," 333; "Desolation as Dark Night," 107n6; and "From Impasse to Prophetic Hope," 29n28.

13. John of the Cross, *The Ascent of Mount Carmel*, in *The Collected Works of Saint John of the Cross*, trans. Kieran Kavanaugh and Otilio Rodriguez (Washington, DC: ICS, 1991), prologue, sec. 3, p. 116, and Teresa of Avila, *The Interior Castle*, trans. Kieran Kavanaugh and Otilio Rodriguez (Mahwah, NJ: Paulist Press, 1979), dwelling places 4, ch. 1, sec. 4, p. 68.

make sense to invite them to embrace their impasse as a hidden work of divine transformation. This very particular theological interpretation of impasse as an instance of the contemplative dark night is viable only in some circumstances, correlated with the interior state of the person in question, and does not work well as a general hermeneutic of impasse. Nevertheless, under the appropriate spiritual and psychological conditions, FitzGerald's connection between impasse and dark night may prove very helpful and instructive.

To clarify these two key points and to indicate how they support a better understanding of FitzGerald's overarching argument for a modern or postmodern retrieval of contemplative theology, I shall concentrate in the remainder of this essay on her reading of one recent representative of the Carmelite tradition, namely Edith Stein (1891–1942). I shall set FitzGerald's largely sympathetic reading of Stein in relief against my own highly critical reading of Martin Heidegger (1889–1976).[14] This juxtaposition of two readings of contemplatively inclined phenomenologists—two acquaintances in the orbit of Edmund Husserl who later developed a robust interest in Christian mystical sources while at the same time becoming ensnared in the violence of Nazi Germany in *starkly opposed* ways—highlights certain important details of Stein's thought and FitzGerald's constructive interpretation of it that are more difficult to perceive without such a foil. Despite certain genealogical connections having to do with their inheritances of both phenomenology and Christian mysticism, Heidegger and Stein express very dissimilar spiritualities of self-surrender.

In brief, Heidegger's reconfiguring of the Christian tradition of contemplative surrender through his idiosyncratic reading of Eckhartian *Gelassenheit* omits any serious doctrine of God and foregoes considerations of spiritual progress through prayer, virtue,

14. The critical reading of Heidegger that I indicate here is more fully elaborated in *Thinking Prayer*, 37–69. See also Lilian Alweiss, "Heidegger's Black Notebooks," *Philosophy* 90 (2015): 305–16; Rüdiger Safranski, *Martin Heidegger: Between Good and Evil*, trans. Ewald Osers (Cambridge, MA: Harvard, 1998); and Richard Wolin, *The Politics of Being: The Political Thought of Martin Heidegger* (New York: Columbia, 2016).

and community. His secularized notion of grace, crystallized in his theory of the *es gibt*, leaves him little room to distinguish such grace from the violence of history. He asks one to surrender, not to God's love, but to the event of being and its destiny. And, to make matters worse, these are in his opinion essentially Germanic. They have a national location and identity, which excludes others. Heidegger's philosophy is undeniably connected with his morally callous support for Nazism, a point which has recently become more evident in the *Black Notebooks*. Expressed in FitzGeraldian terms: Heidegger treats the existential impasses of modernity, including even those of Nazi Germany, as the dark night of being's apocalyptic unveiling.

FitzGerald's reading of Stein shows how dramatically both she and Stein diverge from Heidegger on each of these points. Although Stein finds grace in the midst of an extremely violent situation, and although her experience of this grace opens her up to a Christ-like acceptance of her own suffering and death, she does not surrender herself first and foremost to the event of being which has taken on a violent historical form in Nazi Germany but to the God of infinite love who goes to extraordinary lengths in Christ to oppose such violence and to bring healing and love to sufferers. She is prepared to participate in Christ's cruciform repudiation of the sinfulness of the world only by means of a considerable period of communal, intellectual, and religious formation. This preparation builds up the relational self that she will ultimately let go but that, in another sense, she will, through the same solidaristic act, manifest in a highly exalted manner. Her preparation cultivates her sense of a vocation to live and die for the other. It enflames her passion to be nothing but a vessel of God's love. Her impasse as a woman of Jewish heritage in patriarchal, Nazified Europe eventually does become the occasion for a contemplative dark night, that is, for a cruciform experience of grace. But Stein's particular merging of impasse and dark night happens in such a way that the historical wrongdoing of her age is not deified but clearly condemned, and it occurs at an advanced stage of her spiritual formation in the practice of self-transcending solidarity. These details are essential.

How to Read Edith Stein

FitzGerald's essay, "Passion in the Carmelite Tradition: Edith Stein," richly clarifies these two important details. It demonstrates that Stein surrenders herself to God, not the world, and that she surrenders herself in this way only after a period of formation has given her the strength and passion to do so. FitzGerald notes that Stein's early phenomenological work, such as her classic *On the Problem of Empathy*, continued to influence her later contemplative writings.[15] Whereas Heidegger critically develops Husserl's project by refocusing phenomenology on the question of being, Stein takes a more explicitly social and relational path by reorienting phenomenology toward the problem of empathy, that is, the question of how one is able to experience the consciousness of another.[16] For a time in Freiburg, they all inhabited the same intellectual milieu. Stein recalls meeting Heidegger at a social gathering at Husserl's home and reports, "I liked Heidegger very much that evening."[17] Later in their lives, they would each begin to offer phenomenologically informed interpretations of Christian mystical texts, Heidegger focusing on ontological readings of the Eckhartian tradition and Stein on Carmel, particularly John of the Cross.[18]

In addition to sharing a similar philosophical training and developing a later devotion to contemplative thought, the two have shown similar tendencies toward what FitzGerald calls "a total, extreme, chilling dedication to the German State."[19] In Stein's

15. FitzGerald, "Passion in the Carmelite Tradition: Edith Stein," *Spiritus: A Journal of Christian Spirituality* 2, no. 2 (Fall 2002): 217–35, at 224.

16. Edith Stein, *On the Problem of Empathy*, trans. Waltraut Stein (Washington, DC: ICS, 1989).

17. Stein, *Life in a Jewish Family: Edith Stein—An Autobiography, 1891–1916*, ed. L. Gelber and Romaeus Leuven, trans. Josephine Koeppel (Washington, DC: ICS, 2016), 409.

18. Stein, *The Science of the Cross*, trans. Josephine Koeppel (Washington, DC: ICS, 2002).

19. FitzGerald, "Passion in the Carmelite Tradition," 219. See also Stein, *Self-Portrait in Letters, 1916–1942*, ed. L. Gelber and Romaeus Leuven, trans. Josephine Koeppel (Washington, DC: ICS, 1993), 7–10.

case, however, this only occurred early in her intellectual life, around the year 1917 when she reflected on the First World War. It was a nationalist phase of solidaristic thinking she eventually outgrew through a development of a robust Catholic faith. FitzGerald notes that, by 1938, Stein is able to state definitively that "heaven is my glorious homeland."[20] Her intimate relationship with God in Christ now transcends and conditions all of her other relationships and solidarities, including not only those with the German people but also those with her Jewish family and with her Catholic faith community.[21]

The divergence between Heidegger's and Stein's paths depends significantly on anti-Semitism and sexism. FitzGerald expresses Stein's situation poignantly:

> Little of what this truly brilliant Jewish woman philosopher aspired to or was capable of reached fulfillment. Caught in the confluence of personalities, an inflexible German, male, academic structure and pervasive anti-Semitism, she was effectively marginalized as an intellectual not only because she was a woman, but specifically because she was a single woman.[22]

Stein was never able to acquire habilitation, which would have enabled her to pursue an academic career in the German university system. Because no one would support her loftier academic goals, she worked as an instructor at a college for women and remained somewhat insecure for years about her intellectual gifts and purpose, even though she produced significant philosophical and theological works and went on lecture tours.[23] Meanwhile Heidegger, enjoying the privileges of his male, non-Jewish status, rose to international scholarly fame.

To be sure, Stein has been a highly controversial figure in Jewish-Christian relations. Painful rifts already emerged with

20. FitzGerald, "Passion in the Carmelite Tradition," 220. See also Stein, "I Will Remain with You," in *The Hidden Life: Hagiographic Essays, Meditations, Spiritual Texts*, trans. Waltraut Stein (Washington, DC: ICS, 2014), 135.

21. FitzGerald, "Passion in the Carmelite Tradition," 225.

22. Ibid., 220.

23. Ibid., 221.

her Jewish friends and family at the time of her conversion to Catholicism in 1922. These rifts were not mended simply by Stein's commendable decision to write an autobiography called *Life in a Jewish Family,* in which she was, according to FitzGerald, "freely taking her stand with her own persecuted people and publicly recognizing herself as one of them, an outcast."[24] Such autobiographical solidarity with her Jewish community stands in tension with certain statements she made as a Carmelite, such as one in her handwritten will from July 9, 1939, indicating a desire to atone for the supposed "unbelief of the Jewish people."[25] The idea of atoning for Jewish unbelief is highly problematic if one affirms, as postconciliar Catholic teaching does, that God's salvific covenant with Israel remains unbroken and permanent. Prompted by Stein's beatification in 1987 and canonization in 1998, some Jewish and Catholic commentators have raised additional concerns about the way her example could encourage renewed conversion efforts of Jews, the danger of Carmelites appropriating Auschwitz as a site of Christian devotion, and ongoing failures to recognize the Catholic Church's complicity in the Shoah.[26] These concerns are important to keep in mind while assessing Stein's significance and while reading FitzGerald's article, which admittedly has a different focus.

Nonetheless, critics of Stein and her Catholic reception may at least be glad to see FitzGerald demonstrating clear and appropriate moral outrage at the treatment of Jewish people in Nazified Europe. FitzGerald insists that, in any theological reading of Stein, one must not "spiritualize the brutality and anonymity of her death: one among six million, stripped naked, violated at the very least by the eyes of the guards, herded into

24. Ibid., 222.

25. Quoted in Friedrich Georg Friedmann, "Not Like That! On the Beatification of Edith Stein," in *Never Forget: Christian and Jewish Perspectives on Edith Stein,* ed. Waltraud Herbstrith, trans. Susanne Batzdorff (Washington, DC: ICS, 1998), 109–20, at 112.

26. See Susanne Batzdorff, "What Significance Does Edith Stein's Beatification Have for Her Family?," 21–28; Daniel Krochmalnik, "Edith Stein: A Jew's Path to Catholicism," 63–79; and Eugene J. Fisher, "Edith Stein and Catholic-Jewish Relations," 165–70, among the many illuminating essays in *Never Forget.*

the gas chamber, murdered, reduced to smoke billowing into Polish skies."[27] FitzGerald recognizes that Stein was gruesomely murdered for being a member of the Jewish people. The "final solution" of the Nazis was, in a very straightforward sense, the reason why she died when she did and in the manner that she did. FitzGerald walks a fine line in her argument. She does not want to "spiritualize" this horrific historical reality. Yet, as a Carmelite Catholic theologian, she is interested in the way that Stein interprets her experience of violent political impasse in connection with John's contemplative dark night and the Christian experience of the cross more broadly. FitzGerald endeavors to understand how Stein sought and found God in the midst of such tremendous evil, without in any way absurdly identifying this evil with God's salvific action.

FitzGerald quotes a passage from Stein's *The Science of the Cross* that emphasizes her radical conformity to the crucified Christ. Stein writes: "As, in the desolation of his death, Jesus surrendered himself into the hands of the invisible and incomprehensible God, so the soul must enter the midnight darkness of faith, which is the only way to God."[28] The parallel grammatical structure here is fairly straightforward: *as* Christ, *so* the soul. To whom do they surrender? The answer is clear: to the "hands of the invisible and incomprehensible God," hands of an infinite love one cannot fully understand. Yet there is a difference. In Christ's case, he surrenders himself to save the world, to atone for its sins. Remaining sinless in himself, and uniquely the possessor of divine and human natures, he is the agent of transformation for others. In the case of the soul, according to John's mystical theology, it must surrender itself in order to receive purification and transformation from Christ.

Stein's understanding of the relationship between Christology and spirituality is, however, more complicated than this picture of activity and passivity would suggest. FitzGerald quotes another passage from Stein, this one from a short text called "Love of

27. FitzGerald, "Passion in the Carmelite Tradition," 232.

28. Quoted in ibid., 224.

the Cross," which shows that, on the basis of a doctrine of the Mystical Body of Christ, Stein believes that those who surrender themselves as Christ does can thereby participate actively in his salvific work of expiation. It is not merely a question of formally similar cruciform actions but of a shared redemptive agency. Stein writes: "Christ the head effects expiation in these members of his Mystical Body who put themselves body and soul at his disposal for carrying out his work of salvation."[29] FitzGerald speculates, and other commentators have made similar arguments, that Stein's attraction to this idea of participating in Christ's redemptive work builds on her Jewish celebration of Yom Kippur, the Day of Atonement, a holy day that Stein continued to celebrate each year after becoming Christian.[30] FitzGerald argues that Stein was perfectly aware that "God needs no human expiation or atonement." FitzGerald turns to the Girardian theologian, Raymond Schwager, to underscore this important qualification or nuancing of Stein's participative atonement soteriology.[31] God does not feed vampirically on voluntary suffering. Ascetical practice should not be seen as some sort of works righteousness or semi-Pelagianism. Christ is the one true savior. Nevertheless, according to Stein, what one does in loving union with Christ may share in his redemptive gift of self.

Another complication arises insofar as Stein responds to her violent historical situation in the terms provided by this particular contemplative, soteriological framework. FitzGerald cites Stein's address from 1939, "Elevation of the Cross," as a good example. Let me quote a longer passage than appears in FitzGerald's text to illustrate the full logic here:

> The world is in flames. Are you impelled to put them out? Look at the cross. From the open heart gushes the blood of the Savior. This extinguishes the flames of hell. Make your heart free by the faithful fulfillment of your vows; then the flood of divine love will be poured into your heart until it overflows and becomes

29. Quoted in ibid., 227.
30. Ibid., 226. See also Krochmalnik, "Edith Stein," 68–75.
31. FitzGerald, "Passion in the Carmelite Tradition," 227.

> fruitful to all the ends of the earth. Do you hear the groans on the battlefields in the west and the east? You are not a physician and not a nurse and cannot bind up the wounds. You are enclosed in a cell and cannot get to them. Do you hear the anguish of the dying? You would like to be a priest and comfort them. Does the lament of the widows and orphans distress you? You would like to be an angel of mercy and help them. Look at the Crucified. If you are nuptially bound to him by the faithful observance of your holy vows, your *being* is precious blood. Bound to him, you are omnipotent as he is. You cannot help here or there like the physician, the nurse, the priest. You can be at all fronts, wherever there is grief, in the power of the cross. Your compassionate love takes you everywhere, this love from the divine heart. Its precious blood is poured everywhere—soothing, healing, saving.[32]

Stein instructs her Carmelite sisters to surrender themselves fully to the contemplative life, including its dark nights of purification in love, so that they may participate in Christ's healing, salvific work in this time of great violence and suffering. Surrendering to God in this manner is, according to Stein, a spiritual means of dressing the wounds and soothing the afflictions of others. The goal is not masochism—certainly not!—but rather compassion, consolation, and the restoration of life. The contemplative is not only saved by Christ's blood. She becomes this blood in her very being. Her heart is made "free" and "omnipotent" by being one with God's "compassionate love."

This is the mystical spirituality of a merciful, anti-violent, Christoform love that Stein carried with her into the hell of Auschwitz. Whether Stein ever said the infamous line, "Rosa, come, let us go for our people," which has been widely disputed, matters less than what this statement or similar ones would mean for Stein in the larger context of her thought. FitzGerald argues that it would have "signaled her deliberate desire to stand in the face of communal blindness for an unbreakable love and solidarity, for a defiance of the conspiracy of hatred, of exclusion and

32. Stein, "The Elevation of the Cross, September 14, 1939, *Ave Cruz, Spes Unica!*," in *The Hidden Life*, 95–96. See also FitzGerald, "Passion in the Carmelite Tradition," 228.

marginalization, of reprisal, of evil for evil."[33] In short, Stein's prophetic message is to surrender oneself to God so as to become a channel of the pure divine love that alone is capable of defying and defeating violence at its core.

Stein's formation in Carmel, and before that in phenomenological philosophy and in her Jewish family, provides an indispensable basis for her contemplative theology. Without such formation—without such a sustained, relational deepening of virtue, wisdom, and self-understanding—her suffering at the hands of the Nazis would not have been the explicit occasion for solidaristic union with God and with other sufferers in Christ that it *may* have been for her. As a precaution, one must immediately add that her actual, final experiences remain unknown and that, as much as she surrendered herself to God, she also pursued every possible means of escape from the murderous designs of the German state.[34] How close her experience of violent impasse ultimately was to a mystical experience of the dark night must, therefore, be treated as uncertain. But to whatever degree her contemplative spirituality was able to give some meaning to her worldly suffering, this was only possible because she had already been strengthened and prepared for such an eventuality. She was already in a position to believe that she could become one with Christ in love for the other, even if this meant enduring a death like his, and that it was her calling to be so united with him.

Some of Stein's formation happened through the influence and instruction of family, friends, and other companions in academic and religious community. Some of it took place in the quiet of her inner life. But, in fact, there is no strict separation between these two, no firm boundary between her relational experiences and the interior constitution of her highly empathic and solidaristic self. This interplay between self and other can be seen in what FitzGerald calls Stein's "prayer development."[35] FitzGerald argues that Stein "learned to pray in Speyer. . . . During the eight years

33. FitzGerald, "Passion in the Carmelite Tradition," 231.

34. Friedmann, "Not Like That," 118.

35. FitzGerald, "Passion in the Carmelite Tradition," 222.

she taught there she lived like an enclosed nun, dedicating herself to prayer and rarely going out except to lecture. She immersed herself totally in Christ through daily Eucharist, the Liturgy of the Hours, theological study and the intimacy of silent prayer."[36] Such individual and communal experiences of a Catholic prayer life are central to Stein's own writings on education, including several texts on the education of women. Focusing on what she calls "Eucharistic Formation [*Bildung*]," she argues that we are called to "join in the *sacrifice* [of the Eucharist], abandon ourselves entirely in order to be transformed and offered with [the Eucharistic Lord]." Preparation for the dark night occurs through a full and active participation in the celebration of the Mass. Although such participation requires the interior passion of the individual, it also presupposes solidarity in the Body of Christ. When one does have an isolating experience of the dark night, Stein contends that even and especially then one should not be alone. Rather, "in order not to lose the right way in such afflictions of the soul, there is no better protection, as experience shows, than obedience to an enlightened spiritual director."[37]

The difference it makes to face terrifying historical events and daunting spiritual trials if one has first been strengthened and fortified through learning, through ritual, and through the care of loving guides and companions is inestimable. By this I mean both that such a difference cannot be measured and that it is undeniably great in importance. In contrast to Heidegger, Stein not only refuses to secularize mystical theology. She also refuses to estrange it from the ecclesial conditions of interpersonal relationship, liturgical practice, and gradual interior development that make it bearable and meaningful. Stein and FitzGerald do not ask the finite mortal being simply to receive what manifests itself in the manner in which it does. On the contrary, as faithful Carmelites, Stein and FitzGerald envision a path of spiritual formation that will prepare one to discern the grace of God in such

36. Ibid., 223.

37. Stein, "Religious/Spiritual Formation of the Human Being," in *Edith Stein: Selected Writings*, ed. Marian Maskulak (Mahwah, NJ: Paulist Press, 2016), 193–216, at 202–3 and 216.

a world and that will give one the passion and courage to pursue and embody this grace, even if it means embracing moments of uncertainty and perhaps extreme suffering. This is not ontological fatalism. It is a Christological spirituality of transformation.

Conclusion

Is every impasse, then, an occasion for a contemplative dark night? The foregoing discussion has partly been an effort to explain why thinking so would be highly problematic, in short because this way of thinking would risk treating worldly violence *tout court* as a hidden mode of purgative grace. The preceding argument has also explained why such a simplistic equation of impasse and dark night does not seem to be FitzGerald's true position on the subject. Her reading of Stein suggests that an impasse may become the occasion for a contemplative dark night only when one surrenders oneself to God's love in the midst of this impasse, not to the impasse itself, and only when one has received sufficient formation to do so freely, as the self that one has become, and in an act of self-transcending love for the other.

It is conceivable that some persons will not have an explicitly Christian idea of God but nevertheless have enough of a sense of God's almighty, loving nature to undergo a similar spiritual experience. This would not be out of the question for Jewish persons who, unlike Stein, have not become Christian. Moreover, it need not be the case that one is formed specifically in the Carmelite order or, for that matter, in another vowed religious community. Formation can happen in many different ways in the context of lay spirituality. Nonetheless, the often violent impasses of modernity can become occasions for a contemplative dark night, or some similar experience of gracious divine union, only if there is some discerning theological and formational work well underway in the spiritual life of the impasse sufferer. This is the crucial point.

Although not everyone is called to follow Stein's precise path (and there are limits to how much such imitation would be feasible in any case), there are certain essential elements in Stein's contemplative theology that are missing from Heidegger's contemplative philosophy, and the difference in meaning and outcome is staggering. FitzGerald's contemplative work is on the right side of this divide. She finds grace in a violent world without identifying grace with the mere manifestation of this violent world. This remarkable achievement is just one of the many reasons why her scholarship and her clear spiritual voice will continue to challenge and inspire readers for many years to come. In her reading of Stein, FitzGerald gives us an empowering image of the sort of self-surrendering, compassion-filled discipleship that our patriarchal, racist, militaristic, and ecologically destructive societies desperately need.

15

Preaching the Dark Wisdom of the Cross

Mary Catherine Hilkert, OP

In a 2009 plenary address to the Catholic Theological Society of America, Constance FitzGerald challenged theologians to become contemplative prophets of hope during a time of ecclesial, societal, and ecological impasse. She wagered that, in spite of all of the evidence to the contrary, it is possible that we stand "at the cusp of an evolutionary breakthrough."[1] That challenge is even more radical for those called to the ministry of preaching the Gospel. According to the apostle Paul, all effective preaching comes from the power of God's Spirit who reveals God's own mysterious, hidden wisdom disclosed most fully in Jesus Christ and him crucified (see 1 Cor 2:1-16). The challenge facing the Christian preacher who is called to speak a word of grace in even the most desolate situation is not only how to recognize and analyze the signs of the times in light of the Gospel but also how to announce the wisdom of the cross at the heart of Christian faith as "good news" in a world of suffering and death, hatred and violence, executions and extinction.

1. Constance FitzGerald, "From Impasse to Prophetic Hope: Crisis of Memory," *CTSA Proceedings* 64 (2009): 21–42, at 41–42.

Deeply rooted in Carmelite spirituality, FitzGerald has proposed that the writings of John of the Cross on "dark night" can shed light on both aspects of that dilemma. Contemplative approaches to the wisdom of the cross often turn to mystical expressions of union with the crucified Jesus experienced in silent prayer, an experience sometimes symbolized as "an exchange of hearts."[2] But FitzGerald's writings suggest an alternative path, one more in line with Pope Francis's exhortation that "a preacher has to contemplate the word, but [the preacher] also has to contemplate [the] people, . . . paying attention 'to actual people, to using their language, their signs and symbols, to answering the questions they ask.'"[3] Preachers might discover new depths of the wisdom of the cross if they were first to contemplate what FitzGerald describes as "the dark night of the world" (and, we might add, "the dark night of a Church" complicit in abuse, betrayal, and duplicity) before attempting to speak of the dark wisdom of the cross.[4]

Paying attention to those contemporary dark nights can open preachers to new depths of empathy, solidarity, and communion with those who suffer in profound ways, even as they embrace their own share of the grief that touches every human life. It is

2. FitzGerald confirms that there can be a mystical and transformative experience of "deep intimacy with the suffering, dying Jesus" that nourishes "a profound solidarity with those who suffer," but in her 2017 preaching on Good Friday and elsewhere she calls instead for a preaching of the cross that emerges from the impasse of the world. (Constance FitzGerald, "Near the Cross of Jesus Stood His Mother," Good Friday Preaching 2017, *Baltimore Carmel News* [Summer 2017], 2).

3. Pope Francis, apostolic exhortation *Evangelii Gaudium* (The Joy of the Gospel) (Washington, DC: United States Conference of Catholic Bishops, 2013), par. 154, p. 78. This exhortation includes an explicit echo of Pope Paul VI's 1975 apostolic exhortation *Evangeli Nuntiandi* (On Evangelization in the Modern World).

4. FitzGerald has noted that John of the Cross and Teresa of Avila were no strangers to the experience of impasse in the Church of their day or the Carmelite religious tradition, which they loved but also labored to reform. For reflection on more contemporary ecclesial challenges, see Constance FitzGerald, "Pursuing Our Dreams in Times of Darkness," in *Transformational Leadership*, ed. Annmarie Sanders (Maryknoll, NY: Orbis Books, 2015), 11–15.

only after facing the genuine scandal of the cross, however, that preachers can proclaim a dark wisdom to be found not in the cross itself, nor in the suffering of the passion and death of Jesus, but rather in the love and fidelity that enabled him to extend his arms joining heaven and earth, laying down his life for his friends. Christians believe that God has embraced all of human life, enduring even the horror and depth of suffering brought about by sin and injustice, and broken its power in the life, death, and resurrection of Jesus. Living in the power of his Spirit, witnesses throughout the ages have testified with their lives to the possibility that hope and courage can emerge amid the most desperate of circumstances and they continue to do so today. To proclaim the wisdom of the cross in a way that speaks to suffering hearts, a Church in need of healing, and a violent world, preachers need to attend to the dark night of the world, the scandal of the cross, and the paradoxical forms of wisdom that can emerge amid human finitude and loss and even in the face of radical injustice.

Impasse: The Dark Night of the World

In her 1984 article "Impasse and Dark Night" FitzGerald identifies the depth and dimensions of experiences of impasse:

> There is no way out of, no way around, no rational escape from, what imprisons one, no possibilities in the situation. In a true impasse, every normal manner of acting is brought to a standstill, and ironically, impasse is experienced not only in the problem itself but also in any solution rationally attempted. . . . Any movement out, any next step is canceled.[5]

That experience is unique for each person but includes such anguishing personal struggles as the loss of self-esteem and any sense of meaning or hope for a future that can be different from the past and present. It is often born from painful interpersonal

5. Constance FitzGerald, "Impasse and Dark Night," in *Living with Apocalypse: Spiritual Resources for Social Compassion*, ed. Tilden Edwards (New York: Harper and Row, 1984), 93–116, at 94.

experiences of betrayal, disillusionment, and breakdown of relationships. For religious persons, the most painful impasse may be the experience of the apparent absence of God, the inability to pray, and the psalmist's experience that "my only friend is darkness" (Ps 88:19).[6]

In her now-classic article FitzGerald acknowledges the profound pain of personal and interpersonal suffering, but she highlights in particular *societal* experiences of impasse, including the experience of women (poor women, Black women, White women, exploited women, Asian women, Native American women, etc.), the experience of the poor and oppressed, the experience of the aging, the experience of the fear of nuclear holocaust and nuclear buildup, and the experience of the woundedness of the earth and the environment.[7] Decades later when she was called on to preach on the passion and death of Christ on Good Friday in 2017, FitzGerald turned from the abstract to concrete examples of the persecution of the vulnerable as she reflected on the words addressed to Saul on the road to Damascus in the narrative from the Acts of the Apostles: "Saul, Saul, why are you persecuting me?" (Acts 9:4). Rather than leaving Saul's question, "Who are you, Lord?" and the response, "I am Jesus, whom you are persecuting," in the context of the first-century narrative and Paul's own conversion, FitzGerald extended the challenge to recognize and respond to Christ crucified in countless parts of the world and our own cities today. In response to the haunting question expressed by Paul, she proclaimed:

> I am the migrant, refugee women and children on your borders, in your camps. I am the people of Southern Sudan and Nigeria whose lives are being snuffed out by famine. I am the mother holding my lifeless, dead baby in my arms, one of the 20 million people in Somalia and Yemen who will, without massive aid, die of starvation in the next three months. I am the people caught in the endless, demonic, devasting war in Syria. . . . I am the women, the girls, the children kidnapped, raped and trafficked in every

6. Scripture quotations in this chapter are from the NABRE.
7. FitzGerald, "Impasse and Dark Night," 93.

> part of the world. I am the illegal immigrant mother ruthlessly deported and I am the child, left behind in your country. I am the children caught in the crossfire of poverty and violence in your own city. I am the poor family, the elderly couple, the homeless man, who can't scrape together the means to secure the food and health care we need for life.[8]

FitzGerald also included "the evolving earth, your fragile, threatened home, that cradles all this suffering and death" in her sketch of major fault lines in the "dark night of the world," before returning to the biblical text: "I am Jesus, whom you are [crucifying]" (Acts 9:5).

The Cross: Scandal or Wisdom?

Although she has written eloquently of the transformative power of participation in the suffering of the crucified Jesus and described "dark contemplation" as a process of painful but necessary purification of desire, FitzGerald does not begin there in her writing or her preaching. Neither does she assume that all forms of suffering have that power. On the contrary, in her preaching on Good Friday 2017, she declared that in times of impasse the mystery of Jesus' death on the cross is revealed by first turning to "the shocking enormity of crucified lives":

> It seems as if our powerlessness in the face of so much agony and loss, such rampant cruelty and hard-heartedness, breaks down the protective boundaries of our souls allowing the full impact of senseless, untimely, unfair death to crash in on us.[9]

Although adopting the language of the apostle Paul, many speak of the "wisdom of the cross"; FitzGerald makes an important distinction when she writes instead about "the mystery of Jesus' death" or the wisdom of "dark crucified Sophia." The extent to which Jesus was willing to go in his solidarity with the most

8. FitzGerald, "Near the Cross of Jesus Stood His Mother," 2.
9. Ibid., 3.

vulnerable—even to "lay down his life for his friends"—discloses in the most profound way the unconditional love and mercy of God. But that is not to identify the torture and death of an innocent man whom Christians confess as God's own beloved Son as God's will or to proclaim as "good news" that "God sent his son to die for us." The distinction between the historical event of the crucifixion of Jesus and the love, fidelity, and solidarity with which Jesus endured and accepted his death led to Edward Schillebeeckx's bold reminder: "in one sense we are saved *despite* the death of Jesus."[10]

The God disclosed in the life and ministry of Jesus does not will suffering that is brought about by human sinfulness and injustice—whether speaking about the crucifixion of Jesus or the ongoing passion of contemporary "crucified people" or the exploitation of other creatures and the Earth itself. In his life and ministry, Jesus never appealed to evil as God's will. He did not tell people that suffering was part of God's plan for them. Some point to the fact that the gospel writers, writing after the resurrection, portray Jesus as predicting his own suffering and interpreting it as a necessary dimension of proclaiming the reign of God and ushering in God's final salvation. The core of that insight may well go back to Jesus himself, who chose to stay the course in his preaching ministry when it was leading him toward Jerusalem, where the prophets before him met resistance and death. But in his life and ministry Jesus was active on behalf of healing and reconciliation, of life and flourishing. Reading the icon of Jesus' life and ministry reveals that God's will is that humankind and creation flourish. To borrow and extend the insight of Irenaeus, we might say that "the glory of God is humankind and creation fully alive." The image of God that Jesus enfleshed is a God of love who holds power over evil and who came to bring life in abundance.

The wisdom of God that Jesus preached, lived, and embodied was good news for the poor and the outcast, but that wisdom

10. Edward Schillebeeckx, *Christ: The Experience of Jesus as Lord* (New York: Crossroad, 1980), 724–30, at 729.

was not welcomed by all. Roman authorities perceived this announcement of an alternate kingdom as a clear challenge to their rule and to the political status quo. For those religious leaders who collaborated with the Romans, Jesus and his preaching of the reign of God constituted a threat not only to their power and control but also to their understanding of God and God's will. The suspicion, challenges, and plots to destroy Jesus that echo in the background during his ministry reach a crescendo in the passion narratives. Betrayed by one of his chosen disciples and abandoned by most of his closest friends, Jesus, the preacher of God's unlimited compassion, was handed over to the Romans to be tortured and executed while God remained silent.

Where is the wisdom of the cross to be found in this scene of horror and darkness? Clearly not in the evil of the execution of an innocent man, the final rejection of God's wisdom enfleshed. Rather, the triumph of the cross is to be found in the nonviolent love of Jesus who did not return evil for evil but instead stood in solidarity with all of the victims of historical evil and violence even unto death, breaking the cycle of violence with words of forgiveness.[11] Christians place our hope not in the cross but in the power of the Spirit at work in Jesus in spite of the evil that brought about his execution. The same Spirit of love that empowered and sustained Jesus throughout his ministry enabled him to face rejection and betrayal, to respond to hatred and violence with forgiving love. The wisdom to be found in Christ crucified is the wisdom of the one who kept faith with Abba in the darkness and who embraced solidarity with humankind and all of creation as he stretched out his arms joining heaven and earth. It is the wisdom of the one who laid down his life for his friends (John 15:13).

The love and forgiveness that are the gifts of God's Spirit are the power that Christians believe defeated sin and death. In the words of Australian theologian Denis Edwards, "The Spirit [stayed] with Jesus in his death, enabling him to give his life in love and transforming a brutal and ugly death into life for the

11. For further discussion on this point, see Barbara E. Reid, "The Cross and Cycles of Violence," *Interpretation* 58, no. 4 (2006): 376–85.

world."[12] Pope John Paul II likewise highlighted the role of the Holy Spirit in the death of Jesus as "the Love that works in the depths of the paschal mystery, the source of the salvific power of the cross of Christ, and as the gift of new and eternal life."[13] The love that triumphs over death and evil in the resurrection is God's definitive confirmation of Christian hope for the future, without which the cross remains utter folly.

FitzGerald reminds us that that same Spirit empowers and impels Jesus' disciples to do all that we can to resist injustice, senseless suffering, and violence and to challenge and change the social, economic, and political systems that cause and perpetuate those forms of suffering. In the company of theologians Jon Sobrino, Shawn Copeland, James Cone, and Nancy Pineda-Madrid, among others, she recognizes that it is God's own Spirit who impels us to "take the crucified from their crosses."[14] At the same time, she emphasizes that prophetic action is linked to another dimension, to the paschal mystery—a kind of dark wisdom to be found precisely in the solidarity of communion with other suffering persons, communities, and creatures.

From that perspective she exhorted those gathered at Carmel on Good Friday to "reach with a kind of desperation for the Cross of Christ on behalf of all the victims of human sinfulness who suffer and die counting for so little."[15] Far from an exhortation to masochism, FitzGerald insists that this "communion in the darkest place, at the nadir of human hopelessness," is the place where Jesus' followers can absorb the very compassion of God: "the power of the living God, in Jesus, entering the fray, person-

12. Denis Edwards, *Breath of Life: A Theology of the Creator Spirit* (Maryknoll, NY: Orbis Books, 2004), 82.

13. Pope John Paul II, *The Holy Spirit in the Life of the Church and the World (Dominum et Vivificantem)* (Boston: St. Paul, 1986), par. 41, p. 68.

14. See Jon Sobrino, *The Principle of Mercy: Taking the Crucified People from the Cross* (Maryknoll, NY: Orbis Books, 1994); M. Shawn Copeland, *Knowing Christ Crucified: The Witness of African American Religious Experience* (Maryknoll, NY: Orbis Books, 2018); James Cone, *The Cross and the Lynching Tree* (Maryknoll, NY: Orbis Books, 2011); Nancy Pineda-Madrid, *Suffering + Salvation in Ciudad Juarez* (Minneapolis: Fortress Press, 2011).

15. FitzGerald, "Near the Cross of Jesus Stood His Mother," 3.

ally drinking of the cup of suffering and going down into the nothingness of death, to transform it from within."[16] Speaking in the language of contemplative witness, rather than attempting an impossible explanation, FitzGerald remarks that the transformation of the consciousness of those who embrace this level of solidarity is a participation in the compassion of Christ, the saving love of God enfleshed.

In another preaching event, FitzGerald turned to the work of M. Shawn Copeland for further development of this insight.

> Communion with Jesus who was crucified situates us with him in the darkest places of human suffering and hopelessness absorbing from Jesus God's intimate compassion and unfathomable love, incarnating in our own lives, in spite of the consequences, his solidarity with rejected and despised persons (*Copeland*), one with him in communicating across the vast currents of human consciousness that compassion, that love, the utterly faithful communion, that serves as the thickening of grace that surrounds the victims of human sin and tragedy and strengthens them in their inner depths.[17]

In recent writing and preaching, FitzGerald highlights the experience of impasse at societal, ecological, and ecclesial levels, but always with attention to how social and structural conversion is intertwined with the experience of the paschal journey on personal and interpersonal levels as well. Preachers, pastoral counselors, and spiritual directors know well the dimensions of impasse that touch every dimension of human life and relationships—physical, mental, and emotional forms of illness, forms of addiction, abusive relationships and bullying, infertility or loss of a child, divorce, the death of a spouse or beloved friend, loneliness, the loss of a job, the inability to pray, to name but a few. Can we speak of "dark wisdom" to be discovered there as well?[18]

16. Ibid., 4. Here FitzGerald makes reference to the work of Elizabeth Johnson.

17. Constance FitzGerald, "Profession Exhortation for Sr. Cecilia of the Cosmic Christ, May 12, 2019," *Baltimore Carmel News* (Summer 2019), 4.

18. For one example, see Jessica Coblentz, "The Possibilities of Grace amid Persistent Depression," *Theological Studies* 80, no. 3 (September 2019): 554–71.

Unwanted Wisdom: The Spirit of Life Speaking in the Silence

The existential question that haunts many Christian believers is that of discerning how the power of God to transform human suffering and to defeat even the "last enemy" of death (1 Cor 15:26) relates not only to their call to active discipleship but also to their own concrete life and relationships here and now. What does it mean to participate in the paschal mystery? One woman diagnosed with terminal cancer spoke for many when she said of her struggle: "I don't know what to pray for. Should I be praying for the grace to surrender to death or should I be fighting it and struggling to live? I don't know what to hope for."

In their concrete and diverse experiences of life and suffering, believers participate in multiple aspects of the mystery of the cross. They share in different moments in Jesus' own paschal journey, which according to the gospels included both the anguished cry of "My God, My God, why have you abandoned me?" and the radical trust of "Into your hands, I commit my spirit." Some who have suffered deeply are convinced that cancer or some other serious illness is "God's will for them" and say quite clearly: "I couldn't bear it, if I thought that was not true." For others, their deepest level of anguish comes from questioning why God would allow this to happen to them or to someone they love. Their struggle is made all the more painful when others view them as having failed to come to terms with their illness or the death or the suffering of those they love, especially when described as a failure to accept "God's will."

If the life and ministry as well as the resurrection are the keys to interpreting the death of Jesus, there is a third possibility. Suffering is not God's will for us, nor was it God's will for Jesus. Nevertheless, when suffering befalls us—as it inevitably does in a world of finitude, human malice, and cosmic forces beyond our control—we have God's promise that God's own Spirit will be with us, enabling the courage to endure what we cannot change and holding open a future that we cannot see.[19]

19. For a Thomistic interpretation of this perspective, see Christopher Kiesling, "A Cancer Patient's Vision of Faith," *America* (December 31, 1983), 424–27.

Far from Christian masochism or a romanticization or legitimation of suffering, a genuine participation in the sufferings of Christ requires radical courage and trust in the Spirit of God who raised Jesus from the dead and whom Jesus promised to send to his disciples as his own Advocate. There are, of course, different forms of participation in the sufferings of Christ. At times we are called to embrace the cross as part of our call to conversion, solidarity, and action in a world of sin and suffering. At other times, the Spirit's call is more unfathomable. Our participation in the mystery of the cross is a more direct share in what those who have experienced it have called an "unwanted wisdom."[20] These witnesses of faith testify from their experience that it is possible for wisdom and compassion to be born from experiences that in themselves cannot be attributed to God's will. In each case there is an experience of impasse, but the Spirit may be at work in quite distinct calls to transformation.

Dark Wisdom as Call to Conversion, Solidarity, and Action

In some situations the call to "take up your cross" is a summons to repentance and conversion. It confronts us with the fact that we participate in a world of social as well as personal sin and that Christian discipleship requires self-sacrifice, divestment of power or privilege, and a renewed commitment to solidarity with one's suffering sisters and brothers and with all living creatures. Christians are not only those who have suffered grief and injustice; we are also among those who cause and perpetuate it. Saul considered himself a devout religious believer as he participated in the persecution of another religious group. The wisdom of the cross can be a challenge to lament, which the community does not always want to hear, a word of truth that requires repentance and conversion.[21] Here lament involves not only the naming of pain but also the naming of sin and its consequences as the prophets

20. The phrase is the title of Paul Crowley's book *Unwanted Wisdom* (New York: Continuum, 2005). See also Crowley, *The Unmoored God: Believing in a Time of Dislocation* (Maryknoll, NY: Orbis, 2017), especially chapter 4.

21. Walter Brueggemann, *The Prophetic Imagination* (Philadelphia: Fortress Press, 1978). A number of Brueggemann's later books develop this point.

and Jesus himself did. This form of lament is not a questioning of whether God has been faithful to the covenant and its promises but rather an honest admission that we have not.[22]

The call to conversion for those who hold power in systems of injustice is a call to participate in the self-sacrifice of the cross as the way to genuine liberation. Relinquishment, repentance, and divestment are "necessary losses" for the dominants in any social system if the equal dignity of all members of the human family is to be the criterion for distribution of basic goods and resources. As Pope John Paul II described this call to interdependence and the "virtue" of solidarity,

> This . . . is not a feeling of vague compassion or shallow distress at the misfortunes of so many people, both near and far. On the contrary, it is a *firm and persevering determination* to commit oneself to the *common good*; that is to say to the good of all and of each individual, because we are *all* really responsible *for all*.[23]

Further, as Douglas Meeks and Jürgen Moltmann have noted, "There is no solidarity with the victims of racism, sexism and capitalism without the betrayal of their betrayers. Whoever wants genuine communion with the victims must become the enemy of their enemies. Thus if he or she comes from the ranks of the enemy, he or she will become a betrayer. To become free from the oppressive prison of one's own society means to become a 'stranger among one's own people.'"[24] South African theologian Albert Nolan, who was listed as an enemy of the government—and on a "hit list" for his opposition to the apartheid regime—makes a similar point. He emphasizes that we are called to love even our enemies, but at the same time, he remarks that "the only

22. For a fuller discussion of lament, including forms in which the psalmist or believer does question God's fidelity, see M. C. Hilkert, "Grace at the Edges: Preaching and Lament," in *Naming Grace: Preaching and the Sacramental Imagination* (New York: Continuum, 1997), 108–27.

23. John Paul II, *Sollicitudo Rei Socialis (On Social Concern)*, December 30, 1987 (Boston: Pauline Books and Media, 1987), par. 38, p. 71.

24. Jürgen Moltmann and M. Douglas Meeks, "The Liberation of Oppressors," *Christianity in Crisis* 38 (1978): 310–17.

effective way of loving our enemies is to engage in action that will destroy the system that makes them our enemies."[25]

Here the call to participate in the kenotic power of the cross is a summons to stand in solidarity with those who suffer and to work to change the systems that cause suffering and injustice. This is not to question the salvific efficacy of the life, death, and resurrection of Jesus but rather to recognize that we who are his body—the Church—are called to make his own solidarity with the poor and the marginalized a concrete reality in our time and place. Participation in that mission in a world of sin will inevitably include a participation in his passion as well.

Dark Wisdom Emerging within Impasse

In other situations, however, one's suffering results not from the call to conversion or from active engagement in solidarity with those who suffer or on behalf of life but as a result of circumstances beyond one's choice. Whether because of the actions of others, systems of injustice that block the exercise of freedom, or natural causes, we can find ourselves in situations of anguish, threat, or loss over which we have no control. Where is God's Spirit to be found here in these situations of true impasse? Ranging from the diagnosis of a terminal illness to betrayal by a trusted friend or family member to the violence of genocide and war, these situations are, in the words of Alice Trillin, "realizations of our worst nightmares."[26]

To speak of a wisdom to be discovered even here is dangerous. As many who have written from the context of peoples and nations marked by poverty and multiple forms of oppression have reminded us, suffering inflicted by an oppressor can be destructive and demonic; it can dehumanize and destroy.[27] Any kind of spirituality

25. Albert Nolan, "Taking Sides," in *Hope in an Age of Despair* (Maryknoll, NY: Orbis Books, 2009), 63–71, at 70–71.

26. As quoted by Calvin Trillin in "Alice, Off the Page," *The New Yorker* 82, no. 6 (March 27, 2006), 44–57, at 46.

27. See the distinctions made in the Final Document: Intercontinental Women's Conference, Oaxtepec, Mexico, December 1–6, 1986, in *With Passion and*

or mysticism of the cross faces the danger of romanticizing the terror of brutality or of denying the impact of debilitating illness, not only on the human body, but also on the human spirit and all of the relationships that one holds dear.[28]

Yet there is another side to human experience, sometimes expressed even by those who have suffered radical oppression or affliction. It needs to be honored as testimony to the resilience of the human spirit and, from a Christian perspective, testimony to what grace makes possible. Christians have described this experience as a form of the "wisdom of the cross," even though that experience remains "unwanted wisdom." This testimony, empowered by God's own Spirit of life, comes from the martyrs from the time of Ignatius and Perpetua and Felicity, but also from the letters and words of contemporary martyrs such as Oscar Romero, Maura Clarke, Ita Ford, Jean Donovan, Dorothy Kazel, Ignatio Ellacuría and his companions, and countless Salvadorans who lost their lives in the struggle for human dignity and justice in El Salvador. In the words of Maryknoll Sister Ita Ford,

> The challenge that we live daily is to enter into the paschal mystery with faith. Am I willing to suffer with the people here, the suffering of the powerless? Can I say to my neighbors, "I have no solution to this situation; I don't know the answers, but I will walk with you, search with you, be with you"?[29]

Testimony to this dark and unwanted wisdom of the cross comes also from parents like Bud Welch whose daughter Julie Marie died in the Oklahoma City bombings in April 1995. At first

---

Compassion: Third World Women Doing Theology, ed. Virginia Fabella and Mercy Amba Oduyoye (Maryknoll, NY: Orbis Books, 1988), 184–90, especially 188.

28. On experiences of torture and trauma, see Elaine Scarry, *The Body in Pain: The Making and Unmaking of the World* (Oxford: Oxford University Press, 1985); on the experience of illness, see Eric J. Cassel, "The Nature of Suffering and the Goals of Medicine," *New England Journal of Medicine* 306 (March/April 1982): 639–45.

29. Ita Ford, "Reflections on the Mission Phase," May 1977, as quoted in Judith M. Noone, *The Same Fate as the Poor* (Maryknoll, NY: Orbis Books, 1984, 1995), 82.

he sought vengeance against the man who drove four thousand pounds of explosives into a government building, killing not only Welch's daughter but many of the children in the daycare center housed there. Initially Welch said, "I wanted [Tim McVeigh] to fry. . . . I would have killed him myself."[30] He turned to alcohol and cigarettes to numb the pain. He was angry with God. But after several months, Welch reported recalling his daughter Julie's voice when she was a child telling him that she thought that executions only taught children to hate. That insight led Welch to seek a meeting with another father in pain—Bill McVeigh. According to Welch, that meeting left him feeling somehow closer to God and brought him to the realization that more violence would not bring Julie back. It also led to his own public opposition to the death penalty.

Even more remarkable is the witness that comes from the voices and lives of those who have been the direct victims of cruel systems of injustice. In the face of a resurgence of racism, White supremacy, dehumanizing immigration policies, and xenophobia in the United States and around the world, M. Shawn Copeland has called attention to the dark witness of "slavery's children" as recorded in their narratives, spirituals, and prayers.[31] In their bodies, minds, hearts, and souls, they endured vicious cruelty and dehumanizing abuse. Yet their identification with the crucified Jesus as Lord and Savior was anything but legitimation of that cruelty or internalization of Christian masochism. Rather, the faith they proclaimed was both a radical hope in the God who raised Jesus from the dead and a fierce resistance and defiance of the injustice to which they were subjected. Citing James Cone, Copeland remarks that Jesus is for them "God's Black Slave who had come to put an end to human bondage."[32] The dark wisdom

30. See The Forgiveness Project: http://www.theforgivenessproject.com/stories/bud-welch.

31. See Copeland, *Knowing Christ Crucified*, especially chapter 1.

32. James Hal Cone, *The Spirituals and the Blues* (Maryknoll, NY: Orbis Books, 1991), 49, and John Lovell Jr., *Black Song: The Forge and the Flame; How the African American Spiritual Was Hammered Out* (New York: Macmillan, 1972), 189, as cited by Copeland in *Knowing Christ Crucified*, 35.

that emerged from the hearts and souls of the enslaved people of the United States in spite of the systematic injustice they endured—and of their descendants in our own day—gives witness to the power of the Spirit at work in even the most desperate of circumstances.

The Spirit's Reach and Those Whose Faith Is Known to God Alone

These profiles of unwanted wisdom are not limited to Christian believers who name God's Spirit as the source of their hope and courage. That wisdom is also evident in voices from other faith traditions and from some who make no specific faith claims, as *Gaudium et Spes,* the Pastoral Constitution on the Church in the Modern World, acknowledged.[33] Testimony to that wisdom echoed in the words of black lesbian poet Audre Lorde who spoke frankly to her professional colleagues at a convention after her diagnosis with the breast cancer from which she later died. Confronting the possibility of death freed her to speak the following words:

> In becoming forcibly and essentially aware of my mortality, and of what I wished and wanted for my life, however short it might be, priorities and omissions became strongly etched in a merciless light, and what I most regretted were my silences. Of what had I *ever* been afraid? To question or to speak as I believed could have meant pain, or death. But we all hurt in so many different ways, all the time, and pain will either change or end. Death, on the other hand, is the final silence. . . . And I began to recognize a source of power within myself that comes from the knowledge that while it is most desirable not to be afraid, learning to put fear into a perspective gave me great strength.[34]

33. *Gaudium et Spes* speaks of the grace at work in unseen ways in the hearts of all people of good will. "For since Christ died for all, and since the ultimate human vocation is in fact one, and divine, we ought to believe that the Holy spirit in a manner known only to God offers to every person the possibility of being associated with this paschal mystery" (GS 22).

34. Audre Lorde, "The Transformation of Silence into Language and Action," in *Sister Outsider* (Freedom, CA: The Crossing Press, 1984), 40–44, at 41.

Recall also the testimony of the twenty-nine-year-old Jewish woman Etty Hillesum who penned the following reflections to a friend as the reality of the Holocaust and the impending deaths that both were facing became more real to her:

> Give your sorrow all the space and shelter in yourself that is its due, for if everyone bears his grief honestly and courageously, the sorrow that now fills the world will abate. But if you do not clear a decent shelter for your sorrow, and instead reserve most of the space inside you for hatred and thoughts of revenge—from which new sorrows will be born for others—then sorrow will never cease in this world and will multiply. And if you have given sorrow the space its gentle origins demand, then you may truly say: life is beautiful and so rich. So beautiful and rich that it makes you want to believe in God.[35]

These testimonies offer no systematic explanation for the kind of wisdom that can be born from a share in the experience of suffering because no explanatory language is adequate to express this mystery. Evil has no explanation because it is utterly without meaning. But these voices of wisdom, both those who witness explicitly to the mystery of the cross and those whose faith is known to God alone, cannot be explained for another reason as well. The testimony of their lives and words witnesses to a power at work in the human spirit that surpasses all human understanding. Many speak of the triumph of the human spirit and surely this is true. But from the perspective of Christian faith, each of these witnesses also gives evidence of the power of God's own Spirit dwelling within the human spirit and making possible what, from a human perspective, seems to be impossible.

FitzGerald identifies this kind of experience as a share in the dark wisdom of God. For the Christian mystics, she remarks, that participation involves genuine transformation through personal

35. Etty Hillesum, *An Interrupted Life: The Diaries of Etty Hillesum, 1941–43* (New York: Washington Square Press, 1981), 100–101.

experience of Jesus as "dark Crucified Sophia."[36] Those who preach the Gospel may not be called to a monastic life of unceasing prayer on behalf of a suffering world, but, as prophets of hope, they are called to contemplative prayer and reflection. The shared vocation of all Christians is to bear witness with our words and with our lives to the mystery of God as the dark mystery of love that even death and evil cannot quench.

36. FitzGerald remarks that this dark wisdom of God is not some secret knowledge that we learn or can teach but a personal relationship that deepens and transforms us from within. See Constance FitzGerald, "Transformation in Wisdom: The Subversive Character and Educative Power of Sophia in Contemplation," in *Carmel and Contemplation: Transforming Human Consciousness*, Carmelite Studies 8, ed. Kevin Culligan and Regis Jordan (Washington, DC: Institute of Carmelite Studies, 2000), 281–358. See also Elizabeth A. Johnson, *She Who Is: The Mystery of God in Feminist Theological Discourse* (New York: Crossroad, 1992), 263–64.

16

Dark Night and the Transformative Influence of Wisdom in John of the Cross[1]

Constance Fitzgerald, OCD

The intense interest over the past fifteen years in the Dark Night is certainly part of a much larger retrieval in contemporary theology of the mystical tradition and the classic spiritual texts of the past. More importantly, the current awareness of darkness and the affinity of so many for the dark night experience seem to be a sign of the rebirth and more public valuing of the experience of God in contemplative prayer. There is little doubt, moreover, that over the past twenty years the creative work of the Jesuits in reinterpreting and making available Ignatian prayer, particularly through the medium of the Exercises and directed retreats, has made a significant contribution to this movement toward contemplative prayer in people's lives. This may be why we witness a specific intersection of Ignatian and Carmelite spirituality at the present time, an

1. This was *wrongly* titled, without my knowledge or approval, in *The Way* as "Desolation as Dark Night: The Transformative Influence of Wisdom in John of the Cross." It is not about desolation in the Ignatian sense and is therefore misleading.

intersection related to darkness. This may be why some people, practiced in Ignatian prayer and yet faced with the bewildering experience of darkness, dryness and loss of meaning in their own lives or in the lives of those they guide, find that the dark night teaching of John of the Cross brings to Ignatian prayer an understanding of a critical, contemplative phase of spiritual growth easily misunderstood and not specifically developed by Ignatius.

This intersection or complementarity of Ignatian and Carmelite spirituality reaches back to sixteenth-century Spain when young Jesuits from Ignatius' newly founded Society of Jesus provided spiritual direction for Teresa of Avila as she attempted not only to understand her own disturbing mystical graces but also to reform the ancient Carmelite Order. Thomas H. Green, a loyal son of Ignatius, stands, therefore, within a long history of mutuality and respect when in his second book on prayer, he turns to John of the Cross and Teresa to provide guidance on "prayer beyond the beginnings." For Green, John of the Cross' discussion on the Dark Night "is one of the most important passages in the whole literature of prayer."[2]

In this article, I hope to extend contemporary interpretation of the Dark Night in John of the Cross in two ways: first, by examining the transformative and subversive role of Wisdom (Sophia) in the Dark Night, which is a specifically Christological emphasis suggested by contemporary feminist theologians;[3] and second, by accenting the meaning of the deeper experience of darkness, called by John of the Cross the Dark Night of Spirit.

2. Thomas H. Green, *When the Well Runs Dry* (Notre Dame: Ave Maria Press, 1979), 10 and 110. See pp 110–33.

3. I am using the Greek *Sophia,* not only because feminists prefer it, because the biblical depiction of Wisdom is invariably female suggesting a person rather than a concept or an attribute. Biblical Wisdom is treated not as an it but as a summoning "I," as a "sister, mother, female beloved, . . . and a myriad of other female roles." See Elizabeth Johnson, *She Who Is* (New York: Crossroad, 1992), 87, whose analysis of Sophia has influenced my study, and Roland E. Murphy, *The Tree of Life: An Exploration of Biblical Wisdom Literature* (New York: Doubleday, 1990), 133–49, for a treatment of "Lady Wisdom."

Wisdom in John of the Cross

John moves in the milieu of Wisdom from the beginning of the *Ascent of Mount Carmel* to the end of the *Living Flame of Love*.[4] An analysis of his major writings reveals he is radically influenced by the Wisdom texts of pre-Christian Judaism. Particularly important for John in defining who Sophia is and what she does are the books of Wisdom (chaps. 7–9) and Proverbs (chap. 8). Out of his own distinctive configuration of this Jewish wisdom literature emerge some of the most basic principles of his teaching. It fashions John's understanding of who Jesus is, who God is and how this God functions in the dynamic of human transformation. It suggests the place of Sophia in human suffering and hints at how the beloved of Sophia functions in the world.

It is clear that for John of the Cross, as for St. Paul and the writers of the gospels of John and Matthew, Jesus Christ is divine Wisdom (Sophia), the Word, the Son of God. In the unitive experience of Jesus-Sophia the person is transformed, and in this Jesus the entire creation is gathered into the tender, unifying embrace of Sophia-God who pervades and connects the entire cosmos and every form of life in it.

This means John of the Cross appropriates not only pre-Christian Judaism's understanding of a feminine gestalt of God, Sophia, but he seems to be completely at home with the identification made by New Testament writers of Jesus as Divine Sophia: *Jesus is Sophia incarnate*. To underpin his own cohesive Christology John uses most of the significant New Testament Wisdom texts and he does this in a context that frequently reveals his knowledge of their connection with the Wisdom texts of pre-Christian Judaism. The tradition of personified Wisdom which played a foundational role in the development of Christology in the early Church seems to have been singularly important to him since some of his most profound Christological assertions are couched in its terms. The recognition of the central, critical function of Wisdom is therefore

4. The Institute of Carmelite Studies will publish in late 1995 *Education for Contemplation* in which a more extensive study of Wisdom in John of the Cross will appear. This article is part of that study.

basic to an understanding of John's Christology. Furthermore, to explore the subversive and transformative function of Sophia in the Dark Night is to probe the role of Jesus Christ in the process of transformation.

The Role of Jesus Christ

In John's anthropology the human person is seen as an infinite capacity for God. As long as the great "caverns" of the mind, heart, memory and imagination are filled with human knowledge, loves, dreams and memories that seem or promise to satisfy completely, the person is unable even to feel or imagine the depths of the capacity that is there. Only when we become aware of our emptiness, in the face of the experience of the fragility and breakdown of what or whom we have staked our lives on, the limitation and failure of our life project and life love, the shattering of our dreams and meanings, can the depths of thirst and hunger that exist in the human person, the infinite capacity, really be felt (LF 3.19-22).[5]

Few people understand that John is actually addressing this infinite capacity when he urges them at the end of the first book of the *Ascent* to have an on-going desire to pattern their lives on Christ's.

> Have habitual desire to imitate Christ in all your deeds by bringing your life into conformity with his. You must then study his life in order to know how to imitate him and behave in all things as he would behave. (IA 13.3)[6]

This means only one thing: desire to know Jesus Christ. Human desire is educated by an immersion in the Jesus of the gospels. However, if you channel your desire toward knowing Jesus Christ,

5. Most references to John of the Cross are inserted in text. A=Ascent of Mount Carmel, DN=Dark Night, SC=Spiritual Canticle, LF=Living Flame of Love. Most quotations are from Kieran Kavanaugh and Otilio Rodriguez, *The Collected Works of John of the Cross* (Washington, DC: ICS Publications, 1991).

6. This is a fundamental text indicating the direction of affective transformation and interpreting all that precedes it concerning desire in Book I of the *Ascent*.

the one you will learn to know is loving Sophia who will slowly and secretly redirect and claim your desire and subvert your life. Desire is educated, therefore, by the companionship, the friendship, of Jesus-Sophia. This dynamic underlies John's whole philosophy of prayer and indicates how a conscious decision of the heart for Christ takes place, how a shift in the focus of desire and meaning begins in our lives.

But often the human person is not satisfied with the day to day fidelity to this companionship, nor with its slow, unpretentious, mysterious development. Too many people educated in our culture live with a consuming desire for novelty, excitement, change, new pleasures and extraordinary experiences. But John, appropriating both St. Paul and the Book of Wisdom in one of his most famous Christological passages, affirms that we do not need unusual new revelations, visions or secret truths (IIA 22.5-7). We have everything we desire in the gospel and the unitive companionship of the human Jesus in whom dwells for us the nearness and fullness, the compassionate kindness, of Sophia-God embracing and energizing from within the totality of the human situation.

In accenting the complete sufficiency and unlimited potential of Christ as divine Sophia, John of the Cross validates new possibilities for appropriating the inexhaustible meaning of Jesus. What will we unlock if *in prayer* we experience the life of Jesus in the light of Sophia thereby transforming for our time the symbol of Christ and reclaiming Christ and Christological doctrine in a new way?[7]

> Fasten your eyes on him alone, because in him I have spoken and revealed all, and in him you will discover even more that you ask for and desire. . . . For he is my entire locution and response, vision and revelation, which I have already spoken . . . to you. (IIA 22)

7. Elizabeth Johnson's work is a superb example of this. See also Sandra Schneiders, *The Revelatory Text: Interpreting the New Testament as Sacred Scripture* (San Francisco: Harper and Row, 1991), 180–97 for an example, not of Sophia's retrieval but of feminist interpretation of the meaning of Jesus in John 4.

Image of Jesus Christ and Growth in Wisdom

It is in this walking with the human Jesus that Sophia becomes a life-giving, indwelling image and one's primary focus of affective and cognitive meaning. This image is unique for each person forming a basis for relationship, direction, love, purification and transformation. In fact, a gradual transference of desire occurs as the presence of loving Sophia takes shape within, influencing motivation and affecting imagination.

A principle fundamental to John's wisdom Christology is operative here: love will never reach the fullness of its possibilities, human desire will never stop yearning and aching, until the lovers are so alike that one is transfigured in the love and goodness of the other. This means that a transformative image of Jesus-Sophia is, in a way totally harmonious with human development, gradually etched within the human personality. As I know Jesus-Sophia, this knowledge subverts my life, shows me to myself as in a mirror and redirects and purifies my desire.

If I look long enough at one who truly loves me, I become what I see in the other's eyes. I am transfigured. The image of the loved one, the eyes of the beloved are burnt into my heart and seen with my inner eye. This image is not impersonal! We see this with remarkable clarity in the Spiritual Canticle poem:

> Reveal your presence,
> And may the vision of your beauty be my death;
> For the sickness of love
> Is not cured
> Except by your very presence and image.
>
> O spring like crystal!
> If only, on your silvered over face,
> You would suddenly form
> The eyes I have desired,
> Which I bear sketched deep within my heart. (SC 11-12)

> The soul experiences within herself a certain sketch of love . . . and she desires the completion of the sketch of this image, the image of her Bridegroom, the Word, the Son of God, who as St. Paul says, "is the splendor of [God's] glory and the image of

> [God's] substance," (Heb.1.3) for this is the image into which the soul desires to be transformed through love. (SC 11, 11-12)

Because this is a fundamental experience for John, and not just a concept, it is important to understand the developmental and transformative function of this Wisdom image. Through it the whole creative aspect of Old Testament Sophia is brought to human transformation. If it is not valued relative to spiritual growth, the tender, careful, nurturing creativity of Sophia will be thwarted and we will "damage or lose the sublime image that God [is] painting within [us]."[8]

At first the developing image of Jesus-Sophia is a strength and consolation motivating one toward a generous, self-giving life influenced by the Jesus of the gospels and sensitizing one to this Sophia presence in the world that is energizing and connecting all of reality.[9] As the intimacy with Christ matures, however, this image, within and without, begins to make deeper claims and there is a shift in the way Sophia operates within the depths of human personality.

Dark Night and the Continuing Role of Sophia

In time the presence of Sophia becomes afflictive. The image becomes too threatening. Jesus-Sophia subverts my own self-image and this marks the first level of subversion. I cannot accept the claims of Sophia upon me nor can I accept Wisdom as a life vision

8. See LF 3.41-45 where John castigates those spiritual directors who do not understand the secret, loving wisdom of contemplative prayer, that is "the sublime anointings and shadings of the Holy Spirit," and therefore damage or destroy by poor direction the image God is painting within the human person. "Who will succeed," he says, "in repairing that delicate painting of the Holy Spirit once it is marred by a coarse hand."

9. Here we intersect with John M. Staudemaier's interpretation of the dynamic of the Second Week of the Exercises which "inculcates a form of personal intimacy with Jesus that opens out to intimacy with the larger world, an intimacy of affective engagement that leads to action in the world." See "To Fall in Love with the World," *Studies in the Spirituality of Jesuits* 26 (May 1994): 1–28.

in an unconditional commitment; Sophia is too revolutionary and seditious. Sophia turns life upside-down, challenges my most deeply held beliefs and values, undermines what I have learned, claims whom and what I possess, and highlights the limitations and oppressive character of what I depend on most for satisfaction and assurance.

This brings us to the relationship between the Dark Night and the presence of loving Wisdom.[10] John says very explicitly that Dark Night, infused contemplation, *is* the loving Wisdom of God.[11] It follows that if Jesus Christ *is* Divine Wisdom, Sophia, then *dark contemplation is the presence of Jesus Christ as Wisdom* and Dark Night is the time when the image of Jesus-Sophia takes on all the marks of crucifixion: suffering, isolation, failure, marginality, rejection, abandonment, hopelessness, meaninglessness, death. The image of the Crucified One, reflective of a seemingly silent, incomprehensible God, functions in the Dark Night as incomprehensible, secret, hidden and yet loving Wisdom-Sophia.[12] And this is the second level of subversion: not only has my self-image been subverted but now too the images of Christ and God. Therefore, when John says that the Dark Night is an inflow of God, this inflow is of a God imparting a secret Wisdom who is Jesus Crucified, a unitive, loving knowledge indicative of more intimate relationship (IDN 10.6). Dark Night is not primarily some thing, an impersonal darkness like a difficult situation or distressful psychological condition, but *someone*, a presence leaving an indelible imprint on the human spirit and consequently on one's entire life.

This image is the touch of the hand of God marking, wounding, challenging, shaping, purifying and transforming human

10. When I wrote "Impasse and Dark Night" in *Living with Apocalypse*, ed. Tilden Edwards (San Francisco: Harper and Row, 1984), I did not address the significance of Jesus-Sophia in the Dark Night. This Christological interpretation of Dark Night is a necessary complement to the impasse experience.

11. See IIDN 5.1-2; IIDN 17; IIA 8.6 to study the equivalencies that John sets up.

12. Christ Crucified is seen as the unitive image or pattern of the Dark Night in IIA 7.

personality (LF 2.16). In the mirror of this broken, ambiguous image of suffering Wisdom, we see the miseries and hypocrisies of our lives. This crucified image is the living knowledge of human darkness, limitation, oppression and sinfulness which overpowers our shallow self-confidence, questions what we think we know about God, raises doubts about what we have accomplished and undercuts our entire affective life. In fact, this image subverts our whole individualistic perception of reality, that is, the way we experience not only other people, but also other species, the earth and even the cosmos. It is the language of God (Word) inviting and teaching the human mind and heart, calling us in our confusion and emptiness to pass over into the perspective of loving Sophia by an identification with Jesus Crucified.

It is at this point in development that the images of the poor, the oppressed, the exploited, the suffering take on a clarity and significance that is overpowering. They are clearly a suffering extension of the inner image of Jesus-Sophia, and they make a claim. They are the darkness of humanity; they are *our* darkness. Just as the personal unconscious is revealed in the mirror of suffering Sophia, so is the collective darkness, the shadow of humanity. 'The poor' are recognized and embraced to the degree that the identification with suffering Sophia has taken place in our inner darkness. Thus Sophia, having subverted our images of ourselves and of God, now subverts our understanding of the world. This is the third level of subversion. In the secret, painful, unitive relationship with dark Sophia, a new participatory love-fired knowledge begins to take over human desire and consciousness and to express itself not only in the gradual repudiation of all kinds of personal and socio-cultural violence and oppression but also in an entry, albeit dark and unfinished, into the experience of mutuality, communion, connectedness and kinship with the earth that marks transformed or mystical consciousness.

Richard Tarnas suggests that a "participatory epistemology" that moves beyond the hierarchical dualism characteristic of the Cartesian-Kantian paradigm has been emerging in philosophy for over a century. Common to all its thinkers is an essential conviction that the relation of the human mind to the universe is ultimately not dualistic but participatory.[13] This participatory way of knowing reveals itself in the new paradigm proposed by Thomas Berry, Brian Swimme and many others. They challenge humanity to accept the limitation and death that will usher in the next evolutionary era, when the universe will be experienced not as a collection of objects for human use and mastery but rather as an intimate, interconnected and diverse communion of subjects.[14]

Integral to and one with this participatory way of knowing and understanding life on earth is the tremendous emergence of the feminine in our culture rising out of the unitive energies at work in the universe and heralding the end of the fundamental masculine dominance of the western mind. It appears that we are truly at a highly critical stage of transformation in which the masculine (in all of us) must voluntarily transcend itself in its own dark night of death which will fit it to enter into a fundamentally new relationship of mutuality with the feminine in all its forms.

On the one hand, we observe in the latter years of the twentieth century a massive breakdown of numerous structures, suggestive of the necessary deconstruction or death prior to new birth. On the other hand, we see this participatory vision breaking through on so many levels, in so many disciplines, reflective of a deeper, powerful archetypal process impelled by forces beyond the merely human. This is where the experience of Crucified Sophia intersects and resonates with the current archetypal state of the collective psyche. The unitive relationship with suffering Sophia can be so deep and, consequently, the solidarity with "the other" so profound that not only does the person in this Dark Night carry and bring to consciousness the collective longings of humanity and energies of the cosmos, but brings to them in her very being this participatory, love-fired knowledge which Jesus-Sophia both gives and is. This contribution of mysticism to a broader trans-

13. I draw heavily on the creative thought of Richard Tarnas regarding this "participatory epistemology." See *The Passion of the Western Mind* (New York: Harmony Books, 1991), 433–45.

14. See Brian Swimme and Thomas Berry, *The Universe Story* (San Francisco: Harper, 1992), 243. "Existence itself is derived from and sustained by this intimacy of each being with every other being."

formation must not be overlooked by ecologists, creationists, geologians, scientists or philosophers.

Neither may we forget that this is the time to seek not the consolation and escape of other images or practices or relationships but "the living image of Christ Crucified within" (IIIA 35.5) and to stand open to this transforming imprint of suffering Sophia, which is actually experienced as "no image" but which nonetheless acknowledges, reflects and even accepts our personal and societal darkness. This is the blackest time of night when the last delicate shading of the image of Christ, crucified and abandoned, is being sketched within the human heart in total darkness and silence.

Purification of Spirit

When the invisible, mute God of an abandoned Jesus seems to draw us into lonely introspection where prayer and relationships, as we have known them, are painful or gone; when loss, failure and hopelessness loom large; when all supports drop from one's consciousness and life's deepest meanings and symbol systems are empty and stale; when our inherited language and images no longer reveal the divine, then a dark Wisdom is operative, nurturing the human person with love and confirming values little prized in our society. John throws a stark light on the experience by showing *the whole person* deprived totally in her or his imaginative powers, intellectual intuitions and human sensitivities:

> God divests the faculties, affections and senses, both spiritual and sensory, interior and exterior. God leaves the intellect in darkness, the will in aridity, the memory in emptiness and the affections in supreme affliction, bitterness and anguish by depriving the soul of the feeling and satisfaction it previously enjoyed from spiritual blessings. . . . *For this privation is one of the conditions required that the spiritual form, [the image] which is the union of love, may be introduced into the spirit and united with it.* The Lord works all this in the soul by means of a pure and dark contemplation. (IIDN 3.3)

If in earlier times the dark night wove its way in and out of life bringing dryness, boredom and absence of satisfaction, this darker

Night eclipses the very support systems that have structured our lives, given them meaning and value, and provided a source of affirmation and final assurance.[15]

But what precisely can John mean when he says *the intellect* is emptied and left in darkness? Perhaps he warns us that the time will come when our philosophy of life, our theology and our carefully constructed meanings fall apart before our eyes. All we have accumulated intellectually that has given us "God," "faith" and security loses its significance. Nothing makes any sense. The mind, while *full* on one level of a lifetime of knowledge, is in total darkness on another, the level of meaning. We feel as if we have been duped, and succumb to silence, afraid to shock others by the depth of our cynicism and unbelief.[16]

Our minds stumble over the concept of emptiness in *the memory* because we know human memory is full of experience. But now the imagination can no longer connect life's memories to create meaning and hope. We can speak of emptiness in the memory, not because one remembers nothing, but because all the memory holds, which once provided motivation and security, which engendered trust and promise for the future, seems now an illusion and a mockery. Memories do not mean what one thought they did. The memory is indeed empty, possessing nothing but the scattered remains of cherished experiences and the crushing remembrance of personal failure and defeat (IIDN 5.5-6).

This kind of clarity about one's miseries generates the overwhelming feeling of being rejected and abandoned not only by one's friends but particularly by God. In fact, abandonment and the betrayal of trust are the hallmark of this dark experience. However it happens, what/whom one cherishes most in life is cut off, taken away. The worst thing about this "purification of *the will*" is that the loved one, the very focus of one's love and desire, becomes the cause of one's agony.[17] There is nothing so destructive of affirmation and worth as rejection by one who has loved

15. This interpretation was first begun by me in "A Discipleship of Equals: Voices from a Tradition," in *A Discipleship of Equals: Toward a Christian Feminist Spirituality*, ed. Francis A. Eigo (Villanova: Villanova University Press, 1988).

16. See IIDN 9.3; 5.3-5; IIA 4 & 8.

17. See IIDN 7; IIDN 9.3 & 7; IIIA 16 & 35.5; LF 1.23.

you and on whom you have counted with complete assurance. It leaves one unable to grasp anything affectively. The destruction of mutuality, with its deep frustration of desire, leaves one without any strength of purpose, bereft of motivation and prone to bitterness. A transcendence in which one is not at home and against which one rebels is forced upon the person.

Alternative Vision: Faith, Hope and Love

We face a challenge in this night to throw into gear the kind of radical faith, hope and love that can endure the death dealing "touch of God's hand," the imprint, which is emptying out our isolated self-sufficiency, on the one hand, and our unfree dependence and fear of transformation and evolution on the other. Activated by Sophia's dark presence, the *theological* virtues are our only option, presenting a very uncomfortable alternative vision. Because initially we do not feel faith, hope and love, maintaining this basic contemplative posture in our prayer and life is extremely difficult. It must overcome an anger, fear and rebellion that want to refuse these theological gifts rather than be left with "nothing." Yet the only way the deprivation of the Dark Night will open into a radical change of consciousness and affectivity is by the acceptance of this contemplative posture or vision whereby one actually passes over to the love perspective of Divine Wisdom (IIA 6.6, IIDN 21.11-12).

Faith, however, causes darkness in our very power to understand. Now it is at cross purposes with our ability to make logical sense out of life, death or eternity. When Jesus Christ recedes from consciousness, it is faith that moves us into the Mystery which is unimaginable, incomprehensible and uncontrollable. While we do not set out to empty the mind, imagination or memory, prayer development and life exacts this of us and then faith becomes an opening into a realm of significance far beyond human understanding.[18]

18. John writes in IIDN 21.11: "Faith darkens and empties the intellect of all its natural understanding and thereby prepares it for union with divine wisdom, who is the Word the Son of God." See also IIA 3 for John's teaching on faith and IIA 4.1-3; IIA 8 & 9; IIDN 16.8.2.

The hopelessness and emptiness of the Dark Night is precisely the condition that makes hope, in the strictly theological sense, possible. Hope comes into play when we are really radically at the end unable to find any further resources to connect the memories, feelings, images and experiences of life in a meaningful pattern or a promising future. Then hope, forfeiting the struggle to press meaning out of loss, becomes a free, trustful commitment to the impossible which cannot be built out of what one possesses.[19]

Estrangement and abandonment administer the final test of love. Love prevents us from forcing the loved one into the constraints of our needs and so takes the beloved as he or she is. In the face of seeming rejection and affective loss, theological love will not, in the end, surrender to hate or violence nor forfeit belief in its own worth and lovability. Overcoming the will to die, this love lives honestly with the pain of its own woundedness and longing. It continues to serve others, often with great effectiveness, in spite of profound affective deprivation and loss.[20]

The contemplative posture of faith, hope and love slowly repatterns or transforms desire and consciousness and prepares the human person for the participatory love-driven knowledge Divine Wisdom is and gives. This subversive dynamic of beloved Sophia is set in motion when human suffering, loss and emptiness have reached such a pitch of consciousness, are such a reflection of Jesus silenced, rejected, abused, dismissed or abandoned, that the capacity of the human person is hollowed out for deeper knowing, deeper mutuality, a Wisdom presence and vision in the world. Then the image of Jesus-Sophia Dying, the image of all that is dying within and without, reaches completion.

19. John explains in IIDN 21.11: "Hope empties and withdraws the memory from all creature possessions, for as St. Paul says, hope is for what is not possessed. It withdraws the memory from what can be possessed and fixes it on that for which it hopes. Hence, only hope in God prepares the memory perfectly for union with Him." Karl Rahner has helped me interpret John's thought on hope and on the theological virtues. See "On the Theology of Hope," *Theological Investigations X* and "Theology of Death," *Theological Investigations XIII*.

20. John explains in IIDN 21.11-12: "Charity empties and annihilates the affections and appetites of the will of whatever is not God and centers them on God alone. Thus charity prepares the will and unites it with God through love."

> [This is] the real imitation [imprinting] of the perfect life of the Son of God . . . [through which God] will bring her to the high perfection of union with the Son of God, her spouse, and transformation in Him through love. [Therefore,] When this . . . night (God's communication to the spirit, which usually occurs in extreme darkness of soul) has passed, a union with the Spouse, *Who is the Sophia of God,* then follows . . . [and] love is perfect when the transformation of the soul in God is achieved. (SC 1.10; IA 2.4)[21]

The limits of this article on Dark Night preclude examining what it means in real life to be transfigured in Divine Sophia and to become a prophet of Sophia in the world.

Societal Implications

First, if there is at the present time a participatory world-view crying out for paradigmatic significance, Sophia may well be the God image that resonates with the current archetypal state of the collective psyche.[22] Sophia is the one clear, significant God gestalt emerging out of a long dark night of broken symbols. Thus we may see Jesus more and more taking on the marks of Sophia. This is where the tradition of Wisdom, so long muted and marginalized but embodied with such prophetic power in the mysticism of John of the Cross, will reassure us and enable theology to speak anew about Jesus Christ.

Second, there is a correlation between the intense interest in the Dark Night, the awareness of Sophia and the emergence of feminism, just as there was a correlation in the past between

21. Elizabeth Johnson reminds us of a long-standing tradition of interpretation concerning martyrs, a tradition which Vatican II continues: "Martyrdom 'transforms' a disciple into an intense image of Christ, *imago Christi,* for the martyr 'perfects that image even to the shedding of blood.'" See *She Who Is,* 74 and *Lumen Gentium* 42.

22. What Tarnas writes about paradigms is applicable to our God images: "The birth of every new paradigm begins the process of gestation, growth, crisis and revolution all over again. Each paradigm is a stage in an unfolding evolutionary sequence and when the paradigm has fulfilled its purpose, when it has been developed and exploited to its fullest extent, then it loses its luminosity . . . it becomes oppressive, limiting, opaque, something to be overcome" (*op. cit.,* 439).

the muting of contemplation, the suppression of Sophia and the marginalization of women.

Third, feminists have long been conscious of the darkness of this dying time as they struggled to find meaning in the experience of impasse in their God images, in their churches and in their socio-political lives. But Richard Tarnas emphasizes that the crisis of modern man [*sic*] is essentially not a feminine but a masculine crisis. It is the dominance of the masculine in us that is dying and being called to transcend itself in the Dark Night experience of a Sophia-God. Perhaps now when this pervasive masculinity has become so apparent and when the feminine is welling up with such powerful energy, Sophia is the God image capable of moving with humanity into the next evolutionary era.

Fourth, initially it seemed to me that transformation in Jesus-Sophia or Dark Night was subversive because it radically changed desire, consciousness and ultimately vision and behavior, personal and societal. But perhaps it is subversive, above all, because it could change radically our theological discourse since it is, in fact, a hermeneutic of the very nature of God. These are the questions that contemplative people may face today and those who pray with depth and seriousness under the guidance of St. Ignatius may well encounter these contemporary problems of the Dark Night as they continue to grow in prayer.

17

From Impasse to Prophetic Hope

Crisis of Memory

Constance FitzGerald, OCD

Introduction[1]

In an earlier work I looked at John of the Cross' teaching on the dark night, including the traditional signs marking the passage from meditation to contemplation, through the lens of impasse and applied it to personal spiritual growth as well as to one's relational life, the development of society and culture, and the feminist experience of God.[2] That insight provided a hermeneutical

1. I am grateful to Sue Houchins, Brian McDermott and Mary Catherine Hilkert for their generosity in reading my essay and offering valuable criticism and suggestions, to Leah Hargis for her help with endnotes, and to Shawn Copeland for her generous response. I am especially grateful to Frances Horner who worked with me on an earlier text of this material.

2. Constance FitzGerald, "Impasse and Dark Night," in *Living with Apocalypse*, ed. Tilden H. Edwards (San Francisco: Harper and Row, 1984), 93–116. Article can also be found in *Women's Spirituality: Resources for Christian Development*, ed. Joann Wolski Conn (Mahwah, NJ: Paulist Press, 1986), 287–311. Belden Lane first introduced me to "impasse situations" in his essay "Spirituality and Political Commitment: Notes on a Liberation Theology of Nonviolence" which appeared in *America*, March 14, 1981.

key for many and began changing the perception of the multiple impasses—relational, ecclesial, societal, political, ethical, scientific, economic, environmental and cultural—which engage people today.[3] That it continues to elucidate contemporary experience, prompt new questions, raise radical challenges, and open up fresh avenues of investigation underlines how much the great apophatic mystical traditions of Christianity are a promising source of wisdom and guidance for theology and spirituality.

Now I want to investigate a deeper experience of dark night, what the Carmelite mystical Doctor, John of the Cross, calls the purification of memory,[4] because currently impasse seems centered in great part in memory and imagination, in the conflict between the past and the future. In the first and longest section, I want to reflect on the central importance of memory as well as the limiting and destructive power that memories hold. In that context, I hope to interpret what John of the Cross means by "purification of memory" and then draw briefly on the work of Miroslav Volf and Beverly Lanzetta to illustrate it. Second, I want to point to the goal of this process of purification of memory for John: prophetic hope which expresses itself in what I call "the prayer-of-no-experience" which I will attempt to describe. Finally, I want to suggest that in

3. See, for example, Sandra Schneiders, *Finding the Treasure: Locating Catholic Religious Life in a New Ecclesial and Cultural Context* (Mahwah, NJ: Paulist Press, 2000), 153–83; Nancy Sylvester, IHM, and Mary Jo Click, *Crucible for Change: Engaging Impasse through Communal Contemplation and Dialogue* (San Antonio: Sor Juana Press, 2004); Beverly Lanzetta, *Radical Wisdom: A Feminist Mystical Theology* (Minneapolis, MN: Fortress Press, 2005); Kristine M. Rankka, *Women and the Value of Suffering* (Collegeville, MN: Liturgical Press, 1998), 218–22; Bruce H. Lescher, "Spiritual Direction: Stalking the Boundaries," in *Handbook of Spirituality for Ministers*, vol. 2, ed. Robert J. Wicks (New York and Mahwah, NJ: Paulist Press, 2000), 324; Mary Catherine Hilkert, *Naming Grace: Preaching and the Sacramental Imagination* (New York: Continuum, 1997); M. Shawn Copeland, *The Subversive Power of Love: The Vision of Henriette Delille* (Mahwah, NJ: Paulist Press 2009).

4. John of the Cross, *The Ascent of Mount Carmel*, Book 3, in *The Collected Works of St. John of the Cross*, rev. ed., trans. Kieran Kavanaugh and Otilio Rodriguez (Washington, DC: Institute of Carmelite Studies, 1991), 2.2-3. Unless otherwise noted, all references to the writings of John of the Cross are taken from this volume and refer to the works of John of the Cross given as follows: Ascent = *The Ascent of Mount Carmel*, Dark Night = *The Dark Night*, Canticle = *The Spiritual Canticle*, Living Flame = *The Living Flame of Love*.

this utterly silent *prayer*, a radically new "self" is being worked on and shaped, a dispossessed "self" truly capable of living and loving in a way that realizes more fully our relational evolution and synergistic existence in the universe. My treatment of the self and the evolution of consciousness may be the most perplexing aspect of this study—one where more theological reflection in dialogue with the experience of others is needed.

This presentation of an experience of more profound impasse and deeper contemplative growth is integrally connected to my earlier interpretation. Although my exploration raises its own disturbing questions, I hope it will offer a significant contribution to theological reflection and spiritual experience at a time when polarization, suspicion, denouncement, investigation, silencing, alienation, anger, cynicism and sadness divide our Church, and when our country is rocked with economic suffering precipitated by years of wrong-doing and greed, our political process driven by a cruel bipartisanship that endangers the common good, our earth menaced with global warming and ecological distress that threaten all planetary life with eventual extinction, the religions of the world plagued with extremism and age-old distrust that fuel war and terrorism, the people of the world abused with violence, slavery, and deprivation too great to measure. We are encumbered by old assumptions, burdened by memories that limit our horizons, and, therefore, unfree to see God coming to us from the future. Slow to deal with different levels of complexity of consciousness[5] or to tolerate ambiguity before the Holy Mystery of our lives, the institutional Church, it seems to me, is immersed in an impasse, a crisis of memory, which only a continuing openness to contemplative grace and purification can transform.

Purification of Memory

We are a people of memory. Central to our Christian identity is the memory of the life, death and resurrection of Jesus; as Church we understand our authenticity as historically derived and see

5. See Robert Kegan, *In Over Our Heads: The Mental Demands of Modern Life* (Cambridge, MA: Harvard University Press, 1994), 312–16.

ourselves as guardians of a sacred tradition we dare not forget. Nonetheless, it is no naive accident that John of the Cross writes at such length on the *purification* of memory in the third book of the *Ascent of Mount Carmel* (1-15) and throughout the second book of the *Dark Night*. Nor is it any wonder that this is such a misunderstood and even dangerous part of his teaching considering his counsel both to draw the memory away from its "props and boundaries" and to "forget" both wrongs suffered and good experienced.[6]

Let me sketch in my own words the basic dynamics in this process of purification. In the deeper reaches of a contemplative life, a kind of unraveling or loss of memory occurs which can be more or less conscious. Then one's usual way of harboring memories is incapacitated.[7] A person's past becomes inaccessible as a basis for finding meaning. The experience seems to be not so much an *emptying* of memory, as John describes it, as an unraveling or de-linking of it. A person continues to have memories of the past, she may be bombarded with them, but they are somehow uncoupled from the self. Their significance is altered. Memories do not mean what one thought they did. In a mysterious way there is a cutting off of both past and memory that is inimical to one's personhood. The capacity one loses is the ability to "remember"; that is, to "member" again, bringing past elements together, forward to the present, reconstructed into a newly relevant whole. When memory is "de-constructed" in the dark night, the past can no longer weave its thread of meaning through the person's lived experience into the future. Past, present and future do not fit together. What one remembers, how one remembers, how long one remembers is called into question. The past can seem a mockery or an illusion; the psychological and intellectual structures that have supported or held us together over a life-time, "the beacons by which we have set our course,"[8] the certainties on

6. "It must strip and empty itself of all this knowledge and these forms and strive to lose the imaginative apprehension of them" (Ascent 3.2.4). See also Ascent 3.2.2-4; 3.3.2-6.

7. See Dark Night 2.3.3; 8.1-2.

8. Hein Blommestijn, Jos Huls, Kees Waaijman, *Footprints of Love: John of the Cross as Guide in the Wilderness* (Leuven: Peeters, 2000), 74.

which we have built our lives are seriously undermined or taken away—not only in prayer, but also in and by life, and a profound disorientation results. This is keenly felt as a loss of authenticity, truthfulness and even identity. On a very fundamental level our selfhood—who we are—is threatened.[9] While I have attempted to describe this experience, it has many different faces and is a frightening and seriously destabilizing, liminal experience, leaving a person undone, silenced. How long this turmoil in the memory will last depends on the extent to which one's past encumbers God's approach.

So much that fills our memory blocks this coming of God in love toward us. For John of the Cross the human person is seen as an infinite capacity for God.[10] As long as one is preoccupied with filling the great *caverns* of the mind, heart, memory and imagination with human knowledge, loves, memories and dreams that seem to promise complete satisfaction, or at least more than they can ever deliver, the person is unable to feel or even imagine the vast hollowness one is. Only when one becomes aware of the illusory and limiting character of this fullness in the face of the breakdown of what/whom we have staked our lives on, the limitations of our life project and relationships, the irruption of our unclaimed memories, and the shattering of our dreams and meanings can the depths of hunger and thirst that exist in the human person, the infinite capacity, really be experienced.[11] Therefore, only when the great cavern of the memory is enfeebled by its obsession with the past—past pleasure and past pain—debilitated by its unforgettable suffering over losses and evil inflicted, limited by its inability to come to terms with a complex world, constricted by its need to organize images or to understand and unsay inherited constructs, can the great void of yearning for God really be admit-

9. Dark Night 2.9.5; 2.9.7.

10. Living Flame 3.18-22; consult note 46 in Constance FitzGerald, "Transformation in Wisdom," in *Carmel and Contemplation*, Carmelite Studies 8, ed. Kevin Culligan, OCD, and Regis Jordan, OCD (Washington, DC: ICS Publications, 2000), 351.

11. For a more extensive interpretation of the process of purification in John of the Cross, see FitzGerald, "Transformation in Wisdom," 303–25.

ted. Although triggered by the intimately close presence of the divine,[12] the meaning of this profound pain is hidden from our rational understanding, initially even our spiritual intuition. But for John of the Cross this experience signals that the memory is being deconstructed or dispossessed in a redemptive movement whereby the incredibly slow appropriation of theological hope gradually displaces all that impedes new vision, new possibility, the evolution of a transformed self that is freed from bondage to its confining or destructive past. Crucial to any personal appropriation of hope is the ability to read the signs of what is going on so as to remain with the unfolding process.

The Ambiguity of Memory

Why is this so difficult? Memory is a complex and ambiguous power. Multiple distinctions need to be made. Consider, for example, the distinction between the personal healing of memories and corporate processes of reconciliation, the distinction between memory as dangerous in the sense that liberation theologians speak of the dangerous memory of Jesus Christ, and memory as dangerous in the destructive sense; the distinction between history and memory; or the biblical and liturgical meaning of memory where past, present and future come together. Here I will focus on only one aspect of the ambiguity of memory in light of John of the Cross' treatment of purification of the memory.

Our memories have made us who we are, spiritually and humanly. No-memory makes authentic human relationship virtually impossible and robs us of our identity. I cannot forget the pain of the husband of an Alzheimer's patient, who in despair said of his wife, "She has only the present. To have only the present—that is hell." As Yale theologian Miroslav Volf suggests, however, in

12. This intimately close presence of the divine John of the Cross calls infused contemplation, dark night, an inflow of God, secret Wisdom, mystical theology and loving knowledge. See Dark Night 2.5.1-2; 2.17, and Ascent 2.8.6. Another relevant text is Dark Night 1.10.6 where infused contemplation is, according to Kieran Kavanaugh, mentioned for the first time and equated with "dark and secret contemplation" and "secret and peaceful and loving inflow of God."

The End of Memory: Remembering Rightly in a Violent World, what we remember, what others including our culture remember with us and for us, how we remember, how we weave these memories together into the fabric of our lives matters decisively in shaping our identities.[13]

The difficulty is that memories can lead us to either healing and empathy or hostility and destruction. On the one hand, the human community is saturated with the injunction to remember: not only its triumphs of courage, but especially the unspeakable horrors of the Holocaust, genocide, slavery, rape, ethnic cleansing, torture and abuse precisely so that they never occur again. On the other hand, "the human race as individuals and tribes, at this very moment, is in huge measure bound to the past, to memory, in debilitating and destructive ways."[14] Remembering wrongs suffered seems indispensable to healing, we are told, and is often a means of constructing and consolidating a community that tells the same narrative of anguish; and the memory of past injustices can certainly engender empathy, solidarity and justice for others who are oppressed. However, some victims of such evil, precisely because they remember their own victimization in the past, personally or as members of a persecuted, marginalized group, can feel justified in perpetrating violence, hatred, oppression and even ethnic cleansing in the present. "So easily does the protective shield morph into a sword of violence" that can last for generations, as Volf reminds us.[15]

Conscious of the horrendous evil inflicted upon him and the Jewish people, Elie Wiesel, that eloquent survivor of the Holocaust, is well aware of the ambiguity of remembering. As deeply as anyone, he knows the pain of memory and the desperate "need of many victims to wipe from their memories all traces of days

13. Miroslav Volf, *The End of Memory: Remembering Rightly in a Violent World* (Grand Rapids, MI: Eerdmans, 2006), 25. See also Elizabeth A. Johnson, *Friends of God and Prophets: A Feminist Theological Reading of the Communion of Saints* (New York: Continuum, 1998), 164–65.

14. Brian McDermott, unpublished homily given at Baltimore Carmel, January 18, 2009.

15. Volf, *End of Memory*, 27–33.

that are blacker than nights,"[16] just as he realizes how clinging to the dead can diminish our capacity to live and to love in the present and for the future. He reflects on the effect of the negative use of memory throughout history—as illustrated in Bosnia: "that tormented land," where, he writes, "it is memory that is a problem. It's because they remember what happened to their parents or their sister or their grandparents that they hate each other."[17] While acknowledging the need to redeem memories, still "this passionate prophet of memory" can only continue crying out with glaring, powerful consistency one message: *Remember*![18] He can go no further.

The litany of experiences which cultural critics and survivors, psychologists and historians, theologians and novelists, do not want us to forget has given birth to trauma theory, mimetic theory, non-violent theory, feminist theory and theology, theologies of healing aimed at redeeming memory.[19] All of this (including current neurological research on editing memory) has clouded the lens through which I look at John of the Cross' teaching. Suspended in an intellectual impasse, I struggle to hold in tension both the power of memory and the importance of history in giving us context, on the one hand, *and*, on the other hand, the need to forget and be open to the radical transformation of the self and the memory. I ask how we can remember and forget at the same

16. Elie Wiesel, *Forgotten* (New York: Schoken 1992), 297.

17. Elie Wiesel and Richard D. Heffner, *Conversations with Elie Wiesel*, ed. Thomas J. Vinciguerra (New York: Schoken, 2001), 144–45.

18. Volf, *End of Memory*, 34; see 24–34. Volf reminds us that fifty years after the terrible Kristallnacht, Elie Wiesel spoke these words in the German Reichstag: "We remember Auschwitz and all that it symbolizes because we believe that, in spite of the past and its horrors, the world is worthy of salvation and salvation, like redemption, can be found in memory" (ibid., 19).

19. See, for example, Rene Girard, *Violence and the Sacred*, trans. Patrick Gregory (Baltimore: Johns Hopkins, 1979); Rene Girard, *The Scapegoat*, trans. Yvonne Freccero (Baltimore: Johns Hopkins, 1986); Flora Keshgegian, *Redeeming Memories: A Theology of Healing and Transformation* (Nashville, TN: Abingdon Press, 2000); Judith Lewis Herman, *Trauma and Recovery* (New York: Basic Books, 1992); Jon G. Allen, *Coping with Trauma*, 2nd ed. (Arlington, VA: American Psychiatric Publishing, 2005). See also Johnson, *Friends of God*, 141–70, for the importance of memory in reclaiming women's lost history and rectifying their distorted and silent history.

time. I wrestle with remembering anew so that we can tell the narrative differently, and I wrestle with forgetting when forgetfulness and silence are dangerous; for example, for women who are lower in the social hierarchy, or for those who come out of a heritage of slavery whose potential for being forgotten has been greater than for most. I strive to be faithful to and in solidarity with those who continue to remember indescribable violation and at the same time I am receptive to the transforming power of hope that deconstructs memory and to the fathomless Mystery coming to us from the future. I suggest that in this impasse psychology and the social sciences do not take us far enough. We need the insights of theologians and mystics.

Interpretations of John of the Cross in the Contemporary Context

I turn to the example of John of the Cross' life and his mystical texts on dispossession in the memory to understand how they function for personal and communal transformation. Abused for months in a cold, dark prison cell, humiliated, starved, beaten regularly in the refectory by the other friars, *brainwashed* to persuade him to repudiate Teresa of Avila and the Carmelite Reform, he was saved from certain death only by a daring escape. Clearly John could have been embittered or destroyed by the experience and never moved beyond it. Instead this sixteenth-century Carmelite offers us a mystical inheritance and a provocative challenge.

Almost five centuries later, in his masterful study, *The End of Memory*, Miroslav Volf describes a similar process. He delineates the complex, poignant process whereby he passed from the destructive, confining memory of his intense, dehumanizing interrogation and severe psychic battering in communist Yugoslavia to a realization that the ability to let go of the memories of the evil inflicted by Captain G., his tormentor, would come about only as "a gift of God to the transformed self," a proleptic experience of the new "world of love" to come.[20] Volf's genius lies in his psychological, theological, cultural and spiritual analysis of the deliberate steps involved in his

20. Volf, *End of Memory*, 146–47.

own concrete embodiment of exactly what John of the Cross calls the purification and transformation of memory and Volf's conviction that he would "squander his own soul" if he failed to follow the path toward which Christ called him, if he did not surrender to the redeeming process in all its pain and ambiguity. As he works meticulously through issues of memory and identity, probing the obligation to remember truthfully as a prerequisite for achieving justice for the wronged, the need to remember therapeutically so that wrongs suffered can be integrated into a new narrative and the grip of the past on one's identity broken; as he wonders repeatedly how long one must remember and when, if ever, one can forget, he exposes the severe displacement and the impasse this purifying experience causes.

While it is impossible to synthesize here Volf's careful theological development, he concludes that through the memory of the Passion of Jesus, God will purify his memory of wrongs suffered since his identity as a Christian stems not from the evil done to him, nor from his own false innocence whereby he might justify himself, but from his being beloved of God notwithstanding any sin. So his overriding spiritual intuition anticipates a time when evil suffered will "not come to mind," will be "forgotten," because both wronged and wrongdoer will be forgiven, reconciled, transformed and immersed in the love of God.

If we turn to the night of memory in women's spiritual experience for other examples, we see a multifaceted picture. First, when the purifying touch of secret Wisdom[21] awakens out of numbness a woman's deeply abused humanity, she, first of all, *remembers*. Here again multiple distinctions are needed. Women's experience of chattel slavery or sexual and physical abuse cannot be compared to privileged women's experience of social or ecclesial marginalization. But in any form of systemic injustice, the woman, like Volf, *remembers*: with extraordinary poignancy she remembers all the acts of inequality, dismissal, inferiority, subordination, violence, subjugation and silencing, all the disfiguring assumptions that the dominant culture of patriarchy or

21. See Living Flame 2 for "purifying touch" and FitzGerald "Transformation in Wisdom," 308–18, 326–27.

the majority race or class has projected and continues to inflict on her. Even more, she becomes painfully aware of all the past emotion, passion and feelings associated with these acts that have left her so intensely wounded. Because so many women forget on purpose, or for unconscious reasons fail to see, the initial step of purification is *remembering* and this remembering is a miracle of contemplative grace. Failing to understand the *spiritual* process underway, many go no further.[22]

Only very gradually, under the influence of hidden Sophia drawing a woman deep into herself and her own body memory, does the painful unraveling of her social constructedness, previous spiritual experience, past dependencies and loves, successes and failures, yield to the dark, mysterious, hidden, purifying embrace of intimate divine love effecting woman's radical unsaying of "all the images, understandings and memories that do not name her" or her God.[23] At its nadir this is the experience of the empty tomb, "where the 'follow me' of Jesus comes from a voice which has been effaced,"[24] and from where woman will rise to see herself affirmed in the beauty of divine Wisdom.[25] With powerful

22. I suggest that without an understanding of spiritual development, psychotherapy will have limited and inconclusive results.

23. Beverly Lanzetta, *Radical Wisdom*, 132–35. I appreciate Lanzetta's insights which I have integrated with my own in the preceding section. I believe woman's experience, "via femina," she describes *is* the dark night purification of memory John of the Cross develops even though Lanzetta appears to think "via femina" is something beyond John's (male) descriptions. She seems to suggest, however, that it is Teresa's experience. When Teresa says a specific experience of loneliness and suffering is "beyond" everything she has written, she is referring to her "Life" but not to the "Interior Castle" which she wrote about 15 years later. When she wrote the "Life," she had not experienced the spiritual marriage nor the darkness preceding it. See Constance FitzGerald, "Discipleship of Equals," in *A Discipleship of Equals: Towards a Christian Feminist Spirituality*, ed. Francis A. Eigo (Villanova, PA: Villanova University Press, 1988), 63–97.

24. See Natalie Zeman Davis, "The Quest of Michel de Certeau," *The New York Review of Books* (March 15, 2008), 57–60.

25. In the *Spiritual Canticle*, John of the Cross describes the movement from purification of the memory to its transformation when he writes, "[God] fills her memory with divine knowledge, because it is now alone and empty of all images and fantasies" (35.5). Such transformative self-donation on the part of God embraces the loved one in the beauty of divine Wisdom, in whom the

intensity and considerable clarity, Beverly Lanzetta is, I believe, describing this night of memory in her work, *Radical Wisdom: A Feminine Mystical Theology*, on which I have drawn here, when she discusses the *via femina* of contemporary woman related to the contemplative prayer development of Teresa of Avila. Because this radical emptying out[26] of woman's constructed selfhood is so profoundly united with the kenosis of Jesus,[27] this dispossession in the feminine memory effects a solidarity that reaches far beyond the personal into the communal, into the souls of all women; then deep into the human spirit.[28]

Although I have dwelt on traumatic memories at some length, it is equally important to recall that John extends memory's forfeitures particularly to spiritual gifts and consolation, human achievements and natural endowments and to one's carefully achieved selfhood. The most critical remnant of one's former experience/knowledge of God as well as one's perceived whole-

---

person beholds, as in a mirror her own beauty. Subverted definitively is the confining, hoarding, colonizing power of memory and past assumptions in an affirmation that spirals to seemingly endless degrees of mutual appreciation singularly determined not by the self-possession of the loved person, but by the beauty of Wisdom whose depth and breadth of feeling can gather every absurdity and contradiction into an ever expanding pattern of beauty. John sings: "Let us rejoice, Beloved, and let us go forth to behold ourselves in your beauty . . . that I be so transformed in your beauty and we be alike in beauty possessing then your very beauty . . . in such a way that each looking at the other may see in each other their own beauty, since both are your beauty alone" (36.5).

26. Although I have largely avoided John's language of "emptying" the memory, this experience really is an *emptying* out of memory.

27. For John of the Cross, Jesus Christ is the pattern of the Dark Night: see Ascent 2.7.2-8.

28. In *The Subversive Power of Love*, 49–67, M. Shawn Copeland shows exemplified in Henriette Delille what I am describing. For further explication of solidarity in difference, see also Johnson, *Friends of God*, 175–80, who also references M. Shawn Copeland, "Toward a Critical Christian Feminist Theology of Solidarity," in *Women and Theology*, vol. 3, ed. Mary Ann Hinsdale and Phyllis Kaminski (Maryknoll, NY: Orbis) and "Difference as a Category in Critical Theologies for the Liberation of Women," in *Feminist Theology in Different Contexts*, ed. Elisabeth Schüssler Fiorenza and M. Shawn Copeland (London, UK: SCM Press and Maryknoll, NY: Orbis, 1996), 143.

ness to which one had been clinging without realizing it, is taken away. Listen to one successful, contemporary, American woman's poignant description of her experience of purification of memory. Largely unencumbered by projections of inferiority and subordination, she writes in her journal:[29]

> It is as if I have been robbed profoundly, precisely of the comforting, assuring memory of presence, which is so vital to my self-identity, as it is informed by my past. I no longer own or possess my interior memories of my past (even in some exterior ways). If, like a person with amnesia, I were a complete blank, I would not suffer so. In this way, memory is not exactly "lost." Instead, it is numbed. I remember just enough to be in pain. I still know that I once knew (or thought I knew) God. I still know that I once found meaning and mission in the sense of God's presence and love. I know this but I can no longer connect it with myself. Everything has been de-linked. When I sit for a time of purported prayer, I only feel loss. What I thought I had, now seems like a lie, an illusion. I have been emptied of all claim to authenticity for all that I have lived. I search for a word meaning *to take away the essence of, radically*. The hollowing out is so deep that by its essence it highlights that there are deeper and deeper levels that have not been touched. The only light that is given by this experience shines on the seemingly infinite levels of emptying that are waiting to happen. I find myself wondering how the little acorn of a person I am can possibly have these infinite levels to be emptied. With such a radical process underway within me, how is it possible that something of myself remains? I feel like a shell of a person.[30]
>
> And I am dispossessed in other ways too. My health has been taken away. My considerable financial resources are seriously threatened—this is part of the loss of my past. All that I have accumulated, all the tangible signs of the life I once led are being ground into dust. This vanishing of the product of my work and life removes another layer of evidence for the successful life I once lived. There is no proof, even exterior, of what once was. For years I have known that my intellectual strength has been an ability to use memory to make associations between concepts,

29. From a private spiritual journal shared with me.
30. Dark Night 2.5-6.

> to piece things together to reach good and sometimes insightful conclusions. This part of me seems dead at the moment. Still it is curious to me that throughout this time I have been able to be productive, to work effectively and to concentrate. In my everyday life, I have energy and ability. And so I know at least that this experience is not depression.

Many would see only destruction or psychological illness at work in this woman's life, and the experience of contemplative purification can resemble dark psychological states like depression, so destructive of the self. But Denys Turner, reflecting on depression and dark night, makes an important distinction. While both are malaise of the self, the prognosis is different. The final outcome the depressed person hopes for in therapy or treatment is the restoration of the self which has been lost, albeit a more mature one. But "the dark nights on the other hand are entered into as loss of that same self, for in that consists their pain, but the hope it [the self] acquires is of the non-recovery of that selfhood in any form for what is lost in the passive nights was never the self at all, but only an illusion all along."[31] The selfhood that is lost will never be regained and therein lies its hope. In this purification, the annulling of the memories, we are being dispossessed of the autonomous self, our achieved selfhood put together over a lifetime. The journal concludes:

> As I continue living through this, I have been shown the possibility that this memory unraveling is perhaps a necessary step to true hope. Because the experience denies my past, I have nothing to project on to God for the future or even the present. I experience a poverty that could lead me to hopelessness—to expect nothing of the future because the thread of my past has unraveled, and I no longer have a context for my life.[32] Here the competing directions are despair or a true hope, a hope that is independent of me and my accomplishments, spiritual or otherwise.

31. Denys Turner, "John of the Cross: the dark nights and depression," in *The Darkness of God: Negativity in Western Mysticism* (Cambridge, UK: Cambridge University Press, 1995), 244. See 226-251.

32. Dark Night 2.9.7.

Birth of Theological Hope

John of the Cross does, in fact, make sense of the experience, the purification of the memory, by linking it to theological hope, and this is what I want to emphasize. The cavern of the memory is filled and cluttered with the past—its graces and achievements, its experiences too many and varied to recount. The impotence or muting of this past, authored by the hidden inpouring of God, is precisely the condition that makes hope in the strictly theological sense even possible.[33] As memory slowly becomes a silent space, what very gradually takes over is true theological hope.[34] Activated by divine presence, hope is essential to purification. Without it there is no purification, but only suffering. When the emptiness of the memory on the level of affectivity and imagination becomes a deep void of yearning, it is hope that opens up the possibility of being possessed by the infinite, unimaginable, incomprehensible Mystery of love that is so close. John describes it this way:

> Hope empties and withdraws the memory from all creature possessions, for as St. Paul says, hope is for what is not possessed. It withdraws the memory from what can be possessed and fixes it on what it hopes for. Hence only hope in God prepares the memory perfectly for union with [God].[35]

33. For a clearer understanding of the meaning of theological hope in John of the Cross, consult Karl Rahner, "On the Theology of Hope," in *Theological Investigations*, vol. 10: *Writings of 1965–67 2*, trans. David Bourke (New York: Seabury, 1977), 242–59.

34. Focusing on hope, John of the Cross explains in Ascent 2.6.3: "Hope puts the memory in darkness and emptiness as regards all earthly and heavenly objects. Hope always pertains to the unpossessed object. If something were possessed there could no longer be any hope for it. St. Paul says to the Romans: 'Hope that is seen is not hope, for how does a person hope for what is seen—that is, what is possessed?' As a result, this virtue also occasions emptiness, since it is concerned with unpossessed things and not with the possessed object." See Blommestijn, Huls and Waaijman, *Footprints of Love*, 71–73. I am indebted to the authors' treatment of the purification of memory and specifically here to hope. These Dutch Carmelite scholars have been working with the purification of memory in John as I have.

35. Dark Night 2.21.11.

I believe we can clarify the relationship between memory's deconstruction and theological hope by drawing new insights from the developing theology of evolution, which has been notably synthesized by Templeton scholar John Haught. Building on the work of Karl Rahner, Paul Tillich, Pierre Teilhard de Chardin, and others, Haught speaks compellingly of a "metaphysics of the future." He explains:

> A metaphysics of the future is rooted in the intuition, expressed primordially in the biblical experience, . . . that the abode of ultimate reality is not limited to the causal past nor to a fixed and timeless present "up above." Rather it is to be found most characteristically in the constantly arriving and renewing future. We need a vision of reality that makes sense of the most obvious aspects of life's evolution, in particular the fact that it brings about new forms of being. . . . [This] alternative view of reality . . . is a metaphysics that gives priority to the future rather than to the past or the present . . . and is rooted deeply in the experience that people have of something that to them is overwhelming and incontestably real, namely, what might be called metaphorically the "power of the future." Of course, it is perhaps only by adopting the religious posture of hope that they have been opened to the experience of this power.[36]

Haught would say that this "power of the future," which grasps us and makes us new, might be called "God" who is always alluring us forward from a future that comes to meet us.[37]

Before memory is purified, we can thwart our encounter with the future, without even realizing it, by relying on the images which memory has saved for us—images of our past, joyful or sad, pleasant or unpleasant, fulfilling or detrimental. We project these images onto our vision of the future, we block the limitless possibilities of God by living according to an expectation shaped, not by hope, but by our own desires, needs and past ex-

36. John F. Haught, *God after Darwin: A Theology of Evolution* (Boulder, CO: Westview Press, 2000), 88–89.

37. Ibid., 90.

periences.[38] Dutch Carmelite theologian Kees Waaijman and his colleagues remind us that we have the mistaken notion that we are completely open to the reality around us, whereas we necessarily trim back any new impressions to the images we already carry within ourselves and which provide us with something secure to hold on to. "However much we may open ourselves in self-forgetfulness to the other reality that reveals itself to us, in fact, we do not get beyond the reduction of the other to that which is ours."[39] Bringing a pre-understanding to every dream, we are condemned, without memory's purification, to a predictable and even violent world.

Coming from another tradition, Christopher Bamford articulates even more explicitly how the archives of our images block an authentic encounter with the Other, or any vision for the future. Commenting on Meister Eckhart's instruction on detachment, he says:

> By images Eckhart means the contents of consciousness: the finished fixed forms—past thoughts and memories—which we take

38. John writes: "The spiritual person must continually bear in mind the following precaution; he [*sic*] must not build up an archive of impressions in his memory of all the things he hears, sees, smells, and touches. On the contrary, he must immediately forget them and, if necessary, apply as much energy to forgetting them as others do to remembering them. He must do this in such a way that no communication or idea of these things remains in his memory. He must act as if these things did not exist in the world. Thus he leaves the memory free and unencumbered and unattached to any earthly or heavenly consideration. He then arrives at a state such that it would appear as though he had no memory. He must freely let it sink into oblivion as a hindrance" (Ascent 3.2.14). John further explains: "God displays no form or image that can be encompassed by the memory. Hence also the memory, when it is united with God, is without form or image. . . . Our everyday experience in fact also teaches us this. The memory is devoid of all images and imbued with the supreme good. It has completely forgotten everything and no longer remembers anything. For union with God empties the imagination and sweeps out all forms and communications and elevates it to the supernatural" (Ascent 3.2.4). The translations of these two texts are taken from *Footprints of Love*. I am grateful to Blommestijn, Huls and Waaijman for their articulation of this experience. Their thought is so close to my own. See 71–73.

39. Ibid., 90.

> to be the world but which in fact are not the world in its immediacy and present-ness, but only our own past, our own habits and fixed tendencies. Immured within these images, we feed upon ourselves and take our self-feeling for the world. These images interpose themselves between us and the world, breaking the continuum of being, and making any true meeting or knowledge impossible.[40]

Miroslav Volf's experience led him to the conclusion that if he continued to let the stored impressions of wrongdoing define him, he would take on a distorted identity that would be frozen in time and closed to future growth.[41] Given that the memory of his abuse kept metastasizing itself into his anticipated future, he realized he could not permit his communist interrogator to define the boundary of his expectations forever. Grasped by hope in "Jesus Christ [who] promises to every person a new horizon of possibility, a new world freed from all enmity, a world of love," and believing that those new possibilities for the Christian are defined by that promise and not by past experience or worn out assumptions, Volf was able to open himself to the flame of God's presence; he was able to receive a new identity defined by God's love. Now, as a consequence of God's gift to him of self-transcendence, evil suffered would "not-come-to-mind." In Christ he would live into a future beyond imagining.[42] With his memories undone and absorbed by the fire of contemplative love, he would find the way past the limits of his experience to the truth that has no borders; the meeting that exists beyond his perceptions.

This dynamic of being able to yield unconditionally to God's future is what John of the Cross calls *hope*, a hope that exists without the signature of our life and works, a hope independent of us and our accomplishments (spiritual gifts or ordinary human achievements), a hope that can even embrace and work for a future without us. This theological hope is completely free from the past,

40. *Parabola* 10, no. 3 (1985): 67.

41. See Volf, 12. According to Volf, whether memories multiply pleasure or replicate pain they cut us off from the future (21).

42. Ibid., 81–83, 145–47.

fully liberated from our need to recognize ourselves in the future, to survive, to be someone. When we are laid flat by the deconstruction/silencing of our memory, it is hope that is very gradually taking over the operation of the memory/imagination, hollowing out a place for the "power of the future," for the coming of the Impossible.[43] For hope to extend itself this far by perpetual expectation into the realm of the Invisible and Incomprehensible, its movement will have to be purified of all forms of self-preservation, all efforts to preserve one's selfhood as it is. David F. Ford clarifies this further: "Hope does not desire anything for itself. It does not return to itself but rather remains with that which is hoped for."[44] The key insight here is that it is the limited self, constituted by the past, that needs to yield to the transforming power of God's call into the future.

If this freeing process of purification or forfeiture were up to us we would not, could not, accomplish it. To attempt to unravel one's memory outside of this understanding, unprecipitated by the burning presence of the divine is absolutely destructive and unhealthy, but this purification overtakes us in the events of our lives and God works with us in the depths of these occurrences. When, for example, a theologian is placed under suspicion or silenced, when his/her work is rejected, when his/her identity as a Catholic theologian is threatened, questioned or denied, she/he undoubtedly experiences such dispossession. But however this

43. John explains: " . . . none of the supernatural forms and ideas that can be received by the memory is God, and the soul must empty itself of all that is not God in order to go to God. Consequently, the memory must likewise dismiss all these forms and ideas in order to reach union with God in hope. Every possession is against hope. As St. Paul says, hope is for that which is not possessed (Heb. 2.1). In the measure in which the soul becomes dispossessed of things, in that measure will it have hope, and the more hope it has the greater will be its union with God, for in relation to God, the more a soul hopes the more it attains hope" (Ascent 3.7.2). See Blommestijn, Huls, Waaijman, *Footprints of Love*, 71–73, 79–82.

44. David F. Ford, *Self and Salvation: Being Transformed* (Cambridge, UK: Cambridge University Press, 1998). In *Darkness of God* Denys Turner writes in similar fashion: "As memory we are dispossessed by hope of any power to construct for ourselves an identity of our own" (246).

undoing occurs, it is inevitably accompanied by forfeiture in our spiritual lives and prayer, in all that concerns God. (John calls this the "supernatural memory.") The memory of all our spiritual experiences, above all, creates a pattern of expectation that must yield to the unknown Mystery. And so we experience a draining off of any spiritual meaning in prayer, in our feelings about God, in our experience of liturgy and Church. The inadequacy of theology looms large or even worse seems like an empty shell and all this seems irreversible.

You can see what a radical call this is. Those who answer it must be prepared to leave so much behind, to stop clinging to a security that has been taken away. Perhaps those who finally understand and give their lives over to the dismantling of the archives of memory by accepting the gift of hope eschew keeping a death grip on what has given them assurance of their value and place in the Church.

Prophecy and Prayer of No Experience

The profound and painful purification I have been outlining really does change a person's memory. This dark passage does have an arrival point: prophecy. Obsession with the past gives way to a new undefinable sense of relatedness or intimacy, an experience of ultimate assurance, and this conversion releases creativity and most importantly freedom for the limitless possibilities of God, for hope. This freedom, this posture of hope, is really prophecy, for it enables a person to reveal the vision of a different kind of future than the one we want to construct from our limited capacities. Such a person becomes a prophet when she shows the way; when she is willing to stand on the horizon so that all can see this future, God's future.

It is tempting to envision this emergence from the dark night, this dawn, as a time of wondrous consolation and light, marked by the constant sense of God's presence and highlighted with ecstatic experiences of delight in union with God. But while John of the Cross acknowledges that there may be ecstatic delight, he hints, and I believe, that the actual day-to-day experience in dark night's dawn may be quite different. Perhaps we need to consider anew what we mean by spiritual ecstasy. Perhaps a spiritual ecstasy, in our day, might be defined as any moment when we fully and truly step out of, or are impelled beyond, ourselves.[45]

In fact, from what I have witnessed in spiritual direction and other conversations, openness and freedom in the liberated memory is experienced not so much as consolation but as a profound peace in the silent unknowing and in the dark empty space of encounter with God, the truly Other, an emptiness that is content not to seek fulfillment in its own time. I call this prophetic hope, which "expresses" itself in what I have named the *prayer of no experience*. The depth and prevalence of such prayer begs for interpretation and meaning.

Very often after years of trying to pray and live faithfully, after receiving precious graces, consolations and insight, persons experience not presence, but *nothing*, silence, in their prayer. Many mature, dedicated, seasoned religious people who pray steadfastly and work courageously in the Church describe this phenomenon. They report that there is absolutely nothing discernible going on when they pray and yet they do need prayer; they are faithful to it and actually spend considerable time in silent *there-ness*. But the only experience is *no experience*, the silent place. This is not, I am convinced, the normal season of dryness which earnest people pass through in early prayer development. It is not the loss of enjoyment, pleasure, contentment, sensitivity in life and prayer and ministry, that transitional purification that "dismantle[s] the whole apparatus of sensory ego-compensation."[46]

Though we would probably see these individuals, *pray-ers of no experience*, as remarkably self-possessed and loving, ministerially effective and at the height of their vocational or scholarly achievements, they realize, without dramatization, that they do not quite know who they are anymore. This is not an identity crisis of the young, or not so young adult, or of those who have

45. I am not alone in this interpretation: "[I]n the state of ecstasy," Kees Waaijman and his colleagues suggest, "we are beside ourselves and become strangers and pilgrims who no longer feel at home anywhere and lose our footing" (*Footprints of Love*, 127).

46. Turner, *Darkness of God*, 236.

never discovered themselves, authored their own lives, and borne their own responsibility. It is not even a mid-life crisis with its bid for freedom in sometimes irresponsible escape or heedless self-realization. It is far deeper than these. On one level these persons no longer know what they believe. But on a more profound level, they walk in faith, accustomed to doubt and inner questioning, yet possessed by a hope that is wordless and imageless in its expectation of "what eye has not seen nor ear heard." They are marked by a certain serenity of spirit indicative of the degree to which this dark theological faith has gripped the intellect and pure theological hope has filled the memory obscuring and emptying them and guiding the person toward the "high goal of union with God."[47] While they theoretically, academically and responsibly maintain a hold on their theological underpinnings and remain faithful to their religious tradition and liturgical life, they realize experientially that none of us is meant to know who God is, but only who/what God is not. These people have perhaps made the conclusive passage from extreme desolation of spirit where they felt abandoned by or distant from God to the love opened to them by fathomless Mystery and this is why I think they are on the dawn side of the dark night of the spirit, perhaps the first stage of a truly transformed consciousness. I suggest these prophets of hope are *being worked on*, transformed by love, in profound silence.[48]

Looking through this lens of silence/emptiness, we see that, in fact, these prophets of hope have been able to move beyond the "self of experience" that blocked any true encounter with the Other. Such an encounter requires an "empty space from which

47. Ascent 1.4.1.

48. Commenting on " . . . in solitude he guides her, he alone," John explains "that [t]he meaning of [this line of the *Spiritual Canticle* poem] is not only that he [*sic*] guides her in her solitude, but it is *he alone who works in her* without any means. This is a characteristic of the union of the soul with God in the spiritual marriage: *God works in and communicates himself to her through himself alone*, without using as means the angels or natural ability, for the exterior and interior senses, and all creatures, and even the soul herself do very little toward the reception of the remarkable supernatural favors that God grants in this state" (35.6).

the self has withdrawn"—and this is true in the most radical degree if we are to encounter God, who is the most absolute Other to us.[49] To have "no experience of selfhood" may in fact be the singular hallmark of a transformed self. *No experience pray-ers* are exhibiting in themselves the presence of a purely passive power, a capacity to be attracted by the Future,[50] a movement toward God in love-filled hope no longer grounded in the need to possess, to enjoy or to dominate by words or memory or understanding. This is the ultimate silence, the ultimate empty space and may very well be one kind of ecstatic experience of union. Karl Rahner understood this:

> There is no such thing either in the world or in the heart, as literal vacancy, as a vacuum. And whenever space is really left—by death, by renunciation, by parting, by apparent emptiness, provided the emptiness that cannot remain empty is not filled by the world, or activity, or chatter, or the deadly grief of the world—there is God.[51]

Dispossession of Self

I believe a dispossession of selfhood is being actualized in this silent *prayer of no experience*[52] and I suspect it has a specific prophetic purpose. This is in keeping with my years of sitting with John of the Cross and hints at what I have learned in the intervening time between the writing of "Impasse and Dark Night" and this essay. It is my strong suspicion that the *prayer of no experience,* effecting an essential change in selfhood, may be emerging with such frequency as a response to a world driven by selfishness and self-concern. Any hope for new consciousness and a self-forfeiture driven by

49. Blommestijn, Huls, Waaijman, *Footprints of Love,* 122.

50. "And the memory, which by itself perceived only the figures and phantasms of creatures, is changed through this union so as to have in its mind the eternal years" (Living Flame 2.34.4); and "its memory is the eternal memory of God" (Living Flame 2.34.7).

51. Quoted in *The Tablet* by Daniel O'Leary, "Space for Grace" (November 18, 2006).

52. " . . . the soul is dead to all that it was in itself . . . " (Living Flame 2.34.7).

love stands opposed by a harsh reality: we humans serve our own interests, we hoard resources, we ravage the earth and other species, we scapegoat, we make war, we kill, we torture, we turn a blind eye to the desperation and needs of others, and we allow others to die. We simply are not evolved enough to move into a different future from which God comes to us. Our ability to embody our communion with every human person on the earth and our unassailable connectedness with everything living is limited because we have not yet become these symbiotic "selves." We continue to privilege our personal autonomy and are unable to make the transition from radical individualism to a genuine synergistic community even though we know intellectually we are inseparably and physically connected to every living being in the universe. Yet the future of the entire earth community is riding on whether we can find a way beyond the limits of our present evolutionary trajectory.

I am aware of the discomfort my insistence on dispossession of self might evoke in many of you who rightly ascribe to the principle of personal autonomy and the value of the individual. I am not denying the necessity of growing to healthy autonomy nor of the danger of a selflessness that is unwilling or unable to achieve a strong agency. I value the life's work of very fine scholars, many of them women, who, at the end of modernity, have tried so hard and so successfully through their scholarship and advocacy to claim agency for all women and for disenfranchised groups. But our *present* situation in the world does not allow us to stop at the call for or to cling unreflectively to the idea of such individual autonomy. For if there is any insight that we have gained from postmodernity, it is that radical interdependence can, must, and indeed does co-exist with individuals' power to act. Then, what I am suggesting in this essay speaks of a useful and necessary dispossession that does not deny or stand as obstacle to mutual relationship of persons and community.

The transformation taking place in the *prayer of no experience* opens into a profoundly different realm for which we do not have adequate words: the deconstruction of even healthy forms of autonomy that no longer represent the deepest possibilities of the person herself and the human with God nor the radical need of the human community for a deeper synergy. What this prayer predicts as possibility for what the human person and the human community are to become is far beyond what a coalition of strong willed, autonomous, right thinking, ethical people can ever achieve on their own. I know that with this formulation I have gone into a dangerous space where language fails me and impasse confronts me.

If the process underway in the *prayer of no experience* is silently dispossessing us of our possessive selfhood, might this forfeiture amount to an evolutionary leap toward selflessness? Though we are inclined first to understand John Haught's observation that evolutionary reality brings about "new forms of being" as pertaining just to physical forms, surely we are aware on further consideration that evolution is not so confined. This we know from the emergence of consciousness, our latest evolutionary leap. And analogously if our consciousness develops, then Edith Stein's assertion as early as the 1930s that the human *spirit* evolves too must be true, as must Pierre Teilhard de Chardin's speculation that the next evolutionary stage would be concentrated precisely in the realm of spirit (mind) or consciousness, his "noosphere." His understanding of this next phase reflects his awareness of the interdependence of the spirit and the body for mutual development. Thus, the hypotheses of these great thinkers make me bold to contend that this prayer, expressive of a prophetic hope, is an important contemplative bridge to a new future, to the transformation or evolution of consciousness, and through these *pray-ers of no experience* the human person is being changed radically.[53]

53. What is remarkable in the final section of *The Spiritual Canticle* is the progressive character of transformation and, even more surprising, the differing meanings John ascribes to these almost infinite *transformative* possibilities. The history of these stanzas reveals that in the freer, more passionate and daring first redaction of the Canticle commentary (1584) John situates his marvelous expectations for *continuing transformation* this side of death with only minor gesturing to eternity. In the second, more theologically refined redaction written a year or two later (1585–1586), probably with an eye on the Inquisition, his great hope sees these same transformative consequences taking place largely over the horizon of death. My intuition favors John's first, more spontaneous and "dangerous" explanation in what is known as Canticle A. What I want to note in these mystical texts is John's testimony that silent contemplative

Reaching beyond the horizon of present expectation and imagination, willing to go beyond the boundaries of their lives/selves to make an irrevocable passage into a new place, a new way of "being" in the universe, these prophets of hope stand open to receive the unimaginable future to which God is alluring us, and more: they actually serve as the doorway to it. Emmanuel Levinas, the twentieth-century philosopher and, like Edith Stein, an early disciple of Husserl, understood this movement. Levinas ultimately moved beyond ontological philosophy to emphasize the primacy of the ethical relationship with the Other. In this passage he appropriates radical self-dispossession and locates prophecy precisely in the silent eschatology of profound theological hope:

> What comes to mind is the statement of Leon Blum who, imprisoned in a Nazi camp, wrote: "We work *in* the present, not *for* the present." Genuine dedication in working does not seek the applause of one's own time. It devotes itself in dark trust to "a time which lies past the horizon of my time." Surfacing here is the eschatological meaning of "some work." Our work in this age is fragmentary, part of a whole we cannot take in from where we sit. It is only a completely naked faith which knows that this "some" is bound up with a body of the Messiah I can neither conceive nor organize. By disinterestedly stepping outside of myself in work I exercise myself in darkly trusting the End. As worker I abandon the prospect of "personally experiencing the outcome" of my work. This work is essentially prophetic: it works "without entering the Promised Land." This prophetic eschatology is free: delivered from the snares of calculation, delivered from the

---

union, the *prayer of no experience*, radically changes a person and opens into truly new possibilities, new vision, a vast, bottomless and incomprehensible Future toward which hope reaches and love gives. John writes: "This thicket of wisdom and knowledge of God is so profound and vast that, for all the soul may know thereof, she can ever enter farther still, so vast is it, and so incomprehensible are its riches (A 35.5-6). . . . There we shall enter and be transformed in the transformation of new knowledge and new acts and communications of love. For although it is true that the soul, when she says this, is already transformed . . . in this wisdom . . . it does not therefore follow that she cannot in this estate have new enlightenments and transformations of new kinds of knowledge and divine light" (A 37.5).

> nihilism of uncommitted game-playing and waste. And stronger: in dark trust discerning a triumph "in a time without me. . . ." The prophetism of this work is located precisely in this ["]eschatology without hope for myself. . . ." Really working exceeds the boundaries of one's own time. It is action for a world that is coming, action which surpasses this time, action in which I surpass myself, and in which the yearning for an epiphany of the Other is included.[54]

I want to leave before us in our sad, conflicted Church this image of the self-dispossessed prophet whose face is turned in radical hope toward the God coming from the future. When such prophets overstep the horizon of their own time, their own life, in work, in words, in scholarship, in teaching, in ministry, in who they are as people of silent prayer, not only are they, themselves, reborn on the other side of the boundary, but they are also carriers of the evolution of consciousness for the rest of humanity. We can hope that as more and more people make this dark passage to prophecy, this movement of the human spirit will "selectively activate genetic potentials" different from those operative in our present selfhood.[55] As a result, a critical mass will be generated

54. Adriaan Peperzak, *Het Menselijk Gelaat* (The Human Face) (Bilthoven 1971), 172–73. This is a collection of articles on Emmanuel Levinas. The Levinas text may be found in English in Kees Waaijman, *The Mystical Space of Carmel* (Leuven: Peeters 1999), 209–10. Although Waaijman seems to give this as a direct quote, the quotation marks within the text make it ambiguous. Certainly Levinas discusses *these thoughts* in "Meaning and Sense" in *Emmanuel Levinas, Basic Philosophical Writings*, ed. Adriaan T. Peperzak, Simon Critchley, Robert Bernasconi (Bloomington and Indianapolis: Indiana University Press, 1996), 33–64.

55. In an editorial, "Human Nature Today" in the *New York Times* for June 26, 2009, columnist David Brooks, paraphrasing the thought of Sharon Begley, writes: "The first problem is that far from being preprogrammed with a series of hardwired mental modules, as evolutionary psychologist types assert, our brains are fluid and plastic. We're learning that evolution can be a more rapid process than we thought. It doesn't take hundreds of thousands of years to produce genetic alterations. Moreover, we've evolved to adapt to diverse environments. Different circumstances can *selectively activate different genetic potentials*. . . . Human nature adapts to the continual flow of information—adjusting to the ancient information contained in genes and the current information contained

which will lead all humanity across the frontier into the new epoch that is trying to be born. Only our unpurified memories prevent us from imagining a future in which our descendants are not like the human beings we know ourselves to be.

Like another Carmelite, Edith Stein, whom I mentioned earlier and who died with her people in the extermination camp at Auschwitz, betrayed by the state to which she had vowed a total commitment in her youth, I am suggesting the powerful influence of a *spiritual* generativity. The evolution of spirit or consciousness of which Stein speaks happens not just or mainly through a physical propagation but through a spiritual one in which people "bear fruit by virtue of the atmosphere which radiates from them on their environment and . . . also by means of the works which they produce in common and through which they propagate their spirit."[56] This idea of spiritual generativity may sound far-fetched or ungrounded, until we consider what scientists are discovering and speculating about the true nature of our world. For example, as long ago as 1982 it was reported that "under certain circumstances sub-atomic particles such as electrons are able to instantaneously communicate with each other regardless of the distance separating them, whether an inch, 100 feet, or 10 billion miles apart." Scientist David Bohm's explanation: that there is a deeper and more complex level of reality than we experience, an "implicate order or unbroken wholeness" from which all our perceived reality derives. If such a fabric of interconnectedness exists in nature, it is no stretch of the imagination to apply it to consciousness. Genuine contemplatives have testified to this long before scientists.[57]

---

in today's news [even more the spiritual process of transformation] in a continuous, idiosyncratic blend." (See Sharon Begley, "Don't Blame the Caveman," *Newsweek*, [June 30, 2009]).

56. Edith Stein, *Finite and Eternal Being*, trans. Kurt F. Reinhardt (Washington, DC: Institute of Carmelite Studies, 2002), 266.

57. See, for example, John of the Cross' Living Flame: "The soul feels its ardor strengthen and increase and its love become so refined in this ardor that seemingly there flow seas of loving fire within it, reaching to the heights and depths of the earthly and heavenly spheres, imbuing all with love. It seems to it that the

In a time of unraveling in the Church, when past, present and future do not seem to hold together in a promising continuity, when we stand perhaps at the cusp of an evolutionary breakthrough, we do not know how our work will be used or if it will be accepted or appreciated, nor can we ascertain what benefit it will bring to the Church, religion, American society, or the earth community, now or in a farther future. But I am sure, from my years of keeping company with John of the Cross, that in the personal and communal crisis of memory going on, we are being offered, we are being given, hope for ourselves and humanity—profound, radical theological hope—in a God who is coming anew and calling us forward. We must witness to this in our lives, our work, our scholarship; even in betrayal and suffering.[58] From within the mystical tradition, we are being challenged to be contemplatives willing to be stretched beyond ourselves toward a new epiphany of the Holy, incomprehensible Mystery. We are being challenged to be prophets of hope!

---

entire universe is a sea of love in which it is engulfed, for conscious of the living point or center of love within itself, it is unable to catch sight of the boundaries of this love" (2.10); see also Teresa of Avila, *The Book of Her Life*, vol. 1, rev. ed., in *The Collected Works of St. Teresa of Avila*, trans. Kieran Kavanaugh and Otilio Rodriguez (Washington, DC: Institute of Carmelite Studies, 1987), chap. 40.10.

58. Building on Walter Brueggemann's work on the prophetic imagination, Mary Catherine Hilkert in *Naming Grace* (81–84) describes the task of the prophetic preacher and the prophetic community as that of not only giving language to people's pain and grief in a time of impasse like ours, but also of focusing on the coming of God, the reign of God, and the rekindling of hope.

Contributors

Colette Ackerman, OCD, is currently prioress of the Baltimore Carmel community. She studied anthropology and history at Towson University, Baltimore. Sr. Ackerman is the archivist for Carmelite Communities Associated (CCA), the first association of Carmelite nuns in the United States. She has served CCA in leadership and as a consultant, most recently helping to plan the association's fiftieth anniversary celebration. Sr. Ackerman has served in the ministry of initial formation for her community and has published on St. Therese of Lisieux and other areas of Carmelite spirituality and history. Her areas of special interest include the development of a strong community life based on St. Teresa's model of friendship, inclusion, and care; the transmission of Carmelite spirituality through various forms of outreach; and, especially, the witness of a contemporary, contemplative community sharing liturgy, prayer, and companionship with those seeking a connection with God in their daily lives of struggle and hope.

Susie Paulik Babka is associate professor of theology and religious studies at the University of San Diego, where she teaches courses specializing in the relationship between art and religion, theological aesthetics, the doctrine of God, and the consideration of aesthetics in interreligious encounter. She is the author of *Through the Dark Field: The Incarnation through an Aesthetics of Vulnerability* (Liturgical Press, 2017); is coeditor of *"You Say You Want a Revolution": 1968–2018 in Theological Perspective*, with Elena Procario-Foley and Sandra Yocum (Orbis, 2019); and is currently working on *Ambiguity and Resilience*, which explores the role art plays in empowering communities. She has published articles on a variety of subjects exploring the role of visual art in religious belief, including on Kathe Kollwitz as witness to suffering, the Virgin of Guadalupe and female self-portraiture, Superman and Jesus, Buddhist-Christian dialogue and modern art's influence on the Catholic Church. Her PhD is from the University of Notre Dame.

Laurie Cassidy is a theologian and spiritual director currently teaching in the Christian Spirituality Program at Creighton University. An award-winning author and editor, her books include *Interrupting White Privilege: Catholic Theologians Break the Silence*, edited with Alex Mikulich. Her latest book, *The Scandal of White Complicity and US Hyper-Incarceration: A Nonviolent Spirituality of White Resistance*, is coauthored with Alex Mikulich and Margaret Pfeil (Palgrave Macmillan, 2013). As well as being an antiracist activist, she has ministered in the area of spirituality for the past thirty years and provided spiritual direction, retreats, and workshops across the United States. Her research and writing explore the political and cultural impact of Christian mysticism in personal and social transformation.

M. Shawn Copeland, professor of systematic theology emerita at Boston College, is an internationally recognized and award-winning writer and scholar. She is the author and/or editor of six books including *Knowing Christ Crucified: The Witness of African American Religious Experience* (2018) and *Enfleshing Freedom: Body, Race, and Being* (2010), as well as 130 articles, book chapters, and essays on spirituality, theological anthropology, political theology, social suffering, gender, and race. A former president of the Catholic Theological Society of America (CTSA), Professor Copeland is the recipient of six honorary degrees and has been recognized for outstanding contributions to theology by the Catholic Theological Society of America with the John Courtney Murray Award (2018) and by the University of Dayton with the Marianist Award (2017) and by the Association of Catholic Colleges and Universities with the Monika Hellwig Award for outstanding contributions to Catholic intellectual life.

Constance FitzGerald, OCD, a member of the Carmelite Community in Baltimore, Maryland, is a theologian. Not only has she served her community as prioress, formation director, archivist/historian and treasurer, she was one of the founders of the Association of Contemplative Sisters in the U.S. (1969), a founding member of the Carmelite Forum (1982–2013), and a key consultant to the early work of the Institute for Communal Contemplation and Dialogue. Sr. FitzGerald has devoted her life to the explication and interpretation of the writings of the great Carmelite mystics, with special attention to the writings of Saint John of the Cross. In 2009, she became the first contemplative nun to address the Catholic Theological Society of America (CTSA) and in 2017 the first contemplative nun to be honored by the Leadership Conference of Women Religious (LCWR) with the Outstanding Leadership Award in recognition of her spiritually creative and prophetic contributions to religious life.

Roberto S. Goizueta is the Margaret O'Brien Flatley Professor Emeritus of Catholic Theology at Boston College. Dr. Goizueta is a former president of both the Catholic Theological Society of America and the Academy of Catholic Hispanic Theologians of the United States. The *National Catholic Reporter* named him one of the ten most influential US Latino/a educators, pastors, and theologians. His book *Caminemos con Jesús: Toward a Hispanic/Latino Theology of Accompaniment* (Orbis, 1995) was named one of the "Fifty Foundational Books in Race, Ethnicity, and Religion" by the *Journal of Race, Ethnicity, and Religion.*

Mary Catherine Hilkert, OP, a member of the Dominican Sisters of Peace, is professor of theology at the University of Notre Dame. She is the author of *Naming Grace: Preaching and the Sacramental Imagination* and *Speaking with Authority: Catherine of Siena and the Voices of Women Today* and coeditor with Robert J. Schreiter of *The Praxis of the Reign of God: An Introduction to the Theology of Edward Schillebeeckx*.

Bryan N. Massingale is the James and Nancy Buckman Professor of Theological and Social Ethics, as well as the senior ethics fellow in Fordham's Center for Ethics Education. Professor Massingale is a leader in the field of theological ethics and a noted authority on issues of social and racial justice. He is president-elect of the Society of Christian Ethics, past convener of the Black Catholic Theological Symposium, and a former president of the Catholic Theological Society of America. An award-winning author, Professor Massingale has served on the editorial boards of *Theological Studies*, the *Journal of Moral Theology*, and the *Journal of the Society of Christian Ethics*. The recipient of four honorary degrees, his contributions to justice advocacy have been recognized on numerous occasions, and in 2012 he received Catholic Charities USA's Centennial Gold Medal for leadership and service in the social mission of the Roman Catholic Church and the YWCA's "Eliminating Racism" award in 2014.

Brian O. McDermott, SJ, is currently special assistant to the president of Georgetown University. He received his doctorate in systematic theology from the University of Nijmegen in Holland in 1973. For twenty-seven years he was a professor at Weston Jesuit School of Theology. He is the author of books and articles on Christology and grace and articles on the intersection of authority, leadership, and spirituality.

Alex Mikulich is an antiracist Catholic social ethicist and activist. He coedited and contributed to *The Scandal of White Complicity and US Hyper-Incarceration: A Nonviolent Spirituality of White Resistance* and *Interrupting White Privilege: Catholic Theologians Break the Silence* (Orbis, 2007), which won the 2008 Theological Book of the Year Award from the College Theology Society. He is author of *Embracing Racial Intimacy: A Way of Unlearning White Supremacy* (2021). The *National Catholic Reporter* publishes his monthly column "Decolonizing Faith and Society," which questions the oppressive side of Western modernity and Christianity to imagine communal futures in which the earth and all peoples may thrive. He and his beloved lifetime partner Kara are proud parents of two African American children. He currently cares for adults with special needs in a farm-to-table shared-living community in the Berkshire mountains.

Maria Teresa Morgan is assistant professor of theology at Saint John Vianney College Seminary, where she also coordinates the Humanities Program. She is a frequent contributor to *El Ignaciano,* the online Jesuit magazine of the Pedro Arrupe Institute. Her area of interest lies in Christian spirituality and in theological aesthetics. Her contribution, "The Sentinel," draws from Constance FitzGerald's concept of societal impasse and presents a reflection on the dark night in view of the COVID-19 pandemic. Maria Teresa and her husband Robert reside in Miami, Florida.

Dr. Margaret R. Pfeil holds a joint appointment in the Theology Department and in the Center for Social Concerns at the University of Notre Dame. She is a faculty fellow of the Kroc Institute for International Peace Studies. Her research interests include Catholic social thought, racial justice, ecological ethics, ecumenical dialogue, and peace studies. With Tobias Winright, she coedited *Violence, Transformation, and the Sacred: They Shall Be Called Children of God* (Orbis, 2012). With Gerald Schlabach, she coedited *Sharing Peace: Mennonites and Catholics in Conversation* (Liturgical Press, 2013), and with Laurie Cassidy and Alex Mikulich she is coauthor of *The Scandal of White Complicity and US Hyper-Incarceration: A Nonviolent Spirituality of White Resistance.* With Fr. Don McNeill, CSC, she edited the volume *Act Justly, Love Mercifully, Walk Humbly with Your God* (Andrews McMeel Universal, 2016). She is a cofounder and resident of the St. Peter Claver Catholic Worker Community in South Bend, Indiana.

Andrew Prevot is associate professor of theology at Boston College. His research spans the areas of spiritual and mystical theology, philosophical theology and continental philosophy of religion, and various forms of political, liberation, black, and womanist theology. He is the author of *Theology and Race: Black and Womanist Traditions in the United States* (Brill, 2018) and *Thinking Prayer: Theology and Spirituality amid the Crises of Modernity* (Notre Dame, 2015) and coeditor of *Anti-Blackness and Christian Ethics* (Orbis, 2017). He is currently working on a book-length study on the mysticism of ordinary life.

Selected Writings of Constance FitzGerald, OCD

Major Publications

"Contemplative Life as Charismatic Presence." *Spiritual Life* 29, no. 1 (1983): 18–30.

"Impasse and Dark Night." *Living With Apocalypse*. Ed. Tilden Edwards. San Francisco: Harper & Row, 1984. Reprinted in *Women's Spirituality*. Ed. Joann Wolski Conn. New York: Paulist Press, 1986, 1996.

"A Discipleship of Equals: Voices from Tradition—Teresa of Avila and John of the Cross." *A Discipleship of Equals: Toward a Christian Feminist Spirituality*. Theology Institute Publications. Ed. Francis A. Eigo. Villanova, PA: Villanova University Press, 1988.

"How to Read the Rule: An Interpretation." *Albert's Way*. Ed. Michael Mulhall, OCarm. Rome: Institutum Carmelitanum; Barrington, IL: The Province of the Most Pure Heart of Mary, 1989, 51–69.

The Carmelite Adventure: Carmelite Sources 2. Reno: Carmelite Communities Associated and Carmelite Sisters of Baltimore, 1990. (Critical edition of 1790 Diary of Carmelite founders crossing the ocean to America.) Reprinted in *The Land of Carmel*. Ed. Paul Chandler, OCarm and Keith J. Egan. Rome: Institutum Carmelitanum, 1991, 419–37.

"Desolation as Dark Night, the Transformative Influence of Wisdom in John of the Cross." *Ignatian Prayer*. The Way Supplement 82 (Spring 1995).

"The Mission of Therese of Lisieux." *Contemporary Carmelite Women*. The Way Supplement (Summer 1997).

"Transformation in Wisdom: The Subversive Character and Educative Power of Sophia in Contemplation." *Carmel and Contemplation*. Ed. Kevin Culligan. Washington, DC: ICS Publications, 2000, 281–358.

"The Desire for God and the Transformative Power of Contemplation." *Light Burdens, Heavy Blessings*. Ed. Mary Heather MacKinnon et al. Quincy University: Franciscan Press, 2000, 201–22.

"Passion in the Carmelite Tradition: Edith Stein." *Spiritus: A Journal of Christian Spirituality* 2, no. 2 (Fall 2002). Reprinted in *Carmelite Prayer: A Tradition for the 21st Century*. Ed. Keith Egan. New York: Paulist Press, 2003, 174–201.

"Woodstock 1969: Capturing the Metaphor of Religious Life." *Cloister of the Heart: Association of Contemplative Sisters*. Ed. Ann Denham and Gert Wilkinson. Xlibris Corporation, 2009, 74–88.

"From Impasse to Prophetic Hope: Crisis of Memory." *Catholic Theological Society of America: Proceedings of the Sixty-Fourth Annual Convention*. Ed. Jonathan Y. Tan. Cincinnati, OH: Xavier University Press, 2009, 21–42.

"John of the Cross and Prayer." *Prayer in the Catholic Tradition: A Handbook of Practical Approaches*. Ed. Robert J. Wicks. Cincinnati, OH: Franciscan Media, 2016, 335–51.

Audio/Video

How to Read Teresa and John: Interpretation of Religious Classics. Canfield, OH: Alba House, 1987.

John and Teresa: Voices of a Man and a Woman. Canfield, OH: Alba House, 1987.

The Spiritual Canticle of John of the Cross as the Story of Human Desire: Its Development, Education, Purification, and Transformation. Canfield, OH: Alba House, 1988.

The Desire for God and the Transformative Power of Contemplation. Carmel 200. Kansas City: Credence Cassettes, 1990.

The Meaning and Recognition of the Dark Night Experience. Canfield, OH: Alba House, 1991.

Transformation in Wisdom. Canfield, OH: Alba House, 1992.

Wisdom: The Heart of the Praying Community. Washington, DC: ICS Publications, 1993.

Therese of Lisieux: Saigon and Beyond. Washington, DC: ICS Publications, 1996. Also a video published by Carmelite Institute, 1996.

Into the Thicket: A Hidden God. Washington, DC: ICS Publications, 1997. Also a video published by Carmelite Institute, 1997.

The Passion of the Carmelite Tradition: Edith Stein. Washington, DC: ICS Publications, 2000.

Edith Stein as Scholar and Contemplative: The Truth of Self-Transcendence. Washington DC: ICS Publications, 2004.

Christ Consciousness: Carmelite and Ignatian Spiritualities in Dialogue. With Brian McDermott, SJ. https://www.baltimorecarmel.org/to-the-holy-mountain/. Lectures on Teresa of Avila, 2015.

LCWR Outstanding Leadership Award, 2017. Leadership Conference of Women Religious. https://lcwr.org/about/outstanding-leadership-award.